William Shakespeare

The Tragedy of Hamlet Prince of Denmark

With New and Updated
Critical Essays
and a Revised Bibliography

Edited by Sylvan Barnet

THE SIGNET CLASSIC SHAKESPEARE
General Editor: Sylvan Barnet

A SIGNET CLASSIC

SIGNET CLASSIC
Published by the Penguin Group
Penguin Putnam Inc., 375 Hudson Street, New York, New York 10014, U.S.A.
Penguin Books Ltd, 27 Wrights Lane, London W8 5TZ, England
Penguin Books Australia Ltd, Ringwood, Victoria, Australia
Penguin Books Canada Ltd, 10 Alcorn Avenue, Toronto, Ontario, Canada M4V 3B2
Penguin Books (N.Z.) Ltd, 182–190 Wairau Road, Auckland 10, New Zealand

Penguin Books Ltd, Registered Offices:
Harmondsworth, Middlesex, England

Published by Signet Classic, an imprint of Dutton NAL,
a member of Penguin Putnam Inc.
The Signet Classic edition of *Hamlet* was first published in 1963, and an updated edition
was published in 1986. This new edition has been completely re-edited.

First Signet Classic Printing (Second Revised Edition), June, 1998
10 9 8 7 6 5 4 3

 REGISTERED TRADEMARK—MARCA REGISTRADA

Library of Congress Catalog Card Number: 97-62215

Printed in the United States of America

Contents

Shakespeare: An Overview

Biographical Sketch

Between the record of his baptism in Stratford on 26 April 1564 and the record of his burial in Stratford on 25 April 1616, some forty official documents name Shakespeare, and many others name his parents, his children, and his grandchildren. Further, there are at least fifty literary references to him in the works of his contemporaries. More facts are known about William Shakespeare than about any other playwright of the period except Ben Jonson. The facts should, however, be distinguished from the legends. The latter, inevitably more engaging and better known, tell us that the Stratford boy killed a calf in high style, poached deer and rabbits, and was forced to flee to London, where he held horses outside a playhouse. These traditions are only traditions; they may be true, but no evidence supports them, and it is well to stick to the facts.

Mary Arden, the dramatist's mother, was the daughter of a substantial landowner; about 1557 she married John Shakespeare, a tanner, glove-maker, and trader in wool, grain, and other farm commodities. In 1557 John Shakespeare was a member of the council (the governing body of Stratford), in 1558 a constable of the borough, in 1561 one of the two town chamberlains, in 1565 an alderman (entitling him to the appellation of "Mr."), in 1568 high bailiff— the town's highest political office, equivalent to mayor. After 1577, for an unknown reason he drops out of local politics. What *is* known is that he had to mortgage his wife's property, and that he was involved in serious litigation.

The birthday of William Shakespeare, the third child and the eldest son of this locally prominent man, is unrecorded, but the Stratford parish register records that the infant was baptized on 26 April 1564. (It is quite possible that he was born on 23 April, but this date has probably been assigned by tradition because it is the date on which, fifty-two years later, he died, and perhaps because it is the feast day of St. George, patron saint of England.) The attendance records of the Stratford grammar school of the period are not extant, but it is reasonable to assume that the son of a prominent local official attended the free school—it had been established for the purpose of educating males precisely of his class—and received substantial training in Latin. The masters of the school from Shakespeare's seventh to fifteenth years held Oxford degrees; the Elizabethan curriculum excluded mathematics and the natural sciences but taught a good deal of Latin rhetoric, logic, and literature, including plays by Plautus, Terence, and Seneca.

On 27 November 1582 a marriage license was issued for the marriage of Shakespeare and Anne Hathaway, eight years his senior. The couple had a daughter, Susanna, in May 1583. Perhaps the marriage was necessary, but perhaps the couple had earlier engaged, in the presence of witnesses, in a formal "troth plight" which would render their children legitimate even if no further ceremony were performed. In February 1585, Anne Hathaway bore Shakespeare twins, Hamnet and Judith.

That Shakespeare was born is excellent; that he married and had children is pleasant; but that we know nothing about his departure from Stratford to London or about the beginning of his theatrical career is lamentable and must be admitted. We would gladly sacrifice details about his children's baptism for details about his earliest days in the theater. Perhaps the poaching episode is true (but it is first reported almost a century after Shakespeare's death), or perhaps he left Stratford to be a schoolmaster, as another tradition holds; perhaps he was moved (like Petruchio in *The Taming of the Shrew*) by

> Such wind as scatters young men through the world,
> To seek their fortunes farther than at home
> Where small experience grows.   (1.2.49–51)

In 1592, thanks to the cantankerousness of Robert Greene, we have our first reference, a snarling one, to Shakespeare as an actor and playwright. Greene, a graduate of St. John's College, Cambridge, had become a playwright and a pamphleteer in London, and in one of his pamphlets he warns three university-educated playwrights against an actor who has presumed to turn playwright:

> There is an upstart crow, beautified with our feathers, that with his *tiger's heart wrapped in a player's hide* supposes he is as well able to bombast out a blank verse as the best of you, and being an absolute Johannes-factotum [i.e., jack-of-all-trades] is in his own conceit the only Shake-scene in a country.

The reference to the player, as well as the allusion to Aesop's crow (who strutted in borrowed plumage, as an actor struts in fine words not his own), makes it clear that by this date Shakespeare had both acted and written. That Shakespeare is meant is indicated not only by *Shake-scene* but also by the parody of a line from one of Shakespeare's plays, *3 Henry VI*: "O, tiger's heart wrapped in a woman's hide" (1.4.137). If in 1592 Shakespeare was prominent enough to be attacked by an envious dramatist, he probably had served an apprenticeship in the theater for at least a few years.

In any case, although there are no extant references to Shakespeare between the record of the baptism of his twins in 1585 and Greene's hostile comment about "Shake-scene" in 1592, it is evident that during some of these "dark years" or "lost years" Shakespeare had acted and written. There are a number of subsequent references to him as an actor. Documents indicate that in 1598 he is a "principal comedian," in 1603 a "principal tragedian," in 1608 he is one of the "men players." (We do not have, however, any solid information about which roles he may have played; later traditions say he played Adam in *As You Like It* and the ghost in *Hamlet*, but nothing supports the assertions. Probably his role as dramatist came to supersede his role as actor.) The profession of actor was not for a gentleman, and it occasionally drew the scorn of university men like Greene who resented writing speeches for persons less educated than themselves, but it was respectable enough; players, if prosperous, were in effect members of the bourgeoisie, and there is nothing to suggest that Stratford considered William Shakespeare less than a solid citizen. When, in 1596, the Shakespeares were granted a coat of arms—i.e., the right to be considered gentlemen—the grant was made to Shakespeare's father, but probably William Shakespeare had arranged the matter on his own behalf. In subsequent transactions he is occasionally styled a gentleman.

Although in 1593 and 1594 Shakespeare published two narrative poems dedicated to the Earl of Southampton, *Venus and Adonis* and *The Rape of Lucrece*, and may well have written most or all of his sonnets in the middle nineties, Shakespeare's literary activity seems to have been almost entirely devoted to the theater. (It may be significant that the two narrative poems were written in years when the plague closed the theaters for several months.) In 1594 he was a charter member of a theatrical company called the Chamberlain's Men, which in 1603 became the royal company, the King's Men, making Shakespeare the king's playwright. Until he retired to Stratford (about 1611, apparently), he was with this remarkably stable company. From 1599 the company acted primarily at the Globe theater, in which Shakespeare held a one-tenth interest. Other Elizabethan dramatists are known to have acted, but no other is known also to have been entitled to a share of the profits.

Shakespeare's first eight published plays did not have his name on them, but this is not remarkable; the most popular play of the period, Thomas Kyd's *The Spanish Tragedy*, went through many editions without naming Kyd, and Kyd's authorship is known only because a book on the profession of acting happens to quote (and attribute to Kyd) some lines on the interest of Roman emperors in the drama. What is remarkable is that after 1598 Shakespeare's name commonly appears on printed plays—some of which are not his. Presumably his name was a drawing card, and publishers used it to attract potential buyers. Another indication of his popularity comes from Francis Meres, author of *Palladis Tamia: Wit's Treasury* (1598). In this anthology of snippets accompanied by an essay on literature, many playwrights are mentioned, but Shakespeare's name occurs more often than any other, and Shakespeare is the only playwright whose plays are listed.

From his acting, his play writing, and his share in a playhouse, Shakespeare seems to have made considerable money. He put it to work, making substantial investments in Stratford real estate. As early as 1597 he bought New Place, the second-largest house in Stratford. His family moved in soon afterward, and the house remained in the family until a granddaughter died in 1670. When Shakespeare made his will in 1616, less than a month before he died, he sought to leave his property intact to his descendants. Of small bequests to relatives and to friends (including three actors, Richard Burbage, John Heminges, and Henry Condell), that to his wife of the second-best bed has provoked the most comment. It has sometimes been taken as a sign of an unhappy marriage (other supposed signs are the apparently hasty marriage, his wife's seniority of eight years, and his residence in London without his family). Perhaps the second-best bed was the bed the couple had slept in, the best bed being reserved for visitors. In any case, had Shakespeare not excepted it, the bed would have gone (with the rest of his household possessions) to his daughter and her husband.

On 25 April 1616 Shakespeare was buried within the chancel of the church at Stratford. An unattractive monument to his memory, placed on a wall near the grave, says that he died on 23 April. Over the grave itself are the lines, perhaps by Shakespeare, that (more than his literary fame) have kept his bones undisturbed in the crowded burial ground where old bones were often dislodged to make way for new:

> Good friend, for Jesus' sake forbear
> To dig the dust enclosed here.
> Blessed be the man that spares these stones
> And cursed be he that moves my bones.

A Note on the Anti-Stratfordians, Especially Baconians and Oxfordians

Not until 1769—more than a hundred and fifty years after Shakespeare's death—is there any record of anyone

xii   SHAKESPEARE: AN OVERVIEW

expressing doubt about Shakespeare's authorship of the plays
and poems. In 1769, however, Herbert Lawrence nominated
Francis Bacon (1561–1626) in *The Life and Adventures of
Common Sense*. Since then, at least two dozen other nomi-
nees have been offered, including Christopher Marlowe, Sir
Walter Raleigh, Queen Elizabeth I, and Edward de Vere,
17th earl of Oxford. The impulse behind all anti-Stratfordian
movements is the scarcely concealed snobbish opinion that
"the man from Stratford" simply could not have written the
plays because he was a country fellow without a university
education and without access to high society. Anyone, the
argument goes, who used so many legal terms, medical
terms, nautical terms, and so forth, and who showed some
familiarity with classical writing, must have attended a university, and anyone who knew so much about courtly ele-
gance and courtly deceit must himself have moved among
courtiers. The plays do indeed reveal an author whose interests were exceptionally broad, but specialists in any given
field—law, medicine, arms and armor, and so on—soon find
that the plays do not reveal deep knowledge in specialized
matters; indeed, the playwright often gets technical details
wrong.

The claim on behalf of Bacon, forgotten almost as soon as
it was put forth in 1769, was independently reasserted by
Joseph C. Hart in 1848. In 1856 it was reaffirmed by W. H.
Smith in a book, and also by Delia Bacon in an article; in
1857 Delia Bacon published a book, arguing that Francis
Bacon had directed a group of intellectuals who wrote the
plays.

Francis Bacon's claim has largely faded, perhaps because
it was advanced with such evident craziness by Ignatius
Donnelly, who in *The Great Cryptogram* (1888) claimed to
break a code in the plays that proved Bacon had written not
only the plays attributed to Shakespeare but also other
Renaissance works, for instance the plays of Christopher
Marlowe and the essays of Montaigne.

Consider the last two lines of the Epilogue in *The
Tempest*:

As you from crimes would pardoned be,
Let your indulgence set me free.

What was Shakespeare—sorry, Francis Bacon, Baron Verulam—*really* saying in these two lines? According to Baconians, the lines are an anagram reading, "Tempest of Francis Bacon, Lord Verulam; do ye ne'er divulge me, ye words." Ingenious, and it is a pity that in the quotation the letter *a* appears only twice in the cryptogram, whereas in the deciphered message it appears three times. Oh, no problem; just alter "Verulam" to "Verul'm" and it works out very nicely.

Most people understand that with sufficient ingenuity one can torture any text and find in it what one wishes. For instance: Did Shakespeare have a hand in the King James Version of the Bible? It was nearing completion in 1610, when Shakespeare was forty-six years old. If you look at the 46th Psalm and count forward for forty-six words, you will find the word *shake*. Now if you go to the end of the psalm and count backward forty-six words, you will find the word *spear*. Clear evidence, according to some, that Shakespeare slyly left his mark in the book.

Bacon's candidacy has largely been replaced in the twentieth century by the candidacy of Edward de Vere (1550–1604), 17th earl of Oxford. The basic ideas behind the Oxford theory, advanced at greatest length by Dorothy and Charlton Ogburn in *This Star of England* (1952, rev. 1955), a book of 1297 pages, and by Charlton Ogburn in *The Mysterious William Shakespeare* (1984), a book of 892 pages, are these: (1) The man from Stratford could not possibly have had the mental equipment and the experience to have written the plays—only a courtier could have written them; (2) Oxford had the requisite background (social position, education, years at Queen Elizabeth's court); (3) Oxford did not wish his authorship to be known for two basic reasons: writing for the public theater was a vulgar pursuit, and the plays show so much courtly and royal disreputable behavior that they would have compromised Oxford's position at court. Oxfordians offer countless details to support the claim. For example, Hamlet's phrase "that ever I was born to set it right" (1.5.89) barely conceals "E. Ver, I was born to set it right," an unambiguous announcement of de Vere's authorship, according to *This Star of England* (p. 654). A second example: Consider Ben

Jonson's poem entitled "To the Memory of My Beloved Master William Shakespeare," prefixed to the first collected edition of Shakespeare's plays in 1623. According to Oxfordians, when Jonson in this poem speaks of the author of the plays as the "swan of Avon," he is alluding not to William Shakespeare, who was born and died in Stratford-on-Avon and who throughout his adult life owned property there; rather, he is alluding to Oxford, who, the Ogburns say, used "William Shakespeare" as his pen name, and whose manor at Bilton was on the Avon River. Oxfordians do not offer any evidence that Oxford took a pen name, and they do not mention that Oxford had sold the manor in 1581, forty-two years before Jonson wrote his poem. Surely a reference to the Shakespeare who was born in Stratford, who had returned to Stratford, and who had died there only seven years before Jonson wrote the poem is more plausible. And exactly why Jonson, who elsewhere also spoke of Shakespeare as a playwright, and why Heminges and Condell, who had acted with Shakespeare for about twenty years, should speak of Shakespeare as the author in their dedication in the 1623 volume of collected plays is never adequately explained by Oxfordians. Either Jonson, Heminges and Condell, and numerous others were in on the conspiracy, or they were all duped—equally unlikely alternatives. Another difficulty in the Oxford theory is that Oxford died in 1604, and some of the plays are clearly indebted to works and events later than 1604. Among the Oxfordian responses are: At his death Oxford left some plays, and in later years these were touched up by hacks, who added the material that points to later dates. *The Tempest*, almost universally regarded as one of Shakespeare's greatest plays and pretty clearly dated to 1611, does indeed date from a period after the death of Oxford, but it is a crude piece of work that should not be included in the canon of works by Oxford.

The anti-Stratfordians, in addition to assuming that the author must have been a man of rank and a university man, usually assume two conspiracies: (1) a conspiracy in Elizabethan and Jacobean times, in which a surprisingly large number of persons connected with the theater knew that the actor Shakespeare did not write the plays attributed to him but for some reason or other pretended that he did; (2) a conspiracy of today's Stratfordians, the professors who teach Shakespeare in the colleges and universities, who are said to have a vested interest in preserving Shakespeare as the author of the plays they teach. In fact, (1) it is inconceivable that the secret of Shakespeare's non-authorship could have been preserved by all of the people who supposedly were in on the conspiracy, and (2) academic fame awaits any scholar today who can disprove Shakespeare's authorship.

The Stratfordian case is convincing not only because hundreds or even thousands of anti-Stratford arguments—of the sort that say "ever I was born" has the secret double meaning "E. Ver, I was born"—add up to nothing at all but also because irrefutable evidence connects the man from Stratford with the London theater and with the authorship of particular plays. The anti-Stratfordians do not seem to understand that it is not enough to dismiss the Stratford case by saying that a fellow from the provinces simply couldn't have written the plays. Nor do they understand that it is not enough to dismiss all of the evidence connecting Shakespeare with the plays by asserting that it is perjured.

The Shakespeare Canon

We return to William Shakespeare. Thirty-seven plays as well as some nondramatic poems are generally held to constitute the Shakespeare canon, the body of authentic works. The exact dates of composition of most of the works are highly uncertain, but evidence of a starting point and/or of a final limiting point often provides a framework for informed guessing. For example, *Richard II* cannot be earlier than 1595, the publication date of some material to which it is indebted; *The Merchant of Venice* cannot be later than 1598, the year Francis Meres mentioned it. Sometimes arguments for a date hang on an alleged topical allusion, such as the lines about the unseasonable weather in *A Midsummer Night's Dream*, 2.1.81–117, but such an allusion, if indeed it is an allusion to an event in the real world, can be variously interpreted, and in any case there is always the possibility that a topical allusion was inserted years later, to bring the play up to date. (The issue of alterations in a text between the time that Shakespeare drafted it and the time that it was printed—alterations due to censorship or playhouse practice or Shakespeare's own second thoughts—will be discussed in "The Play Text as a Collaboration" later in this overview.) Dates are often attributed on the basis of style, and although conjectures about style usually rest on other conjectures (such as Shakespeare's development as a playwright, or the appropriateness of lines to character), sooner or later one must rely on one's literary sense. There is no documentary proof, for example, that *Othello* is not as early as *Romeo and Juliet*, but one feels that *Othello* is a later, more mature work, and because the first record of its performance is 1604, one is glad enough to set its composition at that date and not push it back into Shakespeare's early years. (*Romeo and Juliet* was first published in 1597, but evidence suggests that it was written a little earlier.) The following chronology, then, is indebted not only to facts but also to informed guesswork and sensitivity. The dates, necessarily imprecise for some works, indicate something like a scholarly consensus concerning the time of original composition. Some plays show evidence of later revision.

Plays. The first collected edition of Shakespeare, published in 1623, included thirty-six plays. These are all accepted as Shakespeare's, though for one of them, *Henry VIII*, he is thought to have had a collaborator. A thirty-seventh play, *Pericles*, published in 1609 and attributed to Shakespeare on the title page, is also widely accepted as being partly by Shakespeare even though it is not included in the 1623 volume. Still another play not in the 1623 volume, *The Two Noble Kinsmen*, was first published in 1634, with a title page attributing it to John Fletcher and Shakespeare. Probably most students of the subject now believe that Shakespeare did indeed have a hand in it. Of the remaining plays attributed at one time or another to Shakespeare, only one, *Edward III*, anonymously published in 1596, is now regarded by some scholars as a serious candidate. The prevailing opinion, however, is that this rather simpleminded play is not Shakespeare's; at most he may have revised some passages, chiefly scenes with the Countess of

Salisbury. We include *The Two Noble Kinsmen* but do not include *Edward III* in the following list.

1588–94	*The Comedy of Errors*
1588–94	*Love's Labor's Lost*
1589–91	*2 Henry VI*
1590–91	*3 Henry VI*
1589–92	*1 Henry VI*
1592–93	*Richard III*
1589–94	*Titus Andronicus*
1593–94	*The Taming of the Shrew*
1592–94	*The Two Gentlemen of Verona*
1594–96	*Romeo and Juliet*
1595	*Richard II*
1595–96	*A Midsummer Night's Dream*
1596–97	*King John*
1594–96	*The Merchant of Venice*
1596–97	*1 Henry IV*
1597	*The Merry Wives of Windsor*
1597–98	*2 Henry IV*
1598–99	*Much Ado About Nothing*
1598–99	*Henry V*
1599	*Julius Caesar*
1599–1600	*As You Like It*
1599–1600	*Twelfth Night*
1600–1601	*Hamlet*
1601–1602	*Troilus and Cressida*
1602–1604	*All's Well That Ends Well*
1603–1604	*Othello*
1604	*Measure for Measure*
1605–1606	*King Lear*
1605–1606	*Macbeth*
1606–1607	*Antony and Cleopatra*
1605–1608	*Timon of Athens*
1607–1608	*Coriolanus*
1607–1608	*Pericles*
1609–10	*Cymbeline*
1610–11	*The Winter's Tale*
1611	*The Tempest*

1612–13	*Henry VIII*
1613	*The Two Noble Kinsmen*

Poems. In 1989 Donald W. Foster published a book in which he argued that "A Funeral Elegy for Master William Peter," published in 1612, ascribed only to the initials W.S., *may* be by Shakespeare. Foster later published an article in a scholarly journal, *PMLA* 111 (1996), in which he asserted the claim more positively. The evidence begins with the initials, and includes the fact that the publisher and the printer of the elegy had published Shakespeare's *Sonnets* in 1609. But such facts add up to rather little, especially because no one has found any connection between Shakespeare and William Peter (an Oxford graduate about whom little is known, who was murdered at the age of twenty-nine). The argument is based chiefly on statistical examinations of word patterns, which are said to correlate with Shakespeare's known work. Despite such correlations, however, many readers feel that the poem does not sound like Shakespeare. True, Shakespeare has a great range of styles, but his work is consistently imaginative and interesting. Many readers find neither of these qualities in "A Funeral Elegy."

1592–93	*Venus and Adonis*
1593–94	*The Rape of Lucrece*
1593–1600	*Sonnets*
1600–1601	*The Phoenix and the Turtle*

Shakespeare's English

1. Spelling and Pronunciation. From the philologist's point of view, Shakespeare's English is modern English. It requires footnotes, but the inexperienced reader can comprehend substantial passages with very little help, whereas for the same reader Chaucer's Middle English is a foreign language. By the beginning of the fifteenth century the chief grammatical changes in English had taken place, and the final unaccented -*e* of Middle English had been lost (though it survives even today in spelling, as in *name*); during the fif-teenth century the dialect of London, the commercial and political center, gradually displaced the provincial dialects, at least in writing; by the end of the century, printing had helped to regularize and stabilize the language, especially spelling. Elizabethan spelling may seem erratic to us (there were dozens of spellings of *Shakespeare*, and a simple word like *been* was also spelled *beene* and *bin*), but it had much in common with our spelling. Elizabethan spelling was conser-vative in that for the most part it reflected an older pronun-ciation (Middle English) rather than the sound of the language as it was then spoken, just as our spelling continues to reflect medieval pronunciation—most obviously in the now silent but formerly pronounced letters in a word such as *knight*. Elizabethan pronunciation, though not identical with ours, was much closer to ours than to that of the Middle Ages. Incidentally, though no one can be certain about what Elizabethan English sounded like, specialists tend to believe it was rather like the speech of a modern stage Irishman (*time* apparently was pronounced *toime*, *old* pronounced *awld*, *day* pronounced *die*, and *join* pronounced *jine*) and not at all like the Oxford speech that most of us think it was.

An awareness of the difference between our pronuncia-tion and Shakespeare's is crucial in three areas—in accent, or number of syllables (many metrically regular lines may look irregular to us); in rhymes (which may not look like rhymes); and in puns (which may not look like puns). Examples will be useful. Some words that were at least on occasion stressed differently from today are *aspèct*, *còm-plete*, *fòrlorn*, *revènue*, and *sepùlcher*. Words that some-times had an additional syllable are *emp[e]ress*, *Hen[e]ry*, *mon[e]th*, and *villain* (three syllables, *vil-lay-in*). An addi-tional syllable is often found in possessives, like *moon*'s (pronounced *moones*) and in words ending in *-tion* or *-sion*. Words that had one less syllable than they now have are *needle* (pronounced *neel*) and *violet* (pronounced *vilet*). Among rhymes now lost are *one* with *loan*, *love* with *prove*, *beast* with *jest*, *eat* with *great*. (In reading, trust your sense of metrics and your ear, more than your eye.) An example of a pun that has become obliterated by a change in pronuncia-tion is Falstaff's reply to Prince Hal's "Come, tell us your reason" in *1 Henry IV*: "Give you a reason on compulsion? If reasons were as plentiful as blackberries, I would give no man a reason upon compulsion, I" (2.4.237–40). The *ea* in *reason* was pronounced rather like a long *a,* like the *ai* in *raisin,* hence the comparison with blackberries.

Puns are not merely attempts to be funny; like metaphors they often involve bringing into a meaningful relationship areas of experience normally seen as remote. In *2 Henry IV,* when Feeble is conscripted, he stoically says, "I care not. A man can die but once. We owe God a death" (3.2.242–43), punning on *debt,* which was the way *death* was pronounced. Here an enormously significant fact of life is put into simple commercial imagery, suggesting its commonplace quality. Shakespeare used the same pun earlier in *1 Henry IV,* when Prince Hal says to Falstaff, "Why, thou owest God a death," and Falstaff replies, " 'Tis not due yet: I would be loath to pay him before his day. What need I be so forward with him that calls not on me?" (5.1.126–29).

Sometimes the puns reveal a delightful playfulness; sometimes they reveal aggressiveness, as when, replying to Claudius's "But now, my cousin Hamlet, and my son," Hamlet says, "A little more than kin, and less than kind!" (1.2.64–65). These are Hamlet's first words in the play, and we already hear him warring verbally against Claudius. Hamlet's "less than kind" probably means (1) Hamlet is not of Claudius's family or nature, *kind* having the sense it still has in our word *mankind*; (2) Hamlet is not kindly (affectionately) disposed toward Claudius; (3) Claudius is not naturally (but rather unnaturally, in a legal sense incestuously) Hamlet's father. The puns evidently were not put in as sops to the groundlings; they are an important way of communicating a complex meaning.

2. *Vocabulary.* A conspicuous difficulty in reading Shakespeare is rooted in the fact that some of his words are no longer in common use—for example, words concerned with armor, astrology, clothing, coinage, hawking, horsemanship, law, medicine, sailing, and war. Shakespeare had a large vocabulary—something near thirty thousand words—but it was not so much a vocabulary of big words as a vocabulary drawn from a wide range of life, and it is partly

his ability to call upon a great body of concrete language that gives his plays the sense of being in close contact with life. When the right word did not already exist, he made it up. Among words thought to be his coinages are *accommodation, all-knowing, amazement, bare-faced, countless, dexterously, dislocate, dwindle, fancy-free, frugal, indistinguishable, lackluster, laughable, overawe, premeditated, sea change, star-crossed*. Among those that have not survived are the verb *convive,* meaning to feast together, and *smilet,* a little smile.

Less overtly troublesome than the technical words but more treacherous are the words that seem readily intelligible to us but whose Elizabethan meanings differ from their modern ones. When Horatio describes the Ghost as an "erring spirit," he is saying not that the ghost has sinned or made an error but that it is wandering. Here is a short list of some of the most common words in Shakespeare's plays that often (but not always) have a meaning other than their most usual modern meaning:

'a	he
abuse	deceive
accident	occurrence
advertise	inform
an, and	if
annoy	harm
appeal	accuse
artificial	skillful
brave	fine, splendid
censure	opinion
cheer	(1) face (2) frame of mind
chorus	a single person who comments on the events
closet	small private room
competitor	partner
conceit	idea, imagination
cousin	kinsman
cunning	skillful
disaster	evil astrological influence
doom	judgment
entertain	receive into service

envy	malice
event	outcome
excrement	outgrowth (of hair)
fact	evil deed
fancy	(1) love (2) imagination
fell	cruel
fellow	(1) companion (2) low person (often an insulting term if addressed to someone of approximately equal rank)
fond	foolish
free	(1) innocent (2) generous
glass	mirror
hap, haply	chance, by chance
head	army
humor	(1) mood (2) bodily fluid thought to control one's psychology
imp	child
intelligence	news
kind	natural, acting according to nature
let	hinder
lewd	base
mere(ly)	utter(ly)
modern	commonplace
natural	a fool, an idiot
naughty	(1) wicked (2) worthless
next	nearest
nice	(1) trivial (2) fussy
noise	music
policy	(1) prudence (2) stratagem
presently	immediately
prevent	anticipate
proper	handsome
prove	test
quick	alive
sad	serious
saw	proverb
secure	without care, incautious
silly	innocent

sensible	capable of being perceived by the senses
shrewd	sharp
so	provided that
starve	die
still	always
success	that which follows
tall	brave
tell	count
tonight	last night
wanton	playful, careless
watch	keep awake
will	lust
wink	close both eyes
wit	mind, intelligence

All glosses, of course, are mere approximations; sometimes one of Shakespeare's words may hover between an older meaning and a modern one, and as we have seen, his words often have multiple meanings.

3. Grammar. A few matters of grammar may be surveyed, though it should be noted at the outset that Shakespeare sometimes made up his own grammar. As E.A. Abbott says in *A Shakespearian Grammar,* "Almost any part of speech can be used as any other part of speech": a noun as a verb ("he childed as I fathered"); a verb as a noun ("She hath made compare"); or an adverb as an adjective ("a seldom pleasure"). There are hundreds, perhaps thousands, of such instances in the plays, many of which at first glance would not seem at all irregular and would trouble only a pedant. Here are a few broad matters.

Nouns: The Elizabethans thought the *-s* genitive ending for nouns (as in *man's*) derived from *his*; thus the line "'gainst the count his galleys I did some service," for "the count's galleys."

Adjectives: By Shakespeare's time adjectives had lost the endings that once indicated gender, number, and case. About the only difference between Shakespeare's adjectives and ours is the use of the now redundant *more* or *most* with the comparative ("some more fitter place") or superlative

("This was the most unkindest cut of all"). Like double comparatives and double superlatives, double negatives were acceptable; Mercutio "will not budge for no man's pleasure."

Pronouns: The greatest change was in pronouns. In Middle English *thou, thy,* and *thee* were used among familiars and in speaking to children and inferiors; *ye, your,* and *you* were used in speaking to superiors (servants to masters, nobles to the king) or to equals with whom the speaker was not familiar. Increasingly the "polite" forms were used in all direct address, regardless of rank, and the accusative *you* displaced the nominative *ye.* Shakespeare sometimes uses *ye* instead of *you,* but even in Shakespeare's day *ye* was archaic, and it occurs mostly in rhetorical appeals.

Thou, thy, and *thee* were not completely displaced, however, and Shakespeare occasionally makes significant use of them, sometimes to connote familiarity or intimacy and sometimes to connote contempt. In *Twelfth Night* Sir Toby advises Sir Andrew to insult Cesario by addressing him as *thou:* "If thou thou'st him some thrice, it shall not be amiss" (3.2.46–47). In *Othello* when Brabantio is addressing an unidentified voice in the dark he says, "What are you?" (1.1.91), but when the voice identifies itself as the foolish suitor Roderigo, Brabantio uses the contemptuous form, saying, "I have charged thee not to haunt about my doors" (93). He uses this form for a while, but later in the scene, when he comes to regard Roderigo as an ally, he shifts back to the polite *you,* beginning in line 163, "What said she to you?" and on to the end of the scene. For reasons not yet satisfactorily explained, Elizabethans used *thou* in addresses to God—"O God, thy arm was here," the king says in *Henry V* (4.8.108)—and to supernatural characters such as ghosts and witches. A subtle variation occurs in *Hamlet.* When Hamlet first talks with the Ghost in 1.5, he uses *thou,* but when he sees the Ghost in his mother's room, in 3.4, he uses *you,* presumably because he is now convinced that the ghost is not a counterfeit but is his father.

Perhaps the most unusual use of pronouns, from our point of view, is the neuter singular. In place of our *its, his* was often used, as in "How far that little candle throws *his* beams." But the use of a masculine pronoun for a neuter noun came to seem unnatural, and so *it* was used for the possessive as well as the nominative: "The hedge-sparrow fed the cuckoo so long / That it had it head bit off by it young." In the late sixteenth century the possessive form *its* developed, apparently by analogy with the *-s* ending used to indicate a genitive noun, as in *book*'s, but *its* was not yet common usage in Shakespeare's day. He seems to have used *its* only ten times, mostly in his later plays. Other usages, such as "you have seen Cassio and she together" or the substitution of *who* for *whom,* cause little problem even when noticed.

Verbs, Adverbs, and Prepositions: Verbs cause almost no difficulty: The third person singular present form commonly ends in *-s,* as in modern English (e.g., "He blesses"), but sometimes in *-eth* (Portia explains to Shylock that mercy "blesseth him that gives and him that takes"). Broadly speaking, the *-eth* ending was old-fashioned or dignified or "literary" rather than colloquial, except for the words *doth, hath,* and *saith.* The *-eth* ending (regularly used in the King James Bible, 1611) is very rare in Shakespeare's dramatic prose, though not surprisingly it occurs twice in the rather formal prose summary of the narrative poem *Lucrece.* Sometimes a plural subject, especially if it has collective force, takes a verb ending in *-s,* as in "My old bones aches." Some of our strong or irregular preterites (such as *broke*) have a different form in Shakespeare (*brake*); some verbs that now have a weak or regular preterite (such as *helped*) in Shakespeare have a strong or irregular preterite (*holp*). Some adverbs that today end in *-ly* were not inflected: "grievous sick," "wondrous strange." Finally, prepositions often are not the ones we expect: "We are such stuff as dreams are made on," "I have a king here to my flatterer."

Again, none of the differences (except meanings that have substantially changed or been lost) will cause much difficulty. But it must be confessed that for some elliptical passages there is no widespread agreement on meaning. Wise editors resist saying more than they know, and when they are uncertain they add a question mark to their gloss.

Shakespeare's Theater

In Shakespeare's infancy, Elizabethan actors performed wherever they could—in great halls, at court, in the courtyards of inns. These venues implied not only different audiences but also different playing conditions. The innyards must have made rather unsatisfactory theaters: on some days they were unavailable because carters bringing goods to London used them as depots; when available, they had to be rented from the innkeeper. In 1567, presumably to avoid such difficulties, and also to avoid regulation by the Common Council of London, which was not well disposed toward theatricals, one John Brayne, brother-in-law of the carpenter turned actor James Burbage, built the Red Lion in an eastern suburb of London. We know nothing about its shape or its capacity; we can say only that it may have been the first building in Europe constructed for the purpose of giving plays since the end of antiquity, a thousand years earlier. Even after the building of the Red Lion theatrical activity continued in London in makeshift circumstances, in marketplaces and inns, and always uneasily. In 1574 the Common Council required that plays and playing places in London be licensed because

> sundry great disorders and inconveniences have been found to ensue to this city by the inordinate haunting of great multitudes of people, specially youth, to plays, interludes, and shows, namely occasion of frays and quarrels, evil practices of incontinency in great inns having chambers and secret places adjoining to their open stages and galleries.

The Common Council ordered that innkeepers who wished licenses to hold performance put up a bond and make contributions to the poor.

The requirement that plays and innyard theaters be licensed, along with the other drawbacks of playing at inns and presumably along with the success of the Red Lion, led James Burbage to rent a plot of land northeast of the city walls, on property outside the jurisdiction of the city. Here he built England's second playhouse, called simply the Theatre. About all that is known of its construction is that it was wood. It soon had imitators, the most famous being the Globe (1599), essentially an amphitheater built across the Thames (again outside the city's jurisdiction), constructed with timbers of the Theatre, which had been dismantled when Burbage's lease ran out.

Admission to the theater was one penny, which allowed spectators to stand at the sides and front of the stage that jutted into the yard. An additional penny bought a seat in a covered part of the theater, and a third penny bought a more comfortable seat and a better location. It is notoriously difficult to translate prices into today's money, since some things that are inexpensive today would have been expensive in the past and vice versa—a pipeful of tobacco (imported, of course) cost a lot of money, about three pennies, and an orange (also imported) cost two or three times what a chicken cost—but perhaps we can get some idea of the low cost of the penny admission when we realize that a penny could also buy a pot of ale. An unskilled laborer made about five or sixpence a day, an artisan about twelve pence a day, and the hired actors (as opposed to the sharers in the company, such as Shakespeare) made about ten pence a performance. A printed play cost five or sixpence. Of course a visit to the theater (like a visit to a baseball game today) usually cost more than the admission since the spectator probably would also buy food and drink. Still, the low entrance fee meant that the theater was available to all except the very poorest people, rather as movies and most athletic events are today. Evidence indicates that the audience ranged from apprentices who somehow managed to scrape together the minimum entrance fee and to escape from their masters for a few hours, to prosperous members of the middle class and aristocrats who paid the additional fee for admission to the galleries. The exact proportion of men to women cannot be determined, but women of all classes certainly were present. Theaters were open every afternoon but Sundays for much of the year, except in times of plague, when they were closed because of fear of infection. By the way, no evidence suggests the presence of toilet facilities. Presumably the patrons relieved themselves by making a quick trip to the fields surrounding the playhouses.

There are four important sources of information about the

structure of Elizabethan public playhouses—drawings, a contract, recent excavations, and stage directions in the plays. Of drawings, only the so-called de Witt drawing (c. 1596) of the Swan—really his friend Aernout van Buchell's copy of Johannes de Witt's drawing—is of much significance. The drawing, the only extant representation of the interior of an Elizabethan theater, shows an amphitheater of three tiers, with a stage jutting from a wall into the yard or

Johannes de Witt, a Continental visitor to London, made a drawing of the Swan theater in about the year 1596. The original drawing is lost; this is Aernout van Buchell's copy of it.

center of the building. The tiers are roofed, and part of the stage is covered by a roof that projects from the rear and is supported at its front on two posts, but the groundlings, who paid a penny to stand in front of the stage or at its sides, were exposed to the sky. (Performances in such a playhouse were held only in the daytime; artificial illumination was not used.) At the rear of the stage are two massive doors; above the stage is a gallery.

The second major source of information, the contract for the Fortune (built in 1600), specifies that although the Globe (built in 1599) is to be the model, the Fortune is to be square, eighty feet outside and fifty-five inside. The stage is to be forty-three feet broad, and is to extend into the middle of the yard, i.e., it is twenty-seven and a half feet deep.

The third source of information, the 1989 excavations of the Rose (built in 1587), indicate that the Rose was fourteen-sided, about seventy-two feet in diameter with an inner yard almost fifty feet in diameter. The stage at the Rose was about sixteen feet deep, thirty-seven feet wide at the rear, and twenty-seven feet wide downstage. The relatively small dimensions and the tapering stage, in contrast to the rectangular stage in the Swan drawing, surprised theater historians and have made them more cautious in generalizing about the Elizabethan theater. Excavations at the Globe have not yielded much information, though some historians believe that the fragmentary evidence suggests a larger theater, perhaps one hundred feet in diameter.

From the fourth chief source, stage directions in the plays, one learns that entrance to the stage was by the doors at the rear (*"Enter one citizen at one door, and another at the other"*). A curtain hanging across the doorway—or a curtain hanging between the two doorways—could provide a place where a character could conceal himself, as Polonius does, when he wishes to overhear the conversation between Hamlet and Gertrude. Similarly, withdrawing a curtain from the doorway could "discover" (reveal) a character or two. Such discovery scenes are very rare in Elizabethan drama, but a good example occurs in *The Tempest* (5.1.171), where a stage direction tells us, *"Here Prospero discovers Ferdinand and Miranda playing at chess."* There was also some sort of playing space "aloft" or "above" to represent, for instance, the top of a city's walls or a room above the street. Doubtless each theater had its own peculiarities, but perhaps we can talk about a "typical" Elizabethan theater if we realize that no theater need exactly fit the description, just as no mother is the average mother with 2.7 children.

This hypothetical theater is wooden, round, or polygonal (in *Henry V* Shakespeare calls it a "wooden *O*") capable of holding some eight hundred spectators who stood in the yard around the projecting elevated stage—these spectators were the "groundlings"—and some fifteen hundred additional spectators who sat in the three roofed galleries. The stage, protected by a "shadow" or "heavens" or roof, is entered from two doors; behind the doors is the "tiring house" (attiring house, i.e., dressing room), and above the stage is some sort of gallery that may sometimes hold spectators but can be used (for example) as the bedroom from which Romeo—according to a stage direction in one text—"goeth down." Some evidence suggests that a throne can be lowered onto the platform stage, perhaps from the "shadow"; certainly characters can descend from the stage through a trap or traps into the cellar or "hell." Sometimes this space beneath the stage accommodates a sound-effects man or musician (in *Antony and Cleopatra "music of the hautboys* [oboes] *is under the stage"*) or an actor (in *Hamlet* the *"Ghost cries under the stage"*). Most characters simply walk on and off through the doors, but because there is no curtain in front of the platform, corpses will have to be carried off (Hamlet obligingly clears the stage of Polonius's corpse, when he says, "I'll lug the guts into the neighbor room"). Other characters may have fallen at the rear, where a curtain on a doorway could be drawn to conceal them.

Such may have been the "public theater," so called because its inexpensive admission made it available to a wide range of the populace. Another kind of theater has been called the "private theater" because its much greater admission charge (sixpence versus the penny for general admission at the public theater) limited its audience to the wealthy or the prodigal. The private theater was basically a large room, entirely roofed and therefore artificially illuminated, with a stage at one end. The theaters thus were distinct in two ways: One was essentially an amphitheater that catered to the general public; the other was a hall that catered to the wealthy. In 1576 a hall theater was established in Blackfriars, a Dominican priory in London that had been suppressed in 1538 and confiscated by the Crown and thus was not under the city's jurisdiction. All the actors in this Blackfriars theater were boys about eight to thirteen years old (in the public theaters similar boys played female parts; a boy Lady Macbeth played to a man Macbeth). Near the end of this section on Shakespeare's theater we will talk at some length about possible implications in this convention of using boys to play female roles, but for the moment we should say that it doubtless accounts for the relative lack of female roles in Elizabethan drama. Thus, in *A Midsummer Night's Dream*, out of twenty-one named roles, only four are female; in *Hamlet*, out of twenty-four, only two (Gertrude and Ophelia) are female. Many of Shakespeare's characters have fathers but no mothers—for instance, King Lear's daughters. We need not bring in Freud to explain the disparity; a dramatic company had only a few boys in it.

To return to the private theaters, in some of which all of the performers were children—the "eyrie of . . . little eyases" (nest of unfledged hawks—2.2.347–48) which Rosencrantz mentions when he and Guildenstern talk with Hamlet. The theater in Blackfriars had a precarious existence, and ceased operations in 1584. In 1596 James Burbage, who had already made theatrical history by building the Theatre, began to construct a second Blackfriars theater. He died in 1597, and for several years this second Blackfriars theater was used by a troupe of boys, but in 1608 two of Burbage's sons and five other actors (including Shakespeare) became joint operators of the theater, using it in the winter when the open-air Globe was unsuitable. Perhaps such a smaller theater, roofed, artificially illuminated, and with a tradition of a wealthy audience, exerted an influence in Shakespeare's late plays.

Performances in the private theaters may well have had intermissions during which music was played, but in the public theaters the action was probably uninterrupted, flowing from scene to scene almost without a break. Actors would enter, speak, exit, and others would immediately enter and establish (if necessary) the new locale by a few properties and by words and gestures. To indicate that the scene took place at night, a player or two would carry a torch. Here are some samples of Shakespeare establishing the scene:

> This is Illyria, lady.   (*Twelfth Night*, 1.2.2)

> Well, this is the Forest of Arden.   (*As You Like It*, 2.4.14)

> This castle has a pleasant seat; the air
> Nimbly and sweetly recommends itself
> Unto our gentle senses.   (*Macbeth*, 1.6.1–3)

> The west yet glimmers with some streaks of day.
> (*Macbeth*, 3.3.5)

Sometimes a speech will go far beyond evoking the minimal setting of place and time, and will, so to speak, evoke the social world in which the characters move. For instance, early in the first scene of *The Merchant of Venice* Salerio suggests an explanation for Antonio's melancholy. (In the following passage, *pageants* are decorated wagons, floats, and *cursy* is the verb "to curtsy," or "to bow.")

> Your mind is tossing on the ocean,
> There where your argosies with portly sail—
> Like signiors and rich burghers on the flood,
> Or as it were the pageants of the sea—
> Do overpeer the petty traffickers
> That cursy to them, do them reverence,
> As they fly by them with their woven wings.   (1.1.8–14)

Late in the nineteenth century, when Henry Irving produced the play with elaborate illusionistic sets, the first scene showed a ship moored in the harbor, with fruit vendors and dock laborers, in an effort to evoke the bustling and exotic life of Venice. But Shakespeare's words give us this exotic, rich world of commerce in his highly descriptive language when Salerio speaks of "argosies with portly sail" that fly with "woven wings"; equally important, through Salerio Shakespeare conveys a sense of the orderly, hierarchical society in which the lesser ships, "the petty traffickers," curtsy and thereby "do . . . reverence" to their superiors, the merchant prince's ships, which are "Like signiors and rich burghers."

On the other hand, it is a mistake to think that except for verbal pictures the Elizabethan stage was bare. Although Shakespeare's Chorus in *Henry V* calls the stage an "unworthy scaffold" (Prologue 1.10) and urges the spectators to "eke out our performance with your mind" (Prologue 3.35), there was considerable spectacle. The last act of *Macbeth,* for instance, has five stage directions calling for *"drum and colors,"* and another sort of appeal to the eye is indicated by the stage direction *"Enter Macduff, with Macbeth's head."* Some scenery and properties may have been substantial; doubtless a throne was used, but the pillars supporting the roof would have served for the trees on which Orlando pins his poems in *As You Like It*.

Having talked about the public theater—"this wooden *O*"—at some length, we should mention again that Shakespeare's plays were performed also in other locales. Alvin Kernan, in *Shakespeare, the King's Playwright: Theater in the Stuart Court 1603–1613* (1995) points out that "several of [Shakespeare's] plays contain brief theatrical performances, set always in a court or some noble house. When Shakespeare portrayed a theater, he did not, except for the choruses in *Henry V*, imagine a public theater" (p. 195). (Examples include episodes in *The Taming of the Shrew*, *A Midsummer Night's Dream*, *Hamlet*, and *The Tempest*.)

A Note on the Use of Boy Actors in Female Roles

Until fairly recently, scholars were content to mention that the convention existed; they sometimes also mentioned that it continued the medieval practice of using males in female roles, and that other theaters, notably in ancient Greece and in China and Japan, also used males in female roles. (In classical Noh drama in Japan, males still play the female roles.) Prudery may have been at the root of the academic failure to talk much about the use of boy actors, or maybe there really is not much more to say than that it was a convention of a male-centered culture (Stephen Greenblatt's view, in *Shakespearean Negotiations* [1988]). Further, the very nature of a convention is that it is not thought about: Hamlet is a Dane and Julius Caesar is a Roman, but in Shakespeare's plays they speak English, and we in the audience never give this odd fact a thought. Similarly, a character may speak in the presence of others and we understand, again without thinking about it, that he or she is not heard by the figures on the stage (the aside); a character alone on the stage may speak (the soliloquy), and we do not take the character to be unhinged; in a realistic (box) set, the fourth wall, which allows us to see what is going on, is miraculously missing. The no-nonsense view, then, is that the boy actor was an accepted convention, accepted unthinkingly—just as today we know that Kenneth Branagh is not Hamlet, Al Pacino is not Richard III, and Denzel Washington is not the Prince of Aragon. In this view, the audience takes the performer for the role, and that is that; such is the argument we now make for race-free casting, in which African-Americans and Asians can play roles of persons who lived in medieval Denmark and ancient Rome. But gender perhaps is different, at least today. It is a matter of abundant academic study: The Elizabethan theater is now sometimes called a transvestite theater, and we hear much about cross-dressing.

Shakespeare himself in a very few passages calls attention to the use of boys in female roles. At the end of *As You Like It* the boy who played Rosalind addresses the audience, and says, "O men, . . . if I were a woman, I would kiss as many of you as had beards that pleased me." But this is in the Epilogue; the plot is over, and the actor is stepping out of the play and into the audience's everyday world. A second reference to the practice of boys playing female roles occurs in *Antony and Cleopatra*, when Cleopatra imagines that she and Antony will be the subject of crude plays, her role being performed by a boy:

> The quick comedians
> Extemporally will stage us, and present
> Our Alexandrian revels: Antony
> Shall be brought drunken forth, and I shall see
> Some squeaking Cleopatra boy my greatness.   (5.2.216–20)

In a few other passages, Shakespeare is more indirect. For instance, in *Twelfth Night* Viola, played of course by a boy, disguises herself as a young man and seeks service in the house of a lord. She enlists the help of a Captain, and (by way of explaining away her voice and her beardlessness) says,

> I'll serve this duke
> Thou shalt present me as an eunuch to him.　　　(1.2.55–56)

In *Hamlet*, when the players arrive in 2.2, Hamlet jokes with the boy who plays a female role. The boy has grown since Hamlet last saw him: "By'r Lady, your ladyship is nearer to heaven than when I saw you last by the altitude of a chopine" (a lady's thick-soled shoe). He goes on: "Pray God your voice . . . be not cracked" (434–38).

Exactly how sexual, how erotic, this material was and is, is now much disputed. Again, the use of boys may have been unnoticed, or rather not thought about—an unexamined convention—by most or all spectators most of the time, perhaps *all* of the time, except when Shakespeare calls the convention to the attention of the audience, as in the passages just quoted. Still, an occasional bit seems to invite erotic thoughts. The clearest example is the name that Rosalind takes in *As You Like It*, Ganymede—the beautiful youth whom Zeus abducted. Did boys dressed to play female roles carry homoerotic appeal for straight men (Lisa Jardine's view, in *Still Harping on Daughters* [1983]), or for gay men, or for some or all women in the audience? Further, when the boy actor played a woman who (for the purposes of the plot) disguised herself as a male, as Rosalind, Viola, and Portia do—so we get a boy playing a woman playing a man—what sort of appeal was generated, and for what sort of spectator?

Some scholars have argued that the convention empowered women by letting female characters display a freedom unavailable in Renaissance patriarchal society; the convention, it is said, undermined rigid gender distinctions. In this view, the convention (along with plots in which female characters for a while disguised themselves as young men) allowed Shakespeare to say what some modern gender

critics say: Gender is a constructed role rather than a bio-
logical given, something we make, rather than a fixed binary
opposition of male and female (see Juliet Dusinberre, in
Shakespeare and the Nature of Women [1975]). On the other
hand, some scholars have maintained that the male disguise
assumed by some female characters serves only to reaffirm
traditional social distinctions since female characters who
don male garb (notably Portia in *The Merchant of Venice*
and Rosalind in *As You Like It*) return to their female garb
and at least implicitly (these critics say) reaffirm the status
quo. (For this last view, see Clara Claiborne Park, in an
essay in *The Woman's Part*, ed. Carolyn Ruth Swift Lenz et
al. [1980].) Perhaps no one answer is right for all plays; in
As You Like It cross-dressing empowers Rosalind, but in
Twelfth Night cross-dressing comically traps Viola.

Shakespeare's Dramatic Language: Costumes, Gestures and Silences; Prose and Poetry

Because Shakespeare was a dramatist, not merely a poet,
he worked not only with language but also with costume,
sound effects, gestures, and even silences. We have already
discussed some kinds of spectacle in the preceding section,
and now we will begin with other aspects of visual language;
a theater, after all, is literally a "place for seeing." Consider
the opening stage direction in *The Tempest*, the first play in
the first published collection of Shakespeare's plays: *"A
tempestuous noise of thunder and Lightning heard: Enter a
Ship-master, and a Boteswain."*

Costumes: What did that shipmaster and that boatswain
wear? Doubtless they wore something that identified them
as men of the sea. Not much is known about the costumes
that Elizabethan actors wore, but at least three points are
clear: (1) many of the costumes were splendid versions of
contemporary Elizabethan dress; (2) some attempts were
made to approximate the dress of certain occupations and of
antique or exotic characters such as Romans, Turks, and
Jews; (3) some costumes indicated that the wearer was

supernatural. Evidence for elaborate Elizabethan clothing can be found in the plays themselves and in contemporary comments about the "sumptuous" players who wore the discarded clothing of noblemen, as well as in account books that itemize such things as "a scarlet cloak with two broad gold laces, with gold buttons down the sides."

The attempts at approximation of the dress of certain occupations and nationalities also can be documented from the plays themselves, and it derives additional confirmation from a drawing of the first scene of Shakespeare's *Titus Andronicus*—the only extant Elizabethan picture of an identifiable episode in a play. (See pp. xxxviii–xxxix.) The drawing, probably done in 1594 or 1595, shows Queen Tamora pleading for mercy. She wears a somewhat medieval-looking robe and a crown; Titus wears a toga and a wreath, but two soldiers behind him wear costumes fairly close to Elizabethan dress. We do not know, however, if the drawing represents an actual stage production in the public theater, or perhaps a private production, or maybe only a reader's visualization of an episode. Further, there is some conflicting evidence: In *Julius Caesar* a reference is made to Caesar's doublet (a close-fitting jacket), which, if taken literally, suggests that even the protagonist did not wear Roman clothing; and certainly the lesser characters, who are said to wear hats, did not wear Roman garb.

It should be mentioned, too, that even ordinary clothing can be symbolic: Hamlet's "inky cloak," for example, sets him apart from the brightly dressed members of Claudius's court and symbolizes his mourning; the fresh clothes that are put on King Lear partly symbolize his return to sanity. Consider, too, the removal of disguises near the end of some plays. For instance, Rosalind in *As You Like It* and Portia and Nerissa in *The Merchant of Venice* remove their male attire, thus again becoming fully themselves.

Gestures and Silences: Gestures are an important part of a dramatist's language. King Lear kneels before his daughter Cordelia for a benediction (4.7.57–59), an act of humility that contrasts with his earlier speeches banishing her and that contrasts also with a comparable gesture, his ironic

kneeling before Regan (2.4.153–55). Northumberland's failure to kneel before King Richard II (3.3.71–72) speaks volumes. As for silences, consider a moment in *Coriolanus*: Before the protagonist yields to his mother's entreaties (5.3.182), there is this stage direction: *"Holds her by the hand, silent."* Another example of "speech in dumbness" occurs in *Macbeth*, when Macduff learns that his wife and children have been murdered. He is silent at first, as Malcolm's speech indicates: "What, man! Ne'er pull your hat upon your brows. Give sorrow words" (4.3.208–09). (For a discussion of such moments, see Philip C. McGuire's *Speechless Dialect: Shakespeare's Open Silences* [1985].)

Of course when we think of Shakespeare's work, we think primarily of his language, both the poetry and the prose.

Prose: Although two of his plays (*Richard II* and *King John*) have no prose at all, about half the others have at least one quarter of the dialogue in prose, and some have notably more: *1 Henry IV* and *2 Henry IV*, about half; *As You Like It*

and *Twelfth Night*, a little more than half; *Much Ado About Nothing*, more than three quarters; and *The Merry Wives of Windsor*, a little more than five sixths. We should remember that despite Molière's joke about M. Jourdain, who was amazed to learn that he spoke prose, most of us do not speak prose. Rather, we normally utter repetitive, shapeless, and often ungrammatical torrents; prose is something very different—a sort of literary imitation of speech at its most coherent.

Today we may think of prose as "natural" for drama; or even if we think that poetry is appropriate for high tragedy we may still think that prose is the right medium for comedy. Greek, Roman, and early English comedies, however, were written in verse. In fact, prose was not generally considered a literary medium in England until the late fifteenth century; Chaucer tells even his bawdy stories in verse. By the end of the 1580s, however, prose had established itself on the English comic stage. In tragedy, Marlowe made some use of prose, not simply in the speeches of clownish servants but even in the speech of a tragic hero, Doctor Faustus. Still, before Shakespeare, prose normally was used in the theater only for special circumstances: (1) letters and proclamations, to set them off from the poetic dialogue; (2) mad characters, to indicate that normal thinking has become disordered; and (3) low comedy, or speeches uttered by clowns even when they are not being comic. Shakespeare made use of these conventions, but he also went far beyond them. Sometimes he begins a scene in prose and then shifts into verse as the emotion is heightened; or conversely, he may shift from verse to prose when a speaker is lowering the emotional level, as when Brutus speaks in the Forum.

Shakespeare's prose usually is not prosaic. Hamlet's prose includes not only small talk with Rosencrantz and Guildenstern but also princely reflections on "What a piece of work is a man" (2.2.312). In conversation with Ophelia, he shifts from light talk in verse to a passionate prose denunciation of women (3.1.103), though the shift to prose here is perhaps also intended to suggest the possibility of madness. (Consult Brian Vickers, *The Artistry of Shakespeare's Prose* [1968].)

Poetry: Drama in rhyme in England goes back to the Middle Ages, but by Shakespeare's day rhyme no longer dominated poetic drama; a finer medium, blank verse (strictly speaking, unrhymed lines of ten syllables, with the stress on every second syllable) had been adopted. But before looking at unrhymed poetry, a few things should be said about the chief uses of rhyme in Shakespeare's plays. (1) A couplet (a pair of rhyming lines) is sometimes used to convey emotional heightening at the end of a blank verse speech; (2) characters sometimes speak a couplet as they leave the stage, suggesting closure; (3) except in the latest plays, scenes fairly often conclude with a couplet, and sometimes, as in *Richard II*, 2.1.145–46, the entrance of a new character within a scene is preceded by a couplet, which wraps up the earlier portion of that scene; (4) speeches of two characters occasionally are linked by rhyme, most notably in *Romeo and Juliet*, 1.5.95–108, where the lovers speak a sonnet between them; elsewhere a taunting reply occasionally rhymes with the

previous speaker's last line; (5) speeches with sententious
or gnomic remarks are sometimes in rhyme, as in the
duke's speech in *Othello* (1.3.199–206); (6) speeches of
sardonic mockery are sometimes in rhyme—for example,
Iago's speech on women in *Othello* (2.1.146–58)—and
they sometimes conclude with an emphatic couplet, as in
Bolingbroke's speech on comforting words in *Richard II*
(1.3.301–2); (7) some characters are associated with rhyme,
such as the fairies in *A Midsummer Night's Dream*; (8) in
the early plays, especially *The Comedy of Errors* and *The
Taming of the Shrew*, comic scenes that in later plays would
be in prose are in jingling rhymes; (9) prologues, choruses,
plays-within-the-play, inscriptions, vows, epilogues, and so
on are often in rhyme, and the songs in the plays are rhymed.

Neither prose nor rhyme immediately comes to mind
when we first think of Shakespeare's medium: It is blank
verse, unrhymed iambic pentameter. (In a mechanically
exact line there are five iambic feet. An iambic foot consists
of two syllables, the second accented, as in *away*; five feet
make a pentameter line. Thus, a strict line of iambic pentameter contains ten syllables, the even syllables being
stressed more heavily than the odd syllables. Fortunately,
Shakespeare usually varies the line somewhat.) The first
speech in *A Midsummer Night's Dream*, spoken by Duke
Theseus to his betrothed, is an example of blank verse:

> Now, fair Hippolyta, our nuptial hour
> Draws on apace. Four happy days bring in
> Another moon; but, O, methinks, how slow
> This old moon wanes! She lingers my desires,
> Like to a stepdame, or a dowager,
> Long withering out a young man's revenue.　　　　(1.1.1–6)

As this passage shows, Shakespeare's blank verse is not
mechanically unvarying. Though the predominant foot is
the iamb (as in *apace* or *desires*), there are numerous varia-
tions. In the first line the stress can be placed on "fair," as the
regular metrical pattern suggests, but it is likely that "Now"
gets almost as much emphasis; probably in the second line
"Draws" is more heavily emphasized than "on," giving us a

trochee (a stressed syllable followed by an unstressed one); and in the fourth line each word in the phrase "This old moon wanes" is probably stressed fairly heavily, conveying by two spondees (two feet, each of two stresses) the oppressive tedium that Theseus feels.

In Shakespeare's early plays much of the blank verse is end-stopped (that is, it has a heavy pause at the end of each line), but he later developed the ability to write iambic pentameter verse paragraphs (rather than lines) that give the illusion of speech. His chief techniques are (1) enjambing, i.e., running the thought beyond the single line, as in the first three lines of the speech just quoted; (2) occasionally replacing an iamb with another foot; (3) varying the position of the chief pause (the caesura) within a line; (4) adding an occasional unstressed syllable at the end of a line, traditionally called a feminine ending; (5) and beginning or ending a speech with a half line.

Shakespeare's mature blank verse has much of the rhythmic flexibility of his prose; both the language, though richly figurative and sometimes dense, and the syntax seem natural. It is also often highly appropriate to a particular character. Consider, for instance, this speech from *Hamlet*, in which Claudius, King of Denmark ("the Dane"), speaks to Laertes:

> And now, Laertes, what's the news with you?
> You told us of some suit. What is't, Laertes?
> You cannot speak of reason to the Dane
> And lose your voice. What wouldst thou beg, Laertes,
> That shall not be my offer, not thy asking?   (1.2.42–46)

Notice the short sentences and the repetition of the name "Laertes," to whom the speech is addressed. Notice, too, the shift from the royal "us" in the second line to the more intimate "my" in the last line, and from "you" in the first three lines to the more intimate "thou" and "thy" in the last two lines. Claudius knows how to ingratiate himself with Laertes.

For a second example of the flexibility of Shakespeare's blank verse, consider a passage from *Macbeth*. Distressed by the doctor's inability to cure Lady Macbeth and by the imminent battle, Macbeth addresses some of his remarks to the doctor and others to the servant who is arming him. The entire speech, with its pauses, interruptions, and irresolution (in "Pull't off, I say," Macbeth orders the servant to remove the armor that the servant has been putting on him), catches Macbeth's disintegration. (In the first line, *physic* means "medicine," and in the fourth and fifth lines, *cast the water* means "analyze the urine.")

> Throw physic to the dogs, I'll none of it.
> Come, put mine armor on. Give me my staff.
> Seyton, send out.—Doctor, the thanes fly from me.—
> Come, sir, dispatch. If thou couldst, doctor, cast
> The water of my land, find her disease
> And purge it to a sound and pristine health,
> I would applaud thee to the very echo,
> That should applaud again.—Pull't off, I say.—
> What rhubarb, senna, or what purgative drug,
> Would scour these English hence? Hear'st thou of them?
>
> (5.3.47–56)

Blank verse, then, can be much more than unrhymed iambic pentameter, and even within a single play Shakespeare's blank verse often consists of several styles, depending on the speaker and on the speaker's emotion at the moment.

The Play Text as a Collaboration

Shakespeare's fellow dramatist Ben Jonson reported that the actors said of Shakespeare, "In his writing, whatsoever he penned, he never blotted out line," i.e., never crossed out material and revised his work while composing. None of Shakespeare's plays survives in manuscript (with the possible exception of a scene in *Sir Thomas More*), so we cannot fully evaluate the comment, but in a few instances the published work clearly shows that he revised his manuscript. Consider the following passage (shown here in facsimile) from the best early text of *Romeo and Juliet*, the Second Quarto (1599):

Ro. Would I were sleepe and peace so sweet to rest
The grey eyde morne smiles on the frowning night,
Checkring the Easterne Clouds with streaks of light,
And darknesse fleckted like a drunkard reeles,
From forth daies pathway, made by *Tytans* wheeles.
Hence will I to my ghostly Friers close cell,
His helpe to craue, and my deare hap to tell.

                                                    Exit.

Enter Frier alone with a basket.   (night,
Fri. The grey-eyed morne smiles on the frowning
Checking the Easterne clowdes with streaks of light:
And fleckeld darknesse like a drunkard reeles,
From forth daies path, and *Titans* burning wheeles:
Now ere the sun aduance his burning eie,

Romeo rather elaborately tells us that the sun at dawn is
dispelling the night (morning is smiling, the eastern clouds
are checked with light, and the sun's chariot—Titan's
wheels—advances), and he will seek out his spiritual father,
the friar. He exits and, oddly, the Friar enters and says pretty
much the same thing about the sun. Both speakers say that
"the gray-eyed morn smiles on the frowning night," but there
are small differences, perhaps having more to do with the
business of printing the book than with the author's
composition: For Romeo's "checkring," "fleckted," and
"pathway," we get the Friar's "checking," "fleckeld," and
"path." (Notice, by the way, the inconsistency in Elizabethan
spelling: Romeo's "clouds" become the Friar's "clowdes.")

Both versions must have been in the printer's copy, and it
seems safe to assume that both were in Shakespeare's manuscript. He must have written one version—let's say he first
wrote Romeo's closing lines for this scene—and then he
decided, no, it's better to give this lyrical passage to the
Friar, as the opening of a new scene, but he neglected to
delete the first version. Editors must make a choice, and they
may feel that the reasonable thing to do is to print the text as
Shakespeare intended it. But how can we know what he
intended? Almost all modern editors delete the lines from

Romeo's speech, and retain the Friar's lines. They don't do this because they know Shakespeare's intention, however. They give the lines to the Friar because the first published version (1597) of *Romeo and Juliet* gives only the Friar's version, and this text (though in many ways inferior to the 1599 text) is thought to derive from the memory of some actors, that is, it is thought to represent a performance, not just a script. Maybe during the course of rehearsals Shakespeare—an actor as well as an author—unilaterally decided that the Friar should speak the lines; if so (remember that we don't know this to be a fact) his final intention was to give the speech to the Friar. Maybe, however, the actors talked it over and settled on the Friar, with or without Shakespeare's approval. On the other hand, despite the 1597 version, one might argue (if only weakly) on behalf of giving the lines to Romeo rather than to the Friar, thus: (1) Romeo's comment on the coming of the daylight emphasizes his separation from Juliet, and (2) the figurative language seems more appropriate to Romeo than to the Friar. Having said this, in the Signet edition we have decided in this instance to draw on the evidence provided by earlier text and to give the lines to the Friar, on the grounds that since Q1 reflects a production, in the theater (at least on one occasion) the lines were spoken by the Friar.

A playwright sold a script to a theatrical company. The script thus belonged to the company, not the author, and author and company alike must have regarded this script not as a literary work but as the basis for a play that the actors would create on the stage. We speak of Shakespeare as the author of the plays, but readers should bear in mind that the texts they read, even when derived from a single text, such as the First Folio (1623), are inevitably the collaborative work not simply of Shakespeare with his company—doubtless during rehearsals the actors would suggest alterations—but also with other forces of the age. One force was governmental censorship. In 1606 parliament passed "an Act to restrain abuses of players," prohibiting the utterance of oaths and the name of God. So where the earliest text of *Othello* gives us "By heaven" (3.3.106), the first Folio gives "Alas," presumably reflecting the compliance of stage practice with the law. Similarly, the 1623 version of *King Lear* omits the oath "Fut" (probably from "By God's foot") at 1.2.142, again presumably reflecting the line as it was spoken on the stage. Editors who seek to give the reader the play that Shakespeare initially conceived—the "authentic" play conceived by the solitary Shakespeare—probably will restore the missing oaths and references to God. Other editors, who see the play as a collaborative work, a construction made not only by Shakespeare but also by actors and compositors and even government censors, may claim that what counts is the play as it was actually performed. Such editors regard the censored text as legitimate, since it is the play that was (presumably) finally put on. A performed text, they argue, has more historical reality than a text produced by an editor who has sought to get at what Shakespeare initially wrote. In this view, the text of a play is rather like the script of a film; the script is not the film, and the play text is not the performed play. Even if we want to talk about the play that Shakespeare "intended," we will find ourselves talking about a script that he handed over to a company with the intention that it be implemented by actors. The "intended" play is the one that the actors—we might almost say "society"—would help to construct.

Further, it is now widely held that a play is also the work of readers and spectators, who do not simply receive meaning, but who create it when they respond to the play. This idea is fully in accord with contemporary post-structuralist critical thinking, notably Roland Barthes's "The Death of the Author," in *Image-Music-Text* (1977) and Michel Foucault's "What Is an Author?," in *The Foucault Reader* (1984). The gist of the idea is that an author is not an isolated genius; rather, authors are subject to the politics and other social structures of their age. A dramatist especially is a worker in a collaborative project, working most obviously with actors—parts may be written for particular actors—but working also with the audience. Consider the words of Samuel Johnson, written to be spoken by the actor David Garrick at the opening of a theater in 1747:

> The stage but echoes back the public voice;
> The drama's laws, the drama's patrons give,
> For we that live to please, must please to live.

The audience—the public taste as understood by the play-wright—helps to determine what the play is. Moreover, even members of the public who are not part of the playwright's immediate audience may exert an influence through censorship. We have already glanced at governmental censorship, but there are also other kinds. Take one of Shakespeare's most beloved characters, Falstaff, who appears in three of Shakespeare's plays, the two parts of *Henry IV* and *The Merry Wives of Windsor*. He appears with this name in the earliest printed version of the first of these plays, *1 Henry IV*, but we know that Shakespeare originally called him (after an historical figure) Sir John Oldcastle. Oldcastle appears in Shakespeare's source (partly reprinted in the Signet edition of *1 Henry IV*), and a trace of the name survives in Shakespeare's play, 1.2.43–44, where Prince Hal punningly addresses Falstaff as "my old lad of the castle." But for some reason—perhaps because the family of the historical Oldcastle complained—Shakespeare had to change the name. In short, the play as we have it was (at least in this detail) subject to some sort of censorship. If we think that a text should present what we take to be the author's intention, we probably will want to replace *Falstaff* with *Oldcastle*. But if we recognize that a play is a collaboration, we may welcome the change, even if it was forced on Shakespeare. Somehow *Falstaff*, with its hint of *false-staff*, i.e., inadequate prop, seems just right for this fat knight who, to our delight, entertains the young prince with untruths. We can go as far as saying that, at least so far as a play is concerned, an insistence on the author's original intention (even if we could know it) can sometimes impoverish the text.

The tiny example of Falstaff's name illustrates the point that the text we read is inevitably only a version—something in effect produced by the collaboration of the playwright with his actors, audiences, compositors, and editors—of a fluid text that Shakespeare once wrote, just as the *Hamlet* that we see on the screen starring Kenneth Branagh is not the *Hamlet* that Shakespeare saw in an open-air playhouse starring Richard Burbage. *Hamlet* itself, as we shall note in a moment, also exists in several versions. It is not surprising that there is now much talk about the *instability* of Shakespeare's texts.

Because he was not only a playwright but was also an actor and a shareholder in a theatrical company, Shakespeare probably was much involved with the translation of the play from a manuscript to a stage production. He may or may not have done some rewriting during rehearsals, and he may or may not have been happy with cuts that were made. Some plays, notably *Hamlet* and *King Lear*, are so long that it is most unlikely that the texts we read were acted in their entirety. Further, for both of these plays we have more than one early text that demands consideration. In *Hamlet*, the Second Quarto (1604) includes some two hundred lines not found in the Folio (1623). Among the passages missing from the Folio are two of Hamlet's reflective speeches, the "dram of evil" speech (1.4.13–38) and "How all occasions do inform against me" (4.4.32–66). Since the Folio has more numerous and often fuller stage directions, it certainly looks as though in the Folio we get a theatrical version of the play, a text whose cuts were probably made—this is only a hunch, of course—not because Shakespeare was changing his conception of Hamlet but because the playhouse demanded a modified play. (The problem is complicated, since the Folio not only cuts some of the Quarto but adds some material. Various explanations have been offered.)

Or take an example from *King Lear*. In the First and Second Quarto (1608, 1619), the final speech of the play is given to Albany, Lear's surviving son-in-law, but in the First Folio version (1623), the speech is given to Edgar. The Quarto version is in accord with tradition—usually the highest-ranking character in a tragedy speaks the final words. Why does the Folio give the speech to Edgar? One possible answer is this: The Folio version omits some of Albany's speeches in earlier scenes, so perhaps it was decided (by Shakespeare? by the players?) not to give the final lines to so pale a character. In fact, the discrepancies are so many between the two texts, that some scholars argue we do not simply have texts showing different theatrical productions. Rather, these scholars say, Shakespeare substantially revised the play, and we really have two versions of *King Lear* (and of *Othello* also, say some)—two different plays—not simply two texts, each of which is in some ways imperfect.

In this view, the 1608 version of *Lear* may derive from Shakespeare's manuscript, and the 1623 version may derive from his later revision. The Quartos have almost three hundred lines not in the Folio, and the Folio has about a hundred lines not in the Quartos. It used to be held that all the texts were imperfect in various ways and from various causes—some passages in the Quartos were thought to have been set from a manuscript that was not entirely legible, other passages were thought to have been set by a compositor who was new to setting plays, and still other passages were thought to have been provided by an actor who misremembered some of the lines. This traditional view held that an editor must draw on the Quartos and the Folio in order to get Shakespeare's "real" play. The new argument holds (although not without considerable strain) that we have two authentic plays, Shakespeare's early version (in the Quarto) and Shakespeare's—or his theatrical company's—revised version (in the Folio). Not only theatrical demands but also Shakespeare's own artistic sense, it is argued, called for extensive revisions. Even the titles vary: Q1 is called *True Chronicle Historie of the life and death of King Lear and his three Daughters*, whereas the Folio text is called *The Tragedie of King Lear*. To combine the two texts in order to produce what the editor thinks is the play that Shakespeare intended to write is, according to this view, to produce a text that is false to the history of the play. If the new view is correct, and we do have texts of two distinct versions of *Lear* rather than two imperfect versions of one play, it supports in a textual way the poststructuralist view that we cannot possibly have an unmediated vision of (in this case) a play by Shakespeare; we can only recognize a plurality of visions.

Editing Texts

Though eighteen of his plays were published during his lifetime, Shakespeare seems never to have supervised their publication. There is nothing unusual here; when a playwright sold a play to a theatrical company he surrendered his ownership to it. Normally a company would not publish the play, because to publish it meant to allow competitors to acquire the piece. Some plays did get published: Apparently hard up actors sometimes pieced together a play for a publisher; sometimes a company in need of money sold a play; and sometimes a company allowed publication of a play that no longer drew audiences. That Shakespeare did not concern himself with publication is not remarkable; of his contemporaries, only Ben Jonson carefully supervised the publication of his own plays.

In 1623, seven years after Shakespeare's death, John Heminges and Henry Condell (two senior members of Shakespeare's company, who had worked with him for about twenty years) collected his plays—published and unpublished—into a large volume, of a kind called a folio. (A folio is a volume consisting of large sheets that have been folded once, each sheet thus making two leaves, or four pages. The size of the page of course depends on the size of the sheet—a folio can range in height from twelve to sixteen inches, and in width from eight to eleven; the pages in the 1623 edition of Shakespeare, commonly called the First Folio, are approximately thirteen inches tall and eight inches wide.) The eighteen plays published during Shakespeare's lifetime had been issued one play per volume in small formats called quartos. (Each sheet in a quarto has been folded twice, making four leaves, or eight pages, each page being about nine inches tall and seven inches wide, roughly the size of a large paperback.)

Heminges and Condell suggest in an address "To the great variety of readers" that the republished plays are presented in better form than in the quartos:

> Before you were abused with diverse stolen and surreptitious copies, maimed and deformed by the frauds and stealths of injurious impostors that exposed them; even those, are now offered to your view cured and perfect of their limbs, and all the rest absolute in their numbers, as he [i.e., Shakespeare] conceived them.

There is a good deal of truth to this statement, but some of the quarto versions are better than others; some are in fact preferable to the Folio text.

Whoever was assigned to prepare the texts for publication

in the first Folio seems to have taken the job seriously and yet not to have performed it with uniform care. The sources of the texts seem to have been, in general, good unpublished copies or the best published copies. The first play in the collection, *The Tempest*, is divided into acts and scenes, has unusually full stage directions and descriptions of spectacle, and concludes with a list of the characters, but the editor was not able (or willing) to present all of the succeeding texts so fully dressed. Later texts occasionally show signs of carelessness: in one scene of *Much Ado About Nothing* the names of actors, instead of characters, appear as speech prefixes, as they had in the Quarto, which the Folio reprints; proofreading throughout the Folio is spotty and apparently was done without reference to the printer's copy; the pagination of *Hamlet* jumps from 156 to 257. Further, the proofreading was done while the presses continued to print, so that each play in each volume contains a mix of corrected and uncorrected pages.

Modern editors of Shakespeare must first select their copy; no problem if the play exists only in the Folio, but a considerable problem if the relationship between a Quarto and the Folio—or an early Quarto and a later one—is unclear. In the case of *Romeo and Juliet*, the First Quarto (Q1), published in 1597, is vastly inferior to the Second (Q2), published in 1599. The basis of Q1 apparently is a version put together from memory by some actors. Not surprisingly, it garbles many passages and is much shorter than Q2. On the other hand, occasionally Q1 makes better sense than Q2. For instance, near the end of the play, when the parents have assembled and learned of the deaths of Romeo and Juliet, in Q2 the Prince says (5.3.208–9),

> Come, *Montague;* for thou art early vp
> To see thy sonne and heire, now earling downe.

The last three words of this speech surely do not make sense, and many editors turn to Q1, which instead of "now earling downe" has "more early downe." Some modern editors take only "early" from Q1, and print "now early down"; others take "more early," and print "more early down." Further, Q1 (though, again, quite clearly a garbled and abbreviated text) includes some stage directions that are not found in Q2, and today many editors who base their text on Q2 are glad to add these stage directions, because the directions help to give us a sense of what the play looked like on Shakespeare's stage. Thus, in 4.3.58, after Juliet drinks the potion, Q1 gives us this stage direction, not in Q2: *"She falls upon her bed within the curtains."*

In short, an editor's decisions do not end with the choice of a single copy text. First of all, editors must reckon with Elizabethan spelling. If they are not producing a facsimile, they probably modernize the spelling, but ought they to preserve the old forms of words that apparently were pronounced quite unlike their modern forms—*lanthorn, alablaster*? If they preserve these forms are they really preserving Shakespeare's forms or perhaps those of a compositor in the printing house? What is one to do when one finds *lanthorn* and *lantern* in adjacent lines? (The editors of this series in general, but not invariably, assume that words should be spelled in their modern form, unless, for instance, a rhyme is involved.) Elizabethan punctuation, too, presents problems. For example, in the First Folio, the only text for the play, Macbeth rejects his wife's idea that he can wash the blood from his hand (2.2.60–62):

> No: this my Hand will rather
> The multitudinous Seas incarnardine,
> Making the Greene one, Red.

Obviously an editor will remove the superfluous capitals, and will probably alter the spelling to "incarnadine," but what about the comma before "Red"? If we retain the comma, Macbeth is calling the sea "the green one." If we drop the comma, Macbeth is saying that his bloody hand will make the sea ("the Green") *uniformly* red.

An editor will sometimes have to change more than spelling and punctuation. Macbeth says to his wife (1.7.46–47):

> I dare do all that may become a man,
> Who dares no more, is none.

For two centuries editors have agreed that the second line is unsatisfactory, and have emended "no" to "do": "Who dares do more is none." But when in the same play (4.2.21–22) Ross says that fearful persons

> Floate vpon a wilde and violent Sea
> Each way, and moue,

need we emend the passage? On the assumption that the compositor misread the manuscript, some editors emend "each way, and move" to "and move each way"; others emend "move" to "none" (i.e., "Each way and none"). Other editors, however, let the passage stand as in the original. The editors of the Signet Classic Shakespeare have restrained themselves from making abundant emendations. In their minds they hear Samuel Johnson on the dangers of emendation: "I have adopted the Roman sentiment, that it is more honorable to save a citizen than to kill an enemy." Some departures (in addition to spelling, punctuation, and lineation) from the copy text have of course been made, but the original readings are listed in a note following the play, so that readers can evaluate the changes for themselves.

Following tradition, the editors of the Signet Classic Shakespeare have prefaced each play with a list of characters, and throughout the play have regularized the names of the speakers. Thus, in our text of *Romeo and Juliet*, all speeches by Juliet's mother are prefixed "Lady Capulet," although the 1599 Quarto of the play, which provides our copy text, uses at various points seven speech tags for this one character: *Capu. Wi.* (i.e., Capulet's wife), *Ca. Wi., Wi., Wife, Old La.* (i.e., Old Lady), *La.,* and *Mo.* (i.e., Mother). Similarly, in *All's Well That Ends Well*, the character whom we regularly call "Countess" is in the Folio (the copy text) variously identified as *Mother, Countess, Old Countess, Lady,* and *Old Lady.* Admittedly there is some loss in regularizing, since the various prefixes may give us a hint of the way Shakespeare (or a scribe who copied Shakespeare's manuscript) was thinking of the character in a particular scene—for instance, as a mother, or as an old lady. But too much can be made of these differing prefixes, since the social relationships implied are *not* always relevant to the given scene.

We have also added line numbers and in many cases act and scene divisions as well as indications of locale at the beginning of scenes. The Folio divided most of the plays into acts and some into scenes. Early eighteenth-century editors increased the divisions. These divisions, which provide a convenient way of referring to passages in the plays, have been retained, but when not in the text chosen as the basis for the Signet Classic text they are enclosed within square brackets, [ ], to indicate that they are editorial additions. Similarly, though no play of Shakespeare's was equipped with indications of the locale at the heads of scene divisions, locales have here been added in square brackets for the convenience of readers, who lack the information that costumes, properties, gestures, and scenery afford to spectators. Spectators can tell at a glance they are in the throne room, but without an editorial indication the reader may be puzzled for a while. It should be mentioned, incidentally, that there are a few authentic stage directions—perhaps Shakespeare's, perhaps a prompter's—that suggest locales, such as *"Enter Brutus in his orchard,"* and *"They go up into the Senate house."* It is hoped that the bracketed additions in the Signet text will provide readers with the sort of help provided by these two authentic directions, but it is equally hoped that the reader will remember that the stage was not loaded with scenery.

Shakespeare on the Stage

Each volume in the Signet Classic Shakespeare includes a brief stage (and sometimes film) history of the play. When we read about earlier productions, we are likely to find them eccentric, obviously wrongheaded—for instance, Nahum Tate's version of *King Lear*, with a happy ending, which held the stage for about a century and half, from the late seventeenth century until the end of the first quarter of the nineteenth. We see engravings of David Garrick, the greatest actor of the eighteenth century, in eighteenth-century garb as King Lear, and we smile, thinking how absurd the production must have been. If we are more thoughtful, we say, with the English novelist L. P. Hartley, "The past is a foreign country: they do things differently there." But if the eighteenth-century staging is a foreign country, what of the plays of the late sixteenth and seventeenth centuries? A foreign language, a foreign theater, a foreign audience.

Probably all viewers of Shakespeare's plays, beginning with Shakespeare himself, at times have been unhappy with the plays on the stage. Consider three comments about production that we find in the plays themselves, which suggest Shakespeare's concerns. The Chorus in *Henry V* complains that the heroic story cannot possibly be adequately staged:

> But pardon, gentles all,
> The flat unraisèd spirits that hath dared
> On this unworthy scaffold to bring forth
> So great an object. Can this cockpit hold
> The vasty fields of France? Or may we cram
> Within this wooden *O* the very casques
> That did affright the air at Agincourt?
>
> . . . .
>
> Piece out our imperfections with your thoughts.

(Prologue 1.8–14,23)

Second, here are a few sentences (which may or may not represent Shakespeare's own views) from Hamlet's longish lecture to the players:

> Speak the speech, I pray you, as I pronounced it to you, trippingly on the tongue. But if you mouth it, as many of our players do, I had as lief the town crier spoke my lines. . . . O, it offends me to the soul to hear a robustious periwig-pated fellow tear a passion to tatters, to very rags, to split the ears of the groundlings. . . . And let those that play your clowns speak no more than is set down for them, for there be of them that will themselves laugh, to set on some quantity of barren spectators to laugh too, though in the meantime some necessary question of the play be then to be considered. That's villainous and shows a most pitiful ambition in the fool that uses it. (3.2.1–47)

Finally, we can quote again from the passage cited earlier in this introduction, concerning the boy actors who played the female roles. Cleopatra imagines with horror a theatrical version of her activities with Antony:

> The quick comedians
> Extemporally will stage us, and present
> Our Alexandrian revels: Antony
> Shall be brought drunken forth, and I shall see
> Some squeaking Cleopatra boy my greatness
> I' th' posture of a whore.   (5.2.216–21)

It is impossible to know how much weight to put on such passages—perhaps Shakespeare was just being modest about his theater's abilities—but it is easy enough to think that he was unhappy with some aspects of Elizabethan production. Probably no production can fully satisfy a playwright, and for that matter, few productions can fully satisfy *us;* we regret this or that cut, this or that way of costuming the play, this or that bit of business.

One's first thought may be this: Why don't they just do "authentic" Shakespeare, "straight" Shakespeare, the play as Shakespeare wrote it? But as we read the plays—words written to be performed—it sometimes becomes clear that we do not know *how* to perform them. For instance, in *Antony and Cleopatra* Antony, the Roman general who has succumbed to Cleopatra and to Egyptian ways, says, "The nobleness of life / Is to do thus" (1.1.36–37). But what is "thus"? Does Antony at this point embrace Cleopatra? Does he embrace and kiss her? (There are, by the way, very few scenes of kissing on Shakespeare's stage, possibly because boys played the female roles.) Or does he make a sweeping gesture, indicating the Egyptian way of life?

This is not an isolated example; the plays are filled with lines that call for gestures, but we are not sure what the gestures should be. *Interpretation* is inevitable. Consider a passage in *Hamlet*. In 3.1, Polonius persuades his daughter, Ophelia, to talk to Hamlet while Polonius and Claudius eavesdrop. The two men conceal themselves, and Hamlet encounters Ophelia. At 3.1.131 Hamlet suddenly says to her, "Where's your father?" Why does Hamlet, apparently out of nowhere—they have not been talking about Polonius—ask this question? Is this an example of the "antic disposition" (fantastic behavior) that Hamlet earlier (1.5.172) had told Horatio and others—including us—he would display? That is, is the question about the whereabouts of her father a seemingly irrational one, like his earlier question (3.1.103) to Ophelia, "Ha, ha! Are you honest?" Or, on the other hand, has Hamlet (as in many productions) suddenly glimpsed Polonius's foot protruding from beneath a drapery at the rear? That is, does Hamlet ask the question because he has suddenly seen something suspicious and now is testing Ophelia? (By the way, in productions that do give Hamlet a physical cue, it is almost always Polonius rather than Claudius who provides the clue. This itself is an act of interpretation on the part of the director.) Or (a third possibility) does Hamlet get a clue from Ophelia, who inadvertently betrays the spies by nervously glancing at their place of hiding? This is the interpretation used in the BBC television version, where Ophelia glances in fear toward the hiding place just after Hamlet says "Why wouldst thou be a breeder of sinners?" (121–22). Hamlet, realizing that he is being observed, glances here and there *before* he asks "Where's your father?" The question thus is a climax to what he has been doing while speaking the preceding lines. Or (a fourth interpretation) does Hamlet suddenly, without the aid of any clue whatsoever, intuitively (insightfully, mysteriously, wonderfully) sense that someone is spying? Directors must decide, of course—and so must readers.

Recall, too, the preceding discussion of the texts of the plays, which argued that the texts—though they seem to be before us in permanent black on white—are unstable. The Signet text of *Hamlet*, which draws on the Second Quarto (1604) and the First Folio (1623) is considerably longer than any version staged in Shakespeare's time. Our version, even if spoken very briskly and played without any intermission, would take close to four hours, far beyond "the two hours' traffic of our stage" mentioned in the Prologue to *Romeo and Juliet*. (There are a few contemporary references to the duration of a play, but none mentions more than three hours.) Of Shakespeare's plays, only *The Comedy of Errors*, *Macbeth*, and *The Tempest* can be done in less than three hours without cutting. And even if we take a play that exists only in a short text, *Macbeth*, we cannot claim that we are experiencing the very play that Shakespeare conceived, partly because some of the Witches' songs almost surely are non-Shakespearean additions, and partly because we are not willing to watch the play performed without an intermission and with boys in the female roles.

Further, as the earlier discussion of costumes mentioned, the plays apparently were given chiefly in contemporary, that is, in Elizabethan dress. If today we give them in the costumes that Shakespeare probably saw, the plays seem not contemporary but curiously dated. Yet if we use our own dress, we find lines of dialogue that are at odds with what we see; we may feel that the language, so clearly not our own, is inappropriate coming out of people in today's dress. A common solution, incidentally, has been to set the plays in the nineteenth century, on the grounds that this attractively distances the play (gives them a degree of foreignness, allowing for interesting costumes) and yet doesn't put them into a museum world of Elizabethan England.

Inevitably our productions are adaptations, *our* adaptations, and inevitably they will look dated, not in a century but in twenty years, or perhaps even in a decade. Still, we cannot escape from our own conceptions. As the director Peter Brook has said, in *The Empty Space* (1968):

> It is not only the hair-styles, costumes and make-ups that look dated. All the different elements of staging—the shorthands of behavior that stand for emotions; gestures, gesticulations and tones of voice—are all fluctuating on an invisible stock exchange all the time. . . . A living theatre that thinks it can stand aloof from anything as trivial as fashion will wilt. (p. 16)

As Brook indicates, it is through today's hairstyles, costumes, makeup, gestures, gesticulations, tones of voice—this includes our *conception* of earlier hairstyles, costumes, and so forth if we stage the play in a period other than our own—that we inevitably stage the plays.

It is a truism that every age invents its own Shakespeare, just as, for instance, every age has invented its own classical world. Our view of ancient Greece, a slave-holding society in which even free Athenian women were severely circumscribed, does not much resemble the Victorians' view of ancient Greece as a glorious democracy, just as, perhaps, our view of Victorianism itself does not much resemble theirs. We cannot claim that the Shakespeare on our stage is the true Shakespeare, but in our stage productions we find a Shakespeare that speaks to us, a Shakespeare that our ancestors doubtless did not know but one that seems to us to be the true Shakespeare—at least for a while.

Our age is remarkable for the wide variety of kinds of staging that it uses for Shakespeare, but one development deserves special mention. This is the now common practice of race-blind or color-blind or nontraditional casting, which allows persons who are not white to play in Shakespeare. Previously blacks performing in Shakespeare were limited to a mere three roles, Othello, Aaron (in *Titus Andronicus*), and the Prince of Morocco (in *The Merchant of Venice*), and there were no roles at all for Asians. Indeed, African-Americans rarely could play even one of these three roles, since they were not welcome in white companies. Ira Aldridge (c. 1806–1867), a black actor of undoubted talent, was forced to make his living by performing Shakespeare in England and in Europe, where he could play not only Othello but also—in whiteface—other tragic roles such as King Lear. Paul Robeson (1898–1976) made theatrical history when he played Othello in London in 1930, and there was some talk about bringing the production to the United States, but there was more talk about whether American audiences would tolerate the sight of a black man—a real black man, not a white man in blackface—kissing and then killing a white woman. The idea was tried out in summer stock in 1942, the reviews were enthusiastic, and in the following year Robeson opened on Broadway in a production that ran an astounding 296 performances. An occasional all-black company sometimes performed Shakespeare's plays, but otherwise blacks (and other minority members) were in effect shut out from performing Shakespeare. Only since about 1970 has it been common for nonwhites to play major roles along with whites. Thus, in a 1996–97 production of *Antony and Cleopatra*, a white Cleopatra, Vanessa Redgrave, played opposite a black Antony, David Harewood.

Multiracial casting is now especially common at the New York Shakespeare Festival, founded in 1954 by Joseph Papp, and in England, where even siblings such as Claudio and Isabella in *Measure for Measure* or Lear's three daughters may be of different races. Probably most viewers today soon stop worrying about the lack of realism, and move beyond the color of the performers' skin to the quality of the performance.

Nontraditional casting is not only a matter of color or race; it includes sex. In the past, occasionally a distinguished woman of the theater has taken on a male role—Sarah Bernhardt (1844–1923) as Hamlet is perhaps the most famous example—but such performances were widely regarded as eccentric. Although today there have been some performances involving cross-dressing (a drag *As You Like It* staged by the National Theatre in England in 1966 and in the United States in 1974 has achieved considerable fame in the annals of stage history), what is more interesting is the casting of women in roles that traditionally are male but that need not be. Thus, a 1993–94 English production of *Henry V* used a woman—*not* cross-dressed—in the role of the governor of Harfleur. According to Peter Holland, who reviewed the production in *Shakespeare Survey* 48 (1995), "having a female Governor of Harfleur feminized the city and provided a direct response to the horrendous threat of rape and murder that Henry had offered, his language and her body in direct connection and opposition" (p. 210). Ten years from now the device may not play so effectively, but today it speaks to us. Shakespeare, born in the Elizabethan Age, has been dead nearly four hundred years, yet he is, as Ben Jonson said, "not of an age but for all time." We must understand, however, that he is "for all time" precisely because each age finds in his abundance something for itself and something of itself.

And here we come back to two issues discussed earlier in this introduction—the instability of the text and, curiously, the Bacon/Oxford heresy concerning the authorship of the plays. *Of course* Shakespeare wrote the plays, and we should daily fall on our knees to thank him for them—and yet there is something to the idea that he is not their only author. Every editor, every director and actor, and every reader to some degree shapes them, too, for when we edit, direct, act, or read, we inevitably become Shakespeare's collaborator and re-create the plays. The plays, one might say, are so cunningly contrived that they guide our responses, tell us how we ought to feel, and make a mark on us, but (for better or for worse) we also make a mark on them.

—SYLVAN BARNET
Tufts University

Introduction

"By indirections find directions out" (2.1.66)

Hamlet begins with a question, "Who's there?" and questions continue into the last scene, even after Hamlet's death: "Why does the drum come hither?," "Where is this sight?," and "What is it you would see?" (Later we will discuss this last question, which might be rephrased, "What have we seen?") Hamlet tells the Ghost that it comes in a "questionable shape" (1.4.43)—but even here we get into uncertainties and multiple responses, since "questionable" means "able to respond to questions" and also "dubious." (Some editors would question this assertion, sternly arguing that although the nature of the spirit may be dubious, its shape is not.) So many commentators on *Hamlet* have written so many words on one particular question, "Is Hamlet mad, or only pretending to be?" that Oscar Wilde was moved to ask yet another question, "Are the commentators on *Hamlet* mad, or only pretending to be?" The commentators of course have always been easy game. Almost two hundred years ago William Hazlitt remarked, not without some justice, "If we wish to know the force of human genius, we should read Shakespeare. If we wish to see the insignificance of human learning, we may study his commentators."

Commentary on almost all of Shakespeare's plays is highly varied, but there is at least one excuse for the particularly great range of comments on *Hamlet*. As is explained at some length in A Note on the Texts (p. 145), two early printed texts (1604 and 1623), though differing between themselves in many ways, unquestionably are closely derived from Shakespeare's lost manuscript—and a third text (1603), though far less authoritative, nevertheless is sometimes of use. (By way of contrast, for about half of the plays, including some of the most famous, such as *Julius Caesar, Twelfth Night, As You Like It,* and *Macbeth,* there is only one text, the 1623 text, to take into consideration.) Briefly, the 1604 text of *Hamlet*—the longest, and widely regarded as the best—includes 222 lines not found in the 1623 text, but the 1623 text includes 83 lines not found in the 1604 text. (Methods of counting vary slightly, so these figures must be taken as approximate.) For instance, only in the 1604 text does Hamlet talk, at considerable length, about "some vicious mole of nature" and about the "one defect" (1.4.24–31) that can seem to undo a man—a speech that many critics interpret as Hamlet's meditation on his own "tragic flaw." Indeed, without this speech we might be less inclined to talk about a tragic flaw, in Hamlet's case often said to be procrastination. (Sir Laurence Olivier's film version begins by announcing that the play is about "a man who could not make up his mind.") On the other hand, only in the 1623 text is there a passage in which Hamlet says that "Denmark's a prison," and that "there is nothing either good or bad but thinking makes it so" (2.2.247–54), a passage that, like the "vicious mole" in the other text, has given rise to abundant commentary. Further, there are hundreds of small differences between the texts, the most famous being Hamlet's reference to his "sallied" (i.e. sullied) flesh (1.2.129) in the 1604 text, and his reference to his "solid" flesh in the 1623 text.

Again, the three texts of the play are discussed on pages 145–61, but the point here is that at least some of the controversy over *Hamlet* occurs because critics sometimes are not talking about the same *Hamlet* and therefore are not talking about the same Hamlet. Moreover, the present *Hamlet* (a version made by adding to the 1604 text the eighty-odd lines found only in the 1623 text) is by far the longest of Shakespeare's plays, running to something like 3,900 lines. Hamlet's role is about 1,400 lines, 300 more lines than Shakespeare's next longest role (Richard III). In production, the play is almost always cut, and if one embraces the view that a play text is a mere script, and that *Hamlet* exists only when it is performed, each stage production gives the audience a somewhat different *Hamlet* and a somewhat different Hamlet. Later we will talk about the character of the protagonist, and we will glance briefly at the idea that perhaps the very concept of "character" is part of the problem. We can hardly hope to "pluck out the heart of [Hamlet's] mystery" (3.2.373–74), especially since we can find many mysteries in the play, such as, Why, if Horatio is familiar with current doings in Denmark in 1.1, is he unfamiliar with the notorious Danish habit of heavy drinking in 1.4? Indeed, one can fret with such questions as, How old is Hamlet? (he is explicitly said to be thirty, but this seems strangely old for a person who is an undergraduate), and, Did Rosencrantz and Guildenstern know the contents of the letter they were bringing to the English king? These perhaps are questions of the sort that Sir Thomas Browne had in mind when he said, some fifty years after Shakespeare's death, "What song the Sirens sang, or what name Achilles assumed when he hid himself among women, though puzzling questions, are not beyond all conjecture." We will try to approach the play by looking first at three large questions that have raised the passions of critics, "What is the nature of the ghost?"; "What attitude are we to adopt toward revenge?"; and "Does (or Why does) Hamlet delay?" We will then turn to Hamlet as we see him at the end of the play.

"Enter Ghost" (1.1.39 stage direction)

The earlier prose narratives of the Hamlet story do not include a ghost. Hamlet's uncle openly kills his brother, Hamlet's father, at a banquet (see page 167); there is no secret for any ghost to reveal to the son. But Shakespeare did not invent the ghost; he found the ghost in a lost *Hamlet*—probably written by Thomas Kyd, author of another revenge play, *The Spanish Tragedy*—that is mentioned as early as 1589 (but only mentioned, not described or discussed) and is recorded (in the papers of Philip Henslowe, a theatrical producer) as having been staged in 1594. But the closest we come to glimpsing the play itself is a brief comment made in 1596 by Thomas Lodge, who in *Wit's Misery and the World's Madness* writes of a devil who looked "as pale as the vizard of the ghost, which cried so miserably at the Theatre, like an oyster-wife, 'Hamlet, revenge.' "

Lodge's quotation tells us all we really know about the content of the lost *Hamlet*, commonly called the *Ur-Hamlet* (*The Original Hamlet*): The play included a ghost who called for revenge, and it was performed by Shakespeare's company (the Chamberlain's Men), who performed in an amphitheater called The Theatre. Perhaps we can go a bit further, and conjecture—really read backward from Shakespeare's *Hamlet* into the lost play—that in the lost play the murder was performed in secret and that the ghost revealed the details of the death to Hamlet.

How did ghosts come to be associated with tragedy, and particularly with revenge tragedy, in late sixteenth-century drama? Chiefly through the drama of Seneca, a Roman writer of tragedies. The Renaissance saw itself as giving new birth to the literature of the classical world after the alleged darkness of the Middle Ages. Greek drama continued to be relatively unknown in seventeenth-century England, but Roman drama—the tragedies of Seneca and the comedies of Plautus and Terence—became school texts, and translations were produced for those who could not read Latin. These Latin playwrights were the acknowledged masters, so it is not surprising that Polonius mentions them, assuring his hearers that "Seneca cannot be too heavy, nor Plautus too light" for the Players who have come to Elsinore (2.2.409–10). Polonius was echoing a commonplace; a few years before Shakespeare gave him this line, Francis Meres, in the course of comparing classical and English writers, wrote in *Palladis Tamia* ("Wit's Treasury," 1598), "As Plautus and Seneca are the best for comedy and tragedy among the Latins, so Shakespeare among the English is the most excellent in both kinds for the stage." The first English translation of Seneca was published in 1559, and in 1581, just a few years before Shakespeare must have begun his theatrical career, Thomas Newton collected the work of six translators into a volume called *Seneca, his Tenne Tragedies*. With a book of this sort at hand, even a dramatist who had not attended a university could write a play that included material that passed for classical elements. One of Shakespeare's contemporaries, Thomas Nashe, a university man, jeered at his less-educated fellow writers. In the following passage (1589), "sentences" means "wise sayings"; notice too the pretended slip of the tongue, where Nashe claims that when he said "*Hamlets*" he meant to say "handfuls."

> English Seneca read by candle-light yields many good sentences, as *Blood is a beggar,* and so forth; and if you entreat him fair in a frosty morning, he will afford you whole *Hamlets*—I should say handfuls—of tragical speeches.

For the Elizabethan, Senecan tragedy was characterized by "sentences" (sententious remarks), passionate utterances (especially statements about the pain of living, and also defiances of fate), deeds of horror, and vengeful ghosts. Only two ghosts appear in the plays of Seneca (the ghost of Tantalus in *Thyestes*, and the ghost of Thyestes in *Agamemnon*), and neither ghost interacts with the other characters; rather, these two serve as choral figures, commenting on the horrors they endured on earth and in the afterlife in Tartarus, and expressing the hope that they will be avenged. In Shakespeare's *Hamlet* we hear the influence of Seneca's horrible world when the ghost tells Hamlet how a scab ("tetter") covered ("barked") his body with a leperlike crust:

> . . . a most instant tetter barked about
> Most lazarlike with vile and loathsome crust
> All my smooth body.   (1.5.71–73)

And we get a Christian version of a Senecan hero's mental anguish when the ghost tells us that he was killed "Unhouseled, disappointed, unaneled" (77), that is, without having received the housel (the sacrament of communion), unabsolved ("disappointed"), and without extreme unction

("unaneled"), "With all my imperfections on my head. /
O, horrible! O, horrible! Most horrible!" (77–80).

The horrors done to him, the ghost clearly indicates, demand revenge:

> If thou didst ever thy dear father love—
>
> . . . .
>
> Revenge his foul and most unnatural murder.   (23–25)

Judging from Lodge's comment of 1596 about the revenge
ghost sounding like an oyster-vender, by the time Shakespeare wrote *Hamlet* (c. 1600–1601), this sort of thing had
been said so many times on the Elizabethan stage that it
was a subject of comedy. Additional evidence to the effect
that the revenge ghost had become ridiculous is found in
the Induction (Prologue) to an anonymous play belonging
to Shakespeare's company, *A Warning for Fair Women*,
printed in 1599:

> A filthy whining ghost,
> Lapt in some foul sheet or a leather pilch,*
> Comes screaming like a pig half-sticked.
> And cries "Vindicta! Revenge, revenge."
> With that, a little resin flasheth forth,
> Like smoke out of a tobacco pipe or a boy's squib.

But what are we to make of Shakespeare's ghost? The
question is not whether it is ridiculous—virtually no one
suggests it is—but what is its nature? True, Gertrude does
not see it in 3.4 when Hamlet sees it, but we can eliminate
the view that it is a figment of Hamlet's imagination since
it is seen not only by Hamlet but also by Barnardo, Marcellus, and Horatio. We can also eliminate the idea that the
ghost comes, like Seneca's ghosts, from a pagan under-
world, since it explicitly refers to Christian rituals and the
play includes numerous other references to a Christian
world. The ghost, then, is either what it says it is, or it is a

---

*Leather or coarse woolen garment.

demon who has taken the form of Hamlet's father in order
to do mischief on earth—for instance to destroy Hamlet's
soul by enticing him to wickedness. In Hamlet's words, it is
either a "spirit of health" or a "goblin damned." This second view has been argued by several critics, notably
Eleanor Prosser in *Hamlet and Revenge* (2nd ed., 1971).
The gist is this: (a) Protestants do not believe in Purgatory,
so the ghost is either a Catholic ghost from Purgatory—it
says it is "Doomed for a certain term to walk the
night, / And for the day confined to fast in fires, / Till the
foul crimes [i.e. sins] done in my days of nature / Are burnt
and purged away" (1.5.10–13)—or it is a demon disguised
as a ghost; (b) a ghost released from Purgatory, presumably
for some heavenly purpose, would not seek revenge, so it
must be a demon; (c) further evidence that it is a demon is
its suspicious behavior; for instance, it disappears when
Horatio invokes heaven (1.1.49) and it disappears again at
the crowing of the cock, a bird which Marcellus associates
with Christ (157–64). Certainly some Elizabethans believed
that demons could take the form of a deceased person, and
such demons appear in Elizabethan plays, notably Marlowe's *Doctor Faustus*. Hamlet himself says,

> The spirit that I have seen
> May be a devil, and the devil hath power
> T' assume a pleasing shape, yea, and perhaps
> Out of my weakness and my melancholy,
> As he is very potent with such spirits,
> Abuses me to damn me.   (2.2.610–15)

What can be said against the view that the ghost is a demon disguised as Hamlet's father, presumably intending to
snare Hamlet's soul? Only this: (a) when the ghost first appears to Horatio, and then to Hamlet, they do not raise the
possibility that it may be a demon, so the audience—after
all, we are talking about a play—would not consider this
possibility. Later, they do consider the possibility (Horatio
as early as 1.4.69–74), but nothing in the play confirms this
view. Even when the "Ghost cries under the stage" (1.5.148
stage direction), no one suggests it is a demon; (b) although

at the sound of the cock it "started, like a guilty thing / Upon a fearful summons" (1.1.148–49), Marcellus says, when the ghost disappears, "We do it wrong, being so majestical, / To offer it the show of violence" (143–44); (c) why would a demon say to Hamlet, "Taint not thy mind, nor let thy soul contrive / Against thy mother aught" (1.5.85–86)? Admittedly, one might reply that this wholesome advice itself is proof of the demon's cunning, a bit of truth thrown in to make the deception more believable, but could an audience possibly understand that this figure is not what it says it is?; (d) in every one of Shakespeare's other plays, the ghosts—for instance in *Richard III* the ghosts of Richard's victims, in *Julius Caesar* the ghost of Caesar, and in *Macbeth* the ghost of Banquo—are what they seem to be.

Can the case be definitively proved to everyone's satisfaction? Apparently not, since scholars continue to debate the issue. But can we really see *Hamlet* as a play about a demon who tries to ensnare Hamlet? Doesn't it make more sense to see *Hamlet* as a play about a man who learns, from his father's ghost, that a terrible crime has been committed, and who feels he is obliged to set it right? In the course of facing this great task Hamlet not surprisingly has doubts, including doubts about the ghost, but the play itself provides no substantial evidence to indicate that when Hamlet overcomes his doubts about the ghost he is making a disastrous error. Isn't an audience likely to agree with Hamlet's conclusion that the ghost is "an honest ghost" (138), especially in the absence of any remarks from the trustworthy Horatio? Still, one may conceivably be uneasy with the ghost's demand for revenge, and this brings us to the next issue.

"Revenge his foul and most unnatural murder" (1.5.25)

Revenge, beyond all doubt, is widely condemned in Elizabethan writing, dramatic and otherwise. For instance, Francis Bacon in his essay on "Revenge" says, "The more man's nature runs to [revenge], the more ought law to weed it out." And yet, it is not this simple. Bacon goes on to say,

"Public revenges are for the most part fortunate, as that of the death of Caesar . . . and many more. But in private revenges it is not so." If we look at some of Shakespeare's uses of the word *revenge* we will find that our responses (and surely the responses of the original audiences) must vary, depending on the context. Thus, Othello, mistakenly thinking his wife has been unfaithful, determines to seek "revenge" (3.3.456), and we regard his goal as wicked, but in *Macbeth*, Malcolm, counseling the grief-stricken Macduff (Macbeth has murdered Macduff's wife and children), says, "Let's make us med'cines of our great revenge / To cure this deadly grief" (4.3.214–15), and we clearly regard his goal—killing Macbeth—as proper. Later in the play, calling Macbeth to show himself on the battlefield, Macduff says,

> Tyrant, show thy face!
> If thou be'st slain and with no stroke of mine,
> My wife and children's ghost will haunt me still.   (5.7.14–16)

And, to cite yet another example from *Macbeth*, when Banquo is slain he calls out to his son, Fleance,

> O, treachery! Fly, good Fleance, fly, fly, fly!
> Thou mayst revenge.   (3.3.17–18)

We all know that when we are wronged we should turn the other cheek (Jesus's words in Matthew 5.38–39), but the ancient idea of an eye for an eye continues to hold its appeal. In much popular culture, then and now, revenge is accepted. Consider "Revenge is sweet," a proverb going back at least to Shakespeare's day, and "Don't get mad, get even," a saying attributed to the father of John F. Kennedy. Elizabethan authorities were fond of telling their subjects that "Vengeance is mine; I will repay, saith the Lord" (Paul, Epistle to the Romans, 12.19), but the Elizabethans tolerated revenge in various circumstances. For instance, the "Homily against Disobedience and Wilful Rebellion" prohibited rebellion against lawful princes but not against usurpers, and the Bond of Association, signed by thousands

in 1584, specified that subjects are obliged "to take the uttermost revenge" on anyone who harms the rightful
monarch. Hamlet comes to know that Claudius murdered
the legitimate monarch, so we might conclude that Hamlet,
as dutiful son and as loyal subject, has an obligation to kill
the man who killed his father. We will return to this point
in a moment, but perhaps it is also worth mentioning that
probably the most highly revered ship in British history
was the *Revenge*, commanded for a while by Sir Francis
Drake. The word must have had a positive charge.

On several occasions Hamlet comments on the fact that
he has not yet taken his revenge. Many critics have suggested that he cannot take revenge because his moral and
religious code prevents him from doing so, but only once—
and then very briefly—does Hamlet raise the issue of the
rightness or wrongness of revenge. He is addressing Horatio, just after the passage in which he says he has sent
Rosencrantz and Guildenstern to their deaths but their
deaths are "not near my conscience."

> Does it not, think thee, stand me now upon—
> He that hath killed my king, and whored my mother,
> Popped in between th' election and my hopes,
> Thrown out his angle* for my proper life,
> And with such coz'nage†—is't not perfect conscience
> To quit‡ him with this arm? And is't not to be damned
> To let this canker of our nature come
> In further evil?   (5.2.63–70)

There is a slight complication here; the last three lines, not
in the Second Quarto (1604), appear only in the Folio
(1623) version. Probably the compositor accidentally omitted the lines from the Quarto, or possibly Shakespeare
added them to the text that ultimately was printed in 1623,
but in any case it is clear that Hamlet does not doubt the appropriateness of taking revenge. And that is almost all there
is in the way of discussion of revenge. It's not much, and it

*Fishing line.
†Trickery.
‡Requite, pay back.

is formulated as questions ("Does it not?" "And is't not?"), but if anything it is a justification of revenge. If we give full weight to the word "damned," we can even say that Hamlet, far from doubting the code of revenge, regards it as his sacred duty.

Two other passages in the play, however, might seem to call into doubt the justness of the avenger, and in any case readers and viewers often are keenly aware that revenge can hardly be satisfactory, since even if Hamlet succeeds in killing Claudius, the death of Hamlet's father and the infidelity of his mother cannot be altered. The first passage in the play that calls the justness of revenge into doubt is the whole business of the speech about "the rugged Pyrrhus" that Hamlet requests of the Players in 2.2. The speech describes Pyrrhus's slaughter of Priam, King of Troy. (Pyrrhus is avenging his father, Achilles, who was killed in the Trojan War by Paris, son of King Priam of Troy.) Presumably Hamlet requests the speech because in it he finds a parallel to his own situation. One point of connection is given in the lines where Pyrrhus, who has been seeking out Priam, hears the fall of Troy, and interrupts his action:

> For lo, his sword,
> Which was declining on the milky head
> Of reverend Priam, seemed i' th' air to stick.
> So as a painted tyrant Pyrrhus stood,
> And like a neutral to his will and matter*
> Did nothing.
>
> (488–93)

A second connection that we might make between Hamlet and Pyrrhus, especially if we wish to argue that Shakespeare depicts revenge as damnable or at least as wrong, is this: Pyrrhus is compared to "th' Hyrcanian beast" (i.e. a tiger), his "purpose" is "black," he is "horridly tricked [i.e. adorned] / With blood of fathers, mothers, daughters, sons," he is "o'ersizèd [smeared over] with coagulate gore," and he is explicitly called "the hellish Pyrrhus" (461–74). Here the avenger clearly is depicted unfavorably. On the

---

*Task.

other hand, as the play progresses, if the image of Pyrrhus ever again enters our mind it must be because we see that Hamlet is *not* like Pyrrhus; he does *not* kill a helpless old man.

The other passage in which Shakespeare explicitly calls our attention to revenge has to do with Laertes, who, like Hamlet (and also like Fortinbras) has lost his father. Speaking to Claudius, Laertes demands to know how his father died:

> How came he dead? I'll not be juggled with.
> To hell allegiance, vows to the blackest devil,
> Conscience and grace to the profoundest pit!
> I dare damnation. To this point I stand,
> That both the worlds I give to negligence,
> Let come what comes, only I'll be revenged
> Most throughly for my father.   (4.5.130–36)

Claudius is of course only too happy to direct Laertes's anger, and his quest for vengeance, against Hamlet. Two scenes later Claudius stirs the youth to the point that Laertes says he would cut his foe's "throat i' the' church" (4.7.126), a statement that Claudius sanctimoniously caps:

> No place indeed should murder sanctuarize;
> Revenge should have no bounds.   (127–28)

But do these passages in any way indicate that Hamlet is wrong to seek revenge? If anything, they serve to heighten our sympathy for Hamlet, who is pitted against an unscrupulous foe. We can juxtapose Laertes's exuberant willingness to cut his foe's "throat i' th' church" with the earlier scene in which Hamlet did *not* kill Claudius while Claudius was praying. In that scene, Hamlet gives a dreadful reason for not taking revenge—he says he wants to damn Claudius's soul as well as kill his body—but in any case we in the audience are immensely relieved that he does not act, partly because Claudius is at prayer, and partly because Hamlet's thoughts at this moment are so tainted.

In much tragedy, for instance *King Lear* and *Macbeth*,

the tragic hero sets into motion the chain of events that destroys him. Most tragedy begins with the hero in a situation of power, we might say in a prosperous condition; the play then shows the hero making what Aristotle called a tragic error, and we watch the hero fall into misery. Lear, a commanding figure at the start, wishes to retire; he acts on this wish, and he reaps a whirlwind. Macbeth, a favored general, is told that he will become a king; he acts to ensure this future, and he brings destruction upon himself. We see in such plays what the philosopher Alfred North Whitehead in *Science and the Modern World* called "the remorseless working of things," which in Whitehead's view is "the vision possessed by science." The idea that actions have consequences for the doer is evident, too, in an assertion in the Hebrew Bible, "Whoso diggeth a pit shall fall therein, and he that rolleth a stone, it will return" (Proverbs 26.27).

Revenge tragedy, too, shows us the remorseless working of things, but it necessarily begins very differently from such plays as *Lear* and *Macbeth*. In revenge tragedy the hero does not initiate the action, does not begin in a situation of power; on the contrary, in revenge tragedy the hero is caught up in a situation not at all of his making. In *Hamlet*, the prince's father has been murdered, and his mother has married the murderer. The avenger, especially in Senecan revenge tragedy, begins at a disadvantage and is forced to engage in intrigue. Caught up in a situation not of his own making, and confronted with a powerful and unscrupulous foe, the avenger commonly is forced to perform deeds as monstrous as or even more monstrous than those that goad him into motion. The theme is from crime to greater crime—the digging, so to speak, of a deeper pit, perhaps with spikes in its bottom, or the rolling of a heavier rock onto the initial offender. Thus, Medea's husband deserts her and, maddened, she punishes him by murdering their children as well as his new bride.

We do not know much about the lost *Hamlet* that preceded Shakespeare's play, but we do know that other avengers in Elizabethan drama, forced by circumstances to exceed in guile the villains who have injured them, become deeply tainted, unless we absolve them on the grounds that the injuries they suffered drove them to insanity. (Seneca's heroes are slaves of passion, particularly a rage induced by the Furies. Phaedra, for instance, says, "What can reason do? *Furor* has conquered me. The strong god controls my mind.") In the most important surviving Elizabethan precursor of *Hamlet*, Thomas Kyd's *The Spanish Tragedy* (c. 1587), the demented avenger, Hieronimo, actually (mis)quotes in Latin a line from Seneca's *Agamemnon*, in which Clytemnestra in effect asserts that she must kill lest she be killed: *"Per scelus semper tutum est sceleribus iter"* (3.13.6), i.e. "The safe way for crime is always through crime." Hieronimo's next line, this one in English, sets forth another Senecan motif, "Strike, and strike home, where wrong is offered thee." In a slightly later play, John Marston's *Antonio's Revenge* (1601), the ghost that calls on his son for revenge also quotes Seneca, this time from *Thyestes*, a play that influenced Shakespeare's most Senecan play, *Titus Andronicus* (1592–94). Marston's avenger says, *"Scelera non ulcisceris nisi vincis"* (3.1.51), i.e. "You do not avenge crimes unless you conquer," with the implication that the avenger must go further than his injurer did.

In Seneca, and to a large extent in *The Spanish Tragedy*, *Antonio's Revenge*, and *Titus Andronicus*, revenge is ceremoniously performed, a solemn ritual, but it is a hideously bloody ritual. In *Titus Andronicus*, for instance, the injured tragic hero takes his revenge by inviting his foe, Queen Tamora, to a feast at which he feeds the unwitting Tamora her own children. We don't know how the Romans responded to Seneca's plays (the plays seem to have been written for reading, not for performance), nor do we know how the Elizabethans responded to *The Spanish Tragedy*, *Titus*, or *Antonio's Revenge*, but to a modern viewer the ritual celebrant, inevitably bloodied by the sacrifice, seems tainted, savage, even villainous, though the savagery and the villainy are partly diminished by madness.

In the absence of the *Ur-Hamlet*, we cannot speak with confidence, but it probably was Shakespeare's distinctive idea to present a new sort of avenger: A man who has been horribly wronged succeeds in avenging the wrong without himself becoming deeply corrupted.

Let's begin by recalling Laertes as an avenger. We have seen how easily he is duped, and how corrupt he becomes. He huffily talks of his honor (5.2.247–49), but even while speaking thus he holds a foil that has been tipped with poison. A few moments later, dying from the poison he had prepared for Hamlet, he confesses "the foul practice [i.e. deception]" (318). He regains a bit of his lost honor by revealing that the king has planned the affair, and by forgiving Hamlet for the death of Polonius:

> It is a poison tempered by himself.
> Exchange forgiveness with me, noble Hamlet.
> Mine and my father's death come not upon thee . . .   (329–31)

"I do not know / Why yet I live to say, 'This thing's to do' "(4.4.43–44)

In the earliest extant versions of the Hamlet story (see page 167), delay is not a problem, at least not for readers. The Danish monarch is killed by his brother, who marries the queen; the son feigns insanity so that while contriving revenge he will be ignored as a harmless idiot. He is, however, suspected and tested; he evades the tests, is shipped off to England with a death warrant, alters the letters, and returns to avenge his father. The events in the narrative apparently cover several years, but there is no sense of delay, only a sense of plotting and counterplotting.

In Shakespeare's play, however, rightly or wrongly the question of why Hamlet delays, or even *whether* Hamlet delays, has seemed central to many critics. "But why in the world," A. C. Bradley asked at the beginning of the twentieth century, "did not Hamlet obey the ghost at once, and so save seven of these eight lives?" Bradley's own answer was, "The whole story turns upon the peculiar character of the hero," and indeed most discussions of the delay turn into discussions of Hamlet's character. Among the famous explanations is the one offered in Goethe's novel *Wilhelm Meisters Lehrjahre* (*Wilhelm Meister's Apprenticeship,*

1795). In Book 4, Chapter 13, the hero quotes "The time is out of joint. O cursèd spite, / That ever I was born to set it right" (1.5.188–89), and then says:

> In these words, I imagine, will be found the key to Hamlet's whole procedure. To me it is clear that Shakespeare meant, in the present case, to represent the effects of a great action laid upon a soul unfit for the performance of it. In this view the whole piece seems to me to be composed. There is an oak-tree planted in a costly jar, which should have borne only pleasant flowers in its bosom; the roots expand, the jar is shivered.
>
> A lovely, pure, noble, and most moral nature, without the strength of nerve which forms a hero, sinks beneath a burden which it cannot bear and must not cast away. All duties are holy for him; the present is too hard. Impossibilities have been required of him; not in themselves impossibilities, but such for him. He winds, and turns, and torments himself; he advances and recoils; is ever put in mind, ever puts himself in mind; at last does all but lose his purpose from his thoughts; yet still without recovering his peace of mind.

Samuel Taylor Coleridge, in *The Characters of Shakespear's Plays* (1817) has a similar interpretation:

> In Hamlet I conceive [Shakespeare] to have wished to exemplify the moral necessity of a due balance between our attention to outward objects and our meditation on inward thoughts—a due balance between the real and the imaginary world. In Hamlet this balance does not exist—his thoughts, images, and fancy [being] far more vivid than his perceptions, and his very perceptions instantly passing through the medium of his contemplations, and acquiring as they pass a form and a color not naturally their own. Hence great, enormous, intellectual activity, and a consequent proportionate aversion to real action, with all its symptoms and accompanying qualities.
>
> (Notes for a lecture on *Hamlet*, 1813)

A. C. Bradley, from whose *Shakespearean Tragedy* (1904) we have already quoted, took issue with critics such as these because they believed that "Hamlet's procrastination was the normal response of an overspeculative nature confronted with a difficult practical problem." For Bradley, Hamlet was normally a man of action; his melancholy is not a part of his habitual behavior but, rather, it is a disease produced by particular circumstances, his father's death and especially from his mother's hasty remarriage. "This pathological condition," Bradley says, accounts for Hamlet's procrastination, as well as for his callousness (for instance his harsh treatment of Ophelia and his cool dismissiveness of the dead Polonius and Rosencrantz and Guildenstern). Bradley granted that Hamlet is capable of bursts of activity, such as the killing of Polonius, but he held that the shocks that Hamlet has undergone have changed him into someone who "may truly be called diseased." This melancholy, in Bradley's view, accounts for his delay.

What are the signs that Hamlet delays? One would have thought it evident enough from Hamlet's question to the ghost in the queen's private room: "Do you not come your tardy son to chide . . . ?" (3.4.107). The ghost, apparently agreeing that Hamlet is "tardy," speaks of Hamlet's "almost blunted purpose" (112). Further, in two soliloquies ("O, what a rogue and peasant slave am I," 2.2.560, triggered by the Player's speech, and "How all occasions do inform against me," 4.4.32, triggered by the conversation with Fortinbras's Captain), Hamlet reminds us of his delay.

Why does Hamlet delay? One of the earliest comments on the subject offered a common-sense view that is still occasionally uttered. In an anonymous essay called *Some Remarks on the Tragedy of Hamlet Prince of Denmark* (1736), the author (perhaps Sir Thomas Hanmer, who later edited Shakespeare's plays) said:

> The case indeed is this: Had Hamlet gone naturally to work, as we could suppose such a prince to do in parallel circumstances, there would have been an end of our play. The poet therefore was obliged to delay his hero's revenge; but then he should have contrived some good reason for it.

At least the first sentence is right; in a revenge tragedy, the successful completion of the revenge must be delayed, so that viewers can enjoy the plots and counterplots or, in the case of *Hamlet*, they can enjoy the tragic hero's development. Later scholars have contrived reasons, arguing, for instance, that the king is closely guarded and that Hamlet cannot easily get at him—though Laertes seems to have no trouble when he bursts in "with others" on the king in 4.5.110, despite the king's call for his Swiss bodyguards a few lines earlier. Another argument is that Hamlet must kill the king when the king's guilt is evident to the public, though Hamlet doesn't see fit to tell the audience that this is the special difficulty that causes him to delay. Still another argument is that there is no real delay because indeed he must first test the ghost's veracity, and then when he has the opportunity to kill the praying king, of course he cannot act in this particular circumstance, just as none of us could. Hamlet's self-recriminations (notably that he is "tardy") are said to be unjustified, rather like the recriminations we visit upon ourselves when we mentally say, "I don't know why I am standing for this," though we really know perfectly well that we endure the offensive situation because we are civilized. In fact, some writers have gone so far as to say that Hamlet's announcements of delay in taking revenge are not to be taken as indications that he is delaying, much less as indications of a particular kind of personality, but rather are the playwright's way of reminding us of the important action that we know we soon shall be witnessing. In this view, the talk about delay is a way of heightening the suspense. There surely is something to this theatrical view. Consider the passage (2.2.571–72) in which Hamlet asks himself what the Player would do "Had he the motive and the cue for passion / That I have." Probably the effect of the lines is not to make us wonder about Hamlet's character but to cast our minds forward, to make us wonder what Hamlet will do to fulfill the ghost's command.

Still, the idea that the self-reproaches serve chiefly to increase our interest in what will happen somehow remains unconvincing, and so the hunt continues for an explanation for the delay. "Hamlet's moral code forbids revenge, so that is why he can't easily act." An engaging idea, but nothing in the play supports it; Hamlet never expresses the slightest revulsion against the idea of revenge. On the contrary, in one passage (5.2.68–70) he suggests that he has a religious obligation to kill Claudius: ". . . is't not to be damned / to let this canker of our nature come / In further evil?"

Perhaps the most interesting reason that our century has offered is Freud's suggestion, first made in 1900 in a footnote to *The Interpretation of Dreams*: Hamlet cannot take vengeance on the man who killed his father and possessed his mother, because these actions are fulfillments of Hamlet's own repressed Oedipal wishes. Ernest Jones amplified this point in an article in *American Journal of Psychology*, January 1910, and at greater length in a small book, *Hamlet and Oedipus* (1949). Essentially Jones argues that Hamlet delays because if he killed Claudius he would be killing the man who fulfilled his own desires; to kill Claudius would be to kill part of himself.

Two arguments commonly offered against this view are: (1) Shakespeare did not have the advantage of reading Freud, i.e. he could not have been familiar with this view, and (2) Hamlet abundantly praises his father, rather than harbors aggressive feelings toward him. To the first objection the psychoanalysts (and others) reply, rightly, that of course Shakespeare did not read Freud, but he could have had the insight (consciously or not) that Freud later had; indeed, Freud on several occasions said that Sophocles and Shakespeare were his predecessors. On the second point Freudians reply that Hamlet is guiltily compensating for his Oedipal desires by idealizing his father and directing his aggression toward a father-figure, Claudius. This response, where the words of the play are simply ignored, is not so satisfactory; in effect it holds that the Freudian critic's interpretation must be right, and if the words of the text do not support the interpretation, well, the words are deceptive. (By the way, an amusing illustration of Freud's determination to find facts that confirm the theory is seen in his changing view of authorship. In his early years, when he believed that Shakespeare wrote the play, he connected it with the death of Shakespeare's father in 1601, the probable date of the play. But when Freud came to believe that the plays were written not by Shakespeare but by the Earl of Oxford, he had to find a connection with a different father—and of course he found it, this time in Oxford's boyhood experience of his father's death and his mother's quick remarriage.)

We are, at last, in a position to try to say something useful about the play, or at least about the end of the play.

"The readiness is all" (5.2.223–24)

In talking about delay we noticed that almost inevitably critics relate delay—a matter of plot—to Hamlet's character. The idea of *character* today is unfashionable. If the text of a play is unstable (a point touched on briefly in the Overview, page xlix, and more extensively in A Note on the Texts of *Hamlet*, page 145, where it is explained that *Hamlet* exists in three early texts, as well as in countless differing modern editions and wildly different productions), how can anything as complex as a human being have a stable "character"? We are, it is sometimes said today, not unified selves, not "characters" or "personalities," but rather we are mere sites traversed by the discourses to which we are exposed. We may think that in large measure we have shaped our own characters, but according to this view, we passively (or for the most part passively), absorb our environments, and there is no essential self. The fatuous Polonius may believe in a self ("This above all, to thine own self be true"), but wiser heads (it is said) know that there is no self, only passing fancies. After all, is not Hamlet sometimes the grief-stricken prince, at other times the lover of Ophelia, at other times the scorner of Ophelia, at still other times the impetuous man of action who kills Polonius, and sends Rosencrantz and Guildenstern to their deaths, and even (to cut short what might be a long list) the amateur dramatic critic? What, it may be asked, is Hamlet's "self"? How can we speak, then, of a coherent personality?

Probably most of us believe that indeed we *are* "unified selves." We may go even further, and believe that for most people character becomes fixed in maturity. "In most of us," the psychologist William James said, "by the age of thirty, the character has set like plaster, and will never soften again." The idea that people have a consistent and unchanging character is an ancient one. The ancient Roman historian Tacitus, whose insight into character is praised even today (*The Oxford Companion to Classical Literature* speaks of his "penetrating insight into character"), believed that character is an unchanging essence. He explained the crimes of aging emperors as the manifestations of a character that they had earlier concealed. Few of us probably hold such a view, but (again, probably) most of us do believe that people have a unified personality. On the other hand, we all know we have said things like, "I was beside myself," "I must have been out of my mind," "Something possessed me." Hamlet says something along these lines in his apology to Laertes:

>   . . . you must needs have heard,
> How I am punished with a sore distraction.
> What I have done
> That might your nature, honor, and exception*
> Roughly awake, I here proclaim was madness.
> Was't Hamlet wronged Laertes? Never Hamlet.
> If Hamlet from himself be ta'en away,
> And when he's not himself does wrong Laertes,
> Then Hamlet does it not, Hamlet denies it.
> Who does it then? His madness.   (229–38)

Interestingly, most readers and viewers do *not* find Hamlet's excuse acceptable, unless perhaps they feel that, yes, the ghost's revelations of murder and adultery, along with Ophelia's betrayal and then her death, have been sufficient to unhinge Hamlet at least in some moments—for instance when he grappled with Laertes in the grave.

How is Hamlet to fulfill the ghost's commands, in a way

---

*Disapproval.

that is satisfying to us? Do we, for example, want him to kill Claudius when Claudius is praying (3.3)? Surely not. We may be shocked by the reason he gives for not killing Claudius—he says he wants to catch Claudius in an act of sin, so that Claudius will be damned—but we are nevertheless glad that he does not kill the king at this moment. We want him to fulfill the ghost's command, but we want him to do it in a way that is fully satisfying to us.

Let's begin (as many other commentators have done) by comparing Hamlet with the other figures in the play who avenge their fathers. We have already discussed "the rugged Pyrrhus" in the Player's speech (2.2.461). Pyrrhus's father, Achilles, died in the Trojan war, killed by Paris, son of Priam, the aged King of Troy. Do we want Hamlet to be like Pyrrhus, who is compared to a tiger and who is described as "horridly tricked / With blood of fathers, mothers, daughters, sons"? (468–69) Pyrrhus, all in all, is shown as a dreadful machine wound up for slaughtering. He may be a suitable hero within an ancient epic, but we do not want Hamlet to emulate him.

We have also commented on Laertes, who avenges the death of his father, Polonius. Laertes is certainly a man of action—he bursts in upon the king—and he vows that he would cut Hamlet's throat in the church (4.7.136), a circumstance that may remind us of Hamlet's failure to kill the king at prayer in 3.3. But we soon see that this passionate avenger, this man who is so concerned with honor, is easily manipulated by Claudius into most dishonorable behavior. No, we do not want a Hamlet who has the passion (and the easily adjusted sense of honor) that Laertes shows.

The third figure in the play who might be a model for Hamlet is Fortinbras ("Strong-arm"). Like Pyrrhus, Laertes, and Hamlet, Fortinbras has lost a father. In 4.4 Hamlet encounters a Captain in Fortinbras's army, who tells him that a battle will be fought over a worthless piece of land. In a soliloquy that begins, "How all occasions do inform against me," Hamlet utters recriminations against himself for not having acted, and he goes on to praise Fortinbras, a man "whose spirit, with divine ambition puffed," will act "even

for an eggshell," and who will "find quarrel in a straw /
When honor's at the stake." The speech ends thus:

> How stand I then,
> That have a father killed, a mother stained,
> Excitements of my reason and my blood,
> And let all sleep, while to my shame I see
> The imminent death of twenty thousand men
> That for a fantasy and trick of fame
> Go to their graves like beds, fight for a plot
> Whereon the numbers cannot try the cause,
> Which is not tomb enough and continent
> To hide the slain? O, from this time forth,
> My thoughts be bloody, or be nothing worth!   (56–66)

Meditating on Fortinbras's imminent battle stirs Hamlet to
thoughts of honor, but surely the words he uses (even
though they rouse him) *undercut* this sort of honor, which
is "puffed," and which is connected with an "eggshell,"
"straw," "fantasy and trick of fame" (i.e. illusion and trifle
of reputation), and the deaths of thousands of innocent
men. Furthermore, however eager we are for Hamlet to
avenge his father, we are not sure we want his thoughts to
be "bloody." What *do* we want?

We want Hamlet to avenge his father in a way that we
find satisfying. And Shakespeare satisfies our desire primarily in three ways—by changing Hamlet's mood, by establishing a ritual setting for the act of vengeance, and by
having Hamlet act spontaneously—without plotting—in circumstances that his enemy has established (Claudius, so to
speak, kills himself). We will begin with Hamlet's mood.
There is not space here to go through the play speech by
speech, but most readers agree that when Hamlet returns
from the sea journey, he seems poised, almost serene at
times. There will still be outbursts, notably in the struggle
with Laertes in the grave (5.1), but shortly after this out-
burst, we get Hamlet's report of his sea journey. He could
not sleep, he tells Horatio:

> Sir, in my heart there was a kind of fighting
> That would not let me sleep. . . .
> > > > Rashly
> (And praised be rashness for it) let us know,
> Our indiscretion sometime serves us well
> When our deep plots do pall, and that should learn us
> There's a divinity that shapes our ends,
> Rough-hew them how we will.   (5.2.4–11)

Hamlet goes on to say how, finding he was "benetted round with villains" (29) (Rosencrantz and Guildenstern were carrying letters from Claudius that in effect were a death sentence for Hamlet), he instantly forged a letter, affixed the royal seal ("even in that was heaven ordinant" [48]), and on the next day by chance (or do we think that again heaven was ordinant?) escaped by boarding the pirate ship. When Horatio says that Claudius soon will learn what has happened, Hamlet replies, "It will be short; the interim is mine . . ." (73), a line that reveals an assured rather than an agitated mind. Later in the scene, when the challenge to fence is delivered, we again hear this tone of quiet resolution:

> I am constant to my purposes; they follow the King's pleasure. If his fitness speaks, mine is ready; now or whensoever, provided I be so able as now.   (202–4)

For some readers and viewers, this speech reveals that Hamlet's will has atrophied, and he has collapsed into fatalism. The same has been said of the words he utters a few lines later, "There is special providence in the fall of a sparrow" (220–21) and "The readiness is all" (223–24). But surely this reference to Providence and the fall of the sparrow, with its clear evocation of Matthew 10.29 ("not a sparrow shall fall on the ground without your Father's knowledge") is *not* fatalistic. It reveals a belief that despite the evident evil done by Claudius, the world is not without a principle of goodness, and Hamlet's job is not to scheme. Scheming, such as his earlier plan to catch Claudius at a moment when Claudius is sinning, so that he will be damned, can only involve him more deeply in evil. Hamlet's task is not to contrive a moment when he can avenge his father, but to be ready to act when the moment is presented to him. Behind Hamlet's "the readiness is all" we may hear Jesus's words (Matthew 24:44; Luke 12:40), "Be ye also ready." The change that we see and hear in Hamlet does not strike us as simply another psychological moment, to be added to all of the others that we have seen, and to be displaced by something different. Rather, it is a welcome *development* of his character.

Claudius, the villain, himself presents Hamlet with the right moment. It is, after all, Claudius who contrives the deadly fencing match and who prepares the poisoned cup. True, Laertes adds the envenomed foil, but the plan as a whole is Claudius's. When Claudius and Laertes die from the poison, we are in the mysteriously but justly governed world of the Hebrew Bible, "Whoso diggeth a pit," we recall, "shall fall therein, and he that rolleth a stone, it will return" (Proverbs 26.27).

The ceremoniousness of the fencing match, ironically provided not by a contriving Hamlet but by the criminal himself, adds a ritual dignity to the execution of justice:

> *A table prepared. [Enter] Trumpets, Drums, and Officers with cushions; King, Queen, [Osric,] and all the State, [with] foils, daggers, [and stoups of wine borne in]; and Laertes.*
>
> (226 s.d.)

Then we get further ceremonial actions, notably Hamlet's apology to Laertes, the sound of trumpets when the king drinks, and the fencing match itself, beginning with the choice of foils. After the first hit, we get a stage direction (282) that again emphasizes the solemnity or ritual aspect of the action:

> *Drum, trumpets, and shot. Flourish; a piece goes off.*

Laertes is then wounded with his own weapon, accepts his guilt ("I am justly killed with mine own treachery"—308) and confesses the plot:

> The foul practice*
> Hath turned itself on me. Lo, here I lie,
> Never to rise again. Thy mother's poisoned.
> I can no more. The King, the King's to blame.   (318–21)

Hamlet, armed now with the poisonous weapon prepared by his foe, realizes that the right moment has come:

> The point envenomed too?
> Then, venom, to thy work.   (322–23)

He stabs Claudius and, for good measure, forces him to drink from the poisoned cup that Claudius himself had prepared.

> Here, thou incestuous, murd'rous, damnèd Dane,
> Drink off this potion. Is thy union here?
> Follow my mother.   (326–28)

Laertes voices the audience's thoughts concerning Claudius, "He is justly served," and then Laertes and Hamlet exchange forgiveness. It is hard to imagine how Hamlet could more fittingly—more satisfyingly, in a reader's or a viewer's eyes—have avenged the death of his father and, for that matter, the death that we have just seen Claudius inflict upon Hamlet. Again, if we call to mind the missed opportunity when Claudius was praying, surely we are glad that Hamlet "delayed."

Hamlet has done things that are almost unspeakable—but the ghost delivered to him the otherwise unspeakable news about the murder of his father and the adultery of his mother. Hamlet is not entirely untainted; the ill-treatment of Ophelia and the killing of Polonius are understandable but in these episodes Hamlet's behavior pains us; in some

*Deception.

of his lines in such scenes we can hear something of the un-attractive avenger-become-villain. Consider, for instance, his remarks to his mother about Rosencrantz and Guilden-stern, spoken with the dead—and presumably very bloody—body of Polonius in front of him:

> They must sweep my way
> And marshal me to knavery. Let it work;
> For 'tis the sport to have the enginer
> Hoist with his own petar, and 't shall go hard
> But I will delve one yard below their mines
> And blow them at the moon. O, 'tis most sweet
> When in one line two crafts directly meet.   (3.4.205–11)

In the last quoted line, with its pun on *crafts* (boats; acts of guile), we may feel that Hamlet, who has just killed a rela-tively innocent man, is taking too much relish in thoughts of revenge. We are grateful that he hoists Claudius with Claudius's "own petar," but we are grateful too that no "knavery" and no "craft" on Hamlet's part were brought into play. Similarly, prompted by Fortinbras's willingness to sacrifice thousands of lives for straw, Hamlet had said, "O, from this time forth, / My thoughts be bloody, or be nothing worth!" (4.4.65–66), but surely this is not the Hamlet that we hope to see. The avenging Pyrrhus, covered with "coagu-late gore, / With eyes like carbuncles," becomes "the hell-ish Pyrrhus" (2.2.74). This, too, is not what we want of Hamlet. He is right in saying, shortly before the fencing match, "The readiness is all" (5.2.223–24).

Finally, let's look at Horatio's last speeches and at Fort-inbras's tribute to Hamlet. Hamlet's last words endorse Fortinbras as ruler, and the request that Horatio explain to Fortinbras what has happened. Immediately after Hamlet's death, Horatio says,

> Now cracks a noble heart. Good night, sweet Prince,
> And flights of angels sing thee to thy rest.   (360–61)

When Fortinbras enters, Horatio tells him he has entered upon a scene of "woe" and "wonder" (364). A few lines later Horatio says,

> So shall you hear
> Of carnal, bloody, and unnatural acts,
> Of accidental judgments, casual slaughters,
> Of deaths put on by cunning and forced cause,
> And, in this upshot, purposes mistook
> Fall'n on th' inventors' heads. (381–86)

This speech is densely packed; *carnal*, for instance, presumably refers to the adulterous, incestuous relation of Claudius and Gertrude; *unnatural* to incest and also to Claudius's murder of his brother and of his nephew; *accidental* and *casual slaughters* (*casual* means unplanned, by chance) to Hamlet's killing of Polonius, Ophelia's death, and the death of Gertrude; *deaths put on by cunning and forced cause* to numerous deaths in the play, but perhaps *forced cause* especially refers to Hamlet's killing of Claudius; *purposes mistook / Fall'n on th' inventors' heads* to the deaths of Laertes and Claudius and also the deaths of Rosencrantz and Guildenstern, and, in fact, to many other incidents in the play, for instance to Polonius's death, which is the result of his spying and of Hamlet's mistake.

We are now at the end of the play, except for Fortinbras's ultimate tribute to Hamlet. Perhaps we can look back and take stock: (1) From the graveyard scene onward, Hamlet seems calmer, less anguished and less energized by thoughts of vengeance; (2) Claudius is dead by his own contriving, and yet also by Hamlet's hand, a most satisfactory resolution; (3) Horatio's tribute to Hamlet, with the words that the world has remembered, "Good night, sweet Prince, / And flights of angels sing thee to thy rest," suggest that Hamlet has lived a moral life. Surely these words are meant to guide us in our view of Hamlet. We do *not* want the ghost of Hamlet Senior to return to congratulate his son, though that is just the sort of heavy-handed endorsement that Thomas Kyd provides at the end of *The Spanish Tragedy*, when a supernatural figure, Revenge, in the com-

pany of the ghost of the first victim, promises eternal rewards for the virtuous and punishments for the wicked.

At this point, Fortinbras, the successful warrior, enters. Is
it going too far to say that Hamlet has been a warrior, too,
and has won his battle—though at the cost of his life? We
may be so used to the romantic view of Hamlet as the delicate blond prince in the white shirt with an open collar, the
man who could not make up his mind, that we forget he has
been a combatant in a fierce struggle. Fortinbras, expressing recognition of Hamlet as a fellow-soldier, speaks the
last lines and orders the firing of cannon in salute ("the soldiers' music"). Some critics have said that Fortinbras is
simply mouthing politically appropriate statements, but
why should we not hear in his words a genuine praise of a
worthy soldier in the battle of life? Hamlet, we can suppose, would have preferred to continue as a student in Wittenberg, but he has done what the ghost of his murdered
father instructed him to do. Fortinbras speaks for all of us
when he says,

> Let four captains
> Bear Hamlet like a soldier to the stage,
> For he was likely, had he been put on,
> To have proved most royal; and for his passage
> The soldiers' music and the rite of war
> Speak loudly for him.
> . . . .
> Go, bid the soldiers shoot.
> *Exeunt marching; after the which a peal of ordnance are shot off.*
>
> (396–404)

This is the third time we have heard cannon in *Hamlet*.
The first was when the vulgar Claudius drank (1.4.6 s.d.);
the second was when, earlier in the final act (5.2.282
s.d.), Hamlet scores a hit in fencing; and Claudius, claiming
to drink to Hamlet's success, in reality drinks to Hamlet's
death; now, the third time, the cannon are fired, this time in
tribute to a man who, suffering from the knowledge that his
mother has married his father's murderer, has nevertheless
succeeded in performing an almost unbelievably difficult

and horrible duty. "In this harsh world," the dying Hamlet instructs Horatio, "draw thy breath in pain, / To tell my story" (349–50). As we have seen, Horatio in his brief survey (381–87) chiefly offers a summary ("Deaths put on by cunning and forced cause") rather than an interpretation, although there are glimmers of interpretation ("Unnatural acts"). But in characterizing the plot as one of "woe and wonder" (364), Horatio does as much as any later commentator has done to guide us toward an interpretation. Hamlet's story is woeful, but it is also wonderful.

—SYLVAN BARNET

The Tragedie of

HAMLET

Prince of Den:narke.

Enter Barnardo, and Francisco, two Centinels.

Bar.   VVHo se there?
Fran.   Nay answere me. Stand and vnsolde your selfe.
Bar.   Long liue the King,
Fran.   *Barnardo.*
Bar.   Hee.
Fran.   You come most carefully vpon your houre,
Bar.   Tis now strooke twelse, get thee to bed *Francisco.*
Fran.   For this reliefe much thanks, tis bitter cold,
  And I am sick at hart.
Bar.   Haue you had quiet guard?
Fran.   Not a mouse stirring.
Bar.   Well, good night :
  If you doe meete *Horatio* and *Marcellus,*
  The riualls of my watch, bid them make hast.
              Enter Horatio, and Marcellus.
Fran.   I thinke I heare them, stand ho, who is there?
Hora.   Friends to this ground.
Mar.   And Leedgemen to the Dane,
Fran.   Giue you good night.
Mar.   O, farwell honest souldiers, who hath relieu'd you?
Fran.   *Barnardo* hath my place; giue you good night.   *Exit Fran.*
                      B.   *Mar.*

The opening scene, from the Second Quarto (1604–1605)

The Tragedy of Hamlet
Prince of Denmark

[Dramatis Personae

Hamlet, Prince of Denmark, son of the late king and of
  Gertrude
Claudius, King of Denmark, Hamlet's uncle
Ghost of the late king, Hamlet's father
Gertrude, Queen of Denmark, widow of the late king, now
  wife of Claudius
Polonius, councillor to the king
Laertes, son of Polonius
Ophelia, daughter of Polonius
Reynaldo, servant of Polonius
Horatio, Hamlet's friend and fellow student
Rosencrantz }
Guildenstern } courtiers, former school friends of Hamlet
Voltemand }
Cornelius } Danish ambassadors to Norway
Osric, a foppish courtier
Marcellus }
Barnardo } soldiers
Francisco }
English ambassadors
Fortinbras, prince of Norway
Captain, in Fortinbras's army
Players, performing the roles of Prologue, King, Queen,
  and Lucianus
A Priest
Two Clowns—a Grave-digger and his companion
Lords, Ladies, Soldiers, Sailors, Messengers, Attendants

Scene: In and around the court at Elsinore]

The Tragedy of Hamlet
Prince of Denmark

[ACT 1

Scene 1. *A guard platform of the castle.*]

Enter Barnardo and Francisco, two sentinels.

Barnardo. Who's there?

Francisco. Nay, answer me. Stand and unfold°¹ yourself.

Barnardo. Long live the King!°

Francisco. Barnardo?

Barnardo. He.   5

Francisco. You come most carefully upon your hour.

Barnardo. 'Tis now struck twelve. Get thee to bed,
Francisco.

---

¹The degree sign (°) indicates a footnote, which is keyed to the text by
the line number. Text references are printed in **boldface** type; the anno-
tation follows in roman type.
1.1.2 **unfold** disclose   3 **Long live the King** (perhaps a password, perhaps a greeting)

3

Francisco. For this relief much thanks. 'Tis bitter cold,
  And I am sick at heart.

Barnardo. Have you had quiet guard?

10 *Francisco.*   Not a mouse stirring.

Barnardo. Well, good night.
  If you do meet Horatio and Marcellus,
  The rivals° of my watch, bid them make haste.

                Enter Horatio and Marcellus.

Francisco. I think I hear them. Stand, ho! Who is
  there?

Horatio. Friends to this ground.

15 *Marcellus.*   And liegemen to the Dane.°

Francisco. Give you° good night.

Marcellus.   O, farewell, honest soldier.
  Who hath relieved you?

Francisco.   Barnardo hath my place.
  Give you good night.   *Exit Francisco.*

Marcellus.   Holla, Barnardo!

Barnardo.   Say——
  What, is Horatio there?

Horatio.   A piece of him.

20 *Barnardo.* Welcome, Horatio. Welcome, good Marcellus.

Marcellus. What, has this thing appeared again tonight?

Barnardo. I have seen nothing.

Marcellus. Horatio says 'tis but our fantasy,
  And will not let belief take hold of him
25 Touching this dreaded sight twice seen of us;
  Therefore I have entreated him along
  With us to watch the minutes of this night,
  That, if again this apparition come,
  He may approve° our eyes and speak to it.

---

13 **rivals** partners   15 **liegemen to the Dane** loyal subjects to the King
of Denmark   16 **Give you** God give you   29 **approve** confirm

Horatio. Tush, tush, 'twill not appear.

Barnardo.　　　　　　　　　　　　Sit down awhile,　　*30*
　　And let us once again assail your ears,
　　That are so fortified against our story,
　　What we have two nights seen.

Horatio.　　　　　　　　　　　　Well, sit we down,
　　And let us hear Barnardo speak of this.

Barnardo. Last night of all,　　　　　　　　　　*35*
　　When yond same star that's westward from the
　　　　pole°
　　Had made his course t' illume that part of heaven
　　Where now it burns, Marcellus and myself,
　　The bell then beating one——

Enter Ghost.

Marcellus. Peace, break thee off. Look where it comes
　　again.　　　　　　　　　　　　　　　　　　　　*40*

Barnardo. In the same figure like the king that's dead.

Marcellus. Thou art a scholar; speak to it, Horatio.

Barnardo. Looks 'a not like the king? Mark it, Horatio.

Horatio. Most like: it harrows me with fear and won-
　　der.

Barnardo. It would be spoke to.

Marcellus.　　　　　　　　　　Speak to it, Horatio.　　*45*

Horatio. What art thou that usurp'st this time of night,
　　Together with that fair and warlike form
　　In which the majesty of buried Denmark°
　　Did sometimes march? By heaven I charge thee,
　　　　speak.

Marcellus. It is offended.

Barnardo.　　　　　　　See, it stalks away.　　*50*

Horatio. Stay! Speak, speak. I charge thee, speak.
　　　　　　　　　　　　　　　　　　　　Exit Ghost.

36 **pole** polestar　　48 **buried Denmark** the buried King of Denmark

Marcellus. 'Tis gone and will not answer.

Barnardo. How now, Horatio? You tremble and look
　　pale.
　　Is not this something more than fantasy?
55　　What think you on't?

Horatio. Before my God, I might not this believe
　　Without the sensible and true avouch°
　　Of mine own eyes.

Marcellus.　　　　　　Is it not like the King?

Horatio. As thou art to thyself.
60　　Such was the very armor he had on
　　When he the ambitious Norway° combated:
　　So frowned he once, when, in an angry parle,°
　　He smote the sledded Polacks° on the ice.
　　'Tis strange.

Marcellus. Thus twice before, and jump° at this dead
65　　　hour,
　　With martial stalk hath he gone by our watch.

Horatio. In what particular thought to work I know
　　not;
　　But, in the gross and scope° of my opinion,
　　This bodes some strange eruption to our state.

Marcellus. Good now, sit down, and tell me he that
70　　　knows,
　　Why this same strict and most observant watch
　　So nightly toils the subject° of the land,
　　And why such daily cast of brazen cannon
　　And foreign mart° for implements of war,

---

57 **sensible and true avouch** sensory and true proof　61 **Norway** King
of Norway　62 **parle** parley　63 **sledded Polacks** Poles in sledges
65 **jump** just　68 **gross and scope** general drift　72 **toils the subject**
makes the subjects toil　74 **mart** trading

Why such impress° of shipwrights, whose sore task   75
Does not divide the Sunday from the week,
What might be toward° that this sweaty haste
Doth make the night joint-laborer with the day?
Who is't that can inform me?

Horatio.   That can I.
  At least the whisper goes so: our last king,   80
Whose image even but now appeared to us,
Was, as you know, by Fortinbras of Norway,
Thereto pricked on by a most emulate pride,
Dared to the combat; in which our valiant Hamlet
(For so this side of our known world esteemed him)   85
Did slay this Fortinbras, who, by a sealed compact
Well ratified by law and heraldry,°
Did forfeit, with his life, all those his lands
Which he stood seized° of, to the conqueror;
Against the which a moiety competent°   90
Was gagèd° by our King, which had returned
To the inheritance of Fortinbras,
Had he been vanquisher, as, by the same comart°
And carriage of the article designed,°
His fell to Hamlet. Now, sir, young Fortinbras,   95
Of unimprovèd° mettle hot and full,
Hath in the skirts° of Norway here and there
Sharked up° a list of lawless resolutes,°
For food and diet, to some enterprise
That hath a stomach in't;° which is no other,   100
As it doth well appear unto our state,
But to recover of us by strong hand
And terms compulsatory, those foresaid lands
So by his father lost; and this, I take it,
Is the main motive of our preparations,   105

75 **impress** forced service   77 **toward** in preparation   87 **law and heraldry** heraldic law (governing the combat)   89 **seized** possessed
90 **moiety competent** equal portion   91 **gagèd** engaged, pledged
93 **comart** agreement   94 **carriage of the article designed** import of
the agreement drawn up   96 **unimprovèd** untried   97 **skirts** borders
98 **Sharked up** collected indiscriminately (as a shark gulps its prey)
98 **resolutes** desperadoes   100 **hath a stomach in't** i.e., requires
courage

The source of this our watch, and the chief head°
Of this posthaste and romage° in the land.

Barnardo. I think it be no other but e'en so;
Well may it sort° that this portentous figure
110 Comes armèd through our watch so like the King
That was and is the question of these wars.

Horatio. A mote it is to trouble the mind's eye:
In the most high and palmy state of Rome,
A little ere the mightiest Julius fell,
115 The graves stood tenantless, and the sheeted dead
Did squeak and gibber in the Roman streets;°
As stars with trains of fire and dews of blood,
Disasters° in the sun; and the moist star,°
Upon whose influence Neptune's empire stands,
120 Was sick almost to doomsday with eclipse.
And even the like precurse° of feared events,
As harbingers° preceding still° the fates
And prologue to the omen° coming on,
Have heaven and earth together demonstrated
125 Unto our climatures° and countrymen.

Enter Ghost.

But soft, behold, lo where it comes again!
I'll cross it,° though it blast me.—Stay, illusion.
                    It spreads his° arms.
If thou hast any sound or use of voice,
Speak to me.
130 If there be any good thing to be done
That may to thee do ease and grace to me,
Speak to me.
If thou art privy to thy country's fate,
Which happily° foreknowing may avoid,

---

106 **head** fountainhead, origin   107 **romage** bustle   109 **sort** be-
fit   116 **Did squeak . . . Roman streets** (the break in the sense which
follows this line suggests that a line has dropped out)   118 **Disasters**
threatening signs   118 **moist star** moon   121 **precurse** precursor, fore-
shadowing   122 **harbingers** forerunners   122 **still** always   123 **omen**
calamity   125 **climatures** regions   127 **cross it** (1) cross its path, confront it (2) make the sign of the cross in front of it   127 s.d. **his** i.e., its,
the ghost's (though possibly what is meant is that Horatio spreads his
own arms, making a cross of himself)   134 **happily** haply, perhaps

O, speak! 135
Or if thou hast uphoarded in thy life
Extorted° treasure in the womb of earth,
For which, they say, you spirits oft walk in death,

The cock crows.

Speak of it. Stay and speak. Stop it, Marcellus.

Marcellus. Shall I strike at it with my partisan?° 140

Horatio. Do, if it will not stand.

Barnardo. 'Tis here.

Horatio. 'Tis here.

Marcellus. 'Tis gone. *Exit Ghost.*
We do it wrong, being so majestical,
To offer it the show of violence,
For it is as the air, invulnerable, 145
And our vain blows malicious mockery.

Barnardo. It was about to speak when the cock crew.

Horatio. And then it started, like a guilty thing
Upon a fearful summons. I have heard,
The cock, that is the trumpet to the morn, 150
Doth with his lofty and shrill-sounding throat
Awake the god of day, and at his warning,
Whether in sea or fire, in earth or air,
Th' extravagant and erring° spirit hies
To his confine; and of the truth herein 155
This present object made probation.°

Marcellus. It faded on the crowing of the cock.
Some say that ever 'gainst° that season comes
Wherein our Savior's birth is celebrated,
This bird of dawning singeth all night long, 160
And then, they say, no spirit dare stir abroad,
The nights are wholesome, then no planets strike,°
No fairy takes,° nor witch hath power to charm:
So hallowed and so gracious is that time.

Horatio. So have I heard and do in part believe it. 165

137 **Extorted** ill-won   140 **partisan** pike (a long-handled weapon)
154 **extravagant and erring** out of bounds and wandering   156 **probation** proof   158 **'gainst** just before   162 **strike** exert an evil influence
163 **takes** bewitches

But look, the morn in russet mantle clad
Walks o'er the dew of yon high eastward hill.
Break we our watch up, and by my advice
Let us impart what we have seen tonight
170 Unto young Hamlet, for upon my life
This spirit, dumb to us, will speak to him.
Do you consent we shall acquaint him with it,
As needful in our loves, fitting our duty?

Marcellus. Let's do't, I pray, and I this morning know
175 Where we shall find him most convenient.   *Exeunt.*

[Scene 2. *The castle.*]

*Flourish.° Enter Claudius, King of Denmark, Gertrude
the Queen, Councilors, Polonius and his son Laertes,
Hamlet, cum aliis° [including Voltemand and Cor-
nelius].*

King. Though yet of Hamlet our dear brother's death
The memory be green, and that it us befitted
To bear our hearts in grief, and our whole kingdom
To be contracted in one brow of woe,
5   Yet so far hath discretion fought with nature
That we with wisest sorrow think on him
Together with remembrance of ourselves.
Therefore our sometime sister,° now our Queen,
Th' imperial jointress° to this warlike state,
10   Have we, as 'twere, with a defeated joy,
With an auspicious° and a dropping eye,
With mirth in funeral, and with dirge in marriage,
In equal scale weighing delight and dole,
Taken to wife. Nor have we herein barred
15   Your better wisdoms, which have freely gone

1.2.s.d. **Flourish** fanfare of trumpets   s.d. **cum aliis** with others (Latin)
8 **our sometime sister** my (the royal "we") former sister-in-law
9 **jointress** joint tenant, partner   11 **auspicious** joyful

With this affair along. For all, our thanks.
Now follows that you know young Fortinbras,
Holding a weak supposal of our worth,
Or thinking by our late dear brother's death
Our state to be disjoint and out of frame,°   20
Colleaguèd with this dream of his advantage,°
He hath not failed to pester us with message,
Importing the surrender of those lands
Lost by his father, with all bands of law,
To our most valiant brother. So much for him.   25
Now for ourself and for this time of meeting.
Thus much the business is: we have here writ
To Norway, uncle of young Fortinbras—
Who, impotent and bedrid, scarcely hears
Of this his nephew's purpose—to suppress   30
His further gait° herein, in that the levies,
The lists, and full proportions° are all made
Out of his subject;° and we here dispatch
You, good Cornelius, and you, Voltemand,
For bearers of this greeting to old Norway,   35
Giving to you no further personal power
To business with the King, more than the scope
Of these delated articles° allow.
Farewell, and let your haste commend your duty.

Cornelius, Voltemand. In that, and all things, will we
   show our duty.   40

King. We doubt it nothing. Heartily farewell.
                        Exit Voltemand and Cornelius.
And now, Laertes, what's the news with you?
You told us of some suit. What is't, Laertes?
You cannot speak of reason to the Dane
And lose your voice.° What wouldst thou beg,
   Laertes,   45
That shall not be my offer, not thy asking?
The head is not more native° to the heart,

20 **frame** order   21 **advantage** superiority   31 **gait** proceeding   32 **proportions** supplies for war   33 **Out of his subject** i.e., out of old Norway's subjects and realm   38 **delated articles** detailed documents   45 **lose your voice** waste your breath   47 **native** related

The hand more instrumental to the mouth,
Than is the throne of Denmark to thy father.
What wouldst thou have, Laertes?

50 *Laertes.*   My dread lord,
Your leave and favor to return to France,
From whence, though willingly I came to Denmark
To show my duty in your coronation,
Yet now I must confess, that duty done,
55 My thoughts and wishes bend again toward France
And bow them to your gracious leave and pardon.

King. Have you your father's leave? What says Polonius?

Polonius. He hath, my lord, wrung from me my slow
leave
By laborsome petition, and at last
60 Upon his will I sealed my hard consent.°
I do beseech you give him leave to go.

King. Take thy fair hour, Laertes. Time be thine,
And thy best graces spend it at thy will.
But now, my cousin° Hamlet, and my son——

Hamlet. [*Aside*] A little more than kin, and less than
65 kind!°

King. How is it that the clouds still hang on you?

Hamlet. Not so, my lord. I am too much in the sun.°

Queen. Good Hamlet, cast thy nighted color off,
And let thine eye look like a friend on Denmark.
70 Do not forever with thy vailèd° lids
Seek for thy noble father in the dust.
Thou know'st 'tis common; all that lives must die,
Passing through nature to eternity.

60 **Upon his ... hard consent** to his desire I gave my reluctant
consent   64 **cousin** kinsman   65 **kind** (pun on the meanings "kindly"
and "natural"; though doubly related—**more than kin**—Hamlet asserts
that he neither resembles Claudius in nature nor feels kindly toward
him)   67 **sun** sunshine of royal favor (with a pun on "son")   70 **vailèd**
lowered

Hamlet. Ay, madam, it is common.°

Queen.   If it be,
  Why seems it so particular with thee?   75

Hamlet. Seems, madam? Nay, it is. I know not "seems."
  'Tis not alone my inky cloak, good mother,
  Nor customary suits of solemn black,
  Nor windy suspiration° of forced breath,
  No, nor the fruitful river in the eye,   80
  Nor the dejected havior of the visage,
  Together with all forms, moods, shapes of grief,
  That can denote me truly. These indeed seem,
  For they are actions that a man might play,
  But I have that within which passes show;   85
  These but the trappings and the suits of woe.

King. 'Tis sweet and commendable in your nature,
      Hamlet,
  To give these mourning duties to your father,
  But you must know your father lost a father,
  That father lost, lost his, and the survivor bound   90
  In filial obligation for some term
  To do obsequious° sorrow. But to persever
  In obstinate condolement° is a course
  Of impious stubbornness. 'Tis unmanly grief.
  It shows a will most incorrect to heaven,   95
  A heart unfortified, a mind impatient,
  An understanding simple and unschooled.
  For what we know must be and is as common
  As any the most vulgar° thing to sense,
  Why should we in our peevish opposition   100
  Take it to heart? Fie, 'tis a fault to heaven,
  A fault against the dead, a fault to nature,
  To reason most absurd, whose common theme
  Is death of fathers, and who still hath cried,
  From the first corse° till he that died today,   105
  "This must be so." We pray you throw to earth

74 **common** (1) universal (2) vulgar   79 **windy suspiration** heavy sighing   92 **obsequious** suitable to obsequies (funerals)   93 **condolement**
mourning   99 **vulgar** common   105 **corse** corpse

This unprevailing° woe, and think of us
As of a father, for let the world take note
You are the most immediate to our throne,
110 And with no less nobility of love
Than that which dearest father bears his son
Do I impart toward you. For your intent
In going back to school in Wittenberg,
It is most retrograde° to our desire,
115 And we beseech you, bend you° to remain
Here in the cheer and comfort of our eye,
Our chiefest courtier, cousin, and our son.

Queen. Let not thy mother lose her prayers, Hamlet.
I pray thee stay with us, go not to Wittenberg.

120 *Hamlet.* I shall in all my best obey you, madam.

King. Why, 'tis a loving and a fair reply.
Be as ourself in Denmark. Madam, come.
This gentle and unforced accord of Hamlet
Sits smiling to my heart, in grace whereof
125 No jocund health that Denmark drinks today,
But the great cannon to the clouds shall tell,
And the King's rouse° the heaven shall bruit° again,
Respeaking earthly thunder. Come away.
                    Flourish. Exeunt all but Hamlet.

Hamlet. O that this too too sullied° flesh would melt,
130 Thaw, and resolve itself into a dew,
Or that the Everlasting had not fixed
His canon° 'gainst self-slaughter. O God, God,
How weary, stale, flat, and unprofitable
Seem to me all the uses of this world!
135 Fie on't, ah, fie, 'tis an unweeded garden
That grows to seed. Things rank and gross in nature
Possess it merely.° That it should come to this:
But two months dead, nay, not so much, not two,

---

107 **unprevailing** unavailing   114 **retrograde** contrary   115 **bend
you** incline   127 **rouse** deep drink   127 **bruit** announce noisily
129 **sullied** (Q2 has **sallied,** here modernized to **sullied,** which makes
sense and is therefore given; but the Folio reading, **solid,** which fits better with **melt,** is quite possibly correct)   132 **canon** law   137 **merely**
entirely

So excellent a king, that was to this
Hyperion° to a satyr, so loving to my mother   *140*
That he might not beteem° the winds of heaven
Visit her face too roughly. Heaven and earth,
Must I remember? Why, she would hang on him
As if increase of appetite had grown
By what it fed on; and yet within a month—   *145*
Let me not think on't; frailty, thy name is woman—
A little month, or ere those shoes were old
With which she followed my poor father's body
Like Niobe,° all tears, why, she—
O God, a beast that wants discourse of reason°   *150*
Would have mourned longer—married with my
    uncle,
My father's brother, but no more like my father
Than I to Hercules. Within a month,
Ere yet the salt of most unrighteous tears
Had left the flushing° in her gallèd eyes,   *155*
She married. O, most wicked speed, to post°
With such dexterity to incestuous° sheets!
It is not, nor it cannot come to good.
But break my heart, for I must hold my tongue.

          Enter Horatio, Marcellus, and Barnardo.

Horatio. Hail to your lordship!

Hamlet.   I am glad to see you well.   *160*
    Horatio—or I do forget myself.

Horatio. The same, my lord, and your poor servant
    ever.

Hamlet. Sir, my good friend, I'll change° that name
    with you.
    And what make you from Wittenberg, Horatio?
    Marcellus.   *165*

140 **Hyperion** the sun god, a model of beauty   141 **beteem** allow
149 **Niobe** (a mother who wept profusely at the death of her children)
150 **wants discourse of reason** lacks reasoning power   155 **left the
flushing** stopped reddening   156 **post** hasten   157 **incestuous** (canon
law considered marriage with a deceased brother's widow to be incestuous)   163 **change** exchange

Marcellus. My good lord!

Hamlet. I am very glad to see you. [*To Barnardo*]
      Good even, sir.
    But what, in faith, make you from Wittenberg?

Horatio. A truant disposition, good my lord.

170 *Hamlet.* I would not hear your enemy say so,
      Nor shall you do my ear that violence
      To make it truster° of your own report
      Against yourself. I know you are no truant.
      But what is your affair in Elsinore?
175   We'll teach you to drink deep ere you depart.

Horatio. My lord, I came to see your father's funeral.

Hamlet. I prithee do not mock me, fellow student.
    I think it was to see my mother's wedding.

Horatio. Indeed, my lord, it followed hard upon.

180 *Hamlet.* Thrift, thrift, Horatio. The funeral baked
      meats
      Did coldly furnish forth the marriage tables.
      Would I had met my dearest° foe in heaven
      Or ever I had seen that day, Horatio!
      My father, methinks I see my father.

Horatio. Where, my lord?

185 *Hamlet.*   In my mind's eye, Horatio.

Horatio. I saw him once. 'A° was a goodly king.

Hamlet. 'A was a man, take him for all in all,
    I shall not look upon his like again.

Horatio. My lord, I think I saw him yesternight.

190 *Hamlet.* Saw? Who?

Horatio. My lord, the King your father.

Hamlet.   The King my father?

Horatio. Season your admiration° for a while
    With an attent ear till I may deliver
    Upon the witness of these gentlemen

172 **truster** believer   182 **dearest** most intensely felt   186 **'A** he
192 **Season your admiration** control your wonder

This marvel to you.

Hamlet.   For God's love let me hear!   *195*

Horatio. Two nights together had these gentlemen,
    Marcellus and Barnardo, on their watch
    In the dead waste and middle of the night
    Been thus encountered. A figure like your father,
    Armèd at point exactly, cap-a-pe,°   *200*
    Appears before them, and with solemn march
    Goes slow and stately by them. Thrice he walked
    By their oppressed and fear-surprisèd eyes,
    Within his truncheon's length,° whilst they, distilled°
    Almost to jelly with the act° of fear,   *205*
    Stand dumb and speak not to him. This to me
    In dreadful° secrecy impart they did,
    And I with them the third night kept the watch,
    Where, as they had delivered, both in time,
    Form of the thing, each word made true and good,   *210*
    The apparition comes. I knew your father.
    These hands are not more like.

Hamlet.   But where was this?

Marcellus. My lord, upon the platform where we
    watched.

Hamlet. Did you not speak to it?

Horatio.   My lord, I did;
    But answer made it none. Yet once methought   *215*
    It lifted up it° head and did address
    Itself to motion like as it would speak:
    But even then the morning cock crew loud,
    And at the sound it shrunk in haste away
    And vanished from our sight.

Hamlet.   'Tis very strange.   *220*

Horatio. As I do live, my honored lord, 'tis true,
    And we did think it writ down in our duty
    To let you know of it.

---

200 **cap-a-pe** head to foot   204 **truncheon's length** space of a short
staff   204 **distilled** reduced   205 **act** action   207 **dreadful** terrified
216 **it** its

Hamlet. Indeed, indeed, sirs, but this troubles me.
Hold you the watch tonight?

225 *All.*   We do, my lord.

Hamlet. Armed, say you?

All. Armed, my lord.

Hamlet. From top to toe?

All.   My lord, from head to foot.

Hamlet. Then saw you not his face.

230 *Horatio.* O, yes, my lord. He wore his beaver° up.

Hamlet. What, looked he frowningly?

Horatio. A countenance more in sorrow than in anger.

Hamlet. Pale or red?

Horatio. Nay, very pale.

Hamlet.   And fixed his eyes upon you?

Horatio. Most constantly.

235 *Hamlet.*   I would I had been there.

Horatio. It would have much amazed you.

Hamlet. Very like, very like. Stayed it long?

Horatio. While one with moderate haste might tell° a
hundred.

Both. Longer, longer.

Horatio. Not when I saw't.

240 *Hamlet.*   His beard was grizzled,° no?

Horatio. It was as I have seen it in his life,
A sable silvered.°

Hamlet.   I will watch tonight.
Perchance 'twill walk again.

Horatio.   I warr'nt it will.

Hamlet. If it assume my noble father's person,

---

230 **beaver** visor, face guard   238 **tell** count   240 **grizzled** gray
242 **sable silvered** black mingled with white

I'll speak to it though hell itself should gape   245
And bid me hold my peace. I pray you all,
If you have hitherto concealed this sight,
Let it be tenable° in your silence still,
And whatsomever else shall hap tonight,
Give it an understanding but no tongue;   250
I will requite your loves. So fare you well.
Upon the platform 'twixt eleven and twelve
I'll visit you.

All.   Our duty to your honor.

Hamlet. Your loves, as mine to you. Farewell.
                         Exeunt [all but Hamlet].
My father's spirit—in arms? All is not well.   255
I doubt° some foul play. Would the night were come!
Till then sit still, my soul. Foul deeds will rise,
Though all the earth o'erwhelm them, to men's eyes.
                                        Exit.

[Scene 3. *A room.*]

Enter Laertes and Ophelia, his sister.

Laertes. My necessaries are embarked. Farewell.
And, sister, as the winds give benefit
And convoy° is assistant, do not sleep,
But let me hear from you.

Ophelia.   Do you doubt that?

Laertes. For Hamlet, and the trifling of his favor,   5
Hold it a fashion and a toy° in blood,
A violet in the youth of primy° nature,
Forward,° not permanent, sweet, not lasting,
The perfume and suppliance° of a minute,

248 **tenable** held   256 **doubt** suspect 1.3.3 **convoy** conveyance   6 **toy**
idle fancy   7 **primy** springlike   8 **Forward** premature   9 **suppliance**
diversion

No more.

Ophelia.   No more but so?

10 *Laertes.*   Think it no more.
    For nature crescent° does not grow alone
    In thews° and bulk, but as this temple° waxes,
    The inward service of the mind and soul
    Grows wide withal. Perhaps he loves you now,
15   And now no soil nor cautel° doth besmirch
    The virtue of his will; but you must fear,
    His greatness weighed,° his will is not his own.
    For he himself is subject to his birth.
    He may not, as unvalued° persons do,
20   Carve for himself; for on his choice depends
    The safety and health of this whole state;
    And therefore must his choice be circumscribed
    Unto the voice and yielding of that body
    Whereof he is the head. Then if he says he loves you,
25   It fits your wisdom so far to believe it
    As he in his particular act and place
    May give his saying deed, which is no further
    Than the main voice of Denmark goes withal.
    Then weigh what loss your honor may sustain
30   If with too credent° ear you list his songs,
    Or lose your heart, or your chaste treasure open
    To his unmastered importunity.
    Fear it, Ophelia, fear it, my dear sister,
    And keep you in the rear of your affection,
35   Out of the shot and danger of desire.
    The chariest maid is prodigal enough
    If she unmask her beauty to the moon.
    Virtue itself scapes not calumnious strokes.
    The canker° galls the infants of the spring
40   Too oft before their buttons° be disclosed,
    And in the morn and liquid dew of youth
    Contagious blastments are most imminent.

11 **crescent** growing   12 **thews** muscles and sinews   12 **temple** i.e., the body   15 **cautel** deceit   17 **greatness weighed** high rank considered   19 **unvalued** of low rank   30 **credent** credulous   39 **canker** cankerworm   40 **buttons** buds

Be wary then; best safety lies in fear;
Youth to itself rebels, though none else near.

Ophelia. I shall the effect of this good lesson keep 45
As watchman to my heart, but, good my brother,
Do not, as some ungracious° pastors do,
Show me the steep and thorny way to heaven,
Whiles, like a puffed and reckless libertine,
Himself the primrose path of dalliance treads 50
And recks not his own rede.°

Enter Polonius.

Laertes.   O, fear me not.
I stay too long. But here my father comes.
A double blessing is a double grace;
Occasion smiles upon a second leave.

Polonius. Yet here, Laertes? Aboard, aboard, for
    shame! 55
The wind sits in the shoulder of your sail,
And you are stayed for. There—my blessing with
    thee,
And these few precepts in thy memory
Look thou character.° Give thy thoughts no tongue,
Nor any unproportioned° thought his act. 60
Be thou familiar, but by no means vulgar.
Those friends thou hast, and their adoption tried,
Grapple them unto thy soul with hoops of steel,
But do not dull thy palm with entertainment
Of each new-hatched, unfledged courage.° Beware 65
Of entrance to a quarrel; but being in,
Bear't that th' opposèd may beware of thee.
Give every man thine ear, but few thy voice;
Take each man's censure,° but reserve thy judgment.
Costly thy habit as thy purse can buy, 70
But not expressed in fancy; rich, not gaudy,
For the apparel oft proclaims the man,
And they in France of the best rank and station

---

47 **ungracious** lacking grace   51 **recks not his own rede** does not heed
his own advice   59 **character** inscribe   60 **unproportioned** unbal-
anced   65 **courage** gallant youth   69 **censure** opinion

Are of a most select and generous, chief in that.°
75   Neither a borrower nor a lender be,
      For loan oft loses both itself and friend,
      And borrowing dulleth edge of husbandry.°
      This above all, to thine own self be true,
      And it must follow, as the night the day,
80   Thou canst not then be false to any man.
      Farewell. My blessing season this° in thee!

Laertes. Most humbly do I take my leave, my lord.

Polonius. The time invites you. Go, your servants
      tend.°

Laertes. Farewell, Ophelia, and remember well
      What I have said to you.

85   *Ophelia.*   'Tis in my memory locked,
      And you yourself shall keep the key of it.

Laertes. Farewell.   *Exit Laertes.*

Polonius. What is't, Ophelia, he hath said to you?

Ophelia. So please you, something touching the Lord
      Hamlet.

90   *Polonius.* Marry,° well bethought.
      'Tis told me he hath very oft of late
      Given private time to you, and you yourself
      Have of your audience been most free and bounte-
      ous.
      If it be so—as so 'tis put on me,   .
95   And that in way of caution—I must tell you
      You do not understand yourself so clearly
      As it behooves my daughter and your honor.
      What is between you? Give me up the truth.

Ophelia. He hath, my lord, of late made many tenders°
100   Of his affection to me.

---

74 **Are of ... in that** show their fine taste and their gentlemanly in-
stincts more in that than in any other point of manners (Kittredge)
77 **husbandry** thrift 81 **season this** make fruitful this (advice)
83 **tend** attend 90 **Marry** (a light oath, from "By the Virgin Mary")
99 **tenders** offers (in line 103 it has the same meaning, but in line 106
Polonius speaks of **tenders** in the sense of counters or chips; in line
109 **Tend'ring** means "holding," and **tender** means "give," "present")

Polonius. Affection pooh! You speak like a green girl,
  Unsifted° in such perilous circumstance.
  Do you believe his tenders, as you call them?

Ophelia. I do not know, my lord, what I should think.

Polonius. Marry, I will teach you. Think yourself a
    baby   *105*
  That you have ta'en these tenders for true pay
  Which are not sterling. Tender yourself more dearly,
  Or (not to crack the wind of the poor phrase)
  Tend'ring it thus you'll tender me a fool.°

Ophelia. My lord, he hath importuned me with love   *110*
  In honorable fashion.

Polonius. Ay, fashion you may call it. Go to, go to.

Ophelia. And hath given countenance to his speech, my
    lord,
  With almost all the holy vows of heaven.

Polonius. Ay, springes to catch woodcocks.° I do know,   *115*
  When the blood burns, how prodigal the soul
  Lends the tongue vows. These blazes, daughter,
  Giving more light than heat, extinct in both,
  Even in their promise, as it is a-making,
  You must not take for fire. From this time   *120*
  Be something scanter of your maiden presence.
  Set your entreatments° at a higher rate
  Than a command to parley. For Lord Hamlet,
  Believe so much in him that he is young,
  And with a larger tether may he walk   *125*
  Than may be given you. In few, Ophelia,
  Do not believe his vows, for they are brokers,°
  Not of that dye° which their investments° show,
  But mere implorators° of unholy suits,
  Breathing like sanctified and pious bonds,°   *130*
  The better to beguile. This is for all:

102 **Unsifted** untried   109 **tender me a fool** (1) present me with a fool
(2) present me with a baby   115 **springes to catch woodcocks** snares to
catch stupid birds   122 **entreatments** interviews   127 **brokers** procur-
ers   128 **dye** i.e., kind   128 **investments** garments   129 **implorators**
solicitors   130 **bonds** pledges

I would not, in plain terms, from this time forth
Have you so slander° any moment leisure
As to give words or talk with the Lord Hamlet.

135   Look to't, I charge you. Come your ways.

Ophelia. I shall obey, my lord.   *Exeunt.*

[Scene 4. *A guard platform.*]

Enter Hamlet, Horatio, and Marcellus.

Hamlet. The air bites shrewdly;° it is very cold.

Horatio. It is a nipping and an eager° air.

Hamlet. What hour now?

Horatio.   I think it lacks of twelve.

Marcellus. No, it is struck.

Horatio. Indeed? I heard it not. It then draws near the

5   season
       Wherein the spirit held his wont to walk.
              A flourish of trumpets, and two pieces go off.
       What does this mean, my lord?

Hamlet. The King doth wake° tonight and takes his
       rouse,°
       Keeps wassail, and the swagg'ring upspring° reels,

10   And as he drains his draughts of Rhenish° down
       The kettledrum and trumpet thus bray out
       The triumph of his pledge.°

Horatio.   Is it a custom?

---

133 **slander** disgrace 1.4.1 **shrewdly** bitterly   2 **eager** sharp   8 **wake**
hold a revel by night   8 **takes his rouse** carouses   9 **upspring** (a
dance)   10 **Rhenish** Rhine wine   12 **The triumph of his pledge** the
achievement (of drinking a wine cup in one draught) of his toast

Hamlet. Ay, marry, is't,
But to my mind, though I am native here
And to the manner born, it is a custom   *15*
More honored in the breach than the observance.
This heavy-headed revel east and west
Makes us traduced and taxed of° other nations.
They clepe° us drunkards and with swinish phrase
Soil our addition,° and indeed it takes   *20*
From our achievements, though performed at height,
The pith and marrow of our attribute.°
So oft it chances in particular men
That for some vicious mole° of nature in them,
As in their birth, wherein they are not guilty,   *25*
(Since nature cannot choose his origin)
By the o'ergrowth of some complexion,°
Oft breaking down the pales° and forts of reason,
Or by some habit that too much o'erleavens°
The form of plausive° manners, that (these men,   *30*
Carrying, I say, the stamp of one defect,
Being nature's livery, or fortune's star°)
Their virtues else, be they as pure as grace,
As infinite as man may undergo,
Shall in the general censure° take corruption   *35*
From that particular fault. The dram of evil
Doth all the noble substance of a doubt,
To his own scandal.°

Enter Ghost.

Horatio.   Look, my lord, it comes.

Hamlet. Angels and ministers of grace defend us!
Be thou a spirit of health° or goblin damned,   *40*
Bring with thee airs from heaven or blasts from hell,
Be thy intents wicked or charitable,

18 **taxed of** blamed by   19 **clepe** call   20 **addition** reputation (literally, "title of honor")   22 **attribute** reputation   24 **mole** blemish 27 **complexion** natural disposition   28 **pales** enclosures 29 **o'erleavens** mixes with, corrupts   30 **plausive** pleasing   32 **nature's livery, or fortune's star** nature's equipment (i.e., "innate"), or a person's destiny determined by the stars   35 **general censure** popular judgment 36–38 **The dram . . . own scandal** (though the drift is clear, there is no agreement as to the exact meaning of these lines)   40 **spirit of health** good spirit

Thou com'st in such a questionable° shape
That I will speak to thee. I'll call thee Hamlet,
45 King, father, royal Dane. O, answer me!
Let me not burst in ignorance, but tell
Why thy canonized° bones, hearsèd in death,
Have burst their cerements,° why the sepulcher
Wherein we saw thee quietly interred
50 Hath oped his ponderous and marble jaws
To cast thee up again. What may this mean
That thou, dead corse, again in complete steel,
Revisits thus the glimpses of the moon,
Making night hideous, and we fools of nature
55 So horridly to shake our disposition°
With thoughts beyond the reaches of our souls?
Say, why is this? Wherefore? What should we do?

Ghost beckons Hamlet.

Horatio. It beckons you to go away with it,
As if it some impartment° did desire
To you alone.

60 *Marcellus.* Look with what courteous action
It waves you to a more removèd ground.
But do not go with it.

Horatio. No, by no means.

Hamlet. It will not speak. Then I will follow it.

Horatio. Do not, my lord.

Hamlet. Why, what should be the fear?
65 I do not set my life at a pin's fee,
And for my soul, what can it do to that,
Being a thing immortal as itself?
It waves me forth again. I'll follow it.

Horatio. What if it tempt you toward the flood, my
lord,
70 Or to the dreadful summit of the cliff

43 **questionable** (1) capable of discourse (2) dubious 47 **canonized**
buried according to the canon or ordinance of the church 48 **cerements** waxed linen shroud 55 **shake our disposition** disturb us
59 **impartment** communication

That beetles° o'er his base into the sea,
And there assume some other horrible form,
Which might deprive your sovereignty of reason°
And draw you into madness? Think of it.
The very place puts toys° of desperation,   75
Without more motive, into every brain
That looks so many fathoms to the sea
And hears it roar beneath.

Hamlet.   It waves me still.
Go on; I'll follow thee.

Marcellus. You shall not go, my lord.

Hamlet.   Hold off your hands.   80

Horatio. Be ruled. You shall not go.

Hamlet.   My fate cries out
And makes each petty artere° in this body
As hardy as the Nemean lion's nerve.°
Still am I called! Unhand me, gentlemen.
By heaven, I'll make a ghost of him that lets° me!   85
I say, away! Go on. I'll follow thee.
                    Exit Ghost, and Hamlet.

Horatio. He waxes desperate with imagination.

Marcellus. Let's follow. 'Tis not fit thus to obey him.

Horatio. Have after! To what issue will this come?

Marcellus. Something is rotten in the state of Denmark.   90

Horatio. Heaven will direct it.

Marcellus.   Nay, let's follow him.   *Exeunt.*

71 **beetles** juts out   73 **deprive your sovereignty of reason** destroy the
sovereignty of your reason   75 **toys** whims, fancies   82 **artere** artery
83 **Nemean lion's nerve** sinews of the mythical lion slain by Hercules
85 **lets** hinders

[Scene 5. *The battlements.*]

Enter Ghost and Hamlet.

Hamlet. Whither wilt thou lead me? Speak; I'll go no
    further.

Ghost. Mark me.

Hamlet.   I will.

Ghost.   My hour is almost come,
    When I to sulf'rous and tormenting flames
    Must render up myself.

Hamlet.   Alas, poor ghost.

5   *Ghost.* Pity me not, but lend thy serious hearing
    To what I shall unfold.

Hamlet.   Speak. I am bound to hear.

Ghost. So art thou to revenge, when thou shalt hear.

Hamlet. What?

Ghost. I am thy father's spirit,
10   Doomed for a certain term to walk the night,
    And for the day confined to fast in fires,
    Till the foul crimes° done in my days of nature
    Are burnt and purged away. But that I am forbid
    To tell the secrets of my prison house,
15   I could a tale unfold whose lightest word
    Would harrow up thy soul, freeze thy young blood,
    Make thy two eyes like stars start from their
        spheres,°
    Thy knotted and combinèd locks to part,
    And each particular hair to stand an end

1.5.12 **crimes** sins   17 **spheres** (in Ptolemaic astronomy, each planet
was fixed in a hollow transparent shell concentric with the earth)

Like quills upon the fearful porpentine.°　　　　　　20
But this eternal blazon° must not be
To ears of flesh and blood. List, list, O, list!
If thou didst ever thy dear father love——

Hamlet. O God!

Ghost. Revenge his foul and most unnatural murder.　　25

Hamlet. Murder?

Ghost. Murder most foul, as in the best it is,
But this most foul, strange, and unnatural.

Hamlet. Haste me to know't, that I, with wings as swift
As meditation° or the thoughts of love,　　　　30
May sweep to my revenge.

Ghost.　　　　　　　　　I find thee apt,
And duller shouldst thou be than the fat weed
That roots itself in ease on Lethe wharf,°
Wouldst thou not stir in this. Now, Hamlet, hear.
'Tis given out that, sleeping in my orchard,　　35
A serpent stung me. So the whole ear of Denmark
Is by a forgèd process° of my death
Rankly abused. But know, thou noble youth,
The serpent that did sting thy father's life
Now wears his crown.

Hamlet.　　　　　　　O my prophetic soul!　　40
My uncle?

Ghost. Ay, that incestuous, that adulterate° beast,
With witchcraft of his wits, with traitorous gifts—
O wicked wit and gifts, that have the power
So to seduce!—won to his shameful lust　　　　45
The will of my most seeming-virtuous queen.
O Hamlet, what a falling-off was there,
From me, whose love was of that dignity
That it went hand in hand even with the vow
I made to her in marriage, and to decline　　　　50

---

20 **fearful porpentine** timid porcupine　21 **eternal blazon** revelation
of eternity　30 **meditation** thought　33 **Lethe wharf** bank of the river
of forgetfulness in Hades　37 **forgèd process** false account　42 **adulterate** adulterous

Upon a wretch whose natural gifts were poor
To those of mine.
But virtue, as it never will be moved,
Though lewdness° court it in a shape of heaven,
55 So lust, though to a radiant angel linked,
Will sate itself in a celestial bed
And prey on garbage.
But soft, methinks I scent the morning air;
Brief let me be. Sleeping within my orchard,
60 My custom always of the afternoon,
Upon my secure° hour thy uncle stole
With juice of cursed hebona° in a vial,
And in the porches of my ears did pour
The leperous distillment, whose effect
65 Holds such an enmity with blood of man
That swift as quicksilver it courses through
The natural gates and alleys of the body,
And with a sudden vigor it doth posset°
And curd, like eager° droppings into milk,
70 The thin and wholesome blood. So did it mine,
And a most instant tetter° barked about
Most lazarlike° with vile and loathsome crust
All my smooth body.
Thus was I, sleeping, by a brother's hand
75 Of life, of crown, of queen at once dispatched,
Cut off even in the blossoms of my sin,
Unhouseled, disappointed, unaneled,°
No reck'ning made, but sent to my account
With all my imperfections on my head.
80 O, horrible! O, horrible! Most horrible!
If thou hast nature in thee, bear it not.
Let not the royal bed of Denmark be
A couch for luxury° and damnèd incest.
But howsomever thou pursues this act,
85 Taint not thy mind, nor let thy soul contrive

---

54 **lewdness** lust   61 **secure** unsuspecting   62 **hebona** a poisonous plant   68 **posset** curdle   69 **eager** acid   71 **tetter** scab   72 **lazarlike** leperlike   77 **Unhouseled, disappointed, unaneled** without the sacrament of communion, unabsolved, without extreme unction   83 **luxury** lust

Against thy mother aught. Leave her to heaven
And to those thorns that in her bosom lodge
To prick and sting her. Fare thee well at once.
The glowworm shows the matin° to be near
And 'gins to pale his uneffectual fire. *90*
Adieu, adieu, adieu. Remember me. *Exit.*

Hamlet. O all you host of heaven! O earth! What else?
And shall I couple hell? O fie! Hold, hold, my heart,
And you, my sinews, grow not instant old,
But bear me stiffly up. Remember thee? *95*
Ay, thou poor ghost, whiles memory holds a seat
In this distracted globe.° Remember thee?
Yea, from the table° of my memory
I'll wipe away all trivial fond° records,
All saws° of books, all forms, all pressures° past *100*
That youth and observation copied there,
And thy commandment all alone shall live
Within the book and volume of my brain,
Unmixed with baser matter. Yes, by heaven!
O most pernicious woman! *105*
O villain, villain, smiling, damnèd villain!
My tables—meet it is I set it down
That one may smile, and smile, and be a villain.
At least I am sure it may be so in Denmark. [*Writes.*]
So, uncle, there you are. Now to my word: *110*
It is "Adieu, adieu, remember me."
I have sworn't.

Horatio and Marcellus. (*Within*) My lord, my lord!

   Enter Horatio and Marcellus.

Marcellus.   Lord Hamlet!

Horatio.   Heavens secure him!

Hamlet. So be it!

Marcellus. Illo, ho, ho,° my lord! *115*

Hamlet. Hillo, ho, ho, boy! Come, bird, come.

---

89 **matin** morning 97 **globe** i.e., his head 98 **table** tablet, notebook
99 **fond** foolish 100 **saws** maxims 100 **pressures** impressions 115 **Illo,
ho, ho** (falconer's call to his hawk)

Marcellus. How is't, my noble lord?

Horatio.   What news, my lord?

Hamlet. O, wonderful!

Horatio. Good my lord, tell it.

Hamlet.   No, you will reveal it.

Horatio. Not I, my lord, by heaven.

120 *Marcellus.*   Nor I, my lord.

Hamlet. How say you then? Would heart of man once
    think it?
But you'll be secret?

Both.   Ay, by heaven, my lord.

Hamlet. There's never a villain dwelling in all Denmark
But he's an arrant knave.

Horatio. There needs no ghost, my lord, come from the
125   grave
To tell us this.

Hamlet.   Why, right, you are in the right;
And so, without more circumstance° at all,
I hold it fit that we shake hands and part:
You, as your business and desire shall point you,
130 For every man hath business and desire
Such as it is, and for my own poor part,
Look you, I'll go pray.

Horatio. These are but wild and whirling words, my
    lord.

Hamlet. I am sorry they offend you, heartily;
Yes, faith, heartily.

135 *Horatio.*   There's no offense, my lord.

Hamlet. Yes, by Saint Patrick, but there is, Horatio,
And much offense too. Touching this vision here,
It is an honest ghost,° that let me tell you.
For your desire to know what is between us,
140 O'ermaster't as you may. And now, good friends,

127 **circumstance** details   138 **honest ghost** i.e., not a demon in his father's shape

As you are friends, scholars, and soldiers,
Give me one poor request.

Horatio. What is't, my lord? We will.

Hamlet. Never make known what you have seen to-
    night.

Both. My lord, we will not.

Hamlet.   Nay, but swear't.

Horatio.   In faith,   *145*
    My lord, not I.

Marcellus.   Nor I, my lord—in faith.

Hamlet. Upon my sword.

Marcellus.   We have sworn, my lord, already.

Hamlet. Indeed, upon my sword, indeed.
                  Ghost cries under the stage.

Ghost. Swear.

Hamlet. Ha, ha, boy, say'st thou so? Art thou there,
    truepenny?°   *150*
Come on. You hear this fellow in the cellarage.
Consent to swear.

Horatio.   Propose the oath, my lord.

Hamlet. Never to speak of this that you have seen.
Swear by my sword.

Ghost. [*Beneath*] Swear.   *155*

Hamlet. Hic et ubique?° Then we'll shift our ground;
Come hither, gentlemen,
And lay your hands again upon my sword.
Swear by my sword
Never to speak of this that you have heard.   *160*

Ghost. [*Beneath*] Swear by his sword.

Hamlet. Well said, old mole! Canst work i' th' earth so
    fast?
A worthy pioner!° Once more remove, good friends.

---

150 **truepenny** honest fellow   156 **Hic et ubique** here and everywhere
(Latin)   163 **pioner** digger of mines

Horatio. O day and night, but this is wondrous strange!

165 *Hamlet.* And therefore as a stranger give it welcome.
　　　　There are more things in heaven and earth, Horatio,
　　　　Than are dreamt of in your philosophy.
　　　　But come:
　　　　Here as before, never, so help you mercy,
170　　　How strange or odd some'er I bear myself
　　　　(As I perchance hereafter shall think meet
　　　　To put an antic disposition° on),
　　　　That you, at such times seeing me, never shall
　　　　With arms encumb'red° thus, or this headshake,
175　　　Or by pronouncing of some doubtful phrase,
　　　　As "Well, well, we know," or "We could, an if we
　　　　　　would,"
　　　　Or "If we list to speak," or "There be, an if they
　　　　　　might,"
　　　　Or such ambiguous giving out, to note
　　　　That you know aught of me—this do swear,
180　　　So grace and mercy at your most need help you.

Ghost. [*Beneath*] Swear.　　　　　　　　[*They swear.*]

Hamlet. Rest, rest, perturbèd spirit. So, gentlemen,
　　　　With all my love I do commend me° to you,
　　　　And what so poor a man as Hamlet is
185　　　May do t' express his love and friending to you,
　　　　God willing, shall not lack. Let us go in together,
　　　　And still your fingers on your lips, I pray.
　　　　The time is out of joint. O cursèd spite,
　　　　That ever I was born to set it right!
190　　　Nay, come, let's go together.　　　　　　*Exeunt.*

172 **antic   disposition** fantastic behavior 174 **encumb'red** folded
183 **commend me** entrust myself

[ACT 2

Scene 1. *A room.*]

Enter old Polonius, with his man Reynaldo.

Polonius. Give him this money and these notes, Reynaldo.

Reynaldo. I will, my lord.

Polonius. You shall do marvell's° wisely, good Reynaldo,
Before you visit him, to make inquire
Of his behavior.

Reynaldo.   My lord, I did intend it.   *5*

Polonius. Marry, well said, very well said. Look you sir,
Inquire me first what Danskers° are in Paris,
And how, and who, what means, and where they keep,°
What company, at what expense; and finding
By this encompassment° and drift of question   *10*
That they do know my son, come you more nearer
Than your particular demands° will touch it.
Take you as 'twere some distant knowledge of him,
As thus, "I know his father and his friends,
And in part him." Do you mark this, Reynaldo?   *15*

Reynaldo. Ay, very well, my lord.

2.1.3 **marvell's** marvelous(ly)   7 **Danskers** Danes   8 **keep** dwell
10 **encompassment** circling   12 **demands** questions

Polonius. "And in part him, but," you may say, "not
        well,
    But if't be he I mean, he's very wild,
    Addicted so and so." And there put on him
20   What forgeries° you please; marry, none so rank
    As may dishonor him—take heed of that—
    But, sir, such wanton, wild, and usual slips
    As are companions noted and most known
    To youth and liberty.

Reynaldo.   As gaming, my lord.

Polonius. Ay, or drinking, fencing, swearing, quarrel-
25   ing,
    Drabbing.° You may go so far.

Reynaldo. My lord, that would dishonor him.

Polonius. Faith, no, as you may season it in the charge.
    You must not put another scandal on him,
30   That he is open to incontinency.°
    That's not my meaning. But breathe his faults so
        quaintly°
    That they may seem the taints of liberty,
    The flash and outbreak of a fiery mind,
    A savageness in unreclaimèd blood,
    Of general assault.°

35 *Reynaldo.*   But, my good lord——

Polonius. Wherefore should you do this?

Reynaldo.   Ay, my lord,
    I would know that.

Polonius.   Marry, sir, here's my drift,
    And I believe it is a fetch of warrant.°
    You laying these slight sullies on my son
40   As 'twere a thing a little soiled i' th' working,
    Mark you,
    Your party in converse, him you would sound,

---

20 **forgeries** inventions   26 **Drabbing** wenching   30 **incontinency** habitual licentiousness   31 **quaintly** ingeniously, delicately   35 **Of general assault** common to all men   38 **fetch of warrant** justifiable device

Having ever seen in the prenominate crimes°
The youth you breathe of guilty, be assured
He closes with you in this consequence:°   45
"Good sir," or so, or "friend," or "gentleman"—
According to the phrase or the addition°
Of man and country—

Reynaldo.   Very good, my lord.

Polonius. And then, sir, does 'a° this—'a does—
What was I about to say? By the mass, I was about   50
to say something! Where did I leave?

Reynaldo. At "closes in the consequence," at "friend
or so," and "gentleman."

Polonius. At "closes in the consequence"—Ay, marry!
He closes thus: "I know the gentleman;   55
I saw him yesterday, or t'other day,
Or then, or then, with such or such, and, as you say,
There was 'a gaming, there o'ertook in's rouse,
There falling out at tennis"; or perchance,
"I saw him enter such a house of sale,"   60
Videlicet,° a brothel, or so forth.
See you now—
Your bait of falsehood take this carp of truth,
And thus do we of wisdom and of reach,°
With windlasses° and with assays of bias,°   65
By indirections find directions out.
So, by my former lecture and advice,
Shall you my son. You have me, have you not?

Reynaldo. My lord, I have.

Polonius.   God bye ye, fare ye well.

Reynaldo. Good my lord.   70

Polonius. Observe his inclination in yourself.°

---

43 **Having ... crimes** if he has ever seen in the aforementioned crimes
45 **He closes ... this consequence** he falls in with you in this conclusion
47 **addition** title   49 **'a** he   61 **Videlicet** namely   64 **reach** far-
reaching awareness (?)   65 **windlasses** circuitous courses   65 **assays of
bias** indirect attempts (metaphor from bowling; **bias** = curved course)
71 **in yourself** for yourself

Reynaldo. I shall, my lord.

Polonius. And let him ply his music.

Reynaldo.   Well, my lord.

Polonius. Farewell.   *Exit Reynaldo.*

Enter Ophelia.

How now, Ophelia, what's the matter?

75 *Ophelia.* O my lord, my lord, I have been so affrighted!

Polonius. With what, i' th' name of God?

Ophelia. My lord, as I was sewing in my closet,°
Lord Hamlet, with his doublet all unbraced,°
No hat upon his head, his stockings fouled,
80 Ungartered, and down-gyvèd° to his ankle,
Pale as his shirt, his knees knocking each other,
And with a look so piteous in purport,°
As if he had been loosèd out of hell
To speak of horrors—he comes before me.

Polonius. Mad for thy love?

85 *Ophelia.*   My lord, I do not know,
But truly I do fear it.

Polonius.   What said he?

Ophelia. He took me by the wrist and held me hard;
Then goes he to the length of all his arm,
And with his other hand thus o'er his brow
90 He falls to such perusal of my face
As 'a would draw it. Long stayed he so.
At last, a little shaking of mine arm,
And thrice his head thus waving up and down,
He raised a sigh so piteous and profound
95 As it did seem to shatter all his bulk
And end his being. That done, he lets me go,
And, with his head over his shoulder turned,
He seemed to find his way without his eyes,

---

77 **closet** private room 78 **doublet all unbraced** jacket entirely un-
laced 80 **down-gyvèd** hanging down like fetters 82 **purport** expression

For out o' doors he went without their helps,
And to the last bended their light on me.   *100*

Polonius. Come, go with me. I will go seek the King.
This is the very ecstasy° of love,
Whose violent property fordoes° itself
And leads the will to desperate undertakings
As oft as any passions under heaven   *105*
That does afflict our natures. I am sorry.
What, have you given him any hard words of late?

Ophelia. No, my good lord; but as you did command,
I did repel his letters and denied
His access to me.

Polonius.   That hath made him mad.   *110*
I am sorry that with better heed and judgment
I had not quoted° him. I feared he did but trifle
And meant to wrack thee; but beshrew my jealousy.°
By heaven, it is as proper° to our age
To cast beyond ourselves° in our opinions   *115*
As it is common for the younger sort
To lack discretion. Come, go we to the King.
This must be known, which, being kept close, might
      move
More grief to hide than hate to utter love.°
Come.   *Exeunt.*   *120*

---

102 **ecstasy** madness   103 **property fordoes** quality destroys 112 **quoted** noted   113 **beshrew my jealousy** curse on my suspicions   114 **proper** natural   115 **To cast beyond ourselves** to be overcalculating 117–19 **Come, go ... utter love** (the general meaning is that while telling the King of Hamlet's love may anger the King, more grief would come from keeping it secret)

[Scene 2. *The castle.*]

Flourish. Enter King and Queen, Rosencrantz, and
                Guildenstern [with others].

King. Welcome, dear Rosencrantz and Guildenstern.
          Moreover that° we much did long to see you,
          The need we have to use you did provoke
          Our hasty sending. Something have you heard
5   Of Hamlet's transformation: so call it,
          Sith° nor th' exterior nor the inward man
          Resembles that it was. What it should be,
          More than his father's death, that thus hath put him
          So much from th' understanding of himself,
10   I cannot dream of. I entreat you both
          That, being of so° young days brought up with him,
          And sith so neighbored to his youth and havior,°
          That you vouchsafe your rest° here in our court
          Some little time, so by your companies
15   To draw him on to pleasures, and to gather
          So much as from occasion you may glean,
          Whether aught to us unknown afflicts him thus,
          That opened° lies within our remedy.

Queen. Good gentlemen, he hath much talked of you,
20   And sure I am, two men there is not living
          To whom he more adheres. If it will please you
          To show us so much gentry° and good will
          As to expend your time with us awhile
          For the supply and profit of our hope,
25   Your visitation shall receive such thanks
          As fits a king's remembrance.

Rosencrantz.   Both your Majesties

2.2.2 **Moreover that** beside the fact that   6 **Sith** since   11 **of so** from
such   12 **youth and havior** behavior in his youth   13 **vouchsafe your
rest** consent to remain   18 **opened** revealed   22 **gentry** courtesy

Might, by the sovereign power you have of us,
Put your dread pleasures more into command
Than to entreaty.

Guildenstern.   But we both obey,
    And here give up ourselves in the full bent°   30
    To lay our service freely at your feet,
    To be commanded.

King. Thanks, Rosencrantz and gentle Guildenstern.

Queen. Thanks, Guildenstern and gentle Rosencrantz.
    And I beseech you instantly to visit   35
    My too much changèd son. Go, some of you,
    And bring these gentlemen where Hamlet is.

Guildenstern. Heavens make our presence and our
    practices
    Pleasant and helpful to him!

Queen.   Ay, amen!
        *Exeunt Rosencrantz and Guildenstern [with some
                                        Attendants].*

                Enter Polonius.

Polonius. Th' ambassadors from Norway, my good
    lord,   40
    Are joyfully returned.

King. Thou still° hast been the father of good news.

Polonius. Have I, my lord? Assure you, my good liege,
    I hold my duty, as I hold my soul,
    Both to my God and to my gracious king;   45
    And I do think, or else this brain of mine
    Hunts not the trail of policy so sure°
    As it hath used to do, that I have found
    The very cause of Hamlet's lunacy.

King. O, speak of that! That do I long to hear.   50

Polonius. Give first admittance to th' ambassadors.
    My news shall be the fruit to that great feast.

---

30 **in the full bent** entirely (the figure is of a bow bent to its capacity)   42 **still** always   47 **Hunts not . . . so sure** does not follow clues of
political doings with such sureness

    King. Thyself do grace to them and bring them in.

                    [Exit Polonius.]

    He tells me, my dear Gertrude, he hath found
55   The head and source of all your son's distemper.

    Queen. I doubt° it is no other but the main,°
    His father's death and our o'erhasty marriage.

    King. Well, we shall sift him.

       Enter Polonius, Voltemand, and Cornelius.

                   Welcome, my good friends.
    Say, Voltemand, what from our brother Norway?

60   *Voltemand.* Most fair return of greetings and desires.
    Upon our first,° he sent out to suppress
    His nephew's levies, which to him appeared
    To be a preparation 'gainst the Polack;
    But better looked into, he truly found
65   It was against your Highness, whereat grieved,
    That so his sickness, age, and impotence
    Was falsely borne in hand,° sends out arrests
    On Fortinbras; which he, in brief, obeys,
    Receives rebuke from Norway, and in fine,°
70   Makes vow before his uncle never more
    To give th' assay° of arms against your Majesty.
    Whereon old Norway, overcome with joy,
    Gives him threescore thousand crowns in annual fee
    And his commission to employ those soldiers,
75   So levied as before, against the Polack,
    With an entreaty, herein further shown,

                    [Gives a paper.]

    That it might please you to give quiet pass
    Through your dominions for this enterprise,
    On such regards of safety and allowance°
    As therein are set down.

80   *King.*   It likes us well;
    And at our more considered time° we'll read,
    Answer, and think upon this business.

56 **doubt** suspect   56 **main** principal point   61 **first** first audience
67 **borne in hand** deceived   69 **in fine** finally   71 **assay** trial   79 **re-gards of safety and allowance** i.e., conditions   81 **considered time** time proper for considering

Meantime, we thank you for your well-took labor.
Go to your rest; at night we'll feast together.
Most welcome home!　　　　*Exeunt Ambassadors.*

Polonius.　　　　　　This business is well ended。　　85
My liege and madam, to expostulate°
What majesty should be, what duty is,
Why day is day, night night, and time is time,
Were nothing but to waste night, day, and time.
Therefore, since brevity is the soul of wit,°　　　90
And tediousness the limbs and outward flourishes,
I will be brief. Your noble son is mad.
Mad call I it, for, to define true madness,
What is't but to be nothing else but mad?
But let that go.

Queen.　　　　　　More matter, with less art.　　95

Polonius. Madam, I swear I use no art at all.
That he's mad, 'tis true: 'tis true 'tis pity,
And pity 'tis 'tis true—a foolish figure.°
But farewell it, for I will use no art.
Mad let us grant him then; and now remains　　　100
That we find out the cause of this effect,
Or rather say, the cause of this defect,
For this effect defective comes by cause.
Thus it remains, and the remainder thus.
Perpend.°　　　　　　　　　　　　　　105
I have a daughter: have, while she is mine,
Who in her duty and obedience, mark,
Hath given me this. Now gather, and surmise.
　　　　　　　　　　[Reads] the letter.
"To the celestial, and my soul's idol, the most
beautified Ophelia"—　　　　　　　110
That's an ill phrase, a vile phrase; "beautified" is a
vile phrase. But you shall hear. Thus:
"In her excellent white bosom, these, &c."

Queen. Came this from Hamlet to her?

Polonius. Good madam, stay awhile. I will be faithful.　115
　　　　"Doubt thou the stars are fire,

86 **expostulate** discuss　90 **wit** wisdom, understanding　98 **figure** figure of rhetoric　105 **Perpend** consider carefully

Doubt that the sun doth move;
Doubt° truth to be a liar,
But never doubt I love.

120   Q dear Ophelia, I am ill at these numbers.° I have
not art to reckon my groans; but that I love thee
best, O most best, believe it. Adieu.
Thine evermore, most dear lady, whilst this
machine° is to him, HAMLET."

125   This in obedience hath my daughter shown me,
And more above° hath his solicitings,
As they fell out by time, by means, and place,
All given to mine ear.

King.   But how hath she
Received his love?

Polonius.   What do you think of me?

130   *King.* As of a man faithful and honorable.

Polonius. I would fain prove so. But what might you
think,
When I had seen this hot love on the wing
(As I perceived it, I must tell you that,
Before my daughter told me), what might you,
135   Or my dear Majesty your Queen here, think,
If I had played the desk or table book,°
Or given my heart a winking,° mute and dumb,
Or looked upon this love with idle sight?
What might you think? No, I went round to work
140   And my young mistress thus I did bespeak:
"Lord Hamlet is a prince, out of thy star.°
This must not be." And then I prescripts gave her,
That she should lock herself from his resort,
Admit no messengers, receive no tokens.
145   Which done, she took the fruits of my advice,
And he, repellèd, a short tale to make,

118 **Doubt** suspect   120 **ill at these numbers** unskilled in verses
124 **machine** complex device (here, his body)   126 **more above** in addition   136 **played the desk or table book** i.e., been a passive recipient of
secrets   137 **winking** closing of the eyes   141 **star** sphere

Fell into a sadness, then into a fast,
Thence to a watch,° thence into a weakness,
Thence to a lightness,° and, by this declension,
Into the madness wherein now he raves,   *150*
And all we mourn for.

King.   Do you think 'tis this?

Queen. It may be, very like.

Polonius. Hath there been such a time, I would fain
    know that,
    That I have positively said " 'Tis so,"
    When it proved otherwise?

King.   Not that I know.   *155*

Polonius. [*Pointing to his head and shoulder*] Take
    this from this, if this be otherwise.
    If circumstances lead me, I will find
    Where truth is hid, though it were hid indeed
    Within the center.°

King.   How may we try it further?

Polonius. You know sometimes he walks four hours
    together   *160*
    Here in the lobby.

Queen.   So he does indeed.

Polonius. At such a time I'll loose my daughter to him.
    Be you and I behind an arras° then.
    Mark the encounter. If he love her not,
    And be not from his reason fall'n thereon,   *165*
    Let me be no assistant for a state
    But keep a farm and carters.

King.   We will try it.

Enter Hamlet reading on a book.

Queen. But look where sadly the poor wretch comes
    reading.

Polonius. Away, I do beseech you both, away.

Exit King and Queen.

---

148 **watch** wakefulness   149 **lightness** mental derangement   159 **cen-ter** center of the earth   163 **arras** tapestry hanging in front of a wall

170 I'll board him presently.° O, give me leave.
How does my good Lord Hamlet?

Hamlet. Well, God-a-mercy.

Polonius. Do you know me, my lord?

Hamlet. Excellent well. You are a fishmonger.°

175 *Polonius.* Not I, my lord.

Hamlet. Then I would you were so honest a man.

Polonius. Honest, my lord?

Hamlet. Ay, sir. To be honest, as this world goes, is to
be one man picked out of ten thousand.

180 *Polonius.* That's very true, my lord.

Hamlet. For if the sun breed maggots in a dead dog,
being a good kissing carrion°—— Have you a
daughter?

Polonius. I have, my lord.

185 *Hamlet.* Let her not walk i' th' sun. Conception° is a
blessing, but as your daughter may conceive, friend,
look to't.

Polonius. [*Aside*] How say you by that? Still harping
on my daughter. Yet he knew me not at first. 'A said
190 I was a fishmonger. 'A is far gone, far gone. And
truly in my youth I suffered much extremity for
love, very near this. I'll speak to him again.—What
do you read, my lord?

Hamlet. Words, words, words.

195 *Polonius.* What is the matter, my lord?

Hamlet. Between who?

Polonius. I mean the matter° that you read, my lord.

---

170 **board him presently** accost him at once   174 **fishmonger** dealer
in fish (slang for a procurer). (The joke is in the inappropriateness. Although many editors say that *fishmonger* is slang for a procurer, such usage is undocumented)   182 **a good kissing carrion** (perhaps the
meaning is "a good piece of flesh to kiss," but many editors emend *good*
to *god,* taking the word to refer to the sun)   185 **Conception** (1) understanding (2) becoming pregnant   197 **matter** (Polonius means "subject
matter," but Hamlet pretends to take the word in the sense of "quarrel")

Hamlet. Slanders, sir; for the satirical rogue says here that old men have gray beards, that their faces are wrinkled, their eyes purging thick amber and plum- 200 tree gum, and that they have a plentiful lack of wit, together with most weak hams. All which, sir, though I most powerfully and potently believe, yet I hold it not honesty° to have it thus set down; for you yourself, sir, should be old as I am if, like a 205 crab, you could go backward.

Polonius. [*Aside*] Though this be madness, yet there is method in't. Will you walk out of the air, my lord?

Hamlet. Into my grave.

Polonius. Indeed, that's out of the air. [*Aside*] How 210 pregnant° sometimes his replies are! A happiness° that often madness hits on, which reason and sanity could not so prosperously be delivered of. I will leave him and suddenly contrive the means of meeting between him and my daughter.—My lord, 215 I will take my leave of you.

Hamlet. You cannot take from me anything that I will more willingly part withal—except my life, except my life, except my life.

Enter Guildenstern and Rosencrantz.

Polonius. Fare you well, my lord. 220

Hamlet. These tedious old fools!

Polonius. You go to seek the Lord Hamlet? There he is.

Rosencrantz. [*To Polonius*] God save you, sir!
[*Exit Polonius.*]

Guildenstern. My honored lord! 225

Rosencrantz. My most dear lord!

Hamlet. My excellent good friends! How dost thou, Guildenstern? Ah, Rosencrantz! Good lads, how do you both?

204 **honesty** decency   211 **pregnant** meaningful   211 **happiness** apt turn of phrase

230 *Rosencrantz.* As the indifferent° children of the earth.

Guildenstern. Happy in that we are not overhappy.
    On Fortune's cap we are not the very button.

Hamlet. Nor the soles of her shoe?

Rosencrantz. Neither, my lord.

235 *Hamlet.* Then you live about her waist, or in the middle
    of her favors?

Guildenstern. Faith, her privates° we.

Hamlet. In the secret parts of Fortune? O, most true!
    She is a strumpet. What news?

240 *Rosencrantz.* None, my lord, but that the world's
    grown honest.

Hamlet. Then is doomsday near. But your news is not
    true. Let me question more in particular. What
    have you, my good friends, deserved at the hands of
245 Fortune that she sends you to prison hither?

Guildenstern. Prison, my lord?

Hamlet. Denmark's a prison.

Rosencrantz. Then is the world one.

Hamlet. A goodly one, in which there are many
250 confines, wards,° and dungeons, Denmark being
    one o' th' worst.

Rosencrantz. We think not so, my lord.

Hamlet. Why, then 'tis none to you, for there is nothing
    either good or bad but thinking makes it so. To me
255 it is a prison.

Rosencrantz. Why then your ambition makes it one.
    'Tis too narrow for your mind.

Hamlet. O God, I could be bounded in a nutshell and
    count myself a king of infinite space, were it not
260 that I have bad dreams.

Guildenstern. Which dreams indeed are ambition, for

---

230 **indifferent** ordinary   237 **privates** ordinary men (with a pun on
"private parts")   250 **wards** cells

the very substance of the ambitious is merely the shadow of a dream.

Hamlet. A dream itself is but a shadow.

Rosencrantz. Truly, and I hold ambition of so airy and 265 light a quality that it is but a shadow's shadow.

Hamlet. Then are our beggars bodies, and our monarchs and outstretched heroes the beggars' shadows.° Shall we to th' court? For, by my fay,° I cannot reason. 270

Both. We'll wait upon you.

Hamlet. No such matter. I will not sort you with the rest of my servants, for, to speak to you like an honest man, I am most dreadfully attended. But in the beaten way of friendship, what make you at 275 Elsinore?

Rosencrantz. To visit you, my lord; no other occasion.

Hamlet. Beggar that I am, I am even poor in thanks, but I thank you; and sure, dear friends, my thanks are too dear a halfpenny.° Were you not sent for? 280 Is it your own inclining? Is it a free visitation? Come, come, deal justly with me. Come, come; nay, speak.

Guildenstern. What should we say, my lord?

Hamlet. Why anything—but to th' purpose. You were 285 sent for, and there is a kind of confession in your looks, which your modesties have not craft enough to color. I know the good King and Queen have sent for you.

Rosencrantz. To what end, my lord? 290

Hamlet. That you must teach me. But let me conjure you by the rights of our fellowship, by the consonancy of our youth, by the obligation of our ever-

---

267–69 **Then are . . . beggars' shadows** i.e., by your logic, beggars (lacking ambition) are substantial, and great men are elongated shadows 269 **fay** faith   280 **too dear a halfpenny** i.e., not worth a halfpenny

preserved love, and by what more dear a better
295   proposer can charge you withal, be even and direct
with me, whether you were sent for or no.

Rosencrantz. [*Aside to Guildenstern*] What say you?

Hamlet. [*Aside*] Nay then, I have an eye of you.—If
you love me, hold not off.

300 *Guildenstern.* My lord, we were sent for.

Hamlet. I will tell you why; so shall my anticipation
prevent your discovery,° and your secrecy to the
King and Queen molt no feather. I have of late, but
wherefore I know not, lost all my mirth, forgone all
305   custom of exercises; and indeed, it goes so heavily
with my disposition that this goodly frame, the
earth, seems to me a sterile promontory; this most
excellent canopy, the air, look you, this brave
o'erhanging firmament, this majestical roof fretted°
310   with golden fire: why, it appeareth nothing to me
but a foul and pestilent congregation of vapors.
What a piece of work is a man, how noble in reason,
how infinite in faculties, in form and moving how
express° and admirable, in action how like an angel,
315   in apprehension how like a god: the beauty of the
world, the paragon of animals; and yet to me, what
is this quintessence of dust? Man delights not me;
nor woman neither, though by your smiling you
seem to say so.

320 *Rosencrantz.* My lord, there was no such stuff in my
thoughts.

Hamlet. Why did ye laugh then, when I said "Man
delights not me"?

Rosencrantz. To think, my lord, if you delight not in
325   man, what lenten° entertainment the players shall
receive from you. We coted° them on the way, and
hither are they coming to offer you service.

---

302 **prevent your discovery** forestall your disclosure   309 **fretted**
adorned   314 **express** exact   325 **lenten** meager   326 **coted** overtook

Hamlet. He that plays the king shall be welcome; his
Majesty shall have tribute of me; the adventurous
knight shall use his foil and target;° the lover shall   *330*
not sigh gratis; the humorous man° shall end his
part in peace; the clown shall make those laugh
whose lungs are tickle o' th' sere;° and the lady shall
say her mind freely, or° the blank verse shall halt°
for't. What players are they?   *335*

Rosencrantz. Even those you were wont to take such
delight in, the tragedians of the city.

Hamlet. How chances it they travel? Their residence,
both in reputation and profit, was better both ways.

Rosencrantz. I think their inhibition° comes by the   *340*
means of the late innovation.°

Hamlet. Do they hold the same estimation they did
when I was in the city? Are they so followed?

Rosencrantz. No indeed, are they not.

Hamlet. How comes it? Do they grow rusty?   *345*

Rosencrantz. Nay, their endeavor keeps in the wonted
pace, but there is, sir, an eyrie° of children, little
eyases, that cry out on the top of question° and are
most tyrannically° clapped for't. These are now
the fashion, and so berattle the common stages° (so   *350*
they call them) that many wearing rapiers are afraid
of goosequills° and dare scarce come thither.

Hamlet. What, are they children? Who maintains 'em?
How are they escoted?° Will they pursue the

330 **target** shield   331 **humorous man** i.e., eccentric man (among
stock characters in dramas were men dominated by a "humor" or odd
trait)   333 **tickle o' th' sere** on hair trigger (*sere* = part of the gunlock)
334 **or** else   334 **halt** limp   340 **inhibition** hindrance   341 **innovation** (probably an allusion to the companies of child actors that had become popular and were offering serious competition to the adult actors)
347 **eyrie** nest   348 **eyases, that ... of question** unfledged hawks that
cry shrilly above others in matters of debate   349 **tyrannically** violently   350 **berattle the common stages** cry down the public theaters
(with the adult acting companies)   352 **goosequills** pens (of satirists
who ridicule the public theaters and their audiences)   354 **escoted** financially supported

355   quality° no longer than they can sing? Will they not
say afterwards, if they should grow themselves to
common players (as it is most like, if their means
are no better), their writers do them wrong to make
them exclaim against their own succession?°

360 *Rosencrantz.* Faith, there has been much to-do on
both sides, and the nation holds it no sin to tarre°
them to controversy. There was, for a while, no
money bid for argument° unless the poet and the
player went to cuffs in the question.

365 *Hamlet.* Is't possible?

Guildenstern. O, there has been much throwing about
of brains.

Hamlet. Do the boys carry it away?

Rosencrantz. Ay, that they do, my lord—Hercules and
370   his load° too.

Hamlet. It is not very strange, for my uncle is King of
Denmark, and those that would make mouths at
him while my father lived give twenty, forty, fifty,
a hundred ducats apiece for his picture in little.
375   'Sblood,° there is something in this more than
natural, if philosophy could find it out.

                                A flourish.

Guildenstern. There are the players.

Hamlet. Gentlemen, you are welcome to Elsinore.
Your hands, come then. Th' appurtenance of wel-
380   come is fashion and ceremony. Let me comply°
with you in this garb,° lest my extent° to the players
(which I tell you must show fairly outwards) should
more appear like entertainment than yours. You are
welcome. But my uncle-father and aunt-mother are
385   deceived.

355 **quality** profession of acting   359 **succession** future   361 **tarre** incite   363 **argument** plot of a play   369–70 **Hercules and his load** i.e.,
the whole world (with a reference to the Globe Theatre, which had a
sign that represented Hercules bearing the globe)   375 **'Sblood** by
God's blood   380 **comply** be courteous   381 **garb** outward show
381 **extent** behavior

Guildenstern. In what, my dear lord?

Hamlet. I am but mad north-northwest:° when the
wind is southerly I know a hawk from a handsaw.°

Enter Polonius.

Polonius. Well be with you, gentlemen.

Hamlet. Hark you, Guildenstern, and you too; at each   *390*
ear a hearer. That great baby you see there is not
yet out of his swaddling clouts.

Rosencrantz. Happily° he is the second time come to
them, for they say an old man is twice a child.

Hamlet. I will prophesy he comes to tell me of the   *395*
players. Mark it.—You say right, sir; a Monday
morning, 'twas then indeed.

Polonius. My lord, I have news to tell you.

Hamlet. My lord, I have news to tell you. When
Roscius° was an actor in Rome——   *400*

Polonius. The actors are come hither, my lord.

Hamlet. Buzz, buzz.°

Polonius. Upon my honor——

Hamlet. Then came each actor on his ass——

Polonius. The best actors in the world, either for   *405*
tragedy, comedy, history, pastoral, pastoral-comical,
historical-pastoral, tragical-historical, tragical-comical-historical-pastoral; scene individable,° or poem
unlimited.° Seneca° cannot be too heavy, nor
Plautus° too light. For the law of writ and the   *410*
liberty,° these are the only men.

---

387 **north-northwest** i.e., on one point of the compass only   388 **hawk
from a handsaw** (**hawk** can refer not only to a bird but to a kind of
pickax; **handsaw**—a carpenter's tool—may involve a similar pun on
"hernshaw," a heron)   393 **Happily** perhaps   400 **Roscius** (a famous
Roman comic actor)   402 **Buzz, buzz** (an interjection, perhaps indicating that the news is old)   408 **scene individable** plays observing the
unities of time, place, and action   408–09 **poem unlimited** plays not
restricted by the tenets of criticism   409 **Seneca** (Roman tragic dramatist)   410 **Plautus** (Roman comic dramatist)   410–11 **For the law of
writ and the liberty** (perhaps "for sticking to the text and for improvis-
ing"; perhaps "for classical plays and for modern loosely written plays")

Hamlet. O Jeptha, judge of Israel,° what a treasure hadst thou!

Polonius. What a treasure had he, my lord?

415 *Hamlet.* Why,
"One fair daughter, and no more,
The which he lovèd passing well."

Polonius. [*Aside*] Still on my daughter.

Hamlet. Am I not i' th' right, old Jeptha?

420 *Polonius.* If you call me Jeptha, my lord, I have a daughter that I love passing well.

Hamlet. Nay, that follows not.

Polonius. What follows then, my lord?

Hamlet. Why,
425 "As by lot, God wot,"
and then, you know,
"It came to pass, as most like it was."
The first row of the pious chanson° will show you more, for look where my abridgment° comes.

Enter the Players.

430 You are welcome, masters, welcome, all. I am glad to see thee well. Welcome, good friends. O, old friend, why, thy face is valanced° since I saw thee last. Com'st thou to beard me in Denmark? What, my young lady° and mistress? By'r Lady, your
435 ladyship is nearer to heaven than when I saw you last by the altitude of a chopine.° Pray God your voice, like a piece of uncurrent gold, be not cracked within the ring.°—Masters, you are all welcome. We'll e'en to't like French falconers, fly at any-

---

412 **Jeptha, judge of Israel** (the title of a ballad on the Hebrew judge who sacrificed his daughter; see Judges 11)   428 **row of the pious chanson** stanza of the scriptural song   429 **abridgment** (1) i.e., entertainers, who abridge the time (2) interrupters   432 **valanced** fringed (with a beard)   434 **young lady** i.e., boy for female roles   436 **chopine** thick-soled shoe   437–38 **like a piece . . . the ring** (a coin was unfit for legal tender if a crack extended from the edge through the ring enclosing the monarch's head. Hamlet, punning on *ring,* refers to the change of voice that the boy actor will undergo)

thing we see. We'll have a speech straight. Come,   *440*
give us a taste of your quality. Come, a passionate
speech.

Player. What speech, my good lord?

Hamlet. I heard thee speak me a speech once, but it
was never acted, or if it was, not above once, for   *445*
the play, I remember, pleased not the million; 'twas
caviary to the general,° but it was (as I received it,
and others, whose judgments in such matters cried
in the top of° mine) an excellent play, well digested
in the scenes, set down with as much modesty as   *450*
cunning.° I remember one said there were no
sallets° in the lines to make the matter savory;
nor no matter in the phrase that might indict the
author of affectation, but called it an honest method,
as wholesome as sweet, and by very much more   *455*
handsome than fine.° One speech in't I chiefly loved.
'Twas Aeneas' tale to Dido, and thereabout of it
especially when he speaks of Priam's slaughter. If
it live in your memory, begin at this line—let me
see, let me see: *460*

"The rugged Pyrrhus, like th' Hyrcanian
    beast°——"

'Tis not so; it begins with Pyrrhus:

"The rugged Pyrrhus, he whose sable° arms,
Black as his purpose, did the night resemble
When he lay couchèd in th' ominous horse,°   *465*
Hath now this dread and black complexion
    smeared
With heraldry more dismal.° Head to foot
Now is he total gules, horridly tricked°
With blood of fathers, mothers, daughters, sons,
Baked and impasted° with the parching streets,   *470*

447 **caviary to the general** i.e., too choice for the multitude   449 **in the top of** overtopping   450–51 **modesty as cunning** restraint as art   452 **sallets** salads, spicy jests   455–56 **more handsome than fine** well-proportioned rather than ornamented   461 **Hyrcanian beast** i.e., tiger (Hyrcania was in Asia)   463 **sable** black   465 **ominous horse** i.e., wooden horse at the siege of Troy   467 **dismal** ill-omened   468 **total gules, horridly tricked** all red, horridly adorned   470 **impasted** encrusted

That lend a tyrannous and a damnèd light
To their lord's murder. Roasted in wrath and fire,
And thus o'ersizèd° with coagulate gore,
With eyes like carbuncles, the hellish Pyrrhus
475 Old grandsire Priam seeks."
     So, proceed you.

Polonius. Fore God, my lord, well spoken, with good
accent and good discretion.

Player.   "Anon he finds him,
480 Striking too short at Greeks. His antique sword,
     Rebellious to his arm, lies where it falls,
     Repugnant to command.° Unequal matched,
     Pyrrhus at Priam drives, in rage strikes wide,
     But with the whiff and wind of his fell sword
485 Th' unnervèd father falls. Then senseless Ilium,°
     Seeming to feel this blow, with flaming top
     Stoops to his base,° and with a hideous crash
     Takes prisoner Pyrrhus' ear. For lo, his sword,
     Which was declining on the milky head
490 Of reverend Priam, seemed i' th' air to stick.
     So as a painted tyrant° Pyrrhus stood,
     And like a neutral to his will and matter°
     Did nothing.
     But as we often see, against° some storm,
495 A silence in the heavens, the rack° stand still,
     The bold winds speechless, and the orb below
     As hush as death, anon the dreadful thunder
     Doth rend the region, so after Pyrrhus' pause,
     A rousèd vengeance sets him new awork,
500 And never did the Cyclops' hammer fall
     On Mars's armor, forged for proof eterne,°
     With less remorse than Pyrrhus' bleeding sword
     Now falls on Priam.
     Out, out, thou strumpet Fortune! All you gods,
505 In general synod° take away her power,

473 **o'ersizèd** smeared over   482 **Repugnant to command** disobedient
485 **senseless Ilium** insensate Troy   487 **Stoops to his base** collapses
(*his* = its)   491 **painted tyrant** tyrant in a picture   492 **matter** task
494 **against** just before   495 **rack** clouds   501 **proof eterne** eternal
endurance   505 **synod** council

Break all the spokes and fellies° from her wheel,
And bowl the round nave° down the hill of
   heaven,
As low as to the fiends."

Polonius. This is too long.

Hamlet. It shall to the barber's, with your beard.—   *510*
Prithee say on. He's for a jig or a tale of bawdry,
or he sleeps. Say on; come to Hecuba.

Player. "But who (ah woe!) had seen the mobled°
   queen——"

Hamlet. "The mobled queen"?

Polonius. That's good. "Mobled queen" is good.   *515*

Player. "Run barefoot up and down, threat'ning the
   flames
With bisson rheum;° a clout° upon that head
Where late the diadem stood, and for a robe,
About her lank and all o'erteemèd° loins,
A blanket in the alarm of fear caught up—   *520*
Who this had seen, with tongue in venom steeped
'Gainst Fortune's state would treason have pro-
   nounced.
But if the gods themselves did see her then,
When she saw Pyrrhus make malicious sport
In mincing with his sword her husband's limbs,   *525*
The instant burst of clamor that she made
(Unless things mortal move them not at all)
Would have made milch° the burning eyes of
   heaven
And passion in the gods."

Polonius. Look, whe'r° he has not turned his color,   *530*
and has tears in's eyes. Prithee no more.

Hamlet. 'Tis well. I'll have thee speak out the rest of
this soon. Good my lord, will you see the players
well bestowed?° Do you hear? Let them be well

---

506 **fellies** rims   507 **nave** hub   513 **mobled** muffled   517 **bisson
rheum** blinding tears   517 **clout** rag   519 **o'erteemèd** exhausted with
childbearing   528 **milch** moist (literally, "milk-giving")   530 **whe'r**
whether   534 **bestowed** housed

535 used, for they are the abstract and brief chronicles
of the time. After your death you were better have
a bad epitaph than their ill report while you live.

Polonius. My lord, I will use them according to their
desert.

540 *Hamlet.* God's bodkin,° man, much better! Use every
man after his desert, and who shall scape whipping?
Use them after your own honor and dignity. The
less they deserve, the more merit is in your bounty.
Take them in.

545 *Polonius.* Come, sirs.

Hamlet. Follow him, friends. We'll hear a play tomorrow. [*Aside to Player*] Dost thou hear me, old
friend? Can you play *The Murder of Gonzago*?

Player. Ay, my lord.

550 *Hamlet.* We'll ha't tomorrow night. You could for a
need study a speech of some dozen or sixteen lines
which I would set down and insert in't, could you
not?

Player. Ay, my lord.

555 *Hamlet.* Very well. Follow that lord, and look you
mock him not. My good friends, I'll leave you till
night. You are welcome to Elsinore.

Exeunt Polonius and Players.

Rosencrantz. Good my lord.

Exeunt [Rosencrantz and Guildenstern].

Hamlet. Ay, so, God bye to you.—Now I am alone.
560 O, what a rogue and peasant slave am I!
Is it not monstrous that this player here,
But in a fiction, in a dream of passion,°
Could force his soul so to his own conceit°
That from her working all his visage wanned,
565 Tears in his eyes, distraction in his aspect,
A broken voice, and his whole function° suiting

540 **God's bodkin** by God's little body   562 **dream of passion** imagi-
nary emotion   563 **conceit** imagination   566 **function** action

With forms° to his conceit? And all for nothing!
For Hecuba!
What's Hecuba to him, or he to Hecuba,
That he should weep for her? What would he do   570
Had he the motive and the cue for passion
That I have? He would drown the stage with tears
And cleave the general ear with horrid speech,
Make mad the guilty and appall the free,°
Confound the ignorant, and amaze indeed   575
The very faculties of eyes and ears.
Yet I,
A dull and muddy-mettled° rascal, peak
Like John-a-dreams,° unpregnant of° my cause,
And can say nothing. No, not for a king,   580
Upon whose property and most dear life
A damned defeat was made. Am I a coward?
Who calls me villain? Breaks my pate across?
Plucks off my beard and blows it in my face?
Tweaks me by the nose? Gives me the lie i' th' throat   585
As deep as to the lungs? Who does me this?
Ha, 'swounds,° I should take it, for it cannot be
But I am pigeon-livered° and lack gall
To make oppression bitter, or ere this
I should ha' fatted all the region kites°   590
With this slave's offal. Bloody, bawdy villain!
Remorseless, treacherous, lecherous, kindless° vil-
    lain!
O, vengeance!
Why, what an ass am I! This is most brave,°
That I, the son of a dear father murdered,   595
Prompted to my revenge by heaven and hell,
Must, like a whore, unpack my heart with words
And fall a-cursing like a very drab,°

---

567 **forms** bodily expressions   574 **appall the free** terrify (make pale?)
the guiltless   578 **muddy-mettled** weak-spirited   578–79 **peak/Like
John-a-dreams** mope like a dreamer   579 **unpregnant of** unquickened
by   587 **'swounds** by God's wounds   588 **pigeon-livered** gentle as a
dove   590 **region kites** kites (scavenger birds) of the sky   592 **kindless** unnatural   594 **brave** fine   598 **drab** prostitute

          A scullion!° Fie upon't, foh! About,° my brains.
600   Hum——
          I have heard that guilty creatures sitting at a play
          Have by the very cunning of the scene
          Been struck so to the soul that presently°
          They have proclaimed their malefactions.
605   For murder, though it have no tongue, will speak
          With most miraculous organ. I'll have these players
          Play something like the murder of my father
          Before mine uncle. I'll observe his looks,
          I'll tent° him to the quick. If 'a do blench,°
610   I know my course. The spirit that I have seen
          May be a devil, and the devil hath power
          T' assume a pleasing shape, yea, and perhaps
          Out of my weakness and my melancholy,
          As he is very potent with such spirits,
615   Abuses me to damn me. I'll have grounds
          More relative° than this. The play's the thing
          Wherein I'll catch the conscience of the King.   *Exit.*

599 **scullion** low-ranking kitchen servant, noted for foul language
599 **About** to work 603 **presently** immediately 609 **tent** probe
609 **blench** flinch 616 **relative** (probably "pertinent," but possibly
"able to be related plausibly")

[ACT 3

Scene 1. *The castle*.]

Enter King, Queen, Polonius, Ophelia, Rosencrantz,
Guildenstern, Lords.

King. And can you by no drift of conference°
  Get from him why he puts on this confusion,
  Grating so harshly all his days of quiet
  With turbulent and dangerous lunacy?

Rosencrantz. He does confess he feels himself dis-
    tracted,   5
  But from what cause 'a will by no means speak.

Guildenstern. Nor do we find him forward to be
    sounded,°
  But with a crafty madness keeps aloof
  When we would bring him on to some confession
  Of his true state.

Queen.   Did he receive you well?   10

Rosencrantz. Most like a gentleman.

Guildenstern. But with much forcing of his disposi-
    tion.°

Rosencrantz. Niggard of question,° but of our demands
  Most free in his reply.

3.1.1 **drift of conference** management of conversation   7 **forward to
be sounded** willing to be questioned   12 **forcing of his disposition** effort   13 **Niggard of question** uninclined to talk

Queen.   Did you assay° him
15   To any pastime?

Rosencrantz. Madam, it so fell out that certain players
        We o'erraught° on the way; of these we told him,
        And there did seem in him a kind of joy
        To hear of it. They are here about the court,
20   And, as I think, they have already order
        This night to play before him.

Polonius.   'Tis most true,
        And he beseeched me to entreat your Majesties
        To hear and see the matter.

King. With all my heart, and it doth much content me
25   To hear him so inclined.
        Good gentlemen, give him a further edge
        And drive his purpose into these delights.

Rosencrantz. We shall, my lord.
                    Exeunt Rosencrantz and Guildenstern.

King.   Sweet Gertrude, leave us too,
        For we have closely° sent for Hamlet hither,
30   That he, as 'twere by accident, may here
        Affront° Ophelia.
        Her father and myself (lawful espials°)
        Will so bestow ourselves that, seeing unseen,
        We may of their encounter frankly judge
35   And gather by him, as he is behaved,
        If't be th' affliction of his love or no
        That thus he suffers for.

Queen.   I shall obey you.
        And for your part, Ophelia, I do wish
        That your good beauties be the happy cause
40   Of Hamlet's wildness. So shall I hope your virtues
        Will bring him to his wonted way again,
        To both your honors.

Ophelia.   Madam, I wish it may.
                                        [*Exit Queen.*]

14 **assay** tempt   17 **o'erraught** overtook   29 **closely** secretly   31 **Affront** meet face to face   32 **espials** spies

Polonius. Ophelia, walk you here.—Gracious, so please
   you,
   We will bestow ourselves. [*To Ophelia*] Read on this
     book,
   That show of such an exercise may color°   *45*
   Your loneliness. We are oft to blame in this,
   'Tis too much proved, that with devotion's visage
   And pious action we do sugar o'er
   The devil himself.

King.   [*Aside*] O, 'tis too true.
   How smart a lash that speech doth give my con-
     science!   *50*
   The harlot's cheek, beautied with plast'ring art,
   Is not more ugly to the thing that helps it
   Than is my deed to my most painted word.
   O heavy burden!

Polonius. I hear him coming. Let's withdraw, my lord.   *55*
                    [*Exeunt King and Polonius.*]
                 Enter Hamlet.

Hamlet. To be, or not to be: that is the question:
   Whether 'tis nobler in the mind to suffer
   The slings and arrows of outrageous fortune,
   Or to take arms against a sea of troubles,
   And by opposing end them. To die, to sleep—   *60*
   No more—and by a sleep to say we end
   The heartache, and the thousand natural shocks
   That flesh is heir to! 'Tis a consummation
   Devoutly to be wished. To die, to sleep—
   To sleep—perchance to dream: ay, there's the rub,°   *65*
   For in that sleep of death what dreams may come
   When we have shuffled off this mortal coil,°
   Must give us pause. There's the respect°
   That makes calamity of so long life:°
   For who would bear the whips and scorns of time,   *70*

45 **exercise may color** act of devotion may give a plausible hue to (the
book is one of devotion)   65 **rub** impediment (obstruction to a bowler's
ball)   67 **coil** (1) turmoil (2) a ring of rope (here the flesh encircling the
soul)   68 **respect** consideration   69 **makes calamity of so long life** (1)
makes calamity so long-lived (2) makes living so long a calamity

Th' oppressor's wrong, the proud man's contumely,
The pangs of despised love, the law's delay,
The insolence of office, and the spurns
That patient merit of th' unworthy takes,
75 When he himself might his quietus° make
With a bare bodkin?° Who would fardels° bear,
To grunt and sweat under a weary life,
But that the dread of something after death,
The undiscovered country, from whose bourn°
80 No traveler returns, puzzles the will,
And makes us rather bear those ills we have,
Than fly to others that we know not of?
Thus conscience° does make cowards of us all,
And thus the native hue of resolution
85 Is sicklied o'er with the pale cast° of thought,
And enterprises of great pitch° and moment,
With this regard° their currents turn awry,
And lose the name of action.—Soft you now,
The fair Ophelia!—Nymph, in thy orisons°
Be all my sins remembered.

90 *Ophelia.*   Good my lord,
How does your honor for this many a day?

Hamlet. I humbly thank you; well, well, well.

Ophelia. My lord, I have remembrances of yours
That I have longèd long to redeliver.
I pray you now, receive them.

95 *Hamlet.*   No, not I,
I never gave you aught.

Ophelia. My lord, you know right well you
    did,
And with them words of so sweet breath composed
As made these things more rich. Their perfume lost,
100 Take these again, for to the noble mind

75 **quietus** full discharge (a legal term) 76 **bodkin** dagger 76 **fardels** burdens 79 **bourn** region 83 **conscience** (1) self-consciousness, introspection (2) inner moral voice 85 **cast** color 86 **pitch** height (a term from falconry) 87 **regard** consideration 89 **orisons** prayers

Rich gifts wax poor when givers prove unkind.
There, my lord.

Hamlet. Ha, ha! Are you honest?°

Ophelia. My lord?

Hamlet. Are you fair?   *105*

Ophelia. What means your lordship?

Hamlet. That if you be honest and fair, your honesty
should admit no discourse to your beauty.°

Ophelia. Could beauty, my lord, have better commerce
than with honesty?   *110*

Hamlet. Ay, truly; for the power of beauty will sooner
transform honesty from what it is to a bawd° than
the force of honesty can translate beauty into his
likeness. This was sometime a paradox, but now
the time gives it proof. I did love you once.   *115*

Ophelia. Indeed, my lord, you made me believe so.

Hamlet. You should not have believed me, for virtue
cannot so inoculate° our old stock but we shall relish
of it.° I loved you not.

Ophelia. I was the more deceived.   *120*

Hamlet. Get thee to a nunnery. Why wouldst thou be
a breeder of sinners? I am myself indifferent honest,°
but yet I could accuse me of such things that it were
better my mother had not borne me: I am very
proud, revengeful, ambitious, with more offenses at   *125*
my beck° than I have thoughts to put them in,
imagination to give them shape, or time to act them
in. What should such fellows as I do crawling between earth and heaven? We are arrant knaves all;
believe none of us. Go thy ways to a nunnery.   *130*
Where's your father?

---

103 **Are you honest** (1) are you modest (2) are you chaste (3) have you
integrity   107–08 **your honesty ... to your beauty** your modesty
should permit no approach to your beauty   112 **bawd** procurer
118 **inoculate** graft   118–19 **relish of it** smack of it (our old sinful nature)   122 **indifferent honest** moderately virtuous   126 **beck** call

Ophelia. At home, my lord.

Hamlet. Let the doors be shut upon him, that he may
play the fool nowhere but in's own house. Farewell.

135 *Ophelia.* O help him, you sweet heavens!

Hamlet. If thou dost marry, I'll give thee this plague
for thy dowry: be thou as chaste as ice, as pure as
snow, thou shalt not escape calumny. Get thee to a
nunnery. Go, farewell. Or if thou wilt needs marry,
140 marry a fool, for wise men know well enough what
monsters° you make of them. To a nunnery, go,
and quickly too. Farewell.

Ophelia. Heavenly powers, restore him!

Hamlet. I have heard of your paintings, well enough.
145 God hath given you one face, and you make yourselves another. You jig and amble, and you lisp;
you nickname God's creatures and make your
wantonness your ignorance.° Go to, I'll no more
on't; it hath made me mad. I say we will have no
150 moe° marriage. Those that are married already—all
but one—shall live. The rest shall keep as they are.
To a nunnery, go.   *Exit.*

Ophelia. O what a noble mind is here o'erthrown!
The courtier's, soldier's, scholar's, eye, tongue, sword,
155 Th' expectancy and rose° of the fair state,
The glass of fashion, and the mold of form,°
Th' observed of all observers, quite, quite down!
And I, of ladies most deject and wretched,
That sucked the honey of his musicked vows,
160 Now see that noble and most sovereign reason
Like sweet bells jangled, out of time and harsh,
That unmatched form and feature of blown° youth
Blasted with ecstasy.° O, woe is me
T' have seen what I have seen, see what I see!

Enter King and Polonius.

141 **monsters** horned beasts, cuckolds   147–48 **make your wantonness your ignorance** excuse your wanton speech by pretending ignorance   150 **moe** more   155 **expectancy and rose** i.e., fair hope
156 **The glass . . . of form** the mirror of fashion, and the pattern of excellent behavior   162 **blown** blooming   163 **ecstasy** madness

King. Love? His affections° do not that way tend,   165
　　Nor what he spake, though it lacked form a little,
　　Was not like madness. There's something in his soul
　　O'er which his melancholy sits on brood,
　　And I do doubt° the hatch and the disclose
　　Will be some danger; which for to prevent,   170
　　I have in quick determination
　　Thus set it down: he shall with speed to England
　　For the demand of our neglected tribute.
　　Haply the seas, and countries different,
　　With variable objects, shall expel   175
　　This something-settled° matter in his heart,
　　Whereon his brains still beating puts him thus
　　From fashion of himself. What think you on't?

Polonius. It shall do well. But yet do I believe
　　The origin and commencement of his grief   180
　　Sprung from neglected love. How now, Ophelia?
　　You need not tell us what Lord Hamlet said;
　　We heard it all. My lord, do as you please,
　　But if you hold it fit, after the play,
　　Let his queen mother all alone entreat him   185
　　To show his grief. Let her be round° with him,
　　And I'll be placed, so please you, in the ear
　　Of all their conference. If she find him not,°
　　To England send him, or confine him where
　　Your wisdom best shall think.

King.   It shall be so.   190
　　Madness in great ones must not unwatched go.
　　　　　　　　　　　　　　　　　　　Exeunt.

---

165 **affections** inclinations   169 **doubt**   fear   176 **something-settled**
somewhat settled   186 **round** blunt   188 **find him not** does not find
him out.

[Scene 2. *The castle.*]

Enter Hamlet and three of the Players.

Hamlet. Speak the speech, I pray you, as I pronounced
it to you, trippingly on the tongue. But if you mouth
it, as many of our players do, I had as lief the town
crier spoke my lines. Nor do not saw the air too much
5   with your hand, thus, but use all gently, for in the
very torrent, tempest, and (as I may say) whirlwind
of your passion, you must acquire and beget a temperance that may give it smoothness. O, it offends
me to the soul to hear a robustious periwig-pated°
10   fellow tear a passion to tatters, to very rags, to split
the ears of the groundlings,° who for the most part
are capable of° nothing but inexplicable dumb
shows° and noise. I would have such a fellow
whipped for o'erdoing Termagant. It out-herods
15   Herod.° Pray you avoid it.

Player. I warrant your honor.

Hamlet. Be not too tame neither, but let your own discretion be your tutor. Suit the action to the word, the
word to the action, with this special observance, that
20   you o'erstep not the modesty of nature. For anything
so o'erdone is from° the purpose of playing, whose
end, both at the first and now, was and is, to hold,
as 'twere, the mirror up to nature; to show virtue
her own feature, scorn her own image, and the very
25   age and body of the time his form and pressure.°

3.2.9 **robustious periwig-pated** boisterous wig-headed   11 **groundlings** those who stood in the pit of the theater (the poorest and presumably most ignorant of the audience)   12 **are capable of** are able to
understand   12–13 **dumb shows** (it had been the fashion for actors
to preface plays or parts of plays with silent mime)   14–15 **Termagant ... Herod** (boisterous characters in the old mystery plays)
21 **from** contrary to   25 **pressure** image, impress

Now, this overdone, or come tardy off, though it
makes the unskillful laugh, cannot but make the
judicious grieve, the censure of the which one must
in your allowance o'erweigh a whole theater of
others. O, there be players that I have seen play,   30
and heard others praise, and that highly (not to
speak it profanely), that neither having th' accent of
Christians, nor the gait of Christian, pagan, nor
man, have so strutted and bellowed that I have
thought some of Nature's journeymen° had made   35
men, and not made them well, they imitated humanity so abominably.

Player. I hope we have reformed that indifferently°
with us, sir.

Hamlet. O, reform it altogether! And let those that   40
play your clowns speak no more than is set down
for them, for there be of them that will themselves
laugh, to set on some quantity of barren spectators to
laugh too, though in the meantime some necessary
question of the play be then to be considered. That's   45
villainous and shows a most pitiful ambition in the
fool that uses it. Go make you ready.

            Exit Players.

 Enter Polonius, Guildenstern, and Rosencrantz.

How now, my lord? Will the King hear this piece of
work?

Polonius. And the Queen too, and that presently.   50

Hamlet. Bid the players make haste. *Exit Polonius.*
Will you two help to hasten them?

Rosencrantz. Ay, my lord.   *Exeunt they two.*

Hamlet. What, ho, Horatio!

      Enter Horatio.

Horatio. Here, sweet lord, at your service.   55

Hamlet. Horatio, thou art e'en as just a man

35 **journeymen** workers not yet masters of their craft 38 **indifferently**
tolerably

As e'er my conversation coped withal.°

Horatio. O, my dear lord——

Hamlet.   Nay, do not think I flatter.
For what advancement° may I hope from thee,
60 That no revenue hast but thy good spirits
To feed and clothe thee? Why should the poor be
    flattered?
No, let the candied° tongue lick absurd pomp,
And crook the pregnant° hinges of the knee
Where thrift° may follow fawning. Dost thou hear?
65 Since my dear soul was mistress of her choice
And could of men distinguish her election,
S' hath sealed thee° for herself, for thou hast been
As one, in suff'ring all, that suffers nothing,°
A man that Fortune's buffets and rewards
70 Hast ta'en with equal thanks; and blest are those
Whose blood° and judgment are so well com-
    meddled°
That they are not a pipe for Fortune's finger
To sound what stop she please. Give me that man
That is not passion's slave, and I will wear him
75 In my heart's core, ay, in my heart of heart,
As I do thee. Something too much of this—
There is a play tonight before the King.
One scene of it comes near the circumstance
Which I have told thee, of my father's death.
80 I prithee, when thou seest that act afoot,
Even with the very comment° of thy soul
Observe my uncle. If his occulted° guilt
Do not itself unkennel in one speech,
It is a damnèd ghost that we have seen,
85 And my imaginations are as foul
As Vulcan's stithy.° Give him heedful note,
For I mine eyes will rivet to his face,

57 **coped withal** met with   59 **advancement** promotion   62 **candied**
sugared, flattering   63 **pregnant** (1) pliant (2) full of promise of good
fortune   64 **thrift** profit   67 **S' hath sealed thee** she (the soul) has set
a mark on you   68 **As one . . . nothing** Shakespeare puns on *suffering*:
Horatio *undergoes* all things, but is *harmed* by none   71 **blood** passion   71 **commeddled** blended   81 **very comment** deepest wisdom
82 **occulted** hidden   86 **stithy** forge, smithy

And after we will both our judgments join
In censure of his seeming.°

Horatio.   Well, my lord.
If 'a steal aught the whilst this play is playing,   90
And scape detecting, I will pay the theft.

*Enter Trumpets and Kettledrums, King, Queen,
Polonius, Ophelia, Rosencrantz, Guildenstern,
and other Lords attendant with his Guard carrying
torches. Danish March. Sound a Flourish.*

Hamlet. They are coming to the play: I must be idle;°
Get you a place.

King. How fares our cousin Hamlet?

Hamlet. Excellent, i' faith, of the chameleon's dish;°   95
I eat the air, promise-crammed; you cannot feed
capons so.

King. I have nothing with this answer, Hamlet; these
words are not mine.

Hamlet. No, nor mine now. [*To Polonius*] My lord, you   101
played once i' th' university, you say?

Polonius. That did I, my lord, and was accounted a good
actor.

Hamlet. What did you enact?

Polonius. I did enact Julius Caesar. I was killed i' th'   105
Capitol; Brutus killed me.

Hamlet. It was a brute part of him to kill so capital a
calf there. Be the players ready?

Rosencrantz. Ay, my lord. They stay upon your patience.   110

Queen. Come hither, my dear Hamlet, sit by me.

Hamlet. No, good mother. Here's metal more attractive.°

---

89 **censure of his seeming** judgment on his looks   92 **be idle** play the
fool   95 **the chameleon's dish** air (on which chameleons were thought
to live)   112–13 **attractive** magnetic

Polonius. [*To the King*] O ho! Do you mark that?

115 *Hamlet.* Lady, shall I lie in your lap?

> [*He lies at Ophelia's feet.*]

Ophelia. No, my lord.

Hamlet. I mean, my head upon your lap?

Ophelia. Ay, my lord.

Hamlet. Do you think I meant country matters?°

120 *Ophelia.* I think nothing, my lord.

Hamlet. That's a fair thought to lie between maids' legs.

Ophelia. What is, my lord?

Hamlet. Nothing.

125 *Ophelia.* You are merry, my lord.

Hamlet. Who, I?

Ophelia. Ay, my lord.

Hamlet. O God, your only jig-maker!° What should a man do but be merry? For look you how cheerfully
130 my mother looks, and my father died within's two hours.

Ophelia. Nay, 'tis twice two months, my lord.

Hamlet. So long? Nay then, let the devil wear black, for I'll have a suit of sables.° O heavens! Die two
135 months ago, and not forgotten yet? Then there's hope a great man's memory may outlive his life half a year. But, by'r Lady, 'a must build churches then, or else shall 'a suffer not thinking on, with the hobby-horse,° whose epitaph is "For O, for O, the hobby-
140 horse is forgot!"

> *The trumpets sound. Dumb show follows:*

---

119 **country matters** rustic doings (with a pun on the vulgar word for the pudendum)   128 **jig-maker** composer of songs and dances (often a Fool, who performed them)   134 **sables** (pun on "black" and "luxurious furs")   138–39 **hobbyhorse** mock horse worn by a performer in the morris dance

Enter a King and a Queen very lovingly, the Queen embracing him, and he her. She kneels; and makes show of protestation unto him. He takes her up, and declines his head upon her neck. He lies him down upon a bank of flowers. She, seeing him asleep, leaves him. Anon come in another man: takes off his crown, kisses it, pours poison in the sleeper's ears, and leaves him. The Queen returns, finds the King dead, makes passionate action. The poisoner, with some three or four, come in again, seem to condole with her. The dead body is carried away. The poisoner woos the Queen with gifts; she seems harsh awhile, but in the end accepts love.

Exeunt.

Ophelia. What means this, my lord?

Hamlet. Marry, this is miching mallecho;° it means mischief.

Ophelia. Belike this show imports the argument° of the play.   145

Enter Prologue.

Hamlet. We shall know by this fellow. The players cannot keep counsel; they'll tell all.

Ophelia. Will 'a tell us what this show meant?

Hamlet. Ay, or any show that you will show him. Be not you ashamed to show, he'll not shame to tell you   150
what it means.

Ophelia. You are naught,° you are naught; I'll mark the play.

Prologue. For us, and for our tragedy,
   Here stooping to your clemency,   155
   We beg your hearing patiently.   [*Exit.*]

Hamlet. Is this a prologue, or the posy of a ring?°

Ophelia. 'Tis brief, my lord.

Hamlet. As woman's love.

142 **miching mallecho** sneaking mischief   144 **argument** plot
152 **naught** wicked, improper   157 **posy of a ring** motto inscribed in
a ring.

Enter [two Players as] King and Queen.

Player King. Full thirty times hath Phoebus' cart° gone
160   round
            Neptune's salt wash° and Tellus'° orbèd ground,
            And thirty dozen moons with borrowed sheen
            About the world have times twelve thirties been,
            Since love our hearts, and Hymen did our hands,
165   Unite commutual in most sacred bands.

Player Queen. So many journeys may the sun and
            moon
            Make us again count o'er ere love be done!
            But woe is me, you are so sick of late,
            So far from cheer and from your former state,
170   That I distrust° you. Yet, though I distrust,
            Discomfort you, my lord, it nothing must.
            For women fear too much, even as they love,
            And women's fear and love hold quantity,
            In neither aught, or in extremity.°
175   Now what my love is, proof° hath made you know,
            And as my love is sized, my fear is so.
            Where love is great, the littlest doubts are fear;
            Where little fears grow great, great love grows there.

Player King. Faith, I must leave thee, love, and shortly
            too;
180   My operant° powers their functions leave to do:
            And thou shalt live in this fair world behind,
            Honored, beloved, and haply one as kind
            For husband shalt thou——

Player Queen.   O, confound the rest!
            Such love must needs be treason in my breast.
185   In second husband let me be accurst!
            None wed the second but who killed the first.

---

160 **Phoebus' cart** the sun's chariot   161 **Neptune's salt wash** the sea
161 **Tellus** Roman goddess of the earth   170 **distrust** am anxious
about   173–74 **And women's . . . in extremity** (perhaps the idea is that
women's anxiety is great or little in proportion to their love. The previous line, unrhymed, may be a false start that Shakespeare neglected to
delete)   175 **proof** experience   180 **operant** active

Hamlet. [Aside] That's wormwood.°

Player Queen. The instances° that second marriage move°
Are base respects of thrift,° but none of love.
A second time I kill my husband dead   *190*
When second husband kisses me in bed.

Player King. I do believe you think what now you speak,
But what we do determine oft we break.
Purpose is but the slave to memory,
Of violent birth, but poor validity,°   *195*
Which now like fruit unripe sticks on the tree,
But fall unshaken when they mellow be.
Most necessary 'tis that we forget
To pay ourselves what to ourselves is debt.
What to ourselves in passion we propose,   *200*
The passion ending, doth the purpose lose.
The violence of either grief or joy
Their own enactures° with themselves destroy:
Where joy most revels, grief doth most lament;
Grief joys, joy grieves, on slender accident.   *205*
This world is not for aye, nor 'tis not strange
That even our loves should with our fortunes change,
For 'tis a question left us yet to prove,
Whether love lead fortune, or else fortune love.
The great man down, you mark his favorite flies;   *210*
The poor advanced makes friends of enemies;
And hitherto doth love on fortune tend,
For who not needs shall never lack a friend;
And who in want a hollow friend doth try,
Directly seasons him° his enemy.   *215*
But, orderly to end where I begun,
Our wills and fates do so contrary run
That our devices still are overthrown;
Our thoughts are ours, their ends none of our own.

187 **wormwood** a bitter herb 188 **instances** motives 188 **move** induce 189 **respects of thrift** considerations of profit 195 **validity** strength 203 **enactures** acts 215 **seasons him** ripens him into

220   So think thou wilt no second husband wed,
        But die thy thoughts when thy first lord is dead.

    Player Queen. Nor earth to me give food, nor heaven
        light,
        Sport and repose lock from me day and night,
        To desperation turn my trust and hope,
225   An anchor's° cheer in prison be my scope,
        Each opposite that blanks° the face of joy
        Meet what I would have well, and it destroy:
        Both here and hence pursue me lasting strife,
        If, once a widow, ever I be wife!

230 *Hamlet.* If she should break it now!

    Player King. 'Tis deeply sworn. Sweet, leave me here
        awhile;
        My spirits grow dull, and fain I would beguile
        The tedious day with sleep.

    Player Queen.   Sleep rock thy brain,
                       [He] sleeps.
        And never come mischance between us twain!   *Exit.*

235 *Hamlet.* Madam, how like you this play?

    Queen. The lady doth protest too much, methinks.

    Hamlet. O, but she'll keep her word.

    King. Have you heard the argument?° Is there no
    offense in't?

240 *Hamlet.* No, no, they do but jest, poison in jest; no
    offense i' th' world.

    King. What do you call the play?

    Hamlet. The Mousetrap. Marry, how? Tropically.°
    This play is the image of a murder done in Vienna:
245   Gonzago is the Duke's name; his wife, Baptista. You
    shall see anon. 'Tis a knavish piece of work, but
    what of that? Your Majesty, and we that have free°

---

225 **anchor's** anchorite's, hermit's   226 **opposite that blanks** adverse
thing that blanches   238 **argument** plot   243 **Tropically** figuratively
(with a pun on "trap")   247 **free** innocent

souls, it touches us not. Let the galled jade winch;°
our withers are unwrung.

Enter Lucianus.

This is one Lucianus, nephew to the King.   250

Ophelia. You are as good as a chorus, my lord.

Hamlet. I could interpret° between you and your love,
if I could see the puppets dallying.

Ophelia. You are keen,° my lord, you are keen.

Hamlet. It would cost you a groaning to take off mine   255
edge.

Ophelia. Still better, and worse.

Hamlet. So you mistake° your husbands.—Begin,
murderer. Leave thy damnable faces and begin.
Come, the croaking raven doth bellow for revenge.   260

Lucianus. Thoughts black, hands apt, drugs fit, and
time agreeing,
Confederate season,° else no creature seeing,
Thou mixture rank, of midnight weeds collected,
With Hecate's ban° thrice blasted, thrice infected,
Thy natural magic and dire property°   265
On wholesome life usurps immediately.

Pours the poison in his ears.

Hamlet. 'A poisons him i' th' garden for his estate. His
name's Gonzago. The story is extant, and written in
very choice Italian. You shall see anon how the murderer gets the love of Gonzago's wife.   270

Ophelia. The King rises.

Hamlet. What, frighted with false fire?°

Queen. How fares my lord?

Polonius. Give o'er the play.

248 **galled jade winch** chafed horse wince   252 **interpret** (like a show-
man explaining the action of puppets)   254 **keen** (1) sharp (2) sexually
aroused   258 **mistake** err in taking   262 **Confederate season** the opportunity allied with me   264 **Hecate's ban** the curse of the goddess of
sorcery   265 **property** nature   272 **false fire** blank discharge of
firearms

275 *King.* Give me some light. Away!

Polonius. Lights, lights, lights!

> *Exeunt all but Hamlet and Horatio.*

Hamlet. Why, let the strucken deer go weep,
> The hart ungallèd play:
> For some must watch, while some must sleep;
280 > Thus runs the world away.
> Would not this, sir, and a forest of feathers°—if the rest of my fortunes turn Turk° with me—with two Provincial roses° on my razed° shoes, get me a fellowship in a cry° of players?

285 *Horatio.* Half a share.

Hamlet. A whole one, I.
> For thou dost know, O Damon dear,
> This realm dismantled was
> Of Jove himself; and now reigns here
290 > A very, very—pajock.°

Horatio. You might have rhymed.°

Hamlet. O good Horatio, I'll take the ghost's word for a thousand pound. Didst perceive?

Horatio. Very well, my lord.

295 *Hamlet.* Upon the talk of poisoning?

Horatio. I did very well note him.

Hamlet. Ah ha! Come, some music! Come, the recorders!°
> For if the King like not the comedy,
300 > Why then, belike he likes it not, perdy.°
> Come, some music!

> *Enter Rosencrantz and Guildenstern.*

Guildenstern. Good my lord, vouchsafe me a word with you.

---

281 **feathers** (plumes were sometimes part of a costume)   282 **turn Turk** i.e., go bad, treat me badly   283 **Provincial roses** rosettes like the roses of Provence (?)   283 **razed** ornamented with slashes   284 **cry** pack, company   290 **pajock** peacock   291 **You might have rhymed** i.e., rhymed "was" with "ass"   297–98 **recorders** flutelike instruments   300 **perdy** by God (French: *par dieu*)

Hamlet. Sir, a whole history.

Guildenstern. The King, sir—— 305

Hamlet. Ay, sir, what of him?

Guildenstern. Is in his retirement marvelous distemp'red.

Hamlet. With drink, sir?

Guildenstern. No, my lord, with choler.° 310

Hamlet. Your wisdom should show itself more richer to signify this to the doctor, for for me to put him to his purgation would perhaps plunge him into more choler.

Guildenstern. Good my lord, put your discourse into 315 some frame,° and start not so wildly from my affair.

Hamlet. I am tame, sir; pronounce.

Guildenstern. The Queen, your mother, in most great affliction of spirit hath sent me to you.

Hamlet. You are welcome. 320

Guildenstern. Nay, good my lord, this courtesy is not of the right breed. If it shall please you to make me a wholesome answer, I will do your mother's commandment: if not, your pardon and my return shall be the end of my business. 325

Hamlet. Sir, I cannot.

Rosencrantz. What, my lord?

Hamlet. Make you a wholesome° answer; my wit's diseased. But, sir, such answer as I can make, you shall command, or rather, as you say, my mother. 330 Therefore no more, but to the matter. My mother, you say——

Rosencrantz. Then thus she says: your behavior hath struck her into amazement and admiration.°

---

310 **choler** anger (but Hamlet pretends to take the word in its sense of "biliousness")   316 **frame** order, control   328 **wholesome** sane   334 **admiration** wonder

335 *Hamlet.* O wonderful son, that can so stonish a mother!
    But is there no sequel at the heels of this mother's
    admiration? Impart.

Rosencrantz. She desires to speak with you in her
    closet ere you go to bed.

340 *Hamlet.* We shall obey, were she ten times our mother.
    Have you any further trade with us?

Rosencrantz. My lord, you once did love me.

Hamlet. And do still, by these pickers and stealers.°

Rosencrantz. Good my lord, what is your cause of dis-
345 temper? You do surely bar the door upon your own
    liberty, if you deny your griefs to your friend.

Hamlet. Sir, I lack advancement.°

Rosencrantz. How can that be, when you have the
    voice of the King himself for your succession in
350 Denmark?

Enter the Players with recorders.

Hamlet. Ay, sir, but "while the grass grows"—the
    proverb° is something musty. O, the recorders. Let
    me see one. To withdraw° with you—why do you
    go about to recover the wind° of me as if you would
355 drive me into a toil?°

Guildenstern. O my lord, if my duty be too bold, my
    love is too unmannerly.°

Hamlet. I do not well understand that. Will you play
    upon this pipe?

360 *Guildenstern.* My lord, I cannot.

Hamlet. I pray you.

Guildenstern. Believe me, I cannot.

Hamlet. I pray you.

Guildenstern. Believe me, I cannot.

343 **pickers and stealers** i.e., hands (with reference to the prayer; "Keep
my hands from picking and stealing") 347 **advancement** promotion 352 **proverb** ("While the grass groweth, the horse starveth")
353 **withdraw** speak in private 354 **recover the wind** get on the wind-
ward side (as in hunting) 355 **toil** snare 356–57 **if my duty ... too
unmannerly** i.e., if these questions seem rude, it is because my love for
you leads me beyond good manners.

Hamlet. I do beseech you.

Guildenstern. I know no touch of it, my lord.

Hamlet. It is as easy as lying. Govern these ventages°   *365*
with your fingers and thumb, give it breath with your
mouth, and it will discourse most eloquent music.
Look you, these are the stops.

Guildenstern. But these cannot I command to any
utt'rance of harmony; I have not the skill.   *370*

Hamlet. Why, look you now, how unworthy a thing
you make of me! You would play upon me; you
would seem to know my stops; you would pluck
out the heart of my mystery; you would sound me
from my lowest note to the top of my compass;°   *375*
and there is much music, excellent voice, in this little
organ,° yet cannot you make it speak. 'Sblood, do
you think I am easier to be played on than a pipe?
Call me what instrument you will, though you can
fret° me, you cannot play upon me.   *380*

Enter Polonius.

God bless you, sir!

Polonius. My lord, the Queen would speak with you,
and presently.

Hamlet. Do you see yonder cloud that's almost in
shape of a camel?   *385*

Polonius. By th' mass and 'tis, like a camel indeed.

Hamlet. Methinks it is like a weasel.

Polonius. It is backed like a weasel.

Hamlet. Or like a whale.

Polonius. Very like a whale.   *390*

Hamlet. Then I will come to my mother by and by.

---

365 **ventages** vents, stops on a recorder   375 **compass** range of voice
377 **organ** i.e., the recorder   380 **fret** vex (with a pun alluding to the
frets, or ridges, that guide the fingering on some stringed instruments)

[*Aside*] They fool me to the top of my bent.°—I
will come by and by.°

Polonius. I will say so.   *Exit.*

395 *Hamlet.* "By and by" is easily said. Leave me, friends.
                              [*Exeunt all but Hamlet.*]
'Tis now the very witching time of night,
When churchyards yawn, and hell itself breathes out
Contagion to this world. Now could I drink hot
    blood
And do such bitter business as the day
400 Would quake to look on. Soft, now to my mother.
O heart, lose not thy nature; let not ever
The soul of Nero° enter this firm bosom.
Let me be cruel, not unnatural;
I will speak daggers to her, but use none.
405 My tongue and soul in this be hypocrites:
How in my words somever she be shent,°
To give them seals° never, my soul, consent!   *Exit.*

[Scene 3. *The castle.*]

Enter King, Rosencrantz, and Guildenstern.

King. I like him not, nor stands it safe with us
To let his madness range. Therefore prepare you.
I your commission will forthwith dispatch,
And he to England shall along with you.
5 The terms° of our estate may not endure
Hazard so near's° as doth hourly grow
Out of his brows.

Guildenstern.   We will ourselves provide.

392 **They fool ... my bent** they compel me to play the fool to the
limit of my capacity   393 **by and by** very soon   402 **Nero** (Roman
emperor who had his mother murdered)   406 **shent** rebuked   407 **give
them seals** confirm them with deeds   3.3.5 **terms** conditions   6 **near's**
near us

Most holy and religious fear it is
To keep those many many bodies safe
That live and feed upon your Majesty.   10

Rosencrantz. The single and peculiar° life is bound
  With all the strength and armor of the mind
  To keep itself from noyance,° but much more
  That spirit upon whose weal depends and rests
  The lives of many. The cess of majesty°   15
  Dies not alone, but like a gulf° doth draw
  What's near it with it; or it is a massy wheel
  Fixed on the summit of the highest mount,
  To whose huge spokes ten thousand lesser things
  Are mortised and adjoined, which when it falls,   20
  Each small annexment, petty consequence,
  Attends° the boist'rous ruin. Never alone
  Did the King sigh, but with a general groan.

King. Arm° you, I pray you, to this speedy voyage,
  For we will fetters put about this fear,   25
  Which now goes too free-footed.

Rosencrantz.   We will haste us.
                                Exeunt Gentlemen.

                    Enter Polonius.

Polonius. My lord, he's going to his mother's closet.°
  Behind the arras I'll convey myself
  To hear the process.° I'll warrant she'll tax him
    home,°
  And, as you said, and wisely was it said,   30
  'Tis meet that some more audience than a mother,
  Since nature makes them partial, should o'erhear
  The speech of vantage.° Fare you well, my liege.
  I'll call upon you ere you go to bed
  And tell you what I know.

King.   Thanks, dear my lord.   35
                          · *Exit [Polonius].*

11 **peculiar** individual, private   13 **noyance** injury   15 **cess of majesty** cessation (death) of a king   16 **gulf** whirlpool   22 **Attends** waits on, participates in   24 **Arm** prepare   27 **closet** private room   29 **process** proceedings   29 **tax him home** censure him sharply   33 **of vantage** from an advantageous place

O, my offense is rank, it smells to heaven;
It hath the primal eldest curse° upon't,
A brother's murder. Pray can I not,
Though inclination be as sharp as will.
40 My stronger guilt defeats my strong intent,
And like a man to double business bound
I stand in pause where I shall first begin,
And both neglect. What if this cursèd hand
Were thicker than itself with brother's blood,
45 Is there not rain enough in the sweet heavens
To wash it white as snow? Whereto serves mercy
But to confront° the visage of offense?
And what's in prayer but this twofold force,
To be forestallèd ere we come to fall,
50 Or pardoned being down? Then I'll look up.
My fault is past. But, O, what form of prayer
Can serve my turn? "Forgive me my foul murder"?
That cannot be, since I am still possessed
Of those effects° for which I did the murder,
55 My crown, mine own ambition, and my queen.
May one be pardoned and retain th' offense?
In the corrupted currents of this world
Offense's gilded hand may shove by justice,
And oft 'tis seen the wicked prize itself
60 Buys out the law. But 'tis not so above.
There is no shuffling;° there the action lies
In his true nature, and we ourselves compelled,
Even to the teeth and forehead of our faults,
To give in evidence. What then? What rests?°
65 Try what repentance can. What can it not?
Yet what can it when one cannot repent?
O wretched state! O bosom black as death!
O limèd° soul, that struggling to be free
Art more engaged!° Help, angels! Make assay.°
70 Bow, stubborn knees, and, heart with strings of steel,

---

37 **primal eldest curse** (curse of Cain, who killed Abel)   47 **confront** oppose   54 **effects** things gained   61 **shuffling** trickery   64 **rests** remains   68 **limèd** caught (as with birdlime, a sticky substance spread on boughs to snare birds)   69 **engaged** ensnared   69 **assay** an attempt

    Be soft as sinews of the newborn babe.
    All may be well.   [*He kneels.*]

              Enter Hamlet.

Hamlet. Now might I do it pat, now 'a is a-praying,
    And now I'll do't. And so 'a goes to heaven,
    And so am I revenged. That would be scanned.°   75
    A villain kills my father, and for that
    I, his sole son, do this same villain send
    To heaven.
    Why, this is hire and salary, not revenge.
    'A took my father grossly, full of bread,°   80
    With all his crimes broad blown,° as flush° as May;
    And how his audit° stands, who knows save heaven?
    But in our circumstance and course of thought,
    'Tis heavy with him; and am I then revenged,
    To take him in the purging of his soul,   85
    When he is fit and seasoned for his passage?
    No.
    Up, sword, and know thou a more horrid hent.°
    When he is drunk asleep, or in his rage,
    Or in th' incestuous pleasure of his bed,   90
    At game a-swearing, or about some act
    That has no relish° of salvation in't—
    Then trip him, that his heels may kick at heaven,
    And that his soul may be as damned and black
    As hell, whereto it goes. My mother stays.   95
    This physic° but prolongs thy sickly days.   *Exit.*

King. [*Rises*] My words fly up, my thoughts remain
    below.
    Words without thoughts never to heaven go.   *Exit.*

---

75 **would be scanned** ought to be looked into   80 **bread** i. e., worldly
gratification   81 **crimes broad blown** sins in full bloom   81 **flush** vigorous   82 **audit** account   88 **hent** grasp (here, occasion for seizing)
92   **relish** flavor   96 **physic** (Claudius' purgation by prayer, as Hamlet
thinks in line 85)

[Scene 4. *The Queen's private chamber*.]

Enter [Queen] Gertrude and Polonius.

Polonius. 'A will come straight. Look you lay home°
    to him.
    Tell him his pranks have been too broad° to bear
    with,
    And that your Grace hath screened and stood be-
    tween
    Much heat and him. I'll silence me even here.
5   Pray you be round with him.

Hamlet. (*Within*) Mother, Mother, Mother!

Queen. I'll warrant you; fear me not. Withdraw; I hear
    him coming.   [*Polonius hides behind the arras.*]
                Enter Hamlet.

Hamlet. Now, Mother, what's the matter?

10 *Queen.* Hamlet, thou hast thy father much offended.

Hamlet. Mother, you have my father much offended.

Queen. Come, come, you answer with an idle° tongue.

Hamlet. Go, go, you question with a wicked tongue.

Queen. Why, how now, Hamlet?

Hamlet.   What's the matter now?

Queen. Have you forgot me?

15 *Hamlet.*   No, by the rood,° not so!
    You are the Queen, your husband's brother's wife,
    And, would it were not so, you are my mother.

Queen. Nay, then I'll set those to you that can speak.

Hamlet. Come, come, and sit you down. You shall not
    budge.

3.4.1 **lay home** thrust (rebuke) him sharply 2 **broad** unrestrained
12 **idle** foolish 15 **rood** cross

   You go not till I set you up a glass°   20
   Where you may see the inmost part of you!

Queen. What wilt thou do? Thou wilt not murder me?
   Help, ho!

Polonius. [*Behind*] What, ho! Help!

Hamlet. [*Draws*] How now? A rat? Dead for a ducat,
   dead!   25
   [*Thrusts his rapier through the arras and*] *kills Polonius.*

Polonius. [*Behind*] O, I am slain!

Queen.   O me, what hast thou done?

Hamlet. Nay, I know not. Is it the King?

Queen. O, what a rash and bloody deed is this!

Hamlet. A bloody deed—almost as bad, good Mother,
   As kill a king, and marry with his brother.   30

Queen. As kill a king?

Hamlet.   Ay, lady, it was my word.
             [*Lifts up the arras and sees Polonius.*]
   Thou wretched, rash, intruding fool, farewell!
   I took thee for thy better. Take thy fortune.
   Thou find'st to be too busy is some danger.—
   Leave wringing of your hands. Peace, sit you down   35
   And let me wring your heart, for so I shall
   If it be made of penetrable stuff,
   If damnèd custom have not brazed° it so
   That it be proof° and bulwark against sense.°

Queen. What have I done that thou dar'st wag thy
   tongue   40
   In noise so rude against me?

Hamlet.   Such an act
   That blurs the grace and blush of modesty,
   Calls virtue hypocrite, takes off the rose
   From the fair forehead of an innocent love,
   And sets a blister° there, makes marriage vows   45

---

20 **glass** mirror   38 **brazed** hardened like brass   39 **proof** armor
39 **sense** feeling   45 **sets a blister** brands (as a harlot)

As false as dicers' oaths. O, such a deed
As from the body of contraction° plucks
The very soul, and sweet religion makes
A rhapsody° of words! Heaven's face does glow
50 O'er this solidity and compound mass
With heated visage, as against the doom
Is thoughtsick at the act.°

Queen.   Ay me, what act,
That roars so loud and thunders in the index?°

Hamlet. Look here upon this picture, and on this,
55 The counterfeit presentment° of two brothers.
See what a grace was seated on this brow:
Hyperion's curls, the front° of Jove himself,
An eye like Mars, to threaten and command,
A station° like the herald Mercury
60 New lighted on a heaven-kissing hill—
A combination and a form indeed
Where every god did seem to set his seal
To give the world assurance of a man.
This was your husband. Look you now what follows.
65 Here is your husband, like a mildewed ear
Blasting his wholesome brother. Have you eyes?
Could you on this fair mountain leave to feed,
And batten° on this moor? Ha! Have you eyes?
You cannot call it love, for at your age
70 The heyday° in the blood is tame, it's humble,
And waits upon the judgment, and what judgment
Would step from this to this? Sense° sure you have,
Else could you not have motion, but sure that sense
Is apoplexed,° for madness would not err,
75 Nor sense to ecstasy° was ne'er so thralled
But it reserved some quantity of choice

---

47 **contraction** marriage contract   49 **rhapsody** senseless string
49–52 **Heaven's face . . . the act** i.e., the face of heaven blushes over
this earth (compounded of four elements), the face hot, as if Judgment
Day were near, and it is thoughtsick at the act   53 **index** prologue   55
counterfeit presentment represented image   57 **front** forehead   59
station bearing   68 **batten** feed gluttonously   70 **heyday** excitement
72 **Sense** feeling   74 **apoplexed** paralyzed   75 **ecstasy** madness

To serve in such a difference. What devil was't
That thus hath cozened you at hoodman-blind?°
Eyes without feeling, feeling without sight,
Ears without hands or eyes, smelling sans° all,   80
Or but a sickly part of one true sense
Could not so mope.°
O shame, where is thy blush? Rebellious hell,
If thou canst mutine in a matron's bones,
To flaming youth let virtue be as wax   85
And melt in her own fire. Proclaim no shame
When the compulsive ardor° gives the charge,
Since frost itself as actively doth burn,
And reason panders will.°

Queen.   O Hamlet, speak no more.
Thou turn'st mine eyes into my very soul,   90
And there I see such black and grainèd° spots
As will not leave their tinct.°

Hamlet.   Nay, but to live
In the rank sweat of an enseamèd° bed,
Stewed in corruption, honeying and making love
Over the nasty sty——

Queen.   O, speak to me no more.   95
These words like daggers enter in my ears.
No more, sweet Hamlet.

Hamlet.   A murderer and a villain,
A slave that is not twentieth part the tithe°
Of your precedent lord, a vice° of kings,
A cutpurse of the empire and the rule,   100
That from a shelf the precious diadem stole
And put it in his pocket——

Queen.   No more.

---

78 **cozened you at hoodman-blind** cheated you at blindman's buff
80 **sans** without   82 **mope** be stupid   87 **compulsive ardor** com-
pelling passion   89 **reason panders will** reason acts as a procurer
for desire   91 **grainèd** dyed in grain (fast dyed)   92 **tinct** color   93
enseamèd (perhaps "soaked in grease," i.e., sweaty; perhaps "much
wrinkled")   98 **tithe** tenth part   99 **vice** (like the Vice, a fool and
mischief-maker in the old morality plays)

Enter Ghost.

Hamlet. A king of shreds and patches—
    Save me and hover o'er me with your wings,
    You heavenly guards! What would your gracious
105   figure?

Queen. Alas, he's mad.

Hamlet. Do you not come your tardy son to chide,
    That, lapsed in time and passion, lets go by
    Th' important acting of your dread command?
110   O, say!

Ghost. Do not forget. This visitation
    Is but to whet thy almost blunted purpose.
    But look, amazement on thy mother sits.
    O, step between her and her fighting soul!
115   Conceit° in weakest bodies strongest works.
    Speak to her, Hamlet.

Hamlet.   How is it with you, lady?

Queen. Alas, how is't with you,
    That you do bend your eye on vacancy,
    And with th' incorporal° air do hold discourse?
120   Forth at your eyes your spirits wildly peep,
    And as the sleeping soldiers in th' alarm
    Your bedded hair° like life in excrements°
    Start up and stand an end.° O gentle son,
    Upon the heat and flame of thy distemper
125   Sprinkle cool patience. Whereon do you look?

Hamlet. On him, on him! Look you, how pale he
    glares!
    His form and cause conjoined, preaching to stones,
    Would make them capable.°—Do not look upon
    me,
    Lest with this piteous action you convert
130   My stern effects.° Then what I have to do
    Will want true color; tears perchance for blood.

Queen. To whom do you speak this?

115 **Conceit** imagination   119 **incorporal** bodiless   122 **bedded hair**
hairs laid flat   122 **excrements** outgrowths (here, the hair)   123 **an
end** on end   128 **capable** receptive   129–30 **convert/My stern effects**
divert my stern deeds

Hamlet. Do you see nothing there?

Queen. Nothing at all; yet all that is I see.

Hamlet. Nor did you nothing hear?

Queen. No, nothing but ourselves.

Hamlet. Why, look you there! Look how it steals away!   135
My father, in his habit° as he lived!
Look where he goes even now out at the portal!
                              Exit Ghost.

Queen. This is the very coinage of your brain.
This bodiless creation ecstasy
Is very cunning in.

Hamlet.   Ecstasy?   140
My pulse as yours doth temperately keep time
And makes as healthful music. It is not madness
That I have uttered. Bring me to the test,
And I the matter will reword, which madness
Would gambol° from. Mother, for love of grace,   145
Lay not that flattering unction° to your soul,
That not your trespass but my madness speaks.
It will but skin and film the ulcerous place
Whiles rank corruption, mining° all within,
Infects unseen. Confess yourself to heaven,   150
Repent what's past, avoid what is to come,
And do not spread the compost° on the weeds
To make them ranker. Forgive me this my virtue.
For in the fatness of these pursy° times
Virtue itself of vice must pardon beg,   155
Yea, curb° and woo for leave to do him good.

Queen. O Hamlet, thou hast cleft my heart in twain.

Hamlet. O, throw away the worser part of it,
And live the purer with the other half.
Good night—but go not to my uncle's bed.   160
Assume a virtue, if you have it not.

136 **habit** garment (Q1, though a "bad" quarto, is probably correct in saying that at line 102 the ghost enters "in his nightgown," i.e., dressing gown) 145 **gambol** start away 146 **unction** ointment 149 **mining** undermining 152 **compost** fertilizing substance 154 **pursy** bloated 156 **curb** bow low

That monster custom, who all sense doth eat,
Of habits devil, is angel yet in this,
That to the use° of actions fair and good
165 He likewise gives a frock or livery°
That aptly is put on. Refrain tonight,
And that shall lend a kind of easiness
To the next abstinence; the next more easy;
For use almost can change the stamp of nature,
170 And either° the devil, or throw him out
With wondrous potency. Once more, good night,
And when you are desirous to be blest,
I'll blessing beg of you.—For this same lord,
I do repent; but heaven hath pleased it so,
175 To punish me with this, and this with me,
That I must be their° scourge and minister.
I will bestow° him and will answer well
The death I gave him. So again, good night.
I must be cruel only to be kind.
180 Thus bad begins, and worse remains behind.
One word more, good lady.

Queen.   What shall I do?

Hamlet. Not this, by no means, that I bid you do:
Let the bloat King tempt you again to bed,
Pinch wanton on your cheek, call you his mouse,
185 And let him, for a pair of reechy° kisses,
Or paddling in your neck with his damned fingers,
Make you to ravel° all this matter out,
That I essentially am not in madness,
But mad in craft. 'Twere good you let him know,
190 For who that's but a queen, fair, sober, wise,
Would from a paddock,° from a bat, a gib,°
Such dear concernings hide? Who would do so?
No, in despite of sense and secrecy,

---

164 **use** practice   165 **livery** characteristic garment (punning on "habits" in line 163)   170 **either** (probably a word is missing after *either*; among suggestions are "master," "curb," and "house"; but possibly *either* is a printer's error for *entertain,* i.e. "receive"; or perhaps *either* is a verb meaning "make easier")   176 **their** i.e., the heavens' 177 **bestow** stow, lodge   185 **reechy** foul (literally "smoky")   187 **ravel** unravel, reveal   191 **paddock** toad   191 **gib** tomcat

    Unpeg the basket on the house's top,
    Let the birds fly, and like the famous ape,   *195*
    To try conclusions,° in the basket creep
    And break your own neck down.

Queen. Be thou assured, if words be made of breath,
    And breath of life, I have no life to breathe
    What thou hast said to me.   *200*

Hamlet. I must to England; you know that?

Queen.   Alack,
    I had forgot. 'Tis so concluded on.

Hamlet. There's letters sealed, and my two school-
    fellows,
    Whom I will trust as I will adders fanged,
    They bear the mandate;° they must sweep my way   *205*
    And marshal me to knavery. Let it work;
    For 'tis the sport to have the enginer
    Hoist with his own petar,° and 't shall go hard
    But I will delve one yard below their mines
    And blow them at the moon. O, 'tis most sweet   *210*
    When in one line two crafts° directly meet.
    This man shall set me packing:
    I'll lug the guts into the neighbor room.
    Mother, good night. Indeed, this counselor
    Is now most still, most secret, and most grave,   *215*
    Who was in life a foolish prating knave.
    Come, sir, to draw toward an end with you.
    Good night, Mother.
                [Exit the Queen. Then] exit Hamlet, tugging in
                                     Polonius.

196 **To try conclusions** to make experiments   205 **mandate** command
208 **petar** bomb   211 **crafts** (1) boats (2) acts of guile, crafty schemes

[ACT 4

Scene 1. *The castle.*]

*Enter King and Queen, with Rosencrantz and
Guildenstern.*

King. There's matter in these sighs. These profound
heaves
You must translate; 'tis fit we understand them.
Where is your son?

Queen. Bestow this place on us a little while.
            [*Exeunt Rosencrantz and Guildenstern.*]
5   Ah, mine own lord, what have I seen tonight!

King. What, Gertrude? How does Hamlet?

Queen. Mad as the sea and wind when both contend
Which is the mightier. In his lawless fit,
Behind the arras hearing something stir,
10   Whips out his rapier, cries, "A rat, a rat!"
And in this brainish apprehension° kills
The unseen good old man.

King.   O heavy deed!
It had been so with us, had we been there.
His liberty is full of threats to all,
15   To you yourself, to us, to every one.
Alas, how shall this bloody deed be answered?
It will be laid to us, whose providence°

4.1.11 **brainish apprehension** mad imagination   17 **providence** fore-
sight

Should have kept short, restrained, and out of haunt°
This mad young man. But so much was our love
We would not understand what was most fit,   20
But, like the owner of a foul disease,
To keep it from divulging, let it feed
Even on the pith of life. Where is he gone?

Queen. To draw apart the body he hath killed;
O'er whom his very madness, like some ore   25
Among a mineral° of metals base,
Shows itself pure. 'A weeps for what is done.

King. O Gertrude, come away!
The sun no sooner shall the mountains touch
But we will ship him hence, and this vile deed   30
We must with all our majesty and skill
Both countenance and excuse. Ho, Guildenstern!

Enter Rosencrantz and Guildenstern.

Friends both, go join you with some further aid:
Hamlet in madness hath Polonius slain,
And from his mother's closet hath he dragged him.   35
Go seek him out; speak fair, and bring the body
Into the chapel. I pray you haste in this.
        [*Exeunt Rosencrantz and Guildenstern.*]
Come, Gertrude, we'll call up our wisest friends
And let them know both what we mean to do
And what's untimely done . . .°   40
Whose whisper o'er the world's diameter,
As level as the cannon to his blank°
Transports his poisoned shot, may miss our name
And hit the woundless° air. O, come away!
My soul is full of discord and dismay.   *Exeunt.*   45

---

18 **out of haunt** away from association with others   25–26 **ore/Among a mineral** vein of gold in a mine   40 **done** . . . (evidently something has dropped out of the text. Capell's conjecture, "So, haply slander," is usually printed)   42 **blank** white center of a target   44 **woundless** invulnerable

[Scene 2. *The castle.*]

Enter Hamlet.

Hamlet. Safely stowed.

Gentlemen. (Within) Hamlet! Lord Hamlet!

Hamlet. But soft, what noise? Who calls on Hamlet?
   O, here they come.

Enter Rosencrantz and Guildenstern.

Rosencrantz. What have you done, my lord, with the
5   dead body?

Hamlet. Compounded it with dust, whereto 'tis kin.

Rosencrantz. Tell us where 'tis, that we may take it
   thence
   And bear it to the chapel.

Hamlet. Do not believe it.

10 *Rosencrantz.* Believe what?

Hamlet. That I can keep your counsel and not mine
   own. Besides, to be demanded of° a sponge, what
   replication° should be made by the son of a king?

Rosencrantz. Take you me for a sponge, my lord?

15 *Hamlet.* Ay, sir, that soaks up the King's countenance,°
   his rewards, his authorities. But such officers do the
   King best service in the end. He keeps them, like an
   ape, in the corner of his jaw, first mouthed, to be
   last swallowed. When he needs what you have
20   gleaned, it is but squeezing you and, sponge, you
   shall be dry again.

Rosencrantz. I understand you not, my lord.

Hamlet. I am glad of it: a knavish speech sleeps in a
   foolish ear.

4.2.12 **demanded of** questioned by   13 **replication** reply   15 **countenance** favor

Rosencrantz. My lord, you must tell us where the body *25*
 is and go with us to the King.

Hamlet. The body is with the King, but the King is not
 with the body.° The King is a thing——

Guildenstern. A thing, my lord?

Hamlet. Of nothing. Bring me to him. Hide fox, and *30*
 all after.°   *Exeunt.*

[Scene 3. *The castle.*]

Enter King, and two or three.

King. I have sent to seek him and to find the body:
 How dangerous is it that this man goes loose!
 Yet must not we put the strong law on him:
 He's loved of the distracted° multitude,
 Who like not in their judgment, but their eyes,
 And where 'tis so, th' offender's scourge is weighed,
 But never the offense. To bear° all smooth and even, *5*
 This sudden sending him away must seem
 Deliberate pause.° Diseases desperate grown
 By desperate appliance are relieved,
 Or not at all.

 Enter Rosencrantz, [Guildenstern,] and all the rest. *10*

    How now? What hath befall'n?

Rosencrantz. Where the dead body is bestowed, my
 lord,
 We cannot get from him.

King.   But where is he?

Rosencrantz. Without, my lord; guarded, to know your
 pleasure.

27–28 **The body . . . the body** (an allusion to a contemporary theory of
kingship that distinguished between the king's two bodies, the Body
Natural and the Body Politic. The king [Claudius] has a body, but the
Body Politic [the kingship of Denmark] is not inherent in that body)
30–31 **Hide fox, and all after** (a cry in a game such as hide-
and-seek; Hamlet runs from the stage) 4.3.4 **distracted** bewildered,
senseless 7 **bear** carry out 9 **pause** planning

King. Bring him before us.

15 *Rosencrantz.*   Ho! Bring in the lord.

                    They enter.

King. Now, Hamlet, where's Polonius?

Hamlet. At supper.

King. At supper? Where?

Hamlet. Not where he eats, but where 'a is eaten. A
20   certain convocation of politic° worms are e'en at
     him. Your worm is your only emperor for diet. We
     fat all creatures else to fat us, and we fat ourselves
     for maggots. Your fat king and your lean beggar is
     but variable service°—two dishes, but to one table.
25   That's the end.

King. Alas, alas!

Hamlet. A man may fish with the worm that hath eat of
     a king, and eat of the fish that hath fed of that worm.

King. What dost thou mean by this?

30 *Hamlet.* Nothing but to show you how a king may
     go a progress° through the guts of a beggar.

King. Where is Polonius?

Hamlet. In heaven. Send thither to see. If your mes-
     senger find him not there, seek him i' th' other
35   place yourself. But if indeed you find him not
     within this month, you shall nose him as you go
     up the stairs into the lobby.

King. [*To Attendants*] Go seek him there.

Hamlet. 'A will stay till you come.

                    [*Exeunt Attendants.*]

40 *King.* Hamlet, this deed, for thine especial safety,
     Which we do tender° as we dearly grieve
     For that which thou hast done, must send thee hence
     With fiery quickness. Therefore prepare thyself.

---

20 **politic** statesmanlike, shrewd   24 **variable service** different courses
31 **progress** royal journey   41 **tender** hold dear

The bark is ready and the wind at help,
Th' associates tend,° and everything is bent   45
For England.

Hamlet.   For England?

King.   Ay, Hamlet.

Hamlet.   Good.

King. So is it, if thou knew'st our purposes.

Hamlet. I see a cherub° that sees them. But come, for
England! Farewell, dear Mother.

King. Thy loving father, Hamlet.   50

Hamlet. My mother—father and mother is man and
wife, man and wife is one flesh, and so, my mother.
Come, for England!   *Exit.*

King. Follow him at foot;° tempt him with speed
aboard.
Delay it not; I'll have him hence tonight.   55
Away! For everything is sealed and done
That else leans° on th' affair. Pray you make haste.
                        [*Exeunt all but the King.*]
And, England, if my love thou hold'st at aught—
As my great power thereof may give thee sense,
Since yet thy cicatrice° looks raw and red   60
After the Danish sword, and thy free awe°
Pays homage to us—thou mayst not coldly set
Our sovereign process,° which imports at full
By letters congruing to that effect
The present° death of Hamlet. Do it, England,   65
For like the hectic° in my blood he rages,
And thou must cure me. Till I know 'tis done,
Howe'er my haps,° my joys were ne'er begun.

                                            Exit.

45 **tend** wait 48 **cherub** angel of knowledge 54 **at foot** closely
57 **leans** depends 60 **cicatrice** scar 61 **free awe** uncompelled sub-
mis-sion 62–63 **coldly set/Our sovereign process** regard slightly
our royal command 65 **present** instant 66 **hectic** fever 68 **haps**
chances, fortunes

[Scene 4. *A plain in Denmark.*]

Enter Fortinbras with his Army over the stage.

Fortinbras. Go, Captain, from me greet the Danish king.
  Tell him that by his license Fortinbras
  Craves the conveyance of° a promised march
  Over his kingdom. You know the rendezvous.
5 If that his Majesty would aught with us,
  We shall express our duty in his eye;°
  And let him know so.

Captain.   I will do't, my lord.

Fortinbras. Go softly° on.
                   [*Exeunt all but the Captain.*]
       Enter Hamlet, Rosencrantz, &c.

Hamlet. Good sir, whose powers° are these?

10 *Captain.* They are of Norway, sir.

Hamlet. How purposed, sir, I pray you?

Captain. Against some part of Poland.

Hamlet. Who commands them, sir?

Captain. The nephew to old Norway, Fortinbras.

15 *Hamlet.* Goes it against the main° of Poland, sir,
  Or for some frontier?

Captain. Truly to speak, and with no addition,°
  We go to gain a little patch of ground
  That hath in it no profit but the name.
20 To pay five ducats, five, I would not farm it,
  Nor will it yield to Norway or the Pole
  A ranker° rate, should it be sold in fee.°

4.4.3 **conveyance of** escort for 6 **in his eye** before his eyes (i.e., in his presence) 8 **softly** slowly 9 **powers** forces 15 **main** main part 17 **with no addition** plainly 22 **ranker** higher 22 **in fee** out-right

Hamlet. Why, then the Polack never will defend it.

Captain. Yes, it is already garrisoned.

Hamlet. Two thousand souls and twenty thousand
　　ducats　　　　　　　　　　　　　　　　　　　　25
　　Will not debate° the question of this straw.
　　This is th' imposthume° of much wealth and peace,
　　That inward breaks, and shows no cause without
　　Why the man dies. I humbly thank you, sir.

Captain. God bye you, sir.　　　　　　　　　　[*Exit.*]

Rosencrantz.　　　　　　Will't please you go, my lord?　　30

Hamlet. I'll be with you straight. Go a little before.
　　　　　　　　　　　　　　[*Exeunt all but Hamlet.*]
　　How all occasions do inform against me
　　And spur my dull revenge! What is a man,
　　If his chief good and market° of his time
　　Be but to sleep and feed? A beast, no more.　　35
　　Sure he that made us with such large discourse,°
　　Looking before and after, gave us not
　　That capability and godlike reason
　　To fust° in us unused. Now, whether it be
　　Bestial oblivion,° or some craven scruple　　40
　　Of thinking too precisely on th' event°—
　　A thought which, quartered, hath but one part wis-
　　　　dom
　　And ever three parts coward—I do not know
　　Why yet I live to say, "This thing's to do,"
　　Sith I have cause, and will, and strength, and means　　45
　　To do't. Examples gross° as earth exhort me.
　　Witness this army of such mass and charge,°
　　Led by a delicate and tender prince,
　　Whose spirit, with divine ambition puffed,
　　Makes mouths at the invisible event,°　　50
　　Exposing what is mortal and unsure
　　To all that fortune, death, and danger dare,

26 **debate** settle　27 **imposthume** abscess, ulcer　34 **market** profit
36 **discourse** understanding　39 **fust** grow moldy　40 **oblivion** forgetfulness　41 **event** outcome　46 **gross** large, obvious　47 **charge** expense　50 **Makes mouths at the invisible event** makes scornful faces
(is contemptuous of) the unseen outcome

Even for an eggshell. Rightly to be great
Is not° to stir without great argument,°
55 But greatly° to find quarrel in a straw
When honor's at the stake. How stand I then,
That have a father killed, a mother stained,
Excitements° of my reason and my blood,
And let all sleep, while to my shame I see
60 The imminent death of twenty thousand men
That for a fantasy and trick of fame°
Go to their graves like beds, fight for a plot
Whereon the numbers cannot try the cause,
Which is not tomb enough and continent°
65 To hide the slain? O, from this time forth,
My thoughts be bloody, or be nothing worth!   *Exit.*

[Scene 5. *The castle*.]

Enter Horatio, [Queen] Gertrude, and a Gentleman.

Queen. I will not speak with her.

Gentleman. She is importunate, indeed distract.
  Her mood will needs be pitied.

Queen.   What would she have?

Gentleman. She speaks much of her father, says she
      hears
  There's tricks i' th' world, and hems, and beats her
5   heart,
  Spurns enviously at straws,° speaks things in doubt°
  That carry but half sense. Her speech is nothing,
  Yet the unshapèd use of it doth move

54 **not** (the sense seems to require "not not")   54 **argument** reason
55 **greatly** i.e., nobly   58 **Excitements** incentives   61 **fantasy and
trick of fame** illusion and trifle of reputation   64 **continent** receptacle,
container   4.5.6 **Spurns enviously at straws** objects spitefully to in-
significant matters   6 **in doubt** uncertainly

The hearers to collection;° they yawn° at it,
And botch the words up fit to their own thoughts,   10
Which, as her winks and nods and gestures yield
    them,
Indeed would make one think there might be
    thought,
Though nothing sure, yet much unhappily.

Horatio. 'Twere good she were spoken with, for she
    may strew
Dangerous conjectures in ill-breeding minds.   15

Queen. Let her come in.   [*Exit Gentleman.*]
    [*Aside*] To my sick soul (as sin's true nature is)
    Each toy seems prologue to some great amiss;°
    So full of artless jealousy° is guilt
    It spills° itself in fearing to be spilt.   20

              Enter Ophelia [*distracted.*]°

Ophelia. Where is the beauteous majesty of Denmark?

Queen. How now, Ophelia?

Ophelia. (*She sings.*) How should I your truelove know
                      From another one?
                  By his cockle hat° and staff   25
                  And his sandal shoon.°

Queen. Alas, sweet lady, what imports this song?

Ophelia. Say you? Nay, pray you mark.
                  He is dead and gone, lady,   (*Song*)
                  He is dead and gone;   30
                  At his head a grass-green turf,
                  At his heels a stone.
    O, ho!

Queen. Nay, but Ophelia——

Ophelia. Pray you mark.   35

8–9 **Yet the . . . to collection** i.e., yet the formless manner of it moves her
listeners to gather up some sort of meaning   9 **yawn** gape (?)   18 **amiss**
misfortune   19 **artless jealousy** crude suspicion   20 **spills** destroys   20
s.d. the First Quarto says "Enter Ophelia playing on a lute, and her hair
down, singing."   25 **cockle hat** (a cockleshell on the hat was the sign of
a pilgrim who had journeyed to shrines overseas. The association of
lovers and pilgrims was a common one)   26 **shoon** shoes

[*Sings.*] White his shroud as the mountain snow——
Enter King.

Queen. Alas, look here, my lord.

Ophelia.   Larded° all with sweet flowers (*Song*)
          Which bewept to the grave did not go
40   With truelove showers.

King. How do you, pretty lady?

Ophelia. Well, God dild° you! They say the owl was a
baker's daughter.° Lord, we know what we are, but
know not what we may be. God be at your table!

45 *King.* Conceit° upon her father.

Ophelia. Pray let's have no words of this, but when
they ask you what it means, say you this:
          Tomorrow is Saint Valentine's day.° (*Song*)
           All in the morning betime,
50   And I a maid at your window,
           To be your Valentine.

          Then up he rose and donned his clothes
           And dupped° the chamber door,
          Let in the maid, that out a maid
55   Never departed more.

King. Pretty Ophelia.

Ophelia. Indeed, la, without an oath, I'll make an end
on't:
     [*Sings.*] By Gis° and by Saint Charity,
          Alack, and fie for shame!
60   Young men will do't if they come to't,
          By Cock,° they are to blame.
         Quoth she, "Before you tumbled me,
          You promised me to wed."

---

38 **Larded** decorated   42 **dild** yield, i.e., reward   43 **baker's daughter** (an allusion to a tale of a baker's daughter who begrudged bread to
Christ and was turned into an owl)   45 **Conceit** brooding   48 **Saint
Valentine's day** Feb. 14 (the notion was that a bachelor would become
the trueloveof the first girl he saw on this day)   53 **dupped** opened (did
up)   58 **Gis** (contraction of "Jesus")   61 **Cock** (1) God (2) phallus

He answers:
> "So would I 'a' done, by yonder sun,   65
> An thou hadst not come to my bed."

King. How long hath she been thus?

Ophelia. I hope all will be well. We must be patient,
but I cannot choose but weep to think they would
lay him i' th' cold ground. My brother shall know   70
of it; and so I thank you for your good counsel.
Come, my coach! Good night, ladies, good night.
Sweet ladies, good night, good night.   *Exit.*

King. Follow her close; give her good watch, I pray
you.   [*Exit Horatio.*]
O, this is the poison of deep grief; it springs   75
All from her father's death—and now behold!
O Gertrude, Gertrude,
When sorrows come, they còme not single spies,
But in battalions: first, her father slain;
Next, your son gone, and he most violent author   80
Of his own just remove; the people muddied,°
Thick and unwholesome in their thoughts and
whispers
For good Polonius' death, and we have done but
greenly°
In huggermugger° to inter him; poor Ophelia
Divided from herself and her fair judgment,   85
Without the which we are pictures or mere beasts;
Last, and as much containing as all these,
Her brother is in secret come from France,
Feeds on his wonder,° keeps himself in clouds,
And wants not buzzers° to infect his ear   90
With pestilent speeches of his father's death,
Wherein necessity, of matter beggared,°
Will nothing stick° our person to arraign
In ear and ear. O my dear Gertrude, this,

---

81 **muddied** muddled   83 **greenly** foolishly   84 **huggermugger** secret
haste   89 **wonder** suspicion   90 **wants not buzzers** does not lack tale-
bearers   92 **of matter beggared** unprovided with facts   93 **Will nothing stick** will not hesitate

95 Like to a murd'ring piece,° in many places
Gives me superfluous death.   *A noise within.*

Enter a Messenger.

Queen.   **Alack, what noise is this?**

King. Attend, where are my Switzers?° Let them
    guard the door.
    What is the matter?

Messenger.   **Save yourself, my lord.**
    The ocean, overpeering of his list,°
100 Eats not the flats with more impiteous haste
    Than young Laertes, in a riotous head,°
    O'erbears your officers. The rabble call him lord,
    And, as the world were now but to begin,
    Antiquity forgot, custom not known,
105 The ratifiers and props of every word,
    They cry, "Choose we! Laertes shall be king!"
    Caps, hands, and tongues applaud it to the clouds,
    "Laertes shall be king! Laertes king!" *A noise within.*

Queen. How cheerfully on the false trail they cry!
110 O, this is counter,° you false Danish dogs!

Enter Laertes with others.

King. The doors are broke.

Laertes. Where is this king?—Sirs, stand you all
    without.

All. No, let's come in.

Laertes.   **I pray you give me leave.**

All. We will, we will.

Laertes. I thank you. Keep the door. [*Exeunt his
115   Followers.*] O thou vile King,
    Give me my father.

Queen.   **Calmly, good Laertes.**

---

95 **murd'ring piece** (a cannon that shot a kind of shrapnel) 97
Switzers Swiss guards 99 **list** shore 101 **in a riotous head** with a rebellious force 110 **counter** (a hound runs counter when he follows the
scent backward from the prey)

Laertes. That drop of blood that's calm proclaims me
    bastard,
    Cries cuckold° to my father, brands the harlot
    Even here between the chaste unsmirchèd brow
    Of my true mother.

King.   What is the cause, Laertes,   *120*
    That thy rebellion looks so giantlike?
    Let him go, Gertrude. Do not fear° our person.
    There's such divinity doth hedge a king
    That treason can but peep to° what it would,
    Acts little of his will. Tell me, Laertes,   *125*
    Why thou art thus incensed. Let him go, Gertrude.
    Speak, man.

Laertes. Where is my father?

King.   Dead.

Queen.   But not by him.

King. Let him demand his fill.

Laertes. How came he dead? I'll not be juggled with.   *130*
    To hell allegiance, vows to the blackest devil,
    Conscience and grace to the profoundest pit!
    I dare damnation. To this point I stand,
    That both the worlds I give to negligence,°
    Let come what comes, only I'll be revenged   *135*
    Most throughly for my father.

King.   Who shall stay you?

Laertes. My will, not all the world's.
    And for my means, I'll husband them° so well
    They shall go far with little.

King.   Good Laertes,
    If you desire to know the certainty   *140*
    Of your dear father, is't writ in your revenge
    That swoopstake° you will draw both friend and foe,
    Winner and loser?

---

118 **cuckold** man whose wife is unfaithful   112 **fear** fear for   124
peep to i.e., look at from a distance   134 **That both . . . to negligence**
i.e., I care not what may happen (to me) in this world or the next
138 **husband them** use them economically   142 **swoopstake** in a clean
sweep

Laertes. None but his enemies.

King.   Will you know them then?

Laertes. To his good friends thus wide I'll ope my
145   arms
        And like the kind life-rend'ring pelican°
        Repast° them with my blood.

King.   Why, now you speak
        Like a good child and a true gentleman.
        That I am guiltless of your father's death,
150   And am most sensibly° in grief for it,
        It shall as level to your judgment 'pear
        As day does to your eye.
                         A noise within: "Let her come in."

Laertes. How now? What noise is that?

                         Enter Ophelia.

        O heat, dry up my brains; tears seven times salt
155   Burn out the sense and virtue° of mine eye!
        By heaven, thy madness shall be paid with weight
        Till our scale turn the beam.° O rose of May,
        Dear maid, kind sister, sweet Ophelia!
        O heavens, is't possible a young maid's wits
160   Should be as mortal as an old man's life?
        Nature is fine° in love, and where 'tis fine,
        It sends some precious instance° of itself
        After the thing it loves.

Ophelia. They bore him barefaced on the bier (*Song*)
165   Hey non nony, nony, hey nony
                And in his grave rained many a tear——
        Fare you well, my dove!

Laertes. Hadst thou thy wits, and didst persuade re-
        venge,
        It could not move thus.

170 *Ophelia.* You must sing "A-down a-down, and you call

146 **pelican** (thought to feed its young with its own blood) 147 **Repast**
feed 150 **sensibly** acutely 155 **virtue** power 157 **turn the beam**
weigh down the bar (of the balance) 161 **fine** refined, delicate
162 **instance** sample

him a-down-a." O, how the wheel° becomes it! It is
the false steward, that stole his master's daughter.

Laertes. This nothing's more than matter.°

Ophelia. There's rosemary, that's for remembrance.
Pray you, love, remember. And there is pansies, *175*
that's for thoughts.

Laertes. A document° in madness, thoughts and remembrance fitted.

Ophelia. There's fennel° for you, and columbines.
There's rue for you, and here's some for me. We *180*
may call it herb of grace o' Sundays. O, you must
wear your rue with a difference. There's a daisy. I
would give you some violets, but they withered all
when my father died. They say 'a made a good end.
[*Sings*]   For bonny sweet Robin is all my joy. *185*

Laertes. Thought and affliction, passion, hell itself,
She turns to favor° and to prettiness.

Ophelia. And will 'a not come again?   (*Song*)
    And will 'a not come again?
     No, no, he is dead, *190*
     Go to thy deathbed,
    He never will come again.

    His beard was as white as snow,
    All flaxen was his poll.°
     He is gone, he is gone, *195*
     And we cast away moan.
   God 'a' mercy on his soul!
And of all Christian souls, I pray God. God bye you.
               [*Exit.*]

---

171 **wheel** (of uncertain meaning, but probably a turn or dance of Ophelia's, rather than Fortune's wheel) 173 **This nothing's more than
matter** this nonsense has more meaning than matters of consequence 177 **document** lesson 179 **fennel** (the distribution of flowers
in the ensuing lines has symbolic meaning, but the meaning is disputed.
Perhaps **fennel,** flattery; **columbines,** cuckoldry; **rue,** sorrow for Ophelia and repentance for the Queen; **daisy,** dissembling; **violets,** faithful-
ness. For other interpretations, see J. W. Lever in *Review of English
Studies,* New Series 3 [1952], pp. 123–29) 187 **favor** charm, beauty
194 **All flaxen was his poll** white as flax was his head

Laertes. Do you see this, O God?

200 *King.* Laertes, I must commune with your grief,
Or you deny me right. Go but apart,
Make choice of whom your wisest friends you will,
And they shall hear and judge 'twixt you and me.
If by direct or by collateral° hand
205 They find us touched,° we will our kingdom give,
Our crown, our life, and all that we call ours,
To you in satisfaction; but if not,
Be you content to lend your patience to us,
And we shall jointly labor with your soul
To give it due content.

210 *Laertes.*   Let this be so.
His means of death, his obscure funeral—
No trophy, sword, nor hatchment° o'er his bones,
No noble rite nor formal ostentation°—
Cry to be heard, as 'twere from heaven to earth,
That I must call't in question.

215 *King.*   So you shall;
And where th' offense is, let the great ax fall.
I pray you go with me.   *Exeunt.*

[Scene 6. *The castle.*]

Enter Horatio and others.

Horatio. What are they that would speak with me?

Gentleman. Seafaring men, sir. They say they have
letters for you.

Horatio. Let them come in.   [*Exit Attendant.*]
5 I do not know from what part of the world
I should be greeted, if not from Lord Hamlet.

---

204 **collateral** indirect   205 **touched** implicated   212 **hatchment** tablet bearing the coat of arms of the dead   213 **ostentation** ceremony

Enter Sailors.

Sailor. God bless you, sir.

Horatio. Let Him bless thee too.

Sailor. 'A shall, sir, an't please Him. There's a letter
for you, sir—it came from th' ambassador that was   *10*
bound for England—if your name be Horatio, as
I am let to know it is.

Horatio. [*Reads the letter.*] "Horatio, when thou shalt
have overlooked° this, give these fellows some
means to the King. They have letters for him. Ere   *15*
we were two days old at sea, a pirate of very warlike
appointment° gave us chase. Finding ourselves too
slow of sail, we put on a compelled valor, and in
the grapple I boarded them. On the instant they
got clear of our ship; so I alone became their   *20*
prisoner. They have dealt with me like thieves of
mercy, but they knew what they did: I am to do a
good turn for them. Let the King have the letters
I have sent, and repair thou to me with as much
speed as thou wouldest fly death. I have words to   *25*
speak in thine ear will make thee dumb; yet are they
much too light for the bore° of the matter. These
good fellows will bring thee where I am. Rosencrantz and Guildenstern hold their course for England. Of them I have much to tell thee. Farewell.   *30*

          He that thou knowest thine, HAMLET."
Come, I will give you way for these your letters,
And do't the speedier that you may direct me
To him from whom you brought them.   *Exeunt.*

4.6.14 **overlooked** surveyed   17 **appointment** equipment   27 **bore**
caliber (here, "importance")

[Scene 7. *The castle.*]

Enter King and Laertes.

King. Now must your conscience my acquittance seal,
And you must put me in your heart for friend,
Sith you have heard, and with a knowing ear,
That he which hath your noble father slain
Pursued my life.

5   *Laertes.*   It well appears. But tell me
Why you proceeded not against these feats
So criminal and so capital° in nature,
As by your safety, greatness, wisdom, all things else,
You mainly° were stirred up.

King.   O, for two special reasons,
10   Which may to you perhaps seem much unsinewed,°
But yet to me they're strong. The Queen his mother
Lives almost by his looks, and for myself—
My virtue or my plague, be it either which—
She is so conjunctive° to my life and soul,
15   That, as the star moves not but in his sphere,
I could not but by her. The other motive
Why to a public count° I might not go
Is the great love the general gender° bear him,
Who, dipping all his faults in their affection,
20   Would, like the spring that turneth wood to stone,°
Convert his gyves° to graces; so that my arrows,
Too slightly timbered° for so loud a wind,
Would have reverted to my bow again,
And not where I had aimed them.

4.7.7 **capital** deserving death   9 **mainly** powerfully   10 **unsinewed**
weak   14 **conjunctive** closely united   17 **count** reckoning   18 **general gender** common people   20 **spring that turneth wood to stone** (a
spring in Shakespeare's county was so charged with lime that it would
petrify wood placed in it)   21 **gyves** fetters; G.R. Hibbard's emendation
to *guilts* is attractive   22 **timbered** shafted

Laertes. And so have I a noble father lost,　　　　　25
A sister driven into desp'rate terms,°
Whose worth, if praises may go back again,°
Stood challenger on mount of all the age
For her perfections. But my revenge will come.

King. Break not your sleeps for that. You must not
　think　　　　　30
That we are made of stuff so flat and dull
That we can let our beard be shook with danger,
And think it pastime. You shortly shall hear more.
I loved your father, and we love ourself,
And that, I hope, will teach you to imagine——　　　　　35

　　　　Enter a Messenger with letters.

How now? What news?

Messenger.　　　　　Letters, my lord, from Ham-
　let:
These to your Majesty; this to the Queen.

King. From Hamlet? Who brought them?

Messenger. Sailors, my lord, they say; I saw them not.
They were given me by Claudio; he received them　　　　　40
Of him that brought them.

King.　　　　　Laertes, you shall hear them.——
Leave us.　　　　　*Exit Messenger.*
[*Reads.*] "High and mighty, you shall know I am set
naked° on your kingdom. Tomorrow shall I beg
leave to see your kingly eyes; when I shall (first　　　　　45
asking your pardon thereunto) recount the occasion
of my sudden and more strange return.
　　　　　　　　　　HAMLET."
What should this mean? Are all the rest come back?
Or is it some abuse,° and no such thing?　　　　　50

Laertes. Know you the hand?

King.　　　　　'Tis Hamlet's character.° "Naked"!

---

26 **terms** conditions　27 **go back again** revert to what is past　44
naked destitute　50 **abuse** deception　51 **character** handwriting

And in a postscript here, he says "alone."
Can you devise° me?

Laertes. I am lost in it, my lord. But let him come.
55   It warms the very sickness in my heart
That I shall live and tell him to his teeth,
"Thus did'st thou."

King.   If it be so, Laertes
(As how should it be so? How otherwise?),
Will you be ruled by me?

Laertes.   Ay, my lord,
60   So you will not o'errule me to a peace.

King. To thine own peace. If he be now returned,
As checking at° his voyage, and that he means
No more to undertake it, I will work him
To an exploit now ripe in my device,
65   Under the which he shall not choose but fall;
And for his death no wind of blame shall breathe,
But even his mother shall uncharge the practice°
And call it accident.

Laertes.   My lord, I will be ruled;
The rather if you could devise it so
That I might be the organ.

70   *King.*   It falls right.
You have been talked of since your travel much,
And that in Hamlet's hearing, for a quality
Wherein they say you shine. Your sum of parts
Did not together pluck such envy from him
75   As did that one, and that, in my regard,
Of the unworthiest siege.°

Laertes.   What part is that, my lord?

King. A very riband in the cap of youth,
Yet needful too, for youth no less becomes
The light and careless livery that it wears
80   Than settled age his sables and his weeds,°
Importing health and graveness. Two months since

---

53 **devise** advise 62 **checking at** turning away from (a term in falconry) 67 **uncharge the practice** not charge the device with treachery
76 **siege** rank 80 **sables and his weeds** i.e., sober attire

Here was a gentleman of Normandy.
I have seen myself, and served against, the French,
And they can° well on horseback, but this gallant
Had witchcraft in't. He grew unto his seat,   85
And to such wondrous doing brought his horse
As had he been incorpsed and deminatured
With the brave beast. So far he topped my thought
That I, in forgery° of shapes and tricks,
Come short of what he did.

Laertes.   A Norman was't?   90

King. A Norman.

Laertes. Upon my life, Lamord.°

King.   The very same.

Laertes. I know him well. He is the brooch° indeed
And gem of all the nation.

King. He made confession° of you,   95
And gave you such a masterly report,
For art and exercise in your defense,
And for your rapier most especial,
That he cried out 'twould be a sight indeed
If one could match you. The scrimers° of their
    nation   100
He swore had neither motion, guard, nor eye,
If you opposed them. Sir, this report of his
Did Hamlet so envenom with his envy
That he could nothing do but wish and beg
Your sudden coming o'er to play with you.   105
Now, out of this——

Laertes.   What out of this, my lord?

King. Laertes, was your father dear to you?
Or are you like the painting of a sorrow,
A face without a heart?

Laertes.   Why ask you this?

King. Not that I think you did not love your father, 110

84 **can** do   89 **forgery** invention   92 **Lamord** (the name suggests *la mort*, i.e. death [French])   93 **brooch** ornament   95 **confession** report 100 **scrimers** fencers

But that I know love is begun by time,
And that I see, in passages of proof,°
Time qualifies° the spark and fire of it.
There lives within the very flame of love

115 A kind of wick or snuff° that will abate it,
And nothing is at a like goodness still,°
For goodness, growing to a plurisy,°
Dies in his own too-much. That we would do
We should do when we would, for this "would"
　　changes,

120 And hath abatements and delays as many
As there are tongues, are hands, are accidents,
And then this "should" is like a spendthrift sigh,°
That hurts by easing. But to the quick° of th' ulcer—
Hamlet comes back; what would you undertake

125 To show yourself in deed your father's son
More than in words?

Laertes.　　　　　　　　　To cut his throat i' th' church!

King. No place indeed should murder sanctuarize;°
Revenge should have no bounds. But, good Laertes,
Will you do this? Keep close within your chamber.

130 Hamlet returned shall know you are come home.
We'll put on those° shall praise your excellence
And set a double varnish on the fame
The Frenchman gave you, bring you in fine°
　　together
And wager on your heads. He, being remiss,

135 Most generous, and free from all contriving,
Will not peruse the foils, so that with ease,
Or with a little shuffling, you may choose
A sword unbated,° and, in a pass of practice,°
Requite him for your father.

Laertes.　　　　　　　　　I will do't,

112 **passages of proof** proved cases　113 **qualifies** diminishes　11⁵
snuff residue of burnt wick (which dims the light)　116 **still** alway
117 **plurisy** fullness, excess　122 **spendthrift sigh** (sighing provide⁵
ease, but because it was thought to thin the blood and so shorten life
it was spendthrift)　123 **quick** sensitive flesh　127 **sanctuarize** pro
tect　131 **We'll put on those** we'll incite persons who　133 **in fin⁰**
finally　138 **unbated** not blunted　138 **pass of practice** treacherou⁵
thrust

And for that purpose I'll anoint my sword.   *140*
I bought an unction of a mountebank,°
So mortal that, but dip a knife in it,
Where it draws blood, no cataplasm° so rare,
Collected from all simples° that have virtue°
Under the moon, can save the thing from death   *145*
That is but scratched withal. I'll touch my point
With this contagion, that, if I gall him slightly,
It may be death.

King.   Let's further think of this,
Weigh what convenience both of time and means
May fit us to our shape.° If this should fail,   *150*
And that our drift look through° our bad per-
     formance,
'Twere better not assayed. Therefore this project
Should have a back or second, that might hold
If this did blast in proof.° Soft, let me see.
We'll make a solemn wager on your cunnings—   *155*
I ha't!
When in your motion you are hot and dry—
As make your bouts more violent to that end—
And that he calls for drink, I'll have prepared him
A chalice for the nonce,° whereon but sipping,   *160*
If he by chance escape your venomed stuck,°
Our purpose may hold there.—But stay, what noise?

         Enter Queen.

Queen. One woe doth tread upon another's heel.
   So fast they follow. Your sister's drowned, Laertes.

Laertes. Drowned! O, where?   *165*

Queen. There is a willow grows askant° the brook,
   That shows his hoar° leaves in the glassy stream:
   Therewith° fantastic garlands did she make
   Of crowflowers, nettles, daisies, and long purples,

---

141 **mountebank** quack   143 **cataplasm** poultice   144 **simples** medicinal herbs   144 **virtue power** (to heal)   150 **shape** role   151 **drift look through** purpose show through   154 **blast in proof** burst (fail) in performance   160 **nonce** occasion   161 **stuck** thrust   166 **askant** aslant   167 **hoar** silver-gray   168 **Therewith** i.e., with willow twigs

170   That liberal° shepherds give a grosser name,
       But our cold maids do dead men's fingers call them.
       There on the pendent boughs her crownet° weeds
       Clamb'ring to hang, an envious sliver° broke,
       When down her weedy trophies and herself
175   Fell in the weeping brook. Her clothes spread wide,
       And mermaidlike awhile they bore her up,
       Which time she chanted snatches of old lauds,°
       As one incapable° of her own distress,
       Or like a creature native and indued°
180   Unto that element. But long it could not be
       Till that her garments, heavy with their drink,
       Pulled the poor wretch from her melodious lay
       To muddy death.

Laertes.   Alas, then she is drowned?

Queen. Drowned, drowned.

185 *Laertes.* Too much of water hast thou, poor Ophelia,
       And therefore I forbid my tears; but yet
       It is our trick;° nature her custom holds,
       Let shame say what it will: when these° are gone,
       The woman° will be out. Adieu, my lord.
190   I have a speech o' fire, that fain would blaze,
       But that this folly drowns it.   *Exit.*

King.   Let's follow, Gertrude.
       How much I had to do to calm his rage!
       Now fear I this will give it start again;
       Therefore let's follow.   *Exeunt.*

170 **liberal** free-spoken, coarse-mouthed   172 **crownet** coronet   173
envious sliver malicious branch   177 **lauds** hymns   178 **incapable** un-
aware   179 **indued** in harmony with   187 **trick** trait, way   188 **these**
the tears he is shedding   189 **woman** i.e., womanly part of me

[ACT 5

Scene 1. *A churchyard.*]

Enter two Clowns.°

Clown. Is she to be buried in Christian burial when she
willfully seeks her own salvation?

Other. I tell thee she is. Therefore make her grave
straight.° The crowner° hath sate on her, and finds
it Christian burial.   5

Clown. How can that be, unless she drowned herself
in her own defense?

Other. Why, 'tis found so.

Clown. It must be *se offendendo*;° it cannot be else.
For here lies the point: if I drown myself wittingly,   10
it argues an act, and an act hath three branches—
it is to act, to do, to perform. Argal,° she drowned
herself wittingly.

Other. Nay, but hear you, Goodman Delver.

Clown. Give me leave. Here lies the water—good.   15
Here stands the man—good. If the man go to this
water and drown himself, it is, will he nill he,° he
goes; mark you that. But if the water come to him
and drown him, he drowns not himself. Argal, he

5.1.s.d. **Clowns** rustics (the first clown is a grave-digger)   4 **straight**
straightway   4 **crowner** coroner   9 **se offendendo** (blunder for *se defend-
endo,* a legal term meaning "in self-defense")   12 **Argal** (blunder for
Latin *ergo,* "therefore")   17 **will he nill he** will he or will he not (whether
he will or will not)

119

20   that is not guilty of his own death, shortens not his
     own life.

Other. But is this law?

Clown. Ay marry, is't—crowner's quest° law.

Other. Will you ha' the truth on't? If this had not been
25   a gentlewoman, she should have been buried out
     o' Christian burial.

Clown. Why, there thou say'st. And the more pity
     that great folk should have count'nance° in this
     world to drown or hang themselves more than their
30   even-Christen.° Come, my spade. There is no an-
     cient gentlemen but gard'ners, ditchers, and grave-
     makers. They hold up° Adam's profession.

Other. Was he a gentleman?

Clown. 'A was the first that ever bore arms.°

35 *Other.* Why, he had none.

Clown. What, art a heathen? How dost thou under-
     stand the Scripture? The Scripture says Adam
     digged. Could he dig without arms? I'll put another
     question to thee. If thou answerest me not to the
40   purpose, confess thyself——

Other. Go to.

Clown. What is he that builds stronger than either the
     mason, the shipwright, or the carpenter?

Other. The gallowsmaker, for that frame outlives a
45   thousand tenants.

Clown. I like thy wit well, in good faith. The gallows
     does well. But how does it well? It does well to those
     that do ill. Now thou dost ill to say the gallows
     is built stronger than the church. Argal, the gallows
50   may do well to thee. To't again, come.

Other. Who builds stronger than a mason, a ship-
     wright, or a carpenter?

---

23 **quest** inquest   28 **count'nance** privilege   30 **even-Christen** fellow
Christian   32 **hold up** keep up   34 **bore arms** had a coat of arms (the
sign of a gentleman)

Clown. Ay, tell me that, and unyoke.°

Other. Marry, now I can tell.

Clown. To't.   55

Other. Mass,° I cannot tell.

Enter Hamlet and Horatio afar off.

Clown. Cudgel thy brains no more about it, for your
dull ass will not mend his pace with beating. And
when you are asked this question next, say "a gravemaker." The houses he makes lasts till doomsday.   60
Go, get thee in, and fetch me a stoup° of liquor.

[*Exit Other Clown.*]

In youth when I did love, did love,   (*Song*)
    Methought it was very sweet
To contract—O—the time for—a—my behove,°
    O, methought there—a—was nothing—a—meet.   65

Hamlet. Has this fellow no feeling of his business? 'A
sings in gravemaking.

Horatio. Custom hath made it in him a property of
easiness.°

Hamlet. 'Tis e'en so. The hand of little employment   70
hath the daintier sense.°

Clown.   But age with his stealing steps   (*Song*)
        Hath clawed me in his clutch,
    And hath shipped me into the land,
        As if I had never been such.   75

[*Throws up a skull.*]

Hamlet. That skull had a tongue in it, and could sing
once. How the knave jowls° it to the ground, as if
'twere Cain's jawbone, that did the first murder!
This might be the pate of a politician, which this

---

53 **unyoke** i.e., stop work for the day   56 **Mass** by the mass   61 **stoup**
tankard   64 **behove** advantage   68–69 **in him a property of easiness**
easy for him   71 **hath the daintier sense** is more sensitive (because it
is not calloused)   77 **jowls** hurls

80   ass now o'erreaches,° one that would circumvent
         God, might it not?

Horatio. It might, my lord.

Hamlet. Or of a courtier, which could say "Good
         morrow, sweet lord! How dost thou, sweet lord?"
85   This might be my Lord Such-a-one, that praised
         my Lord Such-a-one's horse when 'a went to beg
         it, might it not?

Horatio. Ay, my lord.

Hamlet. Why, e'en so, and now my Lady Worm's,
90   chapless,° and knocked about the mazzard° with a
         sexton's spade. Here's fine revolution, an we had
         the trick to see't. Did these bones cost no more
         the breeding but to play at loggets° with them?
         Mine ache to think on't.

95 *Clown.*   A pickax and a spade, a spade,   (*Song*)
                  For and a shrouding sheet;
               O, a pit of clay for to be made
                  For such a guest is meet.

                                [*Throws up another skull.*]

Hamlet. There's another. Why may not that be the
100   skull of a lawyer? Where be his quiddities° now, his
         quillities,° his cases, his tenures,° and his tricks?
         Why does he suffer this mad knave now to knock
         him about the sconce° with a dirty shovel, and will
         not tell him of his action of battery? Hum! This
105   fellow might be in's time a great buyer of land, with
         his statutes, his recognizances, his fines,° his double
         vouchers, his recoveries. Is this the fine° of his fines,
         and the recovery of his recoveries, to have his fine
         pate full of fine dirt? Will his vouchers vouch him

---

80 **o'erreaches** (1) reaches over (2) has the advantage over   90 **chapless** lacking the lower jaw   90 **mazzard** head   93 **loggets** (a game in
which small pieces of wood were thrown at an object)   100 **quiddities**
subtle arguments (from Latin *quidditas,* "whatness")   101 **quillities**
fine distinctions   101 **tenures** legal means of holding land   103 **sconce**
head   106 **his statutes, his recognizances, his fines** his documents
giving a creditor control of a debtor's land, his bonds of surety, his documents changing an entailed estate into fee simple (unrestricted ownership)   107 **fine** end

no more of his purchases, and double ones too, than *110*
the length and breadth of a pair of indentures?°
The very conveyances° of his lands will scarcely
lie in this box, and must th' inheritor himself have no
more, ha?

Horatio. Not a jot more, my lord.   *115*

Hamlet. Is not parchment made of sheepskins?

Horatio. Ay, my lord, and of calveskins too.

Hamlet. They are sheep and calves which seek out
assurance° in that. I will speak to this fellow. Whose
grave's this, sirrah?   *120*

Clown. Mine, sir.
[*Sings.*]   O, a pit of clay for to be made
                      For such a guest is meet.

Hamlet. I think it be thine indeed, for thou liest in't.

Clown. You lie out on't, sir, and therefore 'tis not *125*
yours. For my part, I do not lie in't, yet it is mine.

Hamlet. Thou dost lie in't, to be in't and say it is
thine. 'Tis for the dead, not for the quick;° therefore thou liest.

Clown. 'Tis a quick lie, sir; 'twill away again from *130*
me to you.

Hamlet. What man dost thou dig it for?

Clown. For no man, sir.

Hamlet. What woman then?

Clown. For none neither.   *135*

Hamlet. Who is to be buried in't?

Clown. One that was a woman, sir; but, rest her soul,
she's dead.

Hamlet. How absolute° the knave is! We must speak by
the card,° or equivocation° will undo us. By the *140*

---

111 **indentures** contracts   112 **conveyances** legal documents for the
transference of land   119 **assurance** safety   128 **quick** living
139 **absolute** positive, decided   139–40 **by the card** by the compass
card, i.e., exactly   140 **equivocation** ambiguity

Lord, Horatio, this three years I have took note of
it, the age is grown so picked° that the toe of the
peasant comes so near the heel of the courtier he
galls his kibe.° How long hast thou been a grave-
145 maker?

Clown. Of all the days i' th' year, I came to't that day
that our last king Hamlet overcame Fortinbras.

Hamlet. How long is that since?

Clown. Cannot you tell that? Every fool can tell that. It
150 was that very day that young Hamlet was born—
he that is mad, and sent into England.

Hamlet. Ay, marry, why was he sent into England?

Clown. Why, because 'a was mad. 'A shall recover his
wits there; or, if 'a do not, 'tis no great matter there.

155 *Hamlet.* Why?

Clown. 'Twill not be seen in him there. There the men
are as mad as he.

Hamlet. How came he mad?

Clown. Very strangely, they say.

160 *Hamlet.* How strangely?

Clown. Faith, e'en with losing his wits.

Hamlet. Upon what ground?

Clown. Why, here in Denmark. I have been sexton
here, man and boy, thirty years.

165 *Hamlet.* How long will a man lie i' th' earth ere he rot?

Clown. Faith, if 'a be not rotten before 'a die (as we
have many pocky corses° nowadays that will scarce
hold the laying in), 'a will last you some eight year
or nine year. A tanner will last you nine year.

170 *Hamlet.* Why he, more than another?

Clown. Why, sir, his hide is so tanned with his trade

142 **picked** refined   144 **kibe** sore on the back of the heel   167 **pocky
corses** bodies of persons who had been infected with the pox (syphilis)

that 'a will keep out water a great while, and your
water is a sore decayer of your whoreson dead body.
Here's a skull now hath lien you i' th' earth three and
twenty years.   *175*

Hamlet. Whose was it?

Clown. A whoreson mad fellow's it was. Whose do you
think it was?

Hamlet. Nay, I know not.

Clown. A pestilence on him for a mad rogue! 'A poured *180*
a flagon of Rhenish on my head once. This same
skull, sir, was, sir, Yorick's skull, the King's jester.

Hamlet. This?

Clown. E'en that.

Hamlet. Let me see. [*Takes the skull.*] Alas, poor *185*
Yorick! I knew him, Horatio, a fellow of infinite
jest, of most excellent fancy. He hath borne me on
his back a thousand times. And now how abhorred
in my imagination it is! My gorge rises at it. Here
hung those lips that I have kissed I know not how *190*
oft. Where be your gibes now? Your gambols, your
songs, your flashes of merriment that were wont to
set the table on a roar? Not one now to mock your
own grinning? Quite chapfall'n°? Now get you to my
lady's chamber, and tell her, let her paint an inch *195*
thick, to this favor° she must come. Make her laugh
at that. Prithee, Horatio, tell me one thing.

Horatio. What's that, my lord?

Hamlet. Dost thou think Alexander looked o' this
fashion i' th' earth?   *200*

Horatio. E'en so.

Hamlet. And smelt so? Pah!   [*Puts down the skull.*]

Horatio. E'en so, my lord.

---

194 **chapfall'n** (1) down in the mouth (2) jawless . 196 **favor** facial
appearance

Hamlet. To what base uses we may return, Horatio!
205   Why may not imagination trace the noble dust of
        Alexander till 'a find it stopping a bunghole?

Horatio. 'Twere to consider too curiously,° to consider
        so.

Hamlet. No, faith, not a jot, but to follow him thither
210   with modesty enough,° and likelihood to lead it; as
        thus: Alexander died, Alexander was buried, Alex-
        ander returneth to dust; the dust is earth; of earth
        we make loam; and why of that loam whereto he was
        converted might they not stop a beer barrel?
215   Imperious Caesar, dead and turned to clay,
        Might stop a hole to keep the wind away.
        O, that that earth which kept the world in awe
        Should patch a wall t' expel the winter's flaw!°
        But soft, but soft awhile! Here comes the King.

*Enter King, Queen, Laertes, and a coffin, with Lords
     attendant [and a Doctor of Divinity].*

220   The Queen, the courtiers. Who is this they follow?
        And with such maimèd° rites? This doth betoken
        The corse they follow did with desp'rate hand
        Fordo it° own life. 'Twas of some estate.°
        Couch° we awhile, and mark. [*Retires with Horatio.*]

Laertes. What ceremony else?

225 *Hamlet.*   That is Laertes,
        A very noble youth. Mark.

Laertes. What ceremony else?

Doctor. Her obsequies have been as far enlarged
        As we have warranty. Her death was doubtful,°
230   And, but that great command o'ersways the order,
        She should in ground unsanctified been lodged
        Till the last trumpet. For charitable prayers,

---

207 **curiously** minutely   210 **with modesty enough** without exaggera-
tion   218 **flaw** gust   221 **maimèd** incomplete   223 **Fordo it** destroy
its   223 **estate** high rank   224 **Couch** hide   229 **doubtful** suspicious

Shards,° flints, and pebbles should be thrown on her.
Yet here she is allowed her virgin crants,°
Her maiden strewments,° and the bringing home   235
Of bell and burial.

Laertes. Must there no more be done?

Doctor.   No more be done.
We should profane the service of the dead
To sing a requiem and such rest to her
As to peace-parted souls.

Laertes.   Lay her i' th' earth,   240
And from her fair and unpolluted flesh
May violets spring! I tell thee, churlish priest,
A minist'ring angel shall my sister be
When thou liest howling!

Hamlet.   What, the fair Ophelia?

Queen. Sweets to the sweet! Farewell.   245
                           [*Scatters flowers.*]
I hoped thou shouldst have been my Hamlet's wife.
I thought thy bride bed to have decked, sweet maid,
And not have strewed thy grave.

Laertes.   O, treble woe
Fall ten times treble on that cursèd head
Whose wicked deed thy most ingenious sense°   250
Deprived thee of! Hold off the earth awhile,
Till I have caught her once more in mine arms.
                           Leaps in the grave.
Now pile your dust upon the quick and dead
Till of this flat a mountain you have made
T'o'ertop old Pelion° or the skyish head   255
Of blue Olympus.

Hamlet.   [*Coming forward*] What is he whose grief

---

233 **Shards** broken pieces of pottery   234 **crants** garlands   235 **strewments** i.e., of flowers   250 **most ingenious sense** finely endowed mind
255 **Pelion** (according to classical legend, giants in their fight with the gods sought to reach heaven by piling Mount Pelion and Mount Ossa on Mount Olympus)

Bears such an emphasis, whose phrase of sorrow
Conjures the wand'ring stars,° and makes them
  stand
Like wonder-wounded hearers? This is I,
Hamlet the Dane.

260 *Laertes.*   The devil take thy soul!
                    [*Grapples with him.*]°

Hamlet. Thou pray'st not well.
  I prithee take thy fingers from my throat,
  For, though I am not splenitive° and rash,
  Yet have I in me something dangerous,
265   Which let thy wisdom fear. Hold off thy hand.

King. Pluck them asunder.

Queen.   Hamlet, Hamlet!

All. Gentlemen!

Horatio.   Good my lord, be quiet.
                    [*Attendants part them.*]

Hamlet. Why, I will fight with him upon this theme
  Until my eyelids will no longer wag.

270 *Queen.* O my son, what theme?

Hamlet. I loved Ophelia. Forty thousand brothers
  Could not with all their quantity of love
  Make up my sum. What wilt thou do for her?

King. O, he is mad, Laertes.

275 *Queen.* For love of God forbear him.

Hamlet. 'Swounds, show me what thou't do.
  Woo't weep? Woo't fight? Woo't fast? Woo't tear
    thyself?
  Woo't drink up eisel?° Eat a crocodile?

258 **wand'ring stars** planets   260 s.d. **Grapples with him** (Q1, a bad
quarto, presumably reporting a version that toured, has a previous direction saying "Hamlet leaps in after Laertes." Possibly he does so, somewhat hysterically. But such a direction—absent from the two good texts,
Q2 and F—makes Hamlet the aggressor, somewhat contradicting his
next speech. Perhaps Laertes leaps out of the grave to attack Hamlet)   263 **splenitive** fiery (the spleen was thought to be the seat of
anger)   278 **eisel** vinegar

I'll do't. Dost thou come here to whine?
To outface me with leaping in her grave?   *280*
Be buried quick with her, and so will I.
And if thou prate of mountains, let them throw
Millions of acres on us, till our ground,
Singeing his pate against the burning zone,°
Make Ossa like a wart! Nay, an thou'lt mouth,   *285*
I'll rant as well as thou.

Queen.   This is mere madness;
And thus a while the fit will work on him.
Anon, as patient as the female dove
When that her golden couplets are disclosed,°
His silence will sit drooping.

Hamlet.   Hear you, sir.   *290*
What is the reason that you use me thus?
I loved you ever. But it is no matter.
Let Hercules himself do what he may,
The cat will mew, and dog will have his day.

King. I pray thee, good Horatio, wait upon him.   *295*
                        Exit Hamlet and Horatio.
[*To Laertes*] Strengthen your patience in our last
    night's speech.
We'll put the matter to the present push.°
Good Gertrude, set some watch over your son.
This grave shall have a living° monument.
An hour of quiet shortly shall we see;   *300*
Till then in patience our proceeding be.   *Exeunt.*

---

284 **burning zone** sun's orbit   289 **golden couplets are disclosed** (the
dove lays two eggs, and the newly hatched [**disclosed**] young are covered with golden down)   297 **present push** immediate test   299 **living**
lasting (with perhaps also a reference to the plot against Hamlet's life)

[Scene 2. *The castle.*]

Enter Hamlet and Horatio.

Hamlet. So much for this, sir; now shall you see the
    other.
    You do remember all the circumstance?

Horatio. Remember it, my lord!

Hamlet. Sir, in my heart there was a kind of fighting
5   That would not let me sleep. Methought I lay
    Worse than the mutines in the bilboes.° Rashly
    (And praised be rashness for it) let us know,
    Our indiscretion sometime serves us well
    When our deep plots do pall,° and that should learn
    us
10   There's a divinity that shapes our ends,
    Rough-hew them how we will.

Horatio.   •   That is most certain.

Hamlet. Up from my cabin,
    My sea gown scarfed about me, in the dark
    Groped I to find out them, had my desire,
15   Fingered° their packet, and in fine° withdrew
    To mine own room again, making so bold,
    My fears forgetting manners, to unseal
    Their grand commission; where I found, Horatio—
    Ah, royal knavery!—an exact command,
20   Larded° with many several sorts of reasons,
    Importing Denmark's health, and England's too,
    With, ho, such bugs and goblins in my life,°
    That on the supervise,° no leisure bated,°
    No, not to stay the grinding of the ax,

5.2.6 **mutines in the bilboes** mutineers in fetters   9 **pall** fail   15 **Fingered** stole   15 **in fine** finally   20 **Larded** enriched   22 **such bugs and goblins in my life** such bugbears and imagined terrors if I were allowed to live   23 **supervise** reading   23 **leisure bated** delay allowed

My head should be struck off.

Horatio.   Is't possible?   *25*

Hamlet. Here's the commission; read it at more leisure.
  But wilt thou hear now how I did proceed?

Horatio. I beseech you.

Hamlet. Being thus benetted round with villains,
  Or° I could make a prologue to my brains,   *30*
  They had begun the play. I sat me down,
  Devised a new commission, wrote it fair.
  I once did hold it, as our statists° do,
  A baseness to write fair,° and labored much
  How to forget that learning, but, sir, now   *35*
  It did me yeoman's service. Wilt thou know
  Th' effect° of what I wrote?

Horatio.   Ay, good my lord.

Hamlet. An earnest conjuration from the King,
  As England was his faithful tributary,
  As love between them like the palm might flourish,   *40*
  As peace should still her wheaten garland wear
  And stand a comma° 'tween their amities,
  And many suchlike as's of great charge,°
  That on the view and knowing of these contents,
  Without debatement further, more or less,   *45*
  He should those bearers put to sudden death,
  Not shriving° time allowed.

Horatio.   How was this sealed?

Hamlet. Why, even in that was heaven ordinant.°
  I had my father's signet in my purse,
  Which was the model° of that Danish seal,   *50*
  Folded the writ up in the form of th' other,
  Subscribed it, gave't th' impression, placed it safely,
  The changeling never known. Now, the next day
  Was our sea fight, and what to this was sequent
  Thou knowest already.   *55*

---

30 **Or** ere   33 **statists** statesmen   34 **fair** clearly   37 **effect** purport
42 **comma** link   43 **great charge** (1) serious exhortation (2) heavy burden (punning on *as's* and "asses")   47 **shriving** absolution   48 **ordinant** ruling   50 **model** counterpart

Horatio. So Guildenstern and Rosencrantz go to't.

Hamlet. Why, man, they did make love to this employment.
They are not near my conscience; their defeat
Does by their own insinuation° grow.

60 'Tis dangerous when the baser nature comes
Between the pass° and fell incensèd points°
Of mighty opposites.

Horatio.   Why, what a king is this!

Hamlet. Does it not, think thee, stand me now upon°—
He that hath killed my king, and whored my mother,

65 Popped in between th' election° and my hopes,
Thrown out his angle° for my proper life,°
And with such coz'nage°—is't not perfect conscience
To quit° him with this arm? And is't not to be
damned
To let this canker of our nature come

70 In further evil?

Horatio. It must be shortly known to him from England
What is the issue of the business there.

Hamlet. It will be short; the interim's mine,
And a man's life's no more than to say "one."

75 But I am very sorry, good Horatio,
That to Laertes I forgot myself,
For by the image of my cause I see
The portraiture of his. I'll court his favors.
But sure the bravery° of his grief did put me
Into a tow'ring passion.

80 *Horatio.*   Peace, who comes here?

Enter young Osric, a courtier.

Osric. Your lordship is right welcome back to Denmark.

59 **insinuation** meddling 61 **pass** thrust 61 **fell incensèd points**
fiercely angry rapiers 63 **stand me now upon** become incumbent upon
me 65 **election** (the Danish monarchy was elective) 66 **angle** fishing
line 66 **my proper life** my own life 67 **coz'nage** trickery (and with a
pun on *cousinage*, kinship) 68 **quit** pay back 79 **bravery** bravado

Hamlet. I humbly thank you, sir. [*Aside to Horatio*]
   Dost know this waterfly?°

Horatio. [*Aside to Hamlet*] No, my good lord.

Hamlet. [*Aside to Horatio*] Thy state is the more gra-   85
   cious, for 'tis a vice to know him. He hath much
   land, and fertile. Let a beast be lord of beasts, and
   his crib shall stand at the king's mess.° 'Tis a
   chough,° but, as I say, spacious° in the possession
   of dirt.   90

Osric. Sweet lord, if your lordship were at leisure, I
   should impart a thing to you from his Majesty.

Hamlet. I will receive it, sir, with all diligence of spirit.
   Put your bonnet to his right use. 'Tis for the head.

Osric. I thank your lordship, it is very hot.   95

Hamlet. No, believe me, 'tis very cold; the wind is
   northerly.

Osric. It is indifferent cold, my lord, indeed.

Hamlet. But yet methinks it is very sultry and hot for
   my complexion.°   100

Osric. Exceedingly, my lord; it is very sultry, as 'twere—
   I cannot tell how. But, my lord, his Majesty bade
   me signify to you that 'a has laid a great wager on
   your head. Sir, this is the matter——

Hamlet. I beseech you remember.   105
               [*Hamlet moves him to put on his hat.*]

Osric. Nay, good my lord; for my ease, in good faith.
   Sir, here is newly come to court Laertes—believe
   me, an absolute gentleman, full of most excellent
   differences,° of very soft society and great showing.
   Indeed, to speak feelingly° of him, he is the card°   110
   or calendar of gentry; for you shall find in him the
   continent° of what part a gentleman would see.

83 **waterfly** (Osric's costume—perhaps a hat with plumes—suggests an
insect's wings) 88 **mess** table 89 **chough** jackdaw (here, chatterer)
89 **spacious** well off 100 **complexion** temperament 109 **differences**
distinguishing characteristics 110 **feelingly** justly 110 **card** chart
112 **continent** summary

Hamlet. Sir, his definement° suffers no perdition° in
you, though, I know, to divide him inventorially
115 would dozy° th' arithmetic of memory, and yet but
yaw neither in respect of his quick sail.° But, in the
verity of extolment, I take him to be a soul of great
article,° and his infusion° of such dearth and rare-
ness as, to make true diction° of him, his semblable°
120 is his mirror, and who else would trace him, his um-
brage,° nothing more.

Osric. Your lordship speaks most infallibly of him.

Hamlet. The concernancy,° sir? Why do we wrap the
gentleman in our more rawer breath?

125 *Osric.* Sir?

Horatio. Is't not possible to understand in another
tongue? You will to't,° sir, really.

Hamlet. What imports the nomination of this gentleman?

130 *Osric.* Of Laertes?

Horatio. [*Aside to Hamlet*] His purse is empty already.
All's golden words are spent.

Hamlet. Of him, sir.

Osric. I know you are not ignorant——

135 *Hamlet.* I would you did, sir; yet, in faith, if you did, it
would not much approve° me. Well, sir?

Osric. You are not ignorant of what excellence Laertes
is——

Hamlet. I dare not confess that, lest I should compare
140 with him in excellence; but to know a man well were
to know himself.

---

113 **definement** description 113 **perdition** loss 115 **dozy** dizzy
115–16 **and yet . . . quick sail** i.e., and yet only stagger despite all (**yaw
neither**) in trying to overtake his virtues 118 **article** (literally, "item,"
but here perhaps "traits" or "importance") 118 **infusion** essential quality 119 **diction** description 119 **semblable** likeness 120–21 **um-
brage** shadow 123 **concernancy** meaning 127 **will to't** will get there
136 **approve** commend

Osric. I mean, sir, for his weapon; but in the imputa-
tion° laid on him by them, in his meed° he's un-
fellowed.

Hamlet. What's his weapon? 145

Osric. Rapier and dagger.

Hamlet. That's two of his weapons—but well.

Osric. The King, sir, hath wagered with him six Bar-
bary horses, against the which he has impawned,° as
I take it, six French rapiers and poniards, with their 150
assigns,° as girdle, hangers,° and so. Three of the
carriages,° in faith, are very dear to fancy, very re-
sponsive° to the hilts, most delicate carriages, and
of very liberal conceit.°

Hamlet. What call you the carriages? 155

Horatio. [*Aside to Hamlet*] I knew you must be edified
by the margent° ere you had done.

Osric. The carriages, sir, are the hangers.

Hamlet. The phrase would be more germane to the
matter if we could carry a cannon by our sides. I 160
would it might be hangers till then. But on! Six Bar-
bary horses against six French swords, their assigns,
and three liberal-conceited carriages—that's the
French bet against the Danish. Why is this all impawned, as you call it? 165

Osric. The King, sir, hath laid, sir, that in a dozen
passes between yourself and him he shall not exceed
you three hits; he hath laid on twelve for nine, and
it would come to immediate trial if your lordship
would vouchsafe the answer. 170

Hamlet. How if I answer no?

Osric. I mean, my lord, the opposition of your person
in trial.

142–43 **imputation** reputation   143 **meed** merit   149 **impawned** wagered   151 **assigns** accompaniments   151 **hangers** straps hanging the
sword to the belt   152 **carriages** (an affected word for hangers)
152–53 **responsive** corresponding   154 **liberal conceit** elaborate design   57 **margent** i.e., marginal (explanatory) comment

Hamlet. Sir, I will walk here in the hall. If it please
175   his Majesty, it is the breathing time of day with me.°
       Let the foils be brought, the gentleman willing, and
       the King hold his purpose, I will win for him an I
       can; if not, I will gain nothing but my shame and
       the odd hits.

180 *Osric.* Shall I deliver you e'en so?

Hamlet. To this effect, sir, after what flourish your
       nature will.

Osric. I commend my duty to your lordship.

Hamlet. Yours, yours. [*Exit Osric.*] He does well to
185   commend it himself; there are no tongues else for's
       turn.

Horatio. This lapwing° runs away with the shell on his
       head.

Hamlet. 'A did comply, sir, with his dug° before 'a
190   sucked it. Thus has he, and many more of the
       same breed that I know the drossy age dotes on,
       only got the tune of the time and, out of an habit of
       encounter,° a kind of yeasty° collection, which
       carries them through and through the most fanned
195   and winnowed opinions; and do but blow them to
       their trial, the bubbles are out.°

                        Enter a Lord.

Lord. My lord, his Majesty commended him to you by
       young Osric, who brings back to him that you
       attend him in the hall. He sends to know if your
200   pleasure hold to play with Laertes, or that you will
       take longer time.

Hamlet. I am constant to my purposes; they follow the

---

175 **breathing time of day with me** time when I take exercise   187 **lapwing** (the new-hatched lapwing was thought to run around
with half its shell on its head)   189 **'A did comply, sir, with his dug** he
was ceremoniously polite to his mother's breast   192–93 **out of an
habit of encounter** out of his own superficial way of meeting and con-
versing with people   193 **yeasty** frothy   196 **the bubbles are out** i.e.,
they are blown away (the reference is to the "yeasty collection")

King's pleasure. If his fitness speaks, mine is ready;
now or whensoever, provided I be so able as now.

Lord. The King and Queen and all are coming down.   *205*

Hamlet. In happy time.°

Lord. The Queen desires you to use some gentle enter-
tainment° to Laertes before you fall to play.

Hamlet. She well instructs me.   [*Exit Lord.*]

Horatio. You will lose this wager, my lord.   *210*

Hamlet. I do not think so. Since he went into France
I have been in continual practice. I shall win at the
odds. But thou wouldst not think how ill all's here
about my heart. But it is no matter.

Horatio. Nay, good my lord——   *215*

Hamlet. It is but foolery, but it is such a kind of gain-
giving° as would perhaps trouble a woman.

Horatio. If your mind dislike anything, obey it. I will
forestall their repair hither and say you are not fit.

Hamlet. Not a whit, we defy augury. There is special   *220*
providence in the fall of a sparrow.° If it be now,
'tis not to come; if it be not to come, it will be now;
if it be not now, yet it will come. The readiness is
all. Since no man of aught he leaves knows, what
is't to leave betimes?° Let be.   *225*

A table prepared. [*Enter*] *Trumpets, Drums, and*
Officers with cushions; King, Queen, [*Osric,*] *and*
all the State, [*with*] *foils, daggers,* [*and stoups*
of wine borne in]; *and Laertes.*

King. Come, Hamlet, come, and take this hand from
me.

[*The King puts Laertes' hand into Hamlet's.*]

---

206 **In happy time** It is an opportune time   207–08 **to use some gentle**
entertainment to be courteous   217 **gaingiving** misgiving   221 **the**
fall of a sparrow (cf. Matthew 10:29 "Are not two sparrows sold for a
farthing? and one of them shall not fall on the ground without your Father")   225 **betimes** early

Hamlet. Give me your pardon, sir. I have done you
    wrong,
    But pardon't, as you are a gentleman.
    This presence° knows, and you must needs have
      heard,
230   How I am punished with a sore distraction.
    What I have done
    That might your nature, honor, and exception°
    Roughly awake, I here proclaim was madness.
    Was't Hamlet wronged Laertes? Never Hamlet.
235   If Hamlet from himself be ta'en away,
    And when he's not himself does wrong Laertes,
    Then Hamlet does it not, Hamlet denies it.
    Who does it then? His madness. If't be so,
    Hamlet is of the faction° that is wronged;
240   His madness is poor Hamlet's enemy.
    Sir, in this audience,
    Let my disclaiming from a purposed evil
    Free me so far in your most generous thoughts
    That I have shot my arrow o'er the house
    And hurt my brother.

245 *Laertes.*   .   I am satisfied in nature,
    Whose motive in this case should stir me most
    To my revenge. But in my terms of honor
    I stand aloof, and will no reconcilement
    Till by some elder masters of known honor
250   I have a voice and precedent° of peace
    To keep my name ungored. But till that time
    I do receive your offered love like love,
    And will not wrong it.

Hamlet.   I embrace it freely,
    And will this brother's wager frankly play.
    Give us the foils. Come on.

255 *Laertes.*   Come, one for me.

Hamlet. I'll be your foil,° Laertes. In mine ignorance

---

229 **presence** royal assembly   232 **exception** disapproval   239 **faction**
party, side   250 **voice and precedent** authoritative opinion justified by
precedent   256 **foil** (1) blunt sword (2) background (of metallic leaf)
for a jewel

Your skill shall, like a star i' th' darkest night,
Stick fiery off° indeed.

Laertes. You mock me, sir.

Hamlet. No, by this hand.

King. Give them the foils, young Osric. Cousin Hamlet, 260
You know the wager?

Hamlet. Very well, my lord.
Your grace has laid the odds o' th' weaker side.

King. I do not fear it, I have seen you both;
But since he is bettered,° we have therefore odds.

Laertes. This is too heavy; let me see another. 265

Hamlet. This likes me well. These foils have all a
length?

Prepare to play.

Osric. Ay, my good lord.

King. Set me the stoups of wine upon that table.
If Hamlet give the first or second hit,
Or quit° in answer of the third exchange, 270
Let all the battlements their ordnance fire.
The King shall drink to Hamlet's better breath,
And in the cup an union° shall he throw
Richer than that which four successive kings
In Denmark's crown have worn. Give me the cups, 275
And let the kettle° to the trumpet speak,
The trumpet to the cannoneer without,
The cannons to the heavens, the heaven to earth,
"Now the King drinks to Hamlet." Come, begin.
Trumpets the while.
And you, the judges, bear a wary eye. 280

Hamlet. Come on, sir.

Laertes. Come, my lord. *They play.*

Hamlet. One.

Laertes. No.

---

258 **Stick fiery off** stand out brilliantly   264 **bettered** has improved (?)
is regarded as better by the public (?)   270 **quit** repay, hit back
273 **union** pearl   276 **kettle** kettledrum

Hamlet.   Judgment?

Osric. A hit, a very palpable hit.
    Drum, trumpets, and shot. Flourish; a piece goes off.

Laertes.   Well, again.

King. Stay, give me drink. Hamlet, this pearl is thine.
    Here's to thy health. Give him the cup.

285 *Hamlet.* I'll play this bout first; set it by awhile.
    Come. [*They play.*] Another hit. What say you?

Laertes. A touch, a touch; I do confess't.

King. Our son shall win.

Queen.   He's fat,° and scant of breath.
    Here, Hamlet, take my napkin, rub thy brows.
290 The Queen carouses to thy fortune, Hamlet.

Hamlet. Good madam!

King.   Gertrude, do not drink.

Queen. I will, my lord; I pray you pardon me. [*Drinks.*]

King. [*Aside*] It is the poisoned cup; it is too late.

Hamlet. I dare not drink yet, madam—by and by.

295 *Queen.* Come, let me wipe thy face.

Laertes. My lord, I'll hit him now.

King.   I do not think't.

Laertes. [*Aside*] And yet it is almost against my con-
    science.

Hamlet. Come for the third, Laertes. You do but dally.
    I pray you pass with your best violence;
300 I am sure you make a wanton° of me.

Laertes. Say you so? Come on.   [*They*] *play.*

Osric. Nothing neither way.

Laertes. Have at you now!
        In scuffling they change rapiers, [*and both are
                                            wounded*].

288 **fat** (1) sweaty (2) out of training   300 **wanton** spoiled child

King.　　　　　　　　Part them. They are incensed.

Hamlet. Nay, come—again!　　　[*The Queen falls.*]

Osric.　　　　　　　Look to the Queen there, ho!

Horatio. They bleed on both sides. How is it, my lord?　*305*

Osric. How is't, Laertes?

Laertes. Why, as a woodcock to mine own springe,°
　Osric.
I am justly killed with mine own treachery.

Hamlet. How does the Queen?

King.　　　　　　　She sounds° to see them bleed.

Queen. No, no, the drink, the drink! O my dear
　Hamlet!
　The drink, the drink! I am poisoned.　　　[*Dies.*]　*310*

Hamlet. O villainy! Ho! Let the door be locked.
　Treachery! Seek it out.　　　　　[*Laertes falls.*]

Laertes. It is here, Hamlet. Hamlet, thou art slain;
　No med'cine in the world can do thee good.　　*315*
　In thee there is not half an hour's life.
　The treacherous instrument is in thy hand,
　Unbated and envenomed. The foul practice°
　Hath turned itself on me. Lo, here I lie,
　Never to rise again. Thy mother's poisoned.　*320*
　I can no more. The King, the King's to blame.

Hamlet. The point envenomed too?
　Then, venom, to thy work.　　　　*Hurts the King.*

All. Treason! Treason!

King. O, yet defend me, friends. I am but hurt.　*325*

Hamlet. Here, thou incestuous, murd'rous, damnèd
　Dane,
　Drink off this potion. Is thy union° here?
　Follow my mother.　　　　　*King dies.*

Laertes.　　　　　　He is justly served.

307 **springe** snare　309 **sounds** swoons　318 **practice** deception
327 **union** (1) the pearl put into the drink in 5.2.273; (2) the King's
poisonous (incestuous) marriage

It is a poison tempered° by himself.
330 Exchange forgiveness with me, noble Hamlet.
Mine and my father's death come not upon thee,
Nor thine on me!   *Dies.*

Hamlet. Heaven make thee free of it! I follow thee.
I am dead, Horatio. Wretched Queen, adieu!
335 You that look pale and tremble at this chance,
That are but mutes° or audience to this act,
Had I but time (as this fell sergeant,° Death,
Is strict in his arrest) O, I could tell you—
But let it be. Horatio, I am dead;
340 Thou livest; report me and my cause aright
To the unsatisfied.°

Horatio.   Never believe it.
I am more an antique Roman° than a Dane.
Here's yet some liquor left.

Hamlet.   As th' art a man,
Give me the cup. Let go. By heaven, I'll ha't!
345 O God, Horatio, what a wounded name,
Things standing thus unknown, shall live behind me!
If thou didst ever hold me in thy heart,
Absent thee from felicity° awhile,
And in this harsh world draw thy breath in pain,
To tell my story.   *A march afar off.* [*Exit Osric.*]
350   What warlike noise is this?

                                    Enter Osric.

Osric. Young Fortinbras, with conquest come from
      Poland,
To th' ambassadors of England gives
This warlike volley.

Hamlet.   O, I die, Horatio!
The potent poison quite o'ercrows° my spirit.
355 I cannot live to hear the news from England,

---

329 **tempered** mixed   336 **mutes** performers who have no words to
speak   337 **fell sergeant** dread sheriff's officer   341 **unsatisfied** unin-
formed   342 **antique Roman** (with reference to the old Roman fashion
of suicide)   348 **felicity** i.e., the felicity of death   354 **o'ercrows** over-
powers (as a triumphant cock crows over its weak opponent)

But I do prophesy th' election lights
On Fortinbras. He has my dying voice.
So tell him, with th' occurrents,° more and less,
Which have solicited°—the rest is silence.   *Dies.*

Horatio. Now cracks a noble heart. Good night, sweet
    Prince,   360
And flights of angels sing thee to thy rest.
                              [*March within.*]
Why does the drum come hither?

    *Enter Fortinbras, with the Ambassadors with
          Drum, Colors, and Attendants.*

Fortinbras. Where is this sight?

Horatio.   What is it you would see?
    If aught of woe or wonder, cease your search.

Fortinbras. This quarry° cries on havoc.° O proud
    Death,   365
What feast is toward° in thine eternal cell
That thou so many princes at a shot
So bloodily hast struck?

Ambassador.   The sight is dismal;
    And our affairs from England come too late.
The ears are senseless that should give us hearing   370
To tell him his commandment is fulfilled,
That Rosencrantz and Guildenstern are dead.
Where should we have our thanks?

Horatio.   Not from his° mouth,
    Had it th' ability of life to thank you.
He never gave commandment for their death.   375
But since, so jump° upon this bloody question,
You from the Polack wars, and you from England,
Are here arrived, give order that these bodies
High on a stage° be placèd to the view,
And let me speak to th' yet unknowing world   380
How these things came about. So shall you hear

358 **occurrents** occurrences   359 **solicited** incited   365 **quarry** heap
of slain bodies   365 **cries on havoc** proclaims general slaughter
366 **toward** in preparation   373 **his** (Claudius')   376 **jump** precisely
379 **stage** platform

Of carnal, bloody, and unnatural acts,
Of accidental judgments, casual° slaughters,
Of deaths put on by cunning and forced cause,
385 And, in this upshot, purposes mistook
Fall'n on th' inventors' heads. All this can I
Truly deliver.

Fortinbras.   Let us haste to hear it,
And call the noblest to the audience.
For me, with sorrow I embrace my fortune.
390 I have some rights of memory° in this kingdom,
Which now to claim my vantage doth invite me.

Horatio. Of that I shall have also cause to speak,
And from his mouth whose voice will draw on°
          more.
But let this same be presently performed,
Even while men's minds are wild, lest more mis-
395   chance
On° plots and errors happen.

Fortinbras.   Let four captains
Bear Hamlet like a soldier to the stage,
For he was likely, had he been put on,°
To have proved most royal; and for his passage°
400 The soldiers' music and the rite of war
Speak loudly for him.
Take up the bodies. Such a sight as this
Becomes the field,° but here shows much amiss.
Go, bid the soldiers shoot.

          Exeunt marching; after the which a peal of ordnance
                              are shot off.

          FINIS

383 **casual** not humanly planned, chance   390 **rights of memory** remembered claims   393 **voice will draw on** vote will influence
396 **On** on top of   398 **put on** advanced (to the throne)   399 **passage**
death   403 **field** battlefield

A Note on the Texts of *Hamlet*

Probably the most famous line in Western literature is "To be or not to be, that is the question," from Hamlet's soliloquy in 3.1.56–90. But in fact this soliloquy exists in three forms—in a text published in 1603, a text published in 1604–1605, and a text published in 1623. First, let's look at the beginning of the 1603 version. This book is a quarto (a fairly small book whose pages were made by folding a sheet of paper twice, producing four leaves, or eight pages); this edition is called Q1 because it is the first quarto version of *Hamlet*. If you are at all familiar with the speech, the Q1 version may strike you as comic, almost a parody. (Spelling and punctuation are modernized in the three versions given here.)

> To be or not to be, aye, there's the point
> To die, to sleep; is that all? Aye, all.
> No, to sleep, to dream, aye, marry, there it goes,
> For in that dream of death, when we awake,
> And borne before an everlasting judge,
> From whence no passenger ever returned,
> The undiscovered country, at whose sight
> The happy smile, and the accursed damned.
> But for this, the joyful hope of this.
> Who'd bear the scorns and flattery of the world,
> Scorned by the right rich, the rich cursed of the poor?
> The widow being oppressed, the orphan wronged,
> The taste of hunger, or a tyrant's reign. . . .

No, we did not mistakenly omit "That is the question." And even if this version were quoted in full, you would not find such familiar phrases as "the slings and arrows of outrageous fortune," or "take arms against a sea of troubles."

Before we comment on Q1, let's look at the beginning of the next version, from Q2 (i.e., the second quarto version), published in 1604–1605. This version will strike you as familiar. Line numbers keyed to the Signet text are added.

> To be or not to be: that is the question:
> Whether 'tis nobler in the mind to suffer
> The slings and arrows of outrageous fortune,
> Or to take arms against a sea of troubles,
> And by opposing end them. To die, to sleep—   60
> No more—and by a sleep to say we end
> The heartache, and the thousand natural shocks
> That flesh is heir to! 'Tis a consummation
> Devoutly to be wished. To die, to sleep—
> To sleep—perchance to dream: ay, there's the rub,   65
> For in that sleep of death what dreams may come
> When we have shuffled off this mortal coil,
> Must give us pause. There's the respect
> That makes calamity of so long life:
> For who would bear the whips and scorns of time,   70
> Th' oppressor's wrong, the proud man's contumely,
> The pangs of despised love, the law's delay. . . .
>
> (3.1.56–72)

The third version, almost the same as the second, appears in the collection of Shakespeare's plays called the First Folio, printed in 1623. (A folio consists of pages made by folding a large sheet only once rather than twice, thereby producing two leaves or four pages, instead of a quarto's four leaves and eight pages.) In the original printings, the second and third versions (Q2 and F) often differ in spelling and punctuation—for instance, in the first line of the Folio version, the word "question" is capitalized and it is followed by a colon, whereas in Q2 "question" is not capitalized and it is followed by a comma—but despite such differences the two versions of the speech are very close to each other.

Putting aside spelling and punctuation, the two chief differences in the quoted passage are "proud" (Q2) versus "poor" (F) in line 71, and "despised" (Q1) versus "disprized," i.e. "undervalued" (F) in line 72.

Let's now look at the three texts in some detail.

The First Quarto (Q1, 1603).

Only two copies of Q1 are extant. This version has 2,154 lines, which is to say that it is much shorter than Q2 (about 3,764 lines), and than F (about 3,535 lines). (Methods of counting lines differ, so you may find slightly different figures in some other source.) In this version, for example, Laertes's speech to Ophelia in 1.3, warning her against Hamlet (5–44), is less than half the length it is in Q2 and F. The Player's speech about Pyrrhus at 2.2.461–529 is twenty lines shorter, and Hamlet's praise of Horatio at 3.2.58–89 is a dozen lines shorter. In the nineteenth century Q1 was commonly regarded either as a stage version of the pre-Shakespearean *Hamlet* or as the early play with some revisions by Shakespeare, i.e. as a sort of first version of Shakespeare's *Hamlet*. Today almost everyone agrees that, partly because many speeches are much shorter than in Q2 and F, and partly because a fair amount of the text is banal and some passages are close to nonsense, whereas some other passages show Shakespeare at the top of his form, it is not a pre-Shakespearean play and it is not an early version by Shakespeare; rather, it is an actor's garbled memory of what Shakespeare wrote. A still-unexplained feature of this version, however, is the fact that Polonius is called Corambis—something that cannot be attributed to a faulty memory. Adding to the mystery is a German play on the Hamlet story, in which the character corresponding to Polonius is called Corambus. The German version presumably is derived from an English version brought to Germany by English players on tour in the seventeenth century, but why Corambis or Corambus became Polonius, or the other way around, is unclear.

Probably an actor who had performed in an abridged version of the play—maybe a version created for a company that toured the provinces—provided the printer with the copy. Such a text is characterized as a "reported text" or a "post-performance" text or a "memorial reconstruction"—something based on the memory of an actor or actors.

In this instance, it is all but certain that the actor who gave the copy to the printer had played Marcellus. Why Marcellus? Because his lines in Q1 correspond very closely with the two other texts, and indeed the lines of characters who are on stage at the same time as Marcellus correspond pretty well, whereas many other passages depart widely and wildly—presumably because the actor was offstage and he was more or less forced to invent speeches he only vaguely recalled. On the other hand, because Lucianus's six-line speech in 3.2.261–66 is perfect—and because Voltemand's long speech in 2.2.60–79 corresponds closely with the other texts, it is likely that the actor who played Marcellus doubled in these other roles.

Texts that are not derived from Shakespeare's manuscript, or from a scribe's clean copy of either the manuscript or from a prompt book prepared for the company, are called "bad" quartos. Early in the twentieth century, the word "bad" suggested not only that the text was inaccurate but also that the actor who provided it had betrayed his company by selling his memory to an unscrupulous printer. Such a book was said to be "pirated"—but in fact we do not know that treachery or piracy were involved. The title page of Q1 bears the initials of one publisher and the name of a second, which suggests that there was nothing illegitimate in the publication.

What value can such a text have? Only a little, but especially in recent years, when there has been an emphasis on the play as a *performance* rather than as a text, claims have been made that whereas the two other versions are "literary," the Q1 version gives us the play as it was actually produced on the stage. It is thus supposedly closer to the real *Hamlet*, the *Hamlet* that the Elizabethans saw, than are the other texts, which are said in any case to be impossibly long. Thus, Graham Holderness and Bryan Loughrey say in their introduction to a reprint (1992) of Q1, "What we can assume with reasonable confidence is that this text comes closer than the other texts to actual Jacobean stage practice" (page 14). But we *cannot* say that this text gives us the play as it was performed. The title page says that the play "hath beene diuerse times acted by his Highnesse seruants in the Cittie of London: as also in the two Vniuersities of Cambridge and Oxford, and else-where," but this is a statement about the play, not about this particular text; and in any case it is an advertisement, not a document whose truth is beyond question. At best Q1 gives us the play as one actor or perhaps a few actors *remembered* it. Further, we don't have direct access to their memories, but only to the compositor's version, filled with printer's errors. For instance, old Norway in Q1 is said to be "impudent" ("impudent / And bed-rid"), but in Q2 (1.2.29) he is "impotent" ("impotent and bedred"). The context (whether "bed-rid" or "bedred") clearly calls for Q2's "impotent," not Q1's "impudent." Whether the actor's memory failed or the compositor misread the handwriting or the compositor's mind wandered we cannot know, but one hardly wants to say that because Q1 has "impudent," this is the word that was spoken in production, much less that it therefore is quite as legitimate as whatever Shakespeare wrote in his lost manuscript.

On the other hand, we can value Q1 for at least two reasons. First, it includes some stage directions not found in the other texts that do indeed seem to give us a sense of how the play was staged. For instance, Q1 has a stage direction, *"Enter Ofelia playing on a Lute, and her haire downe singing"* (4.5.20 s.d.) where Q2 has merely *"Enter Ophelia,"* and the Folio text (1623) has merely *"Enter Ophelia distracted."* A second example of an interesting stage direction in Q1: only Q1 tells us that Hamlet leaps into Ophelia's grave in 5.1.260: *"Hamlet leapes in after Leartes"* (sic). (This stage direction, by the way, causes uneasiness among some editors because it makes Hamlet the aggressor. See the footnote on the passage.) Again, this is not to say that these stage directions are Shakespeare's; the most that we can say is that they help to give us a glimpse of what an Elizabethan audience may have seen.

The second value that editors find in Q1 is this: It may clarify puzzling passages in Q2 and F. For instance, in one of his soliloquies, "O, what a rogue and peasant slave am I" (2.2.560), in Q2 Hamlet speaks of himself (incoherently?) as "the sonne of a deere murthered," and in F he similarly speaks of himself as "the Sonne of the Deere murthered." In Q1, however, he speaks of himself as "The sonne of my deare father." Editors (including the present editor) who believe that Q2 and F—probably because of a compositor's error—do not make sense, and who believe that Hamlet must be speaking of his "dear murdered father" or "dear father murdered," are glad to find the word "father" in the corresponding passage in Q1, and they use the reading in Q1 to justify their emendation of either Q2 or F. It should be mentioned, however, that Philip Edwards, the editor of *Hamlet* in the New Cambridge Shakespeare (1985), rejects this emendation. Edwards, staying with the Folio, prints "the dear murderèd"; in a footnote he glosses the expression as meaning "the loved victim."

In short, despite those enthusiastic amateur theater groups who occasionally stage Q1 and who say that it plays well on the stage—of course they say it does, since they wouldn't have produced it, nonsense and all, if they didn't think it would play well—the uses of Q1 are extremely limited.

The Second Quarto (Q2, 1604–1605).

Q2, the second published version, printed in 1604 and 1605, contains about 3,764 lines. It is the longest of Shakespeare's texts (it is almost twice as long as *Macbeth*), and it claims to be "Newly imprinted and enlarged to almost as much againe as it was, according to the true and perfect Coppie." (The title page, which makes this claim, is reproduced as our frontispiece.) Despite its length, however, it omits some material that is found in the third text, the Folio, which we will look at later.

There is much dispute about exactly what "the true and perfect Coppie" was, but it may well have been Shakespeare's manuscript—sheets that scholars customarily call "foul papers," as opposed, for instance, to a neat scribal copy (a "fair copy"), or a scribal copy with later annotations

that would serve as a prompt copy for actors. A brief re-
minder is called for at this point: When we speak of Shakespeare's "completed manuscript" or his "final version" we
may be talking about something that never existed. No
Shakespeare play survives in manuscript; we do not know
how he worked, and we do not know if he thought of the
play as finished when he turned over a manuscript, or—a
very different thing—when the play was in some degree reworked during rehearsal. And we do not know if, after the
early productions, he revised the play for later productions.
Fifty years ago almost no one talked of the possibility that
Shakespeare revised plays after they had been staged, but
today some scholars argue that the texts of *Hamlet*, *The
Second Part of Henry IV*, *Troilus and Cressida*, *Othello*,
and *King Lear* all show evidence of revision, i.e. there are
(some people say) two authentic versions for each play.

Now to return to Q2 as "foul papers." At the beginning of
2.1 we get a stage direction: *"Enter old Polonius, with his
man or two."* Such a direction suggests foul papers rather
than a prompt copy; Shakespeare, in the process of beginning the scene, was not yet entirely sure about how the
scene would go—maybe he would need two servants, and
maybe he wouldn't. As it turns out, only one servant, Reynaldo, is needed. Presumably in a copy prepared for a stage
production (a promptbook), such a direction would be corrected to something like *"Enter Polonius, and Reynaldo,"*
and (if we may briefly get ahead of our story) that is exactly
what we do find in the next version we will look at, the Folio version, which surely is a text based on a manuscript
that reflects a production.

Of course *"with his man or two"* might survive from
Shakespeare's manuscript into a clean copy that a scribe
prepared for the theatrical company, but additional evidence that the source of Q2 was Shakespeare's manuscript
is the fact that Q2 prints many words that are obvious mis-
readings of handwriting, or guesses as to what the writer intended. Thus, in 3.2.366 it gives *"the vmber"* where the
sense requires *"thumb"* (Hamlet is talking about fingering a
musical instrument), and in 4.7.6 it gives *"the King"* where
the sense requires *checking*."

Further, Q2 seems to include some material that Shake-speare intended to delete. Consider this passage from the Player Queen's speech in 3.2:

For women feare too much, euen as they loue,
And womens feare and loue hold quantitie,
Eyther none, in neither ought, or in extremitie. . . .   (172–74)

Now, the fact that the first line does not rhyme, in a speech in which all of the other lines rhyme in pairs, is immediately a cause for suspicion. Something is wrong here. In his thoughtful Arden edition, Harold Jenkins suggests that the second quoted line seems to be a restatement of the first line, a fresh start, but the first (unrhymed) line was mistakenly printed. Further, in the third line, "Eyther none" probably was a false start that was replaced by "In neither," but, again, the compositor mistakenly printed words that should have been deleted.

In addition to working from some sort of manuscript, the compositors of Q2 made occasional use of a printed text, Q1; especially in the first five scenes there are otherwise inexplicable similarities in typography and layout. Apparently the compositors of Q2 consulted Q1 when they were puzzled by something in their manuscript.

The Folio (1623).

The third early printed version (3,535 lines), in the posthumous First Folio entitled *Mr. William Shakespeares Comedies, Histories, & Tragedies,* is a little shorter than Q2. The title page says the plays are "Published according to the True Originall Copies," but exactly what the printer's copy was for *Hamlet* is uncertain. Most students of the problem believe the compositor worked from a heavily annotated copy of Q2—the text in F contains some of Q2's errors as well as some new errors, and it also contains some of Q2's unusual spellings—but G. R. Hibbard in his Oxford edition of *Hamlet* (1987) offers strong arguments against his view. Still, even if the compositors of F did not use Q2 (or the 1611 reprint of it, Q3) as printer's copy, they may have consulted it on occasion, when their manuscript was unclear.

In any case, although F is slightly shorter than Q2, it is not simply a shortened version; it contains about eighty lines *not* found in Q2. Consider this small example. In the scene with the grave diggers, in Q2 the grave digger (in the speech prefixes he is called a clown) identifies the skull of Yorick, and we then (5.1.183–85) get this dialogue:

> *Ham.* This?
> *Clow.* Een that.
> *Ham.* Alas poore *Yoricke*, I knew him *Horatio*. . . .

But in the Folio text, Hamlet's second speech is different:

> *Ham.* Let me see. Alas poore *Yorick*, I knew him *Horatio*. . . .

The Folio's addition of "Let me see" is very interesting. Probably the words were not in Shakespeare's foul papers (Q2); we can strongly suspect that "Let me see"—words indicating that Hamlet takes the skull from the grave digger— was a bit of dialogue added during the course of producing the play.

True, some of the lines that appear only in F may have been in the manuscript for Q2 and were accidentally omitted when Q2 was printed, but some of the F-only material must be additions. Additions by whom? Are they revisions that actors made as they worked and reworked the play? Or are they revisions that Shakespeare himself made, perhaps after he saw the early productions of the play? Here are some examples of small additions which to most editors sound like the sorts of things that actors might add. In 2.2.217, where in Q2 Hamlet says, "You cannot take from me . . . ," in F he says, "You cannot, sir, take from me . . ." In Hamlet's second soliloquy, "O, what a rogue and peasant slave am I," in an extended passage of blank verse (unrhymed lines of ten syllables) we get a line that consists only of "O, vengeance" (593). A third example, and the most interesting, concerns Hamlet's last words in 5.2.359. In both Q2 and F they are, "the rest is silence," but F goes on to add, as his utterance, "O, o, o, o." This string of *o*'s probably is meant to represent a sigh, and it may well be something that an actor added to Shakespeare's text.

Consider a slightly longer but still a brief example of an addition in F. In Q2, after Rosencrantz and Guildenstern tell Hamlet he must go with them and inform the king where Polonius's body is, Hamlet says, "Bring me to him." But in F, Hamlet adds to these words, "Hide fox, and all after" (4.2.30–31)—presumably the cry from a game like hide-and-seek—and he probably runs off. Is this an authorial revision, adding liveliness to the scene and also perhaps suggesting (at least to Rosencrantz and Guildenstern) that Hamlet is a bit mad? Or is it, on the other hand, despite its theatrical effectiveness, a showy bit added by actors, and in fact *less* effective as an exit line than the simple "Bring me to him"? Or is it a revision—maybe for the worse—by Shakespeare himself?

Even if we grant that many of the small additions found in F probably are the work of actors, we should remember that Shakespeare was an actor, a member of the company that bought his plays, and we should not be too quick to dismiss the changes as unauthorized additions by meddlesome actors.

What of the longer passages found only in F, notably the thirty-odd lines in 2.2 concerning what is conventionally called The War of the Theaters, lines about the competition that companies of children were offering to the adult companies? No one doubts that the passage is authentic Shakespeare, but is it evidence that Shakespeare revised the play after it had already been on the stage? That is, was this passage absent from the manuscript behind Q2 and added in the manuscript behind F, or was it present in the Q2 ms but omitted from the printed version (perhaps because it seemed to be an undramatic digression), in which case it was not so much *added* to F as it was *restored* by F? The short answer is that inconclusive arguments have been offered on both sides. Similarly, take the passage in 5.2.57—

which is found only in F—where Hamlet, talking to Horatio, says of Rosencrantz and Guildenstern,

Why, man, they did make love to this employment.

Did Q2 accidentally omit this line, or did Shakespeare add it, in the course of revising the play, in order to further reveal Hamlet's character, specifically to show him justifying the action by which he sends these two men to their deaths?

The 220-odd lines *not* in F also raise questions. For instance, the soliloquy beginning "How all occasions do inform against me" (4.4.32), present in Q2, is not in F. Does its omission let us glimpse Shakespeare revising the play? Did Shakespeare come to think (as some readers and viewers think) that the speech is redundant? Or did he decide to alter the character of Hamlet, in this case by revealing less of his thoughts? Or is the omission due merely to the company's attempt to shorten the performance time of the play? The same questions can be asked of another passage not in F, Hamlet's comment to his mother about Rosencrantz and Guildenstern:

There's letters sealed, and my two schoolfellows,
Whom I will trust as I will adders fanged,
They bear the mandate; they must sweep my way
And marshal me to knavery. Let it work;
For 'tis sport to have the enginer
Hoist with his own petar, and 't shall go hard
But I will delve one yard below their mines
And blow them to the moon. O, 'tis most sweet
When in one line two crafts directly meet.   (3.4.203–11)

Did Shakespeare have second thoughts, some time after the play had been on the stage, and decide to delete this passage, perhaps because it showed an unattractive cast to Hamlet's thinking? Or perhaps because it is inconsistent with Hamlet's later speech, when he tells Horatio that during the voyage to England he was suddenly inspired in a moment of "rashness" to forge the papers that send

Rosencrantz and Guildenstern to their deaths? If so, in the course of removing the passage he deleted what was to become one of his most famous phrases, "Hoist with his own petar."

In short, in F, some omissions of material that is present in Q2 are very brief, and may be accidental; other omissions are longer, and must be deliberate cuts, but we do not know if the cuts were made by Shakespeare or by someone or some group of actors charged with preparing a text for production. (It is uncertain how a manuscript became a promptbook.) Conceivably, some omissions are due to Shakespeare, some to the company, and some to carelessness.

There are also several hundred small differences—variants—between Q2 and F, such as the famous "too too solid flesh" of F, versus the "sallied" (i.e. sullied) flesh of Q2. Similarly, in 1.4.49, speaking to the ghost, Hamlet says in Q2 that its bones were "quietly interr'd," but in F he says they were "quietly enurn'd." Did Shakespeare in the course of revising think that "interred" was a bit bland, and therefore substitute "inurned"? Or did an actor make the change—or did a compositor misread the manuscript? Whether such differences are due to Shakespeare revising, actors altering the text, or compositors blundering (perhaps the word was the same in both manuscripts, but one compositor got it right and one got it wrong), cannot be established. Possibly some are authorial revisions, some are alterations made by actors, and some are errors made by compositors; everyone agrees, however, that in *some* instances (as when Q2 gives the nonsensical *"the vmber"* and F gives the meaningful *"thumb"*), Q2 is mistaken and F is correct.

It should also be mentioned that F includes some stage directions, such as "On scuffling they change Rapiers," that suggest it is based on a text prepared for performance—but it also omits many necessary exits and entrances. Perhaps the most we can say about the copy for F is that whoever made it began with Shakespeare's foul papers and added some stage directions and some material—whether by

Shakespeare or by the actors is uncertain—that has come to be part of the play.

The Present Text

Given the fact that Q2 contains about 220 lines not found in F, and that F contains about 80 lines not found in Q2, and that there are hundreds of small differences between these two texts, what text does an editor print? The editors of the Oxford edition of Shakespeare's complete works (1986) chose the Folio as the control text for *Hamlet*, and print the Q2-only passages at the end of the play. This means, to take only one example, that the reader does not encounter the great soliloquy, "How all occasions do inform against me" (4.4.33–66), except out of context, in the appendix. The Oxford decision obviously was considered unsatisfactory by the editors of the Norton Shakespeare (1997), who use the Oxford text, because in the Norton edition the Q2 passages are restored to their appropriate places within the play itself, but (in deference to Oxford?) in a different typeface (italic) and with different numbering, thereby alerting the reader that these passages are, so to speak, stepchildren. In effect the italic typeface causes the passages to stick out; material that Oxford meant to minimize, Norton inadvertently emphasizes.

Harold Jenkins in the excellent Arden edition (1982), on the other hand, uses Q2 as the control text, and he omits F-only passages that he takes to be interpolations by actors. Thus, in the soliloquy known as "O, what a rogue and peasant slave am I" (2.2.560), after the line in which Hamlet says (speaking of Claudius) "Remorseless, treacherous, lecherous, kindless villain!" Jenkins omits the short line that consists only of "O, vengeance" (593). In a footnote he explains: "F's *Oh Vengeance* has all the marks of an actor's addition. Hamlet accuses himself of cursing . . . but not of threats, and his change from self-reproach to the pursuit of retribution occurs only at [600]" (page 272). This reasoning sounds plausible, but let's turn to another excellent edition of *Hamlet*, Philip Edwards's volume in the New Cambridge Shakespeare. Edwards takes F as the control text, and he therefore includes "O vengeance." In a footnote he offers the following comment on the line: "This cry, the great climax of the rant with which Hamlet emulates the Player, exhausts his futile self-recrimination, and he turns, in proper disgust, from a display of verbal histrionics to more practical things. Q2 omits the phrase altogether, and many editors unfortunately follow suit. This short line and the silence after it are the pivot of the speech" (page 142). Edwards, by the way, does include the Q2-only lines within his text, but he encloses them within square brackets.

The lesson that we can learn from these two footnotes is surely this: Editors following F ought not to omit Q2 material simply because their aesthetic sense tells them that Shakespeare must have decided to cut it, nor, if they are following Q2, should they omit F material because their aesthetic sense tells them that an actor must have added it. (An exception to the rule: The present editor could not bear to follow Hamlet's "The rest is silence" with F's "O, o, o, o.")

In the Overview that begins this volume, the general editor comments on the "instability" of the text. No manuscript of a play by Shakespeare survives; we have only printed versions, some perhaps based on his drafts, some perhaps based on prompt copies made for the playhouse by a professional scribe, some perhaps based (this is a relatively new view) on playhouse manuscripts that show Shakespeare's revision of his earlier work. In any case we can be sure only that the printed text is a "socialized" document, the product not only of Shakespeare, but of whoever prepared the copy for the compositors, and of the compositors themselves, who made of the copy what they could. And the product of the editors, too, who (whether they know it or not) make countless decisions that make each text distinctive. In the unattractive idiom of today, a given text, whether Q2 or F or, for that matter, the present edition, is only "a particular instantiation of the play" (David Scott Kastan, in *Shakespeare Studies* 24 [1996], page 35). The great editors early in this century sought to establish a text that revealed "authorial intent," but today, largely under the influence of Michel Foucault's "What Is an Author?" and Roland Barthes's "The Death of the Author," editors are likely to insist that "authorial intent" is a will-o'-the-wisp. Thus, in Kastan's words, editors who give a "socialized" or "theatrical" version of the text can claim to recognize "the very social and material mediations that permit (both authorial and nonauthorial) intentions to be realized in print and in performance" (page 33).

Editors who hold that Q2 and F are two distinct "instantiations" of *Hamlet* rather than two imperfect texts of *Hamlet* argue that if we combine the texts—"conflate" them is the technical term—we accomplish nothing useful and in fact are producing a text that never was printed or staged in Shakespeare's day. Thus, Stanley Wells and Gary Taylor explain in *William Shakespeare: A Textual Companion* (1988), a massive volume that accompanies the Oxford *Complete Works,* that Hamlet's motivation for reconciliation with Laertes differs in the two versions. To combine them, Wells and Taylor argue, is absurd. In the Quarto, and only in the Quarto, an anonymous lord says to Hamlet, "The Queen desires you to use some gentle entertainment to Laertes before you fall to play" (5.2.207–08), whereas in the Folio, and only in the Folio, Hamlet says,

> But I am very sorry, good Horatio,
> That to Laertes I forgot myself.
> For by the image of my cause I see
> The portraiture of his. I'll court his favors.
> But sure the bravery* of his grief did put me
> Into a tow'ring passion. (75–80)

In their *Textual Companion* the Oxford editors say,

> Thus, in Q2 Gertrude tells Hamlet to attempt a reconciliation with Laertes, just before Hamlet attempts such a reconciliation. In F, where this passage does not appear, Gertrude is in no way responsible for prompting this change in Hamlet's behaviour. . . . In F Hamlet himself decides, without the need of any prompting from Gertrude or anyone else, to seek a reconciliation with Laertes. . . . Q2 and F thus give two entirely different motivations for the crucial change in Hamlet's behaviour to Laertes.

*Bravado.

The traditional conflated text, in sorry contrast, instead combines these two explanations, without comment, making the anonymous lord's entrance and his message a wholly superfluous intrusion upon the dramatic progress of the play's final scene. (Page 400)

This is a bit strong. After all, to say that "in Q2 Gertrude tells Hamlet to attempt a reconciliation," when in fact all that we get is an anonymous lord reporting, in one line, a message from the Queen, is to give to one bland line much more weight than is appropriate. Moreover, a conflated text does not produce any contradiction or absurdity; rather, it lets us see Hamlet, entirely on his own, tell Horatio that he will apologize to Laertes, and a little later it lets us hear that the Queen (who, after all, was not privy to the conversation between Hamlet and Horatio) would like Hamlet to apologize. There is not the slightest inconsistency or redundancy.

Given that Wells and Taylor use this instance of conflation as a horrible example, it apparently is a worst-case scenario. Editors (and readers and viewers) must ask themselves which does more violence to *Hamlet*, inclusion of all of the lines of both texts, or omission of passages—some of them consisting of many lines—because either the Q2 or F omitted them. The present editor, with only the mildest of misgivings, has elected to conflate the texts. Readers will find not only Hamlet's statement that he will apologize to Laertes but also Gertrude's expressed wish (through an anonymous lord) that he do so. Readers will also find Hamlet's comment on the conflict between the companies of adult actors and the companies of boy actors in 2.2 (only in F), Hamlet's comment on hoisting enemies with their own petar in 3.4 (only in Q), and dozens of other lines, too, that some editors relegate to an appendix, where of course they are not read within the context of the play.

Finally, truth in packaging requires that readers be reminded that even in reading a conflated text they are not getting all of Shakespeare's words and nothing but those words. Editors must decide, to give only two now-familiar instances out of many instances, whether Hamlet speaks of "solid flesh" or "sallied [i.e. sullied] flesh," and whether he says his father was "interred" or "enurned." Editors try to make intelligent choices, which usually means that they believe they can give good reasons for their choices, but this does not mean that the editor whose decisions are theory-driven necessarily makes the best decisions. Given the facts that no manuscripts of Shakespeare's plays survive, that we do not know how these lost manuscripts were prepared to become texts for the playhouse, and that we can only conjecture about what sorts of copy the printers worked from, informed guesswork must play a role in preparing a modern edition.

The present edition takes the Second Quarto—the longest of the three early versions—as the control text, but, as the preceding discussion indicates, an editor must also make use of the Folio. Neither the First Quarto nor the Second Quarto is divided into scenes; the Folio indicates only 1.1, 1.2, 1.3, 2.1, and 2.2. The Signet Classic edition, to allow for easy reference, follows the traditional divisions of the Globe edition, placing them (as well as indications of locale) within square brackets to indicate that they are editorial, not authorial. Punctuation and spelling are modernized (*and* is given as *an* when if means "if"), obvious typographical errors are corrected, abbreviations are expanded, speech prefixes are regularized, and the positions of stage directions slightly altered where necessary. Other departures from the Second Quarto are listed below. First is given the adopted reading, in italic, and then the Second Quarto reading, in roman. The vast majority of these adopted readings are from the Folio; if an adopted reading is not from the Folio, the fact is indicated by a bracketed remark explaining, for example, that it is drawn from the First Quarto [Q1] or the Second Folio [F2] or an editor's conjecture [ed].

1.1.16 *soldier* souldiers   63 *Polacks* [F has "Pollax"] pollax   68 *my* mine   73 *why* with   73 *cast* cost   88 *those* these   91 *returned* returne   94 *designed* [F2] design   112 *mote* [ed] moth   121 *feared* [ed] feare   138 *you* your   140 *at it* it   142 s.d. *Exit Ghost* [Q2 omits]

1.2.1 s.d. *Councilors* [ed] Counsaile: as   41 s.d. *Exit Voltemand and Cornelius* [Q2 omits]   58 *He hath* Hath   67 *so* so much   77 *good* coold 82 *shapes* [ed; F has "shewes"] chapes 96 *a mind* or minde 132 *self-slaughter* seale slaughter 133 *weary* wary 137 *to this* thus 143 *would* should 175 *to drink deep* for to drinke 178 *to see* to 209 *Where, as* [ed] Whereas 224 *Indeed, indeed, sirs* Indeede Sirs 237 *Very like, very like* Very like 238 *hundred* hundreth 257 *foul* fonde

1.3.3 *convoy is* conuay in 12 *bulk* bulkes 18 *For he himself is subject to his birth* [Q2 omits] 49 *like a* a 68 *thine* thy 74 *Are* Or 75 *be* boy 76 *loan* loue 83 *invites* inuests 109 *Tend'ring* [Q1] Wrong [F has "Roaming"] 115 *springes* springs 123 *parley* parle 125 *tether* tider 131 *beguile* beguide

1.4.1 *shrewdly* shroudly 2 *a nipping* nipping 6 s.d. *go* [ed] goes 19 *clepe* [ed] clip 27 *the* [ed] their 33 *Their* [ed] His 36 *evil* [ed] eale 57 s.d. *Ghost beckons Hamlet* Beckins 69 *my lord* my 70 *summit* [ed] somnet [F has "sonnet"] 82 *artere* [ed] arture [F has "artire"] 87 *imagination* imagion

1.5.47 *what a* what 55 *lust* but 56 *sate* sort 64 *leperous* leaprous 68 *posset* possesse 91 s.d. *Exit* [Q2 omits] 95 *stiffly* swiftly 113 *Horatio and Marcellus (Within)* Enter Horatio and Marcellus [Q2 gives the speech to Horatio] 116 *bird* and 122 *heaven, my lord* heauen 132 *Look you, I'll* I will 170 *some'er* [ed] so mere [F has "so ere"]

2.1. s.d. *Reynaldo* or two 28 *Faith, no* Fayth 38 *warrant* wit 39 *sullies* sallies 40 *i' th'* with 52–53 *at "friend or so," and "gentleman"* [Q2 omits] 112 *quoted* coted

2.2.43 *Assure you* I assure! 57 *o'erhasty* hastie 58 s.d. *Enter Polonius, Voltemand, and Cornelius* Enter Embassadors 90 *since brevity* breuitie 108 s.d. *the letter* [Q2 omits, but has "letter" at side of line 116] 126 *above* about 137 *winking* working 143 *his* her 148 *watch* wath 149 *a lightness* lightnes 151 *'tis this* this 167 s.d. *Enter Hamlet reading on a book* Enter Hamlet 190 *far gone, far gone* far gone 205 *you yourself* your selfe 205 *should be* shall growe 212 *sanity* sanctity 214–15 *and suddenly . . . between him* [Q2 omits] 217 *will* will not 227 *excellent* extent 231 *overhappy* euer happy 232 *cap* lap 240 *but that* but the 243–74 *Let me question . . . dreadfully attended* [Q2 omits] 278 *even* euer 285 *Why anything* Any thing 312 *a piece* peece 318 *woman* women 329 *of me* on me 332–33 *the clown . . . o' th' sere* [from F, but F has "tickled a" for "tickle o' "; Q2 omits] 334 *blank* black 345–70 *Hamlet. How comes . . . load too* [Q2 omits] 350 *berattle* [ed; F has "be-ratled"; Q2 omits] 357 *most like* [ed; F has "like most"; Q2 omits] 381 *lest my* let me 407–08 *tragical-historical, tragical-comical-historical-pastoral* [Q2 omits] 434 *By'r Lady* by lady 439 *French falconers* friendly Fankners 454 *affectation* affection 457 *tale* talke 467 *heraldry* heraldy 485 *Then senseless Ilium* [Q2 omits] 492 *And like* Like 506 *fellies* [ed] follies 515 *Mobled queen is good* [F has "Inobled" for "Mobled"; Q2 omits] 525 *husband's* husband 530 *whe'r* [ed] where 550–51 *a need* neede 551 *or sixteen lines* lines, or sixteene lines 556 *till* tell 564 *his visage* the visage 569 *to Hecuba* to her 571 *the cue* that 590 *ha' fatted* [F has "have fatted"] a fatted 593 *O, vengeance* [Q2 omits] 595 *father* [Q4; Q2 and F omit] 599 *scullion* stallion 611 *devil, and the devil* deale, and the deale

3.1.32–33 *myself (lawful espials) Will* myself Wee'le 46 *loneliness* lowliness 55 *Let's withdraw* with-draw 83 *cowards of us all* cowards 85 *sicklied* sickled 92 *well, well, well* well 107 *your honesty* you 121 *to a nunnery* a Nunry 129 *knaves all* knaues 139 *Go, farewell,* farewell 146 *lisp* list 148 *your ignorance* ignorance 155 *expectancy* expectation 160 *that* what 162 *feature* stature 164 [Q2 concludes the line with a stage direction, "Exit"] 191 *unwatched* vnmatcht

3.2.1 *pronounced* pronound 24 *own feature* feature 28 *the which* which 31 *praise* praysd 39 *us, sir* vs 47 s.d. *Exit Players* [Q2 omits] 51 s.d. *Exit Polonius* [Q2 omits] 54 *ho* [F has "hoa"] howe 91 *detecting* detected 91 s.d. *Rosencrantz . . . Flourish* [Q2 omits] 117–18 *Hamlet. I mean . . . my lord* [Q2 omits] 140 s.d. *sound* [ed] sounds 140 s.d. *very lovingly* [Q2 omits] 140 s.d. *She kneels . . . unto him* [Q2 omits] 140 s.d. *Exeunt* [Q2 omits] 142 *is miching* munching 147 *keep counsel* keepe 161 *ground* the ground 169 *your* our 174 *In neither* Eyther none, in neither 175 *love* Lord 196 *like* the 205 *Grief joys* Greefe ioy 225 *An* [ed] And 229 *a* I be a 233 s.d. *sleeps* [Q2 omits] 234 s.d. *Exit* Exeunt 262 *Confederate* Considerat 264 *infected* inuected 266 s.d. *Pours the poison in his ears* [Q2 omits] 272 *Hamlet. What . . . fire* [Q2 omits] 282–83 *two Provincial* prouinciall 316 *start* stare 325 *my business* busines 366 *and thumb* & the vmber 375 *the top of my* my 379 *you can* you 394–95 *Polonius . . . friends* Leaue me friends. I will, say so. By and by is easily said 397 *breathes* breakes 399 *bitter business as the day* buisnes as the bitter day 404 *daggers* dagger

3.3.19 *huge* hough 22 *ruin* raine 23 *with a* a 50 *pardoned* pardon 58 *shove* showe 73 *pat* but 79 *hire and salary* base and silly

3.4.5–6 *with him . . . Mother, Mother, Mother* [Q2 omits] 7 *warrant* wait 21 *inmost* most 23 *ho* [F has "hoa"] how 23 *ho* [F has "hoa"] how 25 s.d. *kills Polonius* [Q2 omits] 53 *That roars . . . index* [Q2 gives to Hamlet] 60 *heaven-kissing* heaue, a kissing 89 *panders* pardons 90 *mine eyes into my very soul* my very eyes into my soule 91 *grainèd* greeued 92 *will not* will 98 *tithe* kyth 140 *Ecstasy* [Q2 omits] 144 *And I* And 159 *live* leaue 166 *Refrain tonight* to refraine night 180 *Thus* This 187 *ravel* rouell 216 *foolish* most foolish 218 s.d. *exit Hamlet, tugging in Polonius* Exit

4.1.35 *dragged* dreg'd

4.2.1 s.d. *Enter Hamlet* Enter Hamlet, Rosencraus, and others 2 *Gentlemen. (Within) Hamlet! Lord Hamlet!* [Q2 omits] 4 s.d. *Enter Rosencrantz and Guildenstern* [Q2 omits] 6 *Compounded* Compound 18 *ape* apple 30–31 *Hide fox, and all after* [Q2 omits]

4.3.15 *Ho* [F has "Hoa"] How 43 *With fiery quickness* [Q2 omits] 52 *and so* so 68 *were ne'er begun* will nere begin

4.5.16 *Queen* [Q2 gives line 16 as part of the previous speech] 20 s.d. *Enter Ophelia distracted* Enter Ophelia [placed after line 16] 39 *grave* ground 42 *God* good 52 *clothes* close 57 *Indeed, la* Indeede 73 s.d. *Exit* [Q2 omits] 82 *in their* in 89 *his* this 96 *Queen. Alack, what noise is this* [Q2 omits] 97 *are* is 106 *They* The 142 *swoopstake* [ed] soopstake 152 s.d. *Let her come in* [Q2 gives to Laertes] 157 *Till* Tell 160 *an old* a poore 161–63 *Nature . . . loves* [Q2 omits] 165 *Hey . . . hey nony* [Q2 omits] 181 *O, you must* you may 186 *affliction* afflictions 194 *All flaxen* Flaxen 198 *Christian souls, I pray God* Christians soules 199 *see this* this

4.6.9 *an't* and 23 *good turn* turne 27 *bore* bord 31 *He* So 32 *give you* you

4.7.6 *proceeded* proceede 14 *conjunctive* concliue 20 *Would* Worke 22 *loud a wind* loued Arm'd 24 *And* But 24 *had* haue 36 *How now . . . Hamlet* [Q2 omits] 42 s.d. *Exit Messenger* [Q2 omits] 46 *your pardon* you pardon 47 *and more strange return* returne 48 *Hamlet* [Q2 omits] 56 *shall live* liue 62 *checking* the King 88 *my* me 115 *wick* [ed] weeke 119 *changes* change 122 *spendthrift* [ed] spend thrifts 125 *in deed* [ed] indeede 134 *on* ore 138 *pass* pace 140 *for that* for 156 *ha't* hate 159 *prepared* prefard 167 *hoar* horry 171 *cold* cull-cold

5.1.9 *se offendendo* so offended 12 *Argall* or all 35–38 *Other. Why . . . without arms* [Q2 omits] 44 *that frame* that 56 s.d. *Enter Hamlet and Horatio afar off* Enter Hamlet and Horatio [Q2 places after line 65] 61 *stoup* soope 71 *daintier* dintier 90 *mazzard* massene 107–08 *Is this . . . recoveries* [Q2 omits] 109 *his vouchers* vouchers 110 *double ones* doubles 122 *O* or 123 *For such a guest is meet* [Q2 omits]   144–45 *a gravemaker* Graue-maker   146 *all the days* the dayes   167 *corses now-a-days* corses   174–75 *three and twenty* 23   185 *Let me see* [Q2 omits]   187 *borne* bore   195 *chamber* table   210–11 *as thus* [Q2 omits]   218 *winter's* waters   219 s.d. *Enter King . . . Lords attendant* Enter K. Q. Laertes and the corse   233 *Shards, flints* Flints   248 *treble* double   252 s.d. *Leaps in the grave* [Q2 omits]   263 *and rash* rash   279 *Dost thou* doost   287 *thus* this   300 *shortly* thirtie   301 *Till* Tell

5.2.5 *Methought* my thought   6 *bilboes* bilbo   17 *unseal* vnfold   19 *Ah* [ed; F has "Oh"] A   43 *as's* [F has "assis"] as sir   52 *Subscribed* Subcribe   57 *Why, man . . . employment* [Q2 omits]   68–80 *To quit . . . comes here* [Q2 omits]   78 *court* [ed; F has "count"; Q2 omits]   80 s.d. *Young Osric* [Q2 omits]   81 *Osric* [Q2 prints "Cour" consistently as the speech prefix]   83 *humbly* humble   94 *Put your* your   99 *sultry* sully   99 *for* or   102 *But, my* my   108 *gentleman* [ed] gentlemen   110 *feelingly* [ed] sellingly   142 *his weapon* [ed] this weapon   151 *hangers* [ed] hanger   158 *carriages* carriage   161 *might be* be   164–65 *all impawned, as* all   180 *e'en so* so   184 *Yours, yours.* He Yours   189 *did comply* did   193 *yeasty* histy   194 *fanned* [ed; F has "fond"] prophane   195 *winnowed* trennowed   208 *to Laertes* [ed] Laertes   210 *lose this wager* loose   213 *But thou* thou   217 *gaingiving* gamgiuing   221 *If it be now* if it be   223 *will come* well come   241 *Sir, in this audience* [Q2 omits]   251 *keep my* my   251 *till* all   254 *Come on* [Q2 omits]   264 *bettered* better   266 s.d. *Prepare to play* [Q2 omits]   273 *union* Vnice   281 s.d. *They play* [Q2 omits]   287 *A touch, a touch* [Q2 omits]   301 s.d. *play* [Q2 omits]   303 s.d. *In scuffling they change rapiers* [Q2 omits]   304 *ho* [F has "hoa"] howe   312 *Ho* [ed] how   314 *Hamlet.* Hamlet Hamlet   317 *thy* my   323 s.d. *Hurts the King* [Q2 omits]   326 *murd'rous, damnèd* damned   327 *thy union* the Onixe   328 s.d. *King dies* [Q2 omits]   332 s.d. *Dies* [Q2 omits]   346 *live* I leaue 359 *Dies* [Q2 omits]   362 s.d. *with Drum, Colors, and Attendants* [Q2 omits]   380 *th' yet* yet   384 *forced* for no   393 *on* no   400 *rite* [ed; F has "rites"] right   404 s.d. *marching . . . shot off* [Q2 omits]

A Note on the Sources of *Hamlet*

The story of Hamlet is ancient. No doubt it had its origin in one of the family feuds familiar in Northern history and saga. Sailors carried it to Ireland, where it picked up accretions of Celtic folklore and legend, and later returned to Scandinavia to become part of the traditional history of Denmark. It was incorporated into written literature in the second half of the twelfth century when a learned clerk, Saxo Grammaticus, retold it in his *Historiae Danicae*, also called *Historia Danica*. His narrative is a story of early and relatively barbaric times. For instance, the dismembered body of the prototype of Polonius is thrown into an open latrine to be devoured by scavenging hogs, and there is no trace of the ideals of chivalry and courtesy that we find in Shakespeare's play. Still, the basic elements of Shakespeare's plot are there: the killing of the Danish ruler by his brother, the marriage of the brother and the widowed queen, the pretended madness and real craft of the dead king's son, the son's evasion of the sanity tests, his voyage to England with letters bearing his death warrant, his alteration of the letters, his return, and the accomplishment of his revenge: He kills his uncle, and he is acclaimed king. Some years later he dies a heroic death in battle against a descendant of an earlier king. Saxo also gives us, under different names, the chief characters of the story as we know it in Shakespeare: Claudius (Fengo), Gertrude (Gerutha), Hamlet (Amlethus), unnamed prototypes of Ophelia, Polonius, Rosencrantz, and Guildenstern, and perhaps even of Horatio.

Saxo's narrative circulated widely in manuscript. It was printed in Paris in 1514, reprinted elsewhere, and came in time to the attention of François de Belleforest, who in 1576 told his version of the Hamlet story in the fifth volume of his *Histoires Tragiques*. He made one notable addition to the story. He states that the Queen committed adultery with her brother-in-law during her marriage to the King. This remains in Shakespeare in the ghost's epithet for his brother, "adulterate" (1.5.42), and in Hamlet's "He that hath killed my king, and whored my mother" (5.2.64), and it operates as part of the motivation for the revulsion which Hamlet sometimes feels for womankind. Belleforest's *Histoires* seems to have been a popular book. His version was translated very badly into English under the title *The Hystorie of Hamblet* in 1608, too late to serve as a source for Shakespeare. In all likelihood it was called into being by the popularity of Shakespeare's play.

The next version of the Hamlet story was an English play of the 1580's based on Belleforest. It was never printed, and the manuscript seems to be irretrievably lost. Since the late eighteenth century it has been attributed more or less confidently to Thomas Kyd (1557?–1595?). Kyd was a scrivener and playwright, the author of the well-known *Spanish Tragedy*. Kyd's play on the Hamlet story, if, indeed, it is his, served as the immediate source of Shakespeare's play and is called by scholars the *Ur-Hamlet*. The first reference to it is found in Thomas Nashe's preface to Robert Greene's *Menaphon*, 1589. In it Nashe, an established writer, indulged in an attack on certain "trivial translators" and "shifting companions" who "leave the trade of noverint [scribe, copyist] whereto they were born, and busy themselves with the endeavors of art. . . . Yet English Seneca . . . yields many good sentences . . . and if you entreat him fair in a frosty morning, he will afford you whole *Hamlets*, I should say handfuls of tragical speeches. . . . Seneca, let blood, line by line and page by page, at length must needs die to our stage; which makes his famished followers to imitate the Kid in Aesop . . . and these men to intermeddle with Italian translations." The play is next mentioned in the diary of Philip Henslowe, the theatrical producer, who records that a play called *Hamlet* was performed at the suburban theater of Newington Butts in June, 1594, by the Admiral's and the Chamberlain's Men.

The play was next referred to by Thomas Lodge in his *Wit's Misery*, 1596. He speaks there of the "ghost which cried so miserably at The Theatre, like an oyster wife, 'Hamlet, revenge.' " The scorn of Lodge's statement suggests that the play was an outmoded one, and his mention of The Theatre as the playhouse at which the ghost cried out tells us that the Chamberlain's Men, the theatrical company to which Shakespeare belonged, had taken over the drama, for the playhouse at which they were then playing was called The Theatre. The play, then, was the property of Shakespeare's company, and he was free to use the story for his own purposes. Scholars have been assiduous in their attempts to reconstruct the *Ur-Hamlet* from references to it and from the versions of the story which preceded and followed it. And they have yet another version of the story at hand. There is a German play on the Hamlet story called *Der bestrafte Brudermord oder Prinz Hamlet aus Daennemark*. It was first printed in 1781 from a manuscript dated 1710. The manuscript has been lost, but the printed version has survived.

We know that a *Hamlet* was played by English actors at Dresden in 1626 and that there was another performance of the play, probably in German, in 1665. The latter is probably the origin of *Der bestrafte Brudermord*, a play which, by the eighteenth century, had grossly deteriorated from its original. Still, its dependence on an English *Hamlet* is certain. We must ask if it derives from an early version by Shakespeare as misrepresented in the First Quarto or from the *Ur-Hamlet*, and the scholars give us a divided answer. The name Corambus of the German version recalls Corambis of the First Quarto and suggests that as a source. On the other hand, Corambis may well have been the name in the *Ur-Hamlet*. There are other similarities to Shakespeare's quarto, but there are great differences from it. The German play opens with a prologue in which Night calls upon the Furies to spur the revenge against the king. This is Senecan rather than Shakespearean. The ghost tells Hamlet that it was reported that he had died of an apoplexy, whereas in the First Quarto it was said that he had died of a snake bite. There is no trace of Hamlet's great soliloquies which exist in the First Quarto in mangled form. On the whole it seems more likely that *Der bestrafte Brudermord* derives from the *Ur-Hamlet* than from the First Quarto.

What, then, was the immediate source of Shakespeare's *Hamlet* like? In answering this question it must be acknowledged that we are not on firm ground, but we can give some tentative answers. It was Senecan and, in name at least, a tragedy, though probably today we would call it a melodrama. A Senecan play would be gory, with the stage cluttered with corpses in the final scene. It was by Thomas Kyd. Why else should Nashe have associated "Kid" and "noverint" with the play? Kyd had been a scrivener, and unlike Nashe, he was not a university man. He had made translations from both Italian and French, and he had turned dramatist. He was able to read Belleforest in French. He knew Seneca intimately. In the play the ghost calls for revenge, and the revengeful ghost is found in Seneca (see page lxvii). In Saxo Grammaticus there is no ghost. There is no need for one; the murderer of the king was known to be his brother, and there was, therefore, nothing for the ghost to reveal. The ghost is one of Kyd's contributions to the story. He had used a ghost effectively in his *Spanish Tragedy*, and he was here repeating one of his successful devices. In the *Ur-Hamlet* the ghost made the revelation and urged upon Hamlet the obligation of revenge. In Saxo, Hamlet feigned madness in self-protection, in order to be thought a harmless idiot, and in order to get at the person of the king. Kyd retained the pretended madness, but we cannot know what uses he made of it. The play ended, of course, with Hamlet's triumph and death in a bloody massacre.

Bibliographic note: Translations of Saxo and of Belleforest are conveniently available in the seventh volume of Geoffrey Bullough, *Narrative and Dramatic Sources of Shakespeare* (1973).

Commentaries

SAMUEL TAYLOR COLERIDGE

From The Lectures of 1811–1812, Lecture XII

We will now pass to *Hamlet,* in order to obviate some of the general prejudices against the author, in reference to the character of the hero. Much has been objected to, which ought to have been praised, and many beauties of the highest kind have been neglected, because they are somewhat hidden.

The first question we should ask ourselves is—What did Shakespeare mean when he drew the character of Hamlet? He never wrote anything without design, and what was his design when he sat down to produce this tragedy? My belief is that he always regarded his story, before he began to write, much in the same light as a painter regards his canvas, before he begins to paint—as a mere vehicle for his thoughts—as the ground upon which he was to work. What then was the point to which Shakespeare directed himself in Hamlet? He intended to portray a person, in whose view the external world, and all its incidents and objects, were comparatively dim, and of no interest in themselves, and which began to interest only when they were reflected in the mirror of his mind. Hamlet beheld external things in the

From *Shakespearean Criticism* by Samuel Taylor Coleridge. 2nd ed., ed. Thomas Middleton Raysor. 2 vols. (New York: E. P. Dutton and Company, Inc., 1960; London: J. M. Dent & Sons, Ltd., 1961) The exact text of Coleridge's lecture does not exist; what is given here is the transcript of a shorthand report taken by an auditor, J. P. Collier.

same way that a man of vivid imagination, who shuts his eyes, sees what has previously made an impression on his organs.

The poet places him in the most stimulating circumstances that a human being can be placed in. He is the heir apparent of a throne; his father dies suspiciously; his mother excludes her son from his throne by marrying his uncle. This is not enough; but the ghost of the murdered father is introduced, to assure the son that he was put to death by his own brother. What is the effect upon the son?—instant action and pursuit of revenge? No: endless reasoning and hesitating—constant urging and solicitation of the mind to act, and as constant an escape from action; ceaseless reproaches of himself for sloth and negligence, while the whole energy of his resolution evaporates in these reproaches. This, too, not from cowardice, for he is drawn as one of the bravest of his time—not from want of forethought or slowness of apprehension, for he sees through the very souls of all who surround him, but merely from that aversion to action, which prevails among such as have a world in themselves.

How admirable, too, is the judgment of the poet! Hamlet's own disordered fancy has not conjured up the spirit of his father; it has been seen by others: he is prepared by them to witness its reappearance, and when he does see it, Hamlet is not brought forward as having long brooded on the subject. The moment before the Ghost enters, Hamlet speaks of other matters: he mentions the coldness of the night, and observes that he has not heard the clock strike, adding, in reference to the custom of drinking, that it is

More honored in the breach than the observance.

Act I., Scene 4.

Owing to the tranquil state of his mind, he indulges in some moral reflections. Afterwards, the Ghost suddenly enters.

Horatio.   Look, my lord, it comes.
Hamlet. Angels and ministers of grace defend us!

The same thing occurs in *Macbeth*: in the dagger scene, the moment before the hero sees it, he has his mind applied to some indifferent matters; "Go, tell thy mistress," &c. Thus, in both cases, the preternatural appearance has all the effect of abruptness, and the reader is totally divested of the notion, that the figure is a vision of a highly wrought imagination.

Here Shakespeare adapts himself so admirably to the situation—in other words, so puts himself into it—that, though poetry, his language is the very language of nature. No terms, associated with such feelings, can occur to us so proper as those which he has employed, especially on the highest, the most august, and the most awful subjects that can interest a human being in this sentient world. That this is no mere fancy, I can undertake to establish from hundreds, I might say thousands, of passages. No character he has drawn, in the whole list of his plays, could so well and fitly express himself as in the language Shakespeare has put into his mouth.

There is no indecision about Hamlet, as far as his own sense of duty is concerned; he knows well what he ought to do, and over and over again he makes up his mind to do it. The moment the players, and the two spies set upon him, have withdrawn, of whom he takes leave with a line so expressive of his contempt,

Ay so, God bye to you.—Now I am alone,

he breaks out into a delirium of rage against himself for neglecting to perform the solemn duty he had undertaken, and contrasts the factitious and artificial display of feeling by the player with his own apparent indifference;

What's Hecuba to him, or he to Hecuba,
That he should weep for her?

Yet the player did weep for her, and was in an agony of grief at her sufferings, while Hamlet is unable to rouse himself to action, in order that he may perform the command of

his father, who had come from the grave to incite him to revenge:

> This is most brave!
> That I, the son of a dear father murdered,
> Prompted to my revenge by heaven and hell,
> Must, like a whore, unpack my heart with words,
> And fall a-cursing like a very drab,
> A scullion.   *Act II., Scene 2.*

It is the same feeling, the same conviction of what is his
duty, that makes Hamlet exclaim in a subsequent part of the
tragedy:

> How all occasions do inform against me
> And spur my dull revenge! What is a man,
> If his chief good and market of his time,
> Be but to sleep and feed? A beast, no more. . . .
>   . . . . I do not know
> Why yet I live to say—"this thing's to do,"
> Sith I have cause and will and strength and means
> To do't.   *Act IV., Scene 4.*

Yet with all this strong conviction of duty, and with all
this resolution arising out of strong conviction, nothing is
done. This admirable and consistent character, deeply ac-
quainted with his own feelings, painting them with such
wonderful power and accuracy, and firmly persuaded that a
moment ought not to be lost in executing the solemn charge
committed to him, still yields to the same retiring from reality, which is the result of having, what we express by the
terms, a world within himself.

Such a mind as Hamlet's is near akin to madness. Dry-
den has somewhere said,[1]

> Great wit to madness nearly is allied,

---

[1] "Great wits are sure to madness near allied."
    Absalom and Achitophel, 163.

and he was right; for he means by "wit" that greatness of genius, which led Hamlet to a perfect knowledge of his own character, which, with all strength of motive, was so weak as to be unable to carry into act his own most obvious duty.

With all this he has a sense of imperfectness, which becomes apparent when he is moralizing on the skull in the churchyard. Something is wanting to his completeness—something is deficient which remains to be supplied, and he is therefore described as attached to Ophelia. His madness is assumed, when he finds that witnesses have been placed behind the arras to listen to what passes, and when the heroine has been thrown in his way as a decoy.

Another objection has been taken by Dr. Johnson, and Shakespeare has been taxed very severely. I refer to the scene where Hamlet enters and finds his uncle praying, and refuses to take his life, excepting when he is in the height of his iniquity. To assail him at such a moment of confession and repentance, Hamlet declares,

> Why, this is hire and salary, not revenge.
> *Act III., Scene 3.*

He therefore forbears, and postpones his uncle's death, until he can catch him in some act

> That has no relish of salvation in't.

This conduct, and this sentiment, Dr. Johnson has pronounced to be so atrocious and horrible as to be unfit to be put into the mouth of a human being. The fact, however, is that Dr. Johnson did not understand the character of Hamlet, and censured accordingly: the determination to allow the guilty King to escape at such a moment is only part of the indecision and irresoluteness of the hero. Hamlet seizes hold of a pretext for not acting, when he might have acted so instantly and effectually: therefore, he again defers the revenge he was bound to seek, and declares his determination to accomplish it at some time,

> When he is drunk asleep or in his rage,
> Or in th' incestuous pleasures of his bed.

This, allow me to impress upon you most emphatically, was merely the excuse Hamlet made to himself for not taking advantage of this particular and favorable moment for doing justice upon his guilty uncle, at the urgent instance of the spirit of his father.

Dr. Johnson further states that in the voyage to England, Shakespeare merely follows the novel as he found it, as if the poet had no other reason for adhering to his original; but Shakespeare never followed a novel because he found such and such an incident in it, but because he saw that the story, as he read it, contributed to enforce or to explain some great truth inherent in human nature. He never could lack invention to alter or improve a popular narrative; but he did not wantonly vary from it, when he knew that, as it was related, it would so well apply to his own great purpose. He saw at once how consistent it was with the character of Hamlet, that after still resolving, and still deferring, still determining to execute, and still postponing execution, he should finally, in the infirmity of his disposition, give himself up to his destiny, and hopelessly place himself in the power and at the mercy of his enemies.

Even after the scene with Osrick, we see Hamlet still indulging in reflection, and hardly thinking of the task he has just undertaken: he is all dispatch and resolution, as far as words and present intentions are concerned, but all hesitation and irresolution, when called upon to carry his words and intentions into effect; so that, resolving to do everything, he does nothing. He is full of purpose, but void of that quality of mind which accomplishes purpose.

Anything finer than this conception, and working out of a great character, is merely impossible. Shakespeare wished to impress upon us the truth that action is the chief end of existence—that no faculties of intellect, however brilliant, can be considered valuable, or indeed otherwise than as misfortunes, if they withdraw us from or render us repugnant to action, and lead us to think and think of doing, until the time has elapsed when we can do anything effectually.

In enforcing this moral truth, Shakespeare has shown the fullness and force of his powers: all that is amiable and excellent in nature is combined in Hamlet, with the exception of one quality. He is a man living in meditation, called upon to act by every motive human and divine, but the great object of his life is defeated by continually resolving to do, yet doing nothing but resolve.

A. C. BRADLEY

From Shakespearean Tragedy

Let us first ask ourselves what we can gather from the play, immediately or by inference, concerning Hamlet as he was just before his father's death. And I begin by observing that the text does not bear out the idea that he was one-sidedly reflective and indisposed to action. Nobody who knew him seems to have noticed this weakness. Nobody regards him as a mere scholar who has "never formed a resolution or executed a deed." In a court which certainly would not much admire such a person, he is the observed of all observers. Though he has been disappointed of the throne everyone shows him respect; and he is the favorite of the people, who are not given to worship philosophers. Fortinbras, a sufficiently practical man, considered that he was likely, had he been put on, to have proved most royally. He has Hamlet borne by four captains "like a soldier" to his grave; and Ophelia says that Hamlet *was* a soldier. If he was fond of acting, an aesthetic pursuit, he was equally fond of fencing, an athletic one: he practiced it assiduously even in his worst days.[1] So far as we can conjecture from what we see of him in those bad days, he must normally

From *Shakespearean Tragedy* by A. C. Bradley. (London: Macmillan & Co., Ltd., 1904) Reprinted by permission of Macmillan & Co., Ltd. (London), St. Martin's Press, Inc. (New York), and the Macmillan Company of Canada, Ltd.

[1]He says so to Horatio, whom he has no motive for deceiving (5.2. 212). His contrary statement (2.2. 304) is made to Rosencrantz and Guildenstern.

have been charmingly frank, courteous, and kindly to
everyone, of whatever rank, whom he liked or respected,
but by no means timid or deferential to others; indeed, one
would gather that he was rather the reverse, and also that he
was apt to be decided and even imperious if thwarted or in-
terfered with. He must always have been fearless—in the
play he appears insensible to fear of any ordinary kind.
And, finally, he must have been quick and impetuous in action; for it is downright impossible that the man we see
rushing after the Ghost, killing Polonius, dealing with the
King's commission on the ship, boarding the pirate, leaping
into the grave, executing his final vengeance, could *ever*
have been shrinking or slow in an emergency. Imagine
Coleridge doing any of these things!

If we consider all this, how can we accept the notion that
Hamlet's was a weak and one-sided character? "Oh, but he
spent ten or twelve years at a University!" Well, even if he
did, it is possible to do that without becoming the victim of
excessive thought. But the statement that he did rests upon
a most insecure foundation.

Where then are we to look for the seeds of danger?

(1) Trying to reconstruct from the Hamlet of the play,
one would not judge that his temperament was melancholy
in the present sense of the word; there seems nothing to
show that; but one would judge that by temperament he
was inclined to nervous instability, to rapid and perhaps extreme changes of feeling and mood, and that he was disposed to be, for the time, absorbed in the feeling or mood
that possessed him, whether it were joyous or depressed.
This temperament the Elizabethans would have called
melancholic; and Hamlet seems to be an example of it, as
Lear is of a temperament mixedly choleric and sanguine.
And the doctrine of temperaments was so familiar in
Shakespeare's time—as Burton, and earlier prose writers,
and many of the dramatists show—that Shakespeare may
quite well have given this temperament to Hamlet consciously and deliberately. Of melancholy in its developed
form, a habit, not a mere temperament, he often speaks. He
more than once laughs at the passing and half-fictitious
melancholy of youth and love; in Don John in *Much Ado* he

had sketched the sour and surly melancholy of discontent; in Jaques a whimsical self-pleasing melancholy; in Antonio in the *Merchant of Venice* a quiet but deep melancholy, for which neither the victim nor his friends can assign any cause. He gives to Hamlet a temperament which would not develop into melancholy unless under some exceptional strain, but which still involved a danger. In the play we see the danger realized, and find a melancholy quite unlike any that Shakespeare had as yet depicted, because the temperament of Hamlet is quite different.

(2) Next, we cannot be mistaken in attributing to the Hamlet of earlier days an exquisite sensibility, to which we may give the name "moral," if that word is taken in the wide meaning it ought to bear. This, though it suffers cruelly in later days, as we saw in criticizing the sentimental view of Hamlet, never deserts him; it makes all his cynicism, grossness, and hardness appear to us morbidities, and has an inexpressibly attractive and pathetic effect. He had the soul of the youthful poet as Shelley and Tennyson have described it, an unbounded delight and faith in everything good and beautiful. We know this from himself. The world for him was *herrlich wie am ersten Tag*—"this goodly frame the earth, this most excellent canopy the air, this brave o'erhanging firmament, this majestical roof fretted with golden fire." And not nature only: "What a piece of work is a man! how noble in reason! how infinite in faculty! in form and moving how express and admirable! in action how like an angel! in apprehension how like a god!" (2.2.306–15). This is no commonplace to Hamlet; it is the language of a heart thrilled with wonder and swelling into ecstasy.

Doubtless it was with the same eager enthusiasm he turned to those around him. Where else in Shakespeare is there anything like Hamlet's adoration of his father? The words melt into music whenever he speaks of him. And, if there are no signs of any such feeling towards his mother, though many signs of love, it is characteristic that he evidently never entertained a suspicion of anything unworthy in her—characteristic, and significant of his tendency to see only what is good unless he is forced to see the reverse. For we find this tendency elsewhere, and find it going so far that we must call it a disposition to idealize, to see something better than what is there, or at least to ignore deficiencies. He says to Laertes, "I loved you ever," and he describes Laertes as a "very noble youth," which he was far from being. In his first greeting of Rosencrantz and Guildenstern, where his old self revives, we trace the same affectionateness and readiness to take men at their best. His love for Ophelia, too, which seems strange to some, is surely the most natural thing in the world. He saw her innocence, simplicity, and sweetness, and it was like him to ask no more; and it is noticeable that Horatio, though entirely worthy of his friendship, is, like Ophelia, intellectually not remarkable. To the very end, however clouded, this generous disposition, this "free and open nature," this unsuspiciousness survive. They cost him his life; for the King knew them, and was sure that he was too "generous and free from all contriving" to "peruse the foils." To the very end, his soul, however sick and tortured it may be, answers instantaneously when good and evil are presented to it, loving the one and hating the other. He is called a skeptic who has no firm belief in anything, but he is never skeptical about *them*.

And the negative side of his idealism, the aversion to evil, is perhaps even more developed in the hero of the tragedy than in the Hamlet of earlier days. It is intensely characteristic. Nothing, I believe, is to be found elsewhere in Shakespeare (unless in the rage of the disillusioned idealist Timon) of quite the same kind as Hamlet's disgust at his uncle's drunkenness, his loathing of his mother's sensuality, his astonishment and horror at her shallowness, his contempt for everything pretentious or false, his indifference to everything merely external. This last characteristic appears in his choice of the friend of his heart, and in a certain impatience of distinctions of rank or wealth. When Horatio calls his father "a goodly king," he answers, surely with an emphasis on "man,"

> He was a man, take him for all in all,
> I shall not look upon his like again.   (1.2.187–88)

He will not listen to talk of Horatio being his "servant." When the others speak of their "duty" to him, he answers, "Your love, as mine to you." He speaks to the actor precisely as he does to an honest courtier. He is not in the least a revolutionary, but still, in effect, a king and a beggar are all one to him. He cares for nothing but human worth, and his pitilessness towards Polonius and Osric and his "schoolfellows" is not wholly due to morbidity, but belongs in part to his original character.

Now, in Hamlet's moral sensibility there undoubtedly lay a danger. Any great shock that life might inflict on it would be felt with extreme intensity. Such a shock might even produce tragic results. And, in fact, *Hamlet* deserves the title "tragedy of moral idealism" quite as much as the title "tragedy of reflection."

(3) With this temperament and this sensibility we find, lastly, in the Hamlet of earlier days, as of later, intellectual genius. It is chiefly this that makes him so different from all those about him, good and bad alike, and hardly less different from most of Shakespeare's other heroes. And this, though on the whole the most important trait in his nature, is also so obvious and so famous that I need not dwell on it at length. But against one prevalent misconception I must say a word of warning. Hamlet's intellectual power is not a specific gift, like a genius for music or mathematics or philosophy. It shows itself, fitfully, in the affairs of life as unusual quickness of perception, great agility in shifting the mental attitude, a striking rapidity and fertility in resource; so that, when his natural belief in others does not make him unwary, Hamlet easily sees through them and masters them, and no one can be much less like the typical helpless dreamer. It shows itself in conversation chiefly in the form of wit or humor; and, alike in conversation and in soliloquy, it shows itself in the form of imagination quite as much as in that of thought in the stricter sense. Further, where it takes the latter shape, as it very often does, it is not philosophic in the technical meaning of the word. There is really nothing in the play to show that Hamlet ever was "a student of philosophies," unless it be the famous lines

which, comically enough, exhibit this supposed victim of philosophy as its critic:

> There are more things in heaven and earth, Horatio,
> Than are dreamt of in your philosophy.   (1.5.166–67)

His philosophy, if the word is to be used, was, like Shakespeare's own, the immediate product of the wondering and meditating mind; and such thoughts as that celebrated one, "There is nothing either good or bad but thinking makes it so," surely needed no special training to produce them. Or does Portia's remark, "Nothing is good without respect," i.e., out of relation, prove that she had studied metaphysics?

Still Hamlet had speculative genius without being a philosopher, just as he had imaginative genius without being a poet. Doubtless in happier days he was a close and constant observer of men and manners, noting his results in those tables which he afterwards snatched from his breast to make in wild irony his last note of all, that one may smile and smile and be a villain. Again and again we remark that passion for generalization which so occupied him, for instance, in reflections suggested by the King's drunkenness that he quite forgot what it was he was waiting to meet upon the battlements. Doubtless, too, he was always considering things, as Horatio thought, too curiously. There was a necessity in his soul driving him to penetrate below the surface and to question what others took for granted. That fixed habitual look which the world wears for most men did not exist for him. He was forever unmaking his world and rebuilding it in thought, dissolving what to others were solid facts, and discovering what to others were old truths. There were no old truths for Hamlet. It is for Horatio a thing of course that there's a divinity that shapes our ends, but for Hamlet it is a discovery hardly won. And throughout this kingdom of the mind, where he felt that man, who in action is only like an angel, is in apprehension like a god, he moved (we must imagine) more than content, so that even in his dark days he declares he could be bounded in a nutshell and yet count himself a king of infinite space, were it not that he had bad dreams.

If now we ask whether any special danger lurked *here*, how shall we answer? We must answer, it seems to me, "Some danger, no doubt, but, granted the ordinary chances of life, not much." For, in the first place, that idea which so many critics quietly take for granted—the idea that the gift and the habit of meditative and speculative thought tend to produce irresolution in the affairs of life—would be found by no means easy to verify. Can you verify it, for example, in the lives of the philosophers, or again in the lives of men whom you have personally known to be addicted to such speculation? I cannot. Of course, individual peculiarities being set apart, absorption in *any* intellectual interest, together with withdrawal from affairs, may make a man slow and unskillful in affairs; and doubtless, individual peculiarities being again set apart, a mere student is likely to be more at a loss in a sudden and great practical emergency than a soldier or a lawyer. But in all this there is no difference between a physicist, a historian, and a philosopher; and again, slowness, want of skill, and even helplessness are something totally different from the peculiar kind of ir-resolution that Hamlet shows. The notion that speculative thinking specially tends to produce *this* is really a mere illusion.

In the second place, even if this notion were true, it has appeared that Hamlet did *not* live the life of a mere student, much less of a mere dreamer, and that his nature was by no means simply or even one-sidedly intellectual, but was healthily active. Hence, granted the ordinary chances of life, there would seem to be no great danger in his intellectual tendency and his habit of speculation; and I would go further and say that there was nothing in them, taken alone, to unfit him even for the extraordinary call that was made upon him. In fact, if the message of the Ghost had come to him within a week of his father's death, I see no reason to doubt that he would have acted on it as decisively as Othello himself, though probably after a longer and more anxious deliberation. And therefore the Schlegel-Coleridge view (apart from its descriptive value) seems to me fatally untrue, for it implies that Hamlet's procrastination was the normal response of an overspeculative nature confronted with a difficult practical problem.

On the other hand, under conditions of a peculiar kind, Hamlet's reflectiveness certainly might prove dangerous to him, and his genius might even (to exaggerate a little) become his doom. Suppose that violent shock to his moral being of which I spoke; and suppose that under this shock, any possible action being denied to him, he began to sink into melancholy; then, no doubt, his imaginative and generalizing habit of mind might extend the effects of this shock through his whole being and mental world. And if, the state of melancholy being thus deepened and fixed, a sudden demand for difficult and decisive action in a matter connected with the melancholy arose, this state might well have for one of its symptoms an endless and futile mental dissection of the required deed. And, finally, the futility of this process, and the shame of his delay, would further weaken him and enslave him to his melancholy still more. Thus the speculative habit would be *one* indirect cause of the morbid state with hindered action; and it would also reappear in a degenerate form as one of the *symptoms* of this morbid state.

Now this is what actually happens in the play. Turn to the first words Hamlet utters when he is alone; turn, that is to say, to the place where the author is likely to indicate his meaning most plainly. What do you hear?

> O, that this too too sullied flesh would melt,
> Thaw and resolve itself into a dew.
> Or that the Everlasting had not fix'd
> His canon 'gainst self-slaughter! O God, God,
> How weary, stale, flat and unprofitable,
> Seem to me all the uses of this world!
> Fie on't, ah, fie, 'tis an unweeded garden,
> That grows to seed. Things rank and gross in nature
> Possess it merely.   (1.2.129–37)

Here are a sickness of life, and even a longing for death, so intense that nothing stands between Hamlet and suicide ex-

cept religious awe. And what has caused them? The rest of
the soliloquy so thrusts the answer upon us that it might
seem impossible to miss it. It was not his father's death;
that doubtless brought deep grief, but mere grief for some
one loved and lost does not make a noble spirit loathe the
world as a place full only of things rank and gross. It was
not the vague suspicion that we know Hamlet felt. Still less
was it the loss of the crown; for though the subserviency of
the electors might well disgust him, there is not a reference
to the subject in the soliloquy, nor any sign elsewhere that
it greatly occupied his mind. It was the moral shock of the
sudden ghastly disclosure of his mother's true nature,
falling on him when his heart was aching with love, and his
body doubtless was weakened by sorrow. And it is essential, however disagreeable, to realize the nature of this
shock. It matters little here whether Hamlet's age was
twenty or thirty: in either case his mother was a matron of
mature years. All his life he had believed in her, we may be
sure, as such a son would. He had seen her not merely devoted to his father, but hanging on him like a newly wed-
ded bride, hanging on him

> As if increase of appetite had grown
> By what it fed on.   (144–45)

He had seen her following his body "like Niobe, all tears."
And then within a month—"O God! a beast would have
mourned longer"—she married again, and married Hamlet's uncle, a man utterly contemptible and loathsome in his
eyes; married him in what to Hamlet was incestuous wed-
lock; married him not for any reason of state, nor even out
of old family affection, but in such a way that her son was
forced to see in her action not only an astounding shallowness of feeling but an eruption of coarse sensuality, "rank
and gross," speeding posthaste to its horrible delight. Is it
possible to conceive an experience more desolating to a
man such as we have seen Hamlet to be; and is its result
anything but perfectly natural? It brings bewildered horror,
then loathing, then despair of human nature. His whole
mind is poisoned. He can never see Ophelia in the same

light again: she is a woman, and his mother is a woman: if she mentions the word "brief" to him, the answer drops from his lips like venom, "as woman's love." The last words of the soliloquy, which is *wholly* concerned with this subject, are,

> But break my heart, for I must hold my tongue.   (159)

He can do nothing. He must lock in his heart, not any suspicion of his uncle that moves obscurely there, but that horror and loathing; and if his heart ever found relief, it was when those feelings, mingled with the love that never died out in him, poured themselves forth in a flood as he stood in his mother's chamber beside his father's marriage bed.

If we still wonder, and ask why the effect of this shock should be so tremendous, let us observe that *now* the conditions have arisen under which Hamlet's highest endowments, his moral sensibility and his genius, become his enemies. A nature morally blunter would have felt even so dreadful a revelation less keenly. A slower and more limited and positive mind might not have extended so widely through its world the disgust and disbelief that have entered it. But Hamlet has the imagination which, for evil as well as good, feels and sees all things in one. Thought is the element of his life, and his thought is infected. He cannot prevent himself from probing and lacerating the wound in his soul. One idea, full of peril, holds him fast, and he cries out in agony at it, but is impotent to free himself ("Must I remember?" "Let me not think on't"). And when, with the fading of his passion, the vividness of this idea abates, it does so only to leave behind a boundless weariness and a sick longing for death.

And this is the time which his fate chooses. In this hour of uttermost weakness, this sinking of his whole being towards annihilation, there comes on him, bursting the bounds of the natural world with a shock of astonishment and terror, the revelation of his mother's adultery and his father's murder, and, with this, the demand on him, in the name of everything dearest and most sacred, to arise and act. And for a moment, though his brain reels and totters,

his soul leaps up in passion to answer this demand. But it
comes too late. It does but strike home the last rivet in the
melancholy which holds him bound.

> The time is out of joint. O cursèd spite,
> That ever I was born to set it right!   (1.5.188–89)

so he mutters within an hour of the moment when he
vowed to give his life to the duty of revenge; and the rest of
the story exhibits his vain efforts to fulfill this duty, his un-
conscious self-excuses and unavailing self-reproaches, and
the tragic results of his delay.

"Melancholy," I said, not dejection, nor yet insanity.
That Hamlet was not far from insanity is very probable. His
adoption of the pretense of madness may well have been
due in part to fear of the reality; to an instinct of self-
preservation, a forefeeling that the pretense would enable
him to give some utterance to the load that pressed on his
heart and brain, and a fear that he would be unable altogether to repress such utterance. And if the pathologist calls
his state melancholia, and even proceeds to determine its
species, I see nothing to object to in that; I am grateful to
him for emphasizing the fact that Hamlet's melancholy was
no mere common depression of spirits; and I have no doubt
that many readers of the play would understand it better if
they read an account of melancholia in a work on mental
diseases. If we like to use the word "disease" loosely, Hamlet's condition may truly be called diseased. No exertion of
will could have dispelled it. Even if he had been able at
once to do the bidding of the Ghost he would doubtless
have still remained for some time under the cloud. It would
be absurdly unjust to call *Hamlet* a study of melancholy,
but it contains such a study.

But this melancholy is something very different from insanity, in anything like the usual meaning of that word. No
doubt it might develop into insanity. The longing for death
might become an irresistible impulse to self-destruction;
the disorder of feeling and will might extend to sense and
intellect; delusions might arise; and the man might become,

as we say, incapable and irresponsible. But Hamlet's melancholy is some way from this condition. It is a totally different thing from the madness which he feigns; and he never, when alone or in company with Horatio alone, exhibits the signs of that madness. Nor is the dramatic use of this melancholy, again, open to the objections which would justly be made to the portrayal of an insanity which brought the hero to a tragic end. The man who suffers as Hamlet suffers—and thousands go about their business suffering thus in greater or less degree—is considered irresponsible neither by other people nor by himself: he is only too keenly conscious of his responsibility. He is therefore, so far, quite capable of being a tragic agent, which an insane person, at any rate according to Shakespeare's practice, is not. And, finally, Hamlet's state is not one which a healthy mind is unable sufficiently to imagine. It is probably not further from average experience, nor more difficult to realize, than the great tragic passions of Othello, Antony, or Macbeth.

MAYNARD MACK

The World of *Hamlet*

My subject is the world of *Hamlet.* I do not of course mean Denmark, except as Denmark is given a body by the play; and I do not mean Elizabethan England, though this is necessarily close behind the scenes. I mean simply the imaginative environment that the play asks us to enter when we read it or go to see it.

Great plays, as we know, do present us with something that can be called a world, a microcosm—a world like our own in being made of people, actions, situations, thoughts, feelings, and much more, but unlike our own in being perfectly, or almost perfectly, significant and coherent. In a play's world, each part implies the other parts, and each lives, each means, with the life and meaning of the rest.

This is the reason, as we also know, that the worlds of great plays greatly differ. Othello in Hamlet's position, we sometimes say, would have no problem; but what we are really saying is that Othello in Hamlet's position would not exist. The conception we have of Othello is a function of the characters who help define him, Desdemona, honest Iago, Cassio, and the rest; of his history of travel and war; of a great storm that divides his ship from Cassio's, and a handkerchief; of a quiet night in Venice broken by cries

From *The Yale Review* XLI (1952): 502–23. Copyright 1952 by the Yale University Press. Reprinted by permission of the author.

about an old black ram; of a quiet night in Cyprus broken
by swordplay; of a quiet bedroom where a woman goes to
bed in her wedding sheets and a man comes in with a light
to put out the light; and above all, of a language, a language
with many voices in it, gentle, rasping, querulous, or foul,
but all counterpointing the one great voice:

> Keep up your bright swords, for the dew will rust them.
>
> (1.2.58)

>   O thou weed
> Who art so lovely fair, and smell'st so sweet,
> That the sense aches at thee.   (4.2.66–68)

>   Yet I'll not shed her blood,
> Nor scar that whiter skin of hers than snow,
> And smooth as monumental alabaster.   (5.2.3–5)

>   I pray you, in your letters,
> When you shall these unlucky deeds relate,
> Speak of me as I am. Nothing extenuate,
> Nor set down aught in malice. Then must you speak
> Of one that loved not wisely, but too well;
> Of one not easily jealous, but being wrought,
> Perplexed in th' extreme; of one whose hand,
> Like the base Indian, threw a pearl away
> Richer than all his tribe.   (836–43)

Without his particular world of voices, persons, events,
the world that both expresses and contains him, Othello is
unimaginable. And so, I think, are Antony, King Lear,
Macbeth—and Hamlet. We come back then to Hamlet's
world, of all the tragic worlds that Shakespeare made, easily the most various and brilliant, the most elusive. It is with
no thought of doing justice to it that I have singled out three
of its attributes for comment. I know too well, if I may echo
a sentiment of Mr. E. M. W. Tillyard's, that no one is likely
to accept another man's reading of *Hamlet*, that anyone
who tries to throw light on one part of the play usually
throws the rest into deeper shadow, and that what I have to

say leaves out many problems—to mention only one, the knotty problem of the text. All I would say in defense of the materials I have chosen is that they seem to me interesting, close to the root of the matter even if we continue to differ about what the root of the matter is, and explanatory, in a modest way, of this play's peculiar hold on everyone's imagination, its almost mythic status, one might say, as a paradigm of the life of man.

The first attribute that impresses us, I think, is mysteriousness. We often hear it said, perhaps with truth, that every great work of art has a mystery at the heart; but the mystery of *Hamlet* is something else. We feel its presence in the numberless explanations that have been brought forward for Hamlet's delay, his madness, his ghost, his treatment of Polonius, or Ophelia, or his mother; and in the controversies that still go on about whether the play is "undoubtedly a failure" (Eliot's phrase) or one of the greatest artistic triumphs; whether, if it is a triumph, it belongs to the highest order of tragedy; whether, if it is such a tragedy, its hero is to be taken as a man of exquisite moral sensibility (Bradley's view) or an egomaniac (Madariaga's view).

Doubtless there have been more of these controversies and explanations than the play requires; for in Hamlet, to paraphrase a remark of Falstaff's, we have a character who is not only mad in himself but a cause that madness is in the rest of us. Still, the very existence of so many theories and countertheories, many of them formulated by sober heads, gives food for thought. *Hamlet* seems to lie closer to the illogical logic of life than Shakespeare's other tragedies. And while the causes of this situation may be sought by saying that Shakespeare revised the play so often that eventually the motivations were smudged over, or that the original old play has been here or there imperfectly digested, or that the problems of Hamlet lay so close to Shakespeare's heart that he could not quite distance them in the formal terms of art, we have still as critics to deal with effects, not causes. If I may quote again from Mr. Tillyard, the play's very lack of a rigorous type of causal logic seems to be a part of its point.

Moreover, the matter goes deeper than this. Hamlet's world is pre-eminently in the interrogative mood. It reverberates with questions, anguished, meditative, alarmed. There are questions that in this play, to an extent I think unparalleled in any other, mark the phases and even the nuances of the action, helping to establish its peculiar baffled tone. There are other questions whose interrogations, innocent at first glance, are subsequently seen to have reached beyond their contexts and to point towards some pervasive inscrutability in Hamlet's world as a whole. Such is that tense series of challenges with which the tragedy begins: Bernardo's of Francisco, "Who's there?" Francisco's of Horatio and Marcellus, "Who is there?" Horatio's of the ghost, "What art thou . . . ?" And then there are the famous questions. In them the interrogations seem to point not only beyond the context but beyond the play, out of Hamlet's predicaments into everyone's: "What a piece of work is a man! . . . And yet to me what is this quintessence of dust?" "To be, or not to be, that is the question." "Get thee to a nunnery. Why wouldst thou be a breeder of sinners?" "I am very proud, revengeful, ambitious, with more offenses at my beck than I have thoughts to put them in, imagination to give them shape, or time to act them in. What should such fellows as I do crawling between earth and heaven?" "Dost thou think Alexander look'd o' this fashion i' th' earth? . . . And smelt so?"

Further, Hamlet's world is a world of riddles. The hero's own language is often riddling, as the critics have pointed out. When he puns, his puns have receding depths in them, like the one which constitutes his first speech: "A little more than kin, and less than kind." His utterances in madness, even if wild and whirling, are simultaneously, as Polonius discovers, pregnant: "Do you know me, my lord?" "Excellent well. You are a fishmonger." Even the madness itself is riddling: How much is real? How much is feigned? What does it mean? Sane or mad, Hamlet's mind plays restlessly about his world, turning up one riddle upon another. The riddle of character, for example, and how it is that in a man whose virtues else are "pure as grace," some vicious mole of nature, some

"dram of eale," can "all the noble substance oft adulter."
Or the riddle of the player's art, and how a man can so
project himself into a fiction, a dream of passion, that he
can weep for Hecuba. Or the riddle of action: how we
may think too little—"What to ourselves in passion we
propose," says the player-king, "The passion ending, doth
the purpose lose"; and again, how we may think too
much: "Thus conscience does make cowards of us all,
And thus the native hue of resolution Is sicklied o'er with
the pale cast of thought."

There are also more immediate riddles. His mother—
how could she "on this fair mountain leave to feed, And
batten on this moor?" The ghost—which may be a devil,
for "the de'il hath power T' assume a pleasing shape."
Ophelia—what does her behavior to him mean? Surprising
her in her closet, he falls to such perusal of her face as he
would draw it. Even the king at his prayers is a riddle. Will
a revenge that takes him in the purging of his soul be
vengeance, or hire and salary? As for himself, Hamlet realizes, he is the greatest riddle of all—a mystery, he warns
Rosencrantz and Guildenstern, from which he will not have
the heart plucked out. He cannot tell why he has of late lost
all his mirth, forgone all custom of exercises. Still less can
he tell why he delays: "I do not know Why yet I live to say,
'This thing's to do,' Sith I have cause and will and strength
and means To do't."

Thus the mysteriousness of Hamlet's world is of a piece.
It is not simply a matter of missing motivations, to be ex-
punged if only we could find the perfect clue. It is built in.
It is evidently an important part of what the play wishes to
say to us. And it is certainly an element that the play thrusts
upon us from the opening word. Everyone, I think, recalls
the mysteriousness of that first scene. The cold middle of
the night on the castle platform, the muffled sentries, the
uneasy atmosphere of apprehension, the challenges leaping
out of the dark, the questions that follow the challenges,
feeling out the darkness, searching for identities, for relations, for assurance. "Bernardo?" "Have you had quiet
guard?" "Who hath reliev'd you?" "What, is Horatio
there?" "What, has this thing appear'd again tonight?"

"Looks 'a not like the king?" "How now, Horatio! ... Is not this something more than fantasy? What think you on 't?" "Is it not like the king?" "Why this same strict and most observant watch ... ?" "Shall I strike at it with my partisan?" "Do you consent we shall acquaint [young Hamlet] with it?"

We need not be surprised that critics and playgoers alike have been tempted to see in this an evocation not simply of Hamlet's world but of their own. Man in his aspect of bafflement, moving in darkness on a rampart between two worlds, unable to reject, or quite accept, the one that, when he faces it, "to-shakes" his disposition with thoughts beyond the reaches of his soul—comforting himself with hints and guesses. We hear these hints and guesses whispering through the darkness as the several watchers speak. "At least, the whisper goes on," says one. "I think it be no other but e'en so," says another. "I have heard" that on the crowing of the cock "Th' extravagant and erring spirit hies To his confine," says a third. "Some say" at Christmas time "this bird of dawning" sings all night, "And then, they say, no spirit dare stir abroad." "So have I heard," says the first, "and do in part believe it." However we choose to take the scene, it is clear that it creates a world where uncertainties are of the essence.

Meantime, such is Shakespeare's economy, a second attribute of Hamlet's world has been put before us. This is the problematic nature of reality and the relation of reality to appearance. The play begins with an appearance, an "apparition," to use Marcellus's term—the ghost. And the ghost is somehow real, indeed the vehicle of realities. Through its revelation, the glittering surface of Claudius's court is pierced, and Hamlet comes to know, and we do, that the king is not only hateful to him but the murderer of his father, that his mother is guilty of adultery as well as incest. Yet there is a dilemma in the revelation. For possibly the apparition *is* an apparition, a devil who has assumed his father's shape.

This dilemma, once established, recurs on every hand. From the court's point of view, there is Hamlet's madness. Polonius investigates and gets some strange advice about his daughter: "Conception is a blessing, but as your daughter may conceive, friend, look to 't." Rosencrantz and Guildenstern investigate and get the strange confidence that "Man delights not me; no, nor woman neither." Ophelia is "loosed" to Hamlet (Polonius's vulgar word), while Polonius and the king hide behind the arras; and what they hear is a strange indictment of human nature, and a riddling threat: "Those that are married already, all but one, shall live."

On the other hand, from Hamlet's point of view, there is Ophelia. Kneeling here at her prayers, she seems the image of innocence and devotion. Yet she is of the sex for whom he has already found the name Frailty, and she is also, as he seems either madly or sanely to divine, a decoy in a trick. The famous cry—"Get thee to a nunnery"—shows the anguish of his uncertainty. If Ophelia is what she seems, this dirty-minded world of murder, incest, lust, adultery, is no place for her. Were she "as chaste as ice, as pure as snow," she could not escape its calumny. And if she is not what she seems, then a nunnery in its other sense of brothel is relevant to her. In the scene that follows he treats her as if she were indeed an inmate of a brothel.

Likewise, from Hamlet's point of view, there is the enigma of the king. If the ghost is *only* an appearance, then possibly the king's appearance is reality. He must try it further. By means of a second and different kind of "apparition," the play within the play, he does so. But then, immediately after, he stumbles on the king at prayer. This appearance has a relish of salvation in it. If the king dies now, his soul may yet be saved. Yet actually, as we know, the king's efforts to come to terms with heaven have been unavailing; his words fly up, his thoughts remain below. If Hamlet means the conventional revenger's reasons that he gives for sparing Claudius, it was the perfect moment not to spare him—when the sinner was acknowledging his guilt, yet unrepentant. The perfect moment, but it was hidden, like so much else in the play, behind an arras.

There are two arrases in his mother's room. Hamlet thrusts his sword through one of them. Now at last he has got to the heart of the evil, or so he thinks. But now it is the

wrong man; now he himself is a murderer. The other arras
he stabs through with his words—like daggers, says the
queen. He makes her shrink under the contrast he points between her present husband and his father. But as the play
now stands (matters are somewhat clearer in the bad
Quarto), it is hard to be sure how far the queen grasps the
fact that her second husband is the murderer of her first.
And it is hard to say what may be signified by her inability
to see the ghost, who now for the last time appears. In one
sense at least, the ghost is the supreme reality, representa-
tive of the hidden ultimate power, in Bradley's terms—
witnessing from beyond the grave against this hollow
world. Yet the man who is capable of seeing through to this
reality, the queen thinks is mad. "To whom do you speak
this?" she cries to her son. "Do you see nothing there?" he
asks, incredulous. And she replies: "Nothing at all; yet all
that is I see." Here certainly we have the imperturbable
self-confidence of the worldly world, its layers on layers of
habituation, so that when the reality is before its very eyes
it cannot detect its presence.

Like mystery, this problem of reality is central to the
play and written deep into its idiom. Shakespeare's favorite
terms in *Hamlet* are words of ordinary usage that pose the
question of appearances in a fundamental form. "Apparition" I have already mentioned. Another term is "seems."
When we say, as Ophelia says of Hamlet leaving her closet,
"He seem'd to find his way without his eyes," we mean one
thing. When we say, as Hamlet says to his mother in
the first court scene, "Seems, Madam! ... I know not
'seems.' " we mean another. And when we say, as Hamlet
says to Horatio before the play within the play, "And after,
we will both our judgments join In censure of his seeming,"
we mean both at once. The ambiguities of "seem" coil and
uncoil throughout this play, and over against them is set the
idea of "seeing." So Hamlet challenges the king in his triumphant letter announcing his return to Denmark: "Tomorrow shall I beg leave to see your kingly eyes." Yet "seeing"
itself can be ambiguous, as we recognize from Hamlet's
uncertainty about the ghost; or from that statement of his

mother's already quoted: "Nothing at all; yet all that is I see."

Another term of like importance is "assume." What we assume may be what we are not: "The de'il hath power T' assume a pleasing shape." But it may be what we are: "If it assume my noble father's person, I'll speak to it." And it may be what we are not yet, but would become; thus Hamlet advises his mother, "Assume a virtue, if you have it not." The perplexity in the word points to a real perplexity in Hamlet's and our own experience. We assume our habits—and habits are like costumes, as the word implies: "My father in his habit as he liv'd!" Yet these habits become ourselves in time: "That monster, custom, who all sense doth eat Of habits evil, is angel yet in this, That to the use of actions fair and good He likewise gives a frock of livery That aptly is put on."

Two other terms I wish to instance are "put on" and "shape." The shape of something is the form under which we are accustomed to apprehend it: "Do you see yonder cloud that's almost in shape of a camel?" But a shape may also be a disguise—even, in Shakespeare's time, an actor's costume or an actor's role. This is the meaning when the king says to Laertes as they lay the plot against Hamlet's life: "Weigh what convenience both of time and means May fit us to our shape." "Put on" supplies an analogous ambiguity. Shakespeare's mind seems to worry this phrase in the play much as Hamlet's mind worries the problem of acting in a world of surfaces, or the king's mind worries the meaning of Hamlet's transformation. Hamlet has put an antic disposition on, that the king knows. But what does "put on" mean? A mask, or a frock or livery—our "habit"? The king is left guessing, and so are we.

What is found in the play's key terms is also found in its imagery. Miss Spurgeon has called attention to a pattern of disease images in *Hamlet*, to which I shall return. But the play has other patterns equally striking. One of these, as my earlier quotations hint, is based on clothes. In the world of surfaces to which Shakespeare exposes us in *Hamlet*, clothes are naturally a factor of importance. "The apparel oft proclaims the man," Polonius assures Laertes,

cataloguing maxims in the young man's ear as he is about
to leave for Paris. Oft, but not always. And so he sends his
man Reynaldo to look into Laertes' life there—even, if
need be, to put a false dress of accusation upon his son
("What forgeries you please"), the better by indirections to
find directions out. On the same grounds, he takes Hamlet's vows to Ophelia as false apparel. They are bawds, he
tells her—or if we do not like Theobald's emendation,
they are bonds—in masquerade, "Not of that dye which
their investments show, But mere implorators of unholy
suits."

This breach between the outer and the inner stirs no special emotion in Polonius, because he is always either behind an arras or prying into one, but it shakes Hamlet to the
core. Here so recently was his mother in her widow's
weeds, the tears still flushing in her galled eyes; yet now
within a month, a little month, before even her funeral
shoes are old, she has married with his uncle. Her mourning
was all clothes. Not so his own, he bitterly replies, when
she asks him to cast his "nighted color off." " 'Tis not alone
my inky cloak, good mother"—and not alone, he adds, the
sighs, the tears, the dejected havior of the visage—"that can
denote me truly."

> These indeed seem,
> For they are actions that a man might play,
> But I have that within which passes show;
> These but the trappings and the suits of woe. (1.2.83–86)

What we must not overlook here is Hamlet's visible attire, giving the verbal imagery a theatrical extension. Hamlet's apparel now is his inky cloak, mark of his grief for his
father, mark also of his character as a man of melancholy,
mark possibly too of his being one in whom appearance
and reality are attuned. Later, in his madness, with his mind
disordered, he will wear his costume in a corresponding
disarray, the disarray that Ophelia describes so vividly to
Polonius and that producers of the play rarely give sufficient heed to: "Lord Hamlet with his doublet all unbrac'd,

No hat upon his head; his stockings foul'd, Ungarter'd, and down-gyved to his ankle." Here the only question will be, as with the madness itself, how much is studied, how much is real. Still later, by a third costume, the simple traveler's garb in which we find him new come from shipboard, Shakespeare will show us that we have a third aspect of the man.

A second pattern of imagery springs from terms of painting: the paints, the colorings, the varnishes that may either conceal, or, as in the painter's art, reveal. Art in Claudius conceals. "The harlot's cheek," he tells us in his one aside, "beautied with plastering art, Is not more ugly to the thing that helps it Than is my deed to my most painted word." Art in Ophelia, loosed to Hamlet in the episode already noticed to which this speech of the king's is prelude, is more complex. She looks so beautiful—"the celestial, and my soul's idol, the most beautified Ophelia," Hamlet has called her in his love letter. But now, what does beautified mean? Perfected with all the innocent beauties of a lovely woman? Or "beautied" like the harlot's cheek? "I have heard of your paintings too, well enough. God hath given you one face, and you make yourselves another."

Yet art, differently used, may serve the truth. By using an "image" (his own word) of a murder done in Vienna, Hamlet cuts through to the king's guilt; holds "as 'twere, the mirror up to nature," shows "virtue her own feature, scorn her own image, and the very age and body of the time"—which is out of joint—"his form and pressure." Something similar he does again in his mother's bedroom, painting for her in words "the rank sweat of an enseamed bed," making her recoil in horror from his "counterfeit presentment of two brothers," and holding, if we may trust a stage tradition, his father's picture beside his uncle's. Here again the verbal imagery is realized visually on the stage.

The most pervasive of Shakespeare's image patterns in this play, however, is the pattern evolved around the three words, "show," "act," "play." "Show" seems to be Shakespeare's unifying image in *Hamlet*. Through it he pulls together and exhibits in a single focus much of the diverse

material in his play. The ideas of seeming, assuming, and
putting on; the images of clothing, painting, mirroring; the
episode of the dumb show and the play within the play;
the characters of Polonius, Laertes, Ophelia, Claudius,
Gertrude, Rosencrantz and Guildenstern, Hamlet himself—
all these at one time or another, and usually more than
once, are drawn into the range of implications flung round
the play by "show."

"Act," on the other hand, I take to be the play's radical
metaphor. It distills the various perplexities about the character of reality into a residual perplexity about the character of an act. What, this play asks again and again, is an
act? What is its relation to the inner act, the intent? "If I
drown myself wittingly," says the clown in the graveyard,
"it argues an act, and an act hath three branches; it is to
act, to do, to perform." Or again, the play asks, how does
action relate to passion, that "laps'd in time and passion" I
can let "go by Th' important acting of your dread command"; and to thought, which can so sickly o'er the native
hue of resolution that "enterprises of great pitch and moment With this regard their currents turn awry, And lose
the name of action"; and to words, which are not acts, and
so we dare not be content to unpack our hearts with them,
and yet are acts of a sort, for we may speak daggers though
we use none. Or still again, how does an act (a deed) relate
to an act (a pretense)? For an action may be nothing but
pretense. So Polonius readying Ophelia for the interview
with Hamlet, with "pious action," as he phrases it,
"sugar[s] o'er The devil himself." Or it may not be a pretense, yet not what it appears. So Hamlet spares the king,
finding him in an act that has some "relish of salvation
in 't." Or it may be a pretense that is also the first foothold
of a new reality, as when we assume a virtue though we
have it not. Or it may be a pretense that is actually a mirroring of reality, like the play within the play, or the
tragedy of *Hamlet*.

To this network of implications, the third term, "play,"
adds an additional dimension. "Play" is a more precise
word, in Elizabethan parlance at least, for all the elements
in *Hamlet* that pertain to the art of the theater; and it ex-

tends their field of reference till we see that every major personage in the tragedy is a player in some sense, and every major episode a play. The court plays, Hamlet plays, the players play, Rosencrantz and Guildenstern try to play on Hamlet, though they cannot play on his recorders—here we have an extension to a musical sense. And the final duel, by a further extension, becomes itself a play, in which everyone but Claudius and Laertes plays his role in ignorance: "The queen desires you to show some gentle entertainment to Laertes before you fall to play." "I . . . will this brother's wager frankly play." "Give him the cup."—"I'll play this bout first."

The full extension of this theme is best evidenced in the play within the play itself. Here, in the bodily presence of these traveling players, bringing with them the latest playhouse gossip out of London, we have suddenly a situation that tends to dissolve the normal barriers between the fictive and the real. For here on the stage before us is a play of false appearances in which an actor called the player-king is playing. But there is also on the stage, Claudius, another player-king, who is a spectator of this player. And there is on the stage, besides, a prince who is a spectator of both these player-kings and who plays with great intensity a player's role himself. And around these kings and that prince is a group of courtly spectators—Gertrude, Rosencrantz, Guildenstern, Polonius, and the rest—and they, as we have come to know, are players too. And lastly there are ourselves, an audience watching all these audiences who are also players. Where, it may suddenly occur to us to ask, does the playing end? Which *are* the guilty creatures sitting at a play? When is an act not an "act"?

The mysteriousness of Hamlet's world, while it pervades the tragedy, finds its point of greatest dramatic concentration in the first act, and its symbol in the first scene. The problems of appearance and reality also pervade the play as a whole, but come to a climax in Acts 2 and 3, and possibly their best symbol is the play within the play. Our third attribute, though again it is one that crops out everywhere, reaches its full development in Acts 4 and 5. It is not easy to find an appropriate name for this attribute, but perhaps "mortality" will serve, if we remember to mean by mortality the heartache and the thousand natural shocks that flesh is heir to, not simply death.

The powerful sense of mortality in *Hamlet* is conveyed to us, I think, in three ways. First, there is the play's emphasis on human weakness, the instability of human purpose, the subjection of humanity to fortune—all that we might call the aspect of failure in man. Hamlet opens this theme in Act 1, when he describes how from that single blemish, perhaps not even the victim's fault, a man's whole character may take corruption. Claudius dwells on it again, to an extent that goes far beyond the needs of the occasion, while engaged in seducing Laertes to step behind the arras of a seemer's world and dispose of Hamlet by a trick. Time qualifies everything, Claudius says, including love, including purpose. As for love—it has a "plurisy" in it and dies of its own too much. As for purpose—"That we would do, We should do when we would, for this 'would' changes, And hath abatements and delays as many As there are tongues, are hands, are accidents; And then this 'should' is like a spendthrift's sigh, That hurts by easing." The player-king, in his long speeches to his queen in the play within the play, sets the matter in a still darker light. She means these protestations of undying love, he knows, but our purposes depend on our memory, and our memory fades fast. Or else, he suggests, we propose something to ourselves in a condition of strong feeling, but then the feeling goes, and with it the resolve. Or else our fortunes change, he adds, and with these our loves: "The great man down, you mark his favorite flies." The subjection of human aims to fortune is a reiterated theme in *Hamlet*, as subsequently in *Lear*. Fortune is the harlot goddess in whose secret parts men like Rosencrantz and Guildenstern live and thrive; the strumpet who threw down Troy and Hecuba and Priam; the outrageous foe whose slings and arrows a man of principle must suffer or seek release in suicide. Horatio suffers them with composure: he is one of the blessed few "Whose blood and judgment are so well co-mingled That they are not a pipe for fortune's finger To sound what stop she please." For Hamlet the task is of a greater difficulty.

Next, and intimately related to this matter of infirmity, is the emphasis on infection—the ulcer, the hidden abscess, "th' imposthume of much wealth and peace That inward breaks and shows no cause without Why the man dies." Miss Spurgeon, who was the first to call attention to this aspect of the play, has well remarked that so far as Shakespeare's pictorial imagination is concerned, the problem in *Hamlet* is not a problem of the will and reason, "of a mind too philosophical or a nature temperamentally unfitted to act quickly," nor even a problem of an individual at all. Rather, it is a condition—"a condition for which the individual himself is apparently not responsible, any more than the sick man is to blame for the infection which strikes and devours him, but which, nevertheless, in its course and development, impartially and relentlessly, annihilates him and others, innocent and guilty alike." "That," she adds, "is the tragedy of *Hamlet,* as it is perhaps the chief tragic mystery of life." This is a perceptive comment, for it reminds us that Hamlet's situation is mainly not of his own manufacture, as are the situations of Shakespeare's other tragic heroes. He has inherited it; he is "born to set it right."

We must not, however, neglect to add to this what another student of Shakespeare's imagery has noticed—that the infection in Denmark is presented alternatively as poison. Here, of course, responsibility is implied, for the poisoner of the play is Claudius. The juice he pours into the ear of the elder Hamlet is a combined poison and disease, a "leperous distillment" that curds "the thin and wholesome blood." From this fatal center, unwholesomeness spreads out till there is something rotten in all Denmark. Hamlet tells us that his "wit's diseased," the queen speaks of her "sick soul," the king is troubled by "the hectic" in his blood, Laertes meditates revenge to warm "the sickness in my heart," the people of the kingdom grow "muddied, Thick and unwholesome in their thoughts"; and even Ophelia's madness is said to be "the poison of deep grief." In the end, all save Ophelia die of that poison in a literal as well as figurative sense.

But the chief form in which the theme of mortality reaches us, it seems to me, is as a profound consciousness of loss. Hamlet's father expresses something of the kind when he tells Hamlet how his "[most] seeming-virtuous queen," betraying a love which "was of that dignity That it went hand in hand even with the vow I made to her in marriage," had chosen to "decline Upon a wretch whose natural gifts were poor To those of mine." "O Hamlet, what a falling off was there!" Ophelia expresses it again, on hearing Hamlet's denunciation of love and woman in the nunnery scene, which she takes to be the product of a disordered brain:

> O what a noble mind is here o'erthrown!
> The courtier's, soldier's, scholar's, eye, tongue, sword,
> Th' expectancy and rose of the fair state,
> The glass of fashion, and the mold of form,
> Th' observ'd of all observers, quite, quite down!   (3.1.153–57)

The passage invites us to remember that we have never actually seen such a Hamlet—that his mother's marriage has brought a falling off in him before we met him. And then there is that further falling off, if I may call it so, when Ophelia too goes mad—"Divided from herself and her fair judgment, Without the which we are pictures, or mere beasts."

Time was, the play keeps reminding us, when Denmark was a different place. That was before Hamlet's mother took off "the rose From the fair forehead of an innocent love" and set a blister there. Hamlet then was still "Th' expectancy and rose of the fair state"; Ophelia, the "rose of May." For Denmark was a garden then, when his father ruled. There had been something heroic about his father—a king who met the threats to Denmark in open battle, fought with Norway, smote the sledded Polacks on the ice, slew the elder Fortinbras in an honorable trial of strength. There had been something godlike about his father too: "Hyperion's curls, the front of Jove himself, An eye like Mars . . . A station like the herald Mercury." But, the ghost reveals, a serpent was in the garden, and "the serpent that did sting thy father's life Now wears his crown." The martial virtues are put by now. The threats to Denmark are attended to by policy, by agents working deviously for and through an uncle. The moral virtues are put by too. Hyperion's throne is occupied by "a vice of kings," "a king of shreds and patches"; Hyperion's bed, by a satyr, a paddock, a bat, a gib, a bloat king with reechy kisses. The garden is unweeded now, and "grows to seed; things rank and gross in nature Possess it merely." Even in himself he feels the taint, the taint of being his mother's son; and that other taint, from an earlier garden, of which he admonishes Ophelia: "Our virtue cannot so inoculate our old stock but we shall relish of it." "Why wouldst thou be a breeder of sinners?" "What should such fellows as I do crawling between earth and heaven?"

"Hamlet is painfully aware," says Professor Tillyard, "of the baffling human predicament between the angels and the beasts, between the glory of having been made in God's image and the incrimination of being descended from fallen Adam." To this we may add, I think, that Hamlet is more than aware of it; he exemplifies it; and it is for this reason that his problem appeals to us so powerfully as an image of our own.

Hamlet's problem, in its crudest form, is simply the problem of the avenger: He must carry out the injunction of the ghost and kill the king. But this problem, as I ventured to suggest at the outset, is presented in terms of a certain kind of world. The ghost's injunction to act becomes so inextricably bound up for Hamlet with the character of the world in which the action must be taken—its mysteriousness, its baffling appearances, its deep consciousness of infection, frailty, and loss—that he cannot come to terms with either without coming to terms with both.

When we first see him in the play, he is clearly a very young man, sensitive and idealistic, suffering the first shock of growing up. He has taken the garden at face value, we might say, supposing mankind to be only a little lower than the angels. Now in his mother's hasty and incestuous marriage, he discovers evidence of something else, something bestial—though even a beast, he thinks, would have mourned longer. Then comes the revelation of the ghost, bringing a second shock. Not so much because he now knows that his serpent-uncle killed his father; his prophetic soul had almost suspected this. Not entirely, even, because he knows now how far below the angels humanity has fallen in his mother, and how lust—these were the ghost's words—"though to a radiant angel link'd Will sate itself in a celestial bed, And prey on garbage." Rather, because he now sees everywhere, but especially in his own nature, the general taint, taking from life its meaning, from woman her integrity, from the will its strength, turning reason into madness. "Why wouldst thou be a breeder of sinners?" "What should such fellows as I do crawling between earth and heaven?" Hamlet is not the first young man to have felt the heavy and the weary weight of all this unintelligible world; and, like the others, he must come to terms with it.

The ghost's injunction to revenge unfolds a different facet of his problem. The young man growing up is not to be allowed simply to endure a rotten world, he must also act in it. Yet how to begin, among so many enigmatic surfaces? Even Claudius, whom he now knows to be the core of the ulcer, has a plausible exterior. And around Claudius, swathing the evil out of sight, he encounters all those other exteriors, as we have seen. Some of them already deeply infected beneath, like his mother. Some noble, but marked for infection, like Laertes. Some not particularly corrupt but infinitely corruptible, like Rosencrantz and Guildenstern; some mostly weak and foolish like Polonius and Osric. Some, like Ophelia, innocent, yet in their innocence still serving to "skin and film the ulcerous place."

And this is not all. The act required of him, though retributive justice, is one that necessarily involves the doer in the general guilt. Not only because it involves a killing; but because to get at the world of seeming one sometimes has to use its weapons. He himself, before he finishes, has become a player, has put an antic disposition on, has killed a man—the wrong man—has helped drive Ophelia mad, and has sent two friends of his youth to death, mining below their mines, and hoisting the engineer with his own petard. He had never meant to dirty himself with these things, but from the moment of the ghost's challenge to act, this dirtying was inevitable. It is the condition of living at all in such a world. To quote Polonius, who knew that world so well, men become "a little soil'd i' th' working." Here is another matter with which Hamlet has to come to terms.

Human infirmity—all that I have discussed with reference to instability, infection, loss—supplies the problem with its third phase. Hamlet has not only to accept the mystery of man's condition between the angels and the brutes, and not only to act in a perplexing and soiling world. He has also to act within the human limits—"with shabby equipment always deteriorating," if I may adapt some phrases from Eliot's *East Coker*, "In the general mess of imprecision of feeling, Undisciplined squads of emotion." Hamlet is aware of that fine poise of body and mind, feeling and thought, that suits the action to the word, the word to the action; that acquires and begets a temperance in the very torrent, tempest, and whirlwind of passion; but he cannot at first achieve it in himself. He vacillates between undisciplined squads of emotion and thinking too precisely on the event. He learns to his cost how easily action can be lost in "acting," and loses it there for a time himself. But these again are only the terms of every man's life. As Anatole France reminds us in a now famous apostrophe to Hamlet: "What one of us thinks without contradiction and acts without incoherence? What one of us is not mad? What one of us does not say with a mixture of pity, comradeship, admiration, and horror, Goodnight, sweet Prince!"

In the last act of the play (or so it seems to me, for I know there can be differences on this point), Hamlet accepts his world and we discover a different man. Shakespeare does not outline for us the process of acceptance any more than he had done with Romeo or was to do with Othello. But he leads us strongly to expect an altered Hamlet, and then, in my opinion, provides him. We must

recall that at this point Hamlet has been absent from the
stage during several scenes, and that such absences in
Shakespearean tragedy usually warn us to be on the watch
for a new phase in the development of the character. It is
so when we leave King Lear in Gloucester's farmhouse
and find him again in Dover fields. It is so when we leave
Macbeth at the witches' cave and rejoin him at Dunsi-
nane, hearing of the armies that beset it. Furthermore, and
this is an important matter in the theater—especially important in a play in which the symbolism of clothing has
figured largely—Hamlet now looks different. He is
wearing a different dress—probably, as Granville-Barker
thinks, his "seagown scarf'd" about him, but in any case
no longer the disordered costume of his antic disposition.
The effect is not entirely dissimilar to that in *Lear*, when
the old king wakes out of his madness to find fresh garments on him.

Still more important, Hamlet displays a considerable
change of mood. This is not a matter of the way we take
the passage about defying augury, as Mr. Tillyard among
others seems to think. It is a matter of Hamlet's whole de-
portment, in which I feel we may legitimately see the de-
portment of a man who has been "illuminated" in the
tragic sense. Bradley's term for it is fatalism, but if this is
what we wish to call it, we must at least acknowledge that
it is fatalism of a very distinctive kind—a kind that
Shakespeare has been willing to touch with the associa-
tions of the saying in St. Matthew about the fall of a sparrow, and with Hamlet's recognition that a divinity shapes
our ends. The point is not that Hamlet has suddenly become religious; he has been religious all through the play.
The point is that he has now learned, and accepted, the
boundaries in which human action, human judgment, are
enclosed.

Till his return from the voyage he had been trying to act
beyond these, had been encroaching on the role of providence, if I may exaggerate to make a vital point. He had
been too quick to take the burden of the whole world and
its condition upon his limited and finite self. Faced with a
task of sufficient difficulty in its own right, he had dilated it

into a cosmic problem—as indeed every task is, but if we think about this too precisely we cannot act at all. The whole time is out of joint, he feels, and in his young man's egocentricity, he will set it right. Hence he misjudges Ophelia, seeing in her only a breeder of sinners. Hence he misjudges himself, seeing himself a vermin crawling between earth and heaven. Hence he takes it upon himself to be his mother's conscience, though the ghost has warned that this is no fit task for him, and returns to repeat the warning: "Leave her to heaven, And to those thorns that in her bosom lodge." Even with the king, Hamlet has sought to play at God. *He* it must be who decides the issue of Claudius's salvation, saving him for a more damnable occasion. Now, he has learned that there are limits to the before and after that human reason can comprehend. Rashness, even, is sometimes good. Through rashness he has saved his life from the commission for his death, "and prais'd be rashness for it." This happy circumstance and the unexpected arrival of the pirate ship make it plain that the roles of life are not entirely self-assigned. "There is a divinity that shapes our ends, Rough-hew them how we will." Hamlet is ready now for what may happen, seeking neither to foreknow it nor avoid it. "If it be now, 'tis not to come; if it be not to come, it will be now; if it be not now, yet it will come: the readiness is all."

The crucial evidence of Hamlet's new frame of mind, as I understand it, is the graveyard scene. Here, in its ultimate symbol, he confronts, recognizes, and accepts the condition of being man. It is not simply that he now accepts death, though Shakespeare shows him accepting it in ever more poignant forms: first, in the imagined persons of the politician, the courtier, and the lawyer, who laid their little schemes "to circumvent God," as Hamlet puts it, but now lie here; then in Yorick, whom he knew and played with as a child; and then in Ophelia. This last death tears from him a final cry of passion, but the striking contrast between his behavior and Laertes's reveals how deeply he has changed.

Still, it is not the fact of death that invests this scene with its peculiar power. It is instead the haunting mystery of life itself that Hamlet's speeches point to, holding in its inscrutable folds those other mysteries that he has wrestled with so long. These he now knows for what they are, and lays them by. The mystery of evil is present here—for this is after all the universal graveyard, where, as the clown says humorously, he holds up Adam's profession; where the scheming politician, the hollow courtier, the tricky lawyer, the emperor and the clown and the beautiful young maiden, all come together in an emblem of the world; where even, Hamlet murmurs, one might expect to stumble on "Cain's jawbone, that did the first murther." The mystery of reality is here too—for death puts the question, "What is real?" in its irreducible form, and in the end uncovers all appearances: "Is this the fine of his fines and the recovery of his recoveries, to have his fine pate full of fine dirt?" "Now get you to my lady's chamber, and tell her, let her paint an inch thick, to this favor she must come." Or if we need more evidence of this mystery, there is the anger of Laertes at the lack of ceremonial trappings, and the ambiguous character of Ophelia's own death. "Is she to be buried in Christian burial when she willfully seeks her own salvation?" asks the gravedigger. And last of all, but most pervasive of all, there is the mystery of human limitation. The grotesque nature of man's little joys, his big ambitions. The fact that the man who used to bear us on his back is now a skull that smells; that the noble dust of Alexander somewhere plugs a bunghole; that "Imperious Caesar, dead and turn'd to clay, Might stop a hole to keep the wind away." Above all, the fact that a pit of clay is "meet" for such a guest as man, as the gravedigger tells us in his song, and yet that, despite all frailties and limitations, "That skull had a tongue in it and could sing once."

After the graveyard and what it indicates has come to pass in him, we know that Hamlet is ready for the final contest of mighty opposites. He accepts the world as it is, the world as a duel, in which, whether we know it or not, evil holds the poisoned rapier and the poisoned chalice waits; and in which, if we win at all, it costs not less than everything. I think we understand by the close of Shakespeare's *Hamlet* why it is that unlike the other tragic heroes he is given a soldier's rites upon the stage. For as William Butler Yeats once said, "Why should we honor those who die on the field of battle? A man may show as reckless a courage in entering into the abyss of himself."

ROBERT ORNSTEIN

From The Moral Vision of Jacobean Tragedy

The impression of vastness in *Macbeth* is created almost entirely by poetic suggestion. The play lacks the intellectual dimension and richness of thought which make *Hamlet* seem to the critics the most philosophical of Shakespeare's plays. Honor, revenge, justice, political order, Stoicism, friendship, familial piety—how many Renaissance ideas and ideals come under scrutiny in the halls of Elsinore. And yet how little is there in the lines of *Hamlet* which testifies to Shakespeare's intellectual or philosophical powers. Subjected to philosophical analysis the great speeches in *Hamlet* yield commonplaces. We treasure them for their incomparable poetry, not for their depth and originality of thought—for their revelation of Hamlet's soul, not for their discovery of the human condition. Many questions are raised in the play but few are answered. The question of action in an evil society, one might say, is resolved by an expedient dear to Victorian novelists: a change of air, a sea voyage from which the hero returns calm if not resolute, buoyed by a vaguely optimistic fatalism that is half-Christian, half-Stoic.

My point is not that Shakespeare tricks us into accepting a sham or meretricious resolution in *Hamlet*, but that we do

From *The Moral Vision of Jacobean Tragedy* by Robert Ornstein. (Madison, Wisconsin: The University of Wisconsin Press, 1960) Reprinted by permission of the copyright owners, the Regents of The University of Wisconsin.

not find in Shakespearean drama the intellectual schemes of Chapman's tragedies. Even when Shakespeare seems to dramatize a thesis, he does not debate philosophical positions. He is not interested in abstract thought but in characters who think, who have intellectual as well as emotional needs, and who, like Pirandello's characters, cry aloud the reason of their suffering. The "problem" of *Hamlet* is not an intellectual puzzle. It arises because the play creates so marvelous a sense of the actual improvisation of life that we can find no simple logic in its sprawling action. Unable to comprehend or accept the totality of Shakespeare's many-sided hero, we search for a more logical, more consistent, or more pleasant Hamlet than the play affords. We try to arrive at Shakespeare's moral ideas by reading Elizabethan treatises of psychology and moral philosophy, when it is only by studying the total artifice of *Hamlet* that we can understand why its hero seems to us the most noble, pure-minded, and blameless of Shakespeare's tragic protagonists. What is not near Hamlet's conscience is not near our own because he is our moral interpreter. He is the voice of ethical sensibility in a sophisticated, courtly milieu; his bitter asides, which penetrate Claudius' façade of kingly virtue and propriety, initiate, so to speak, the moral action of the play. And throughout the play our identification with Hamlet's moral vision is such that we hate what he hates, admire what he admires. As centuries of Shakespeare criticism reveal, we accuse Hamlet primarily of what he accuses himself: namely, his slowness to revenge.

Our moral impression of Hamlet's character derives primarily from what he says rather than what he does. It is an almost intuitive awareness of the beauty, depth, and refinement of his moral nature, upon which is thrust a savage burden of revenge and of disillusion. If Shakespeare's characters are illusions created by dramatic artifice, then what we love in Hamlet is an illusion within an illusion: i.e., the suggestion of Hamlet's former self, the Hamlet whom Ophelia remembers and who poignantly reappears in the conversations with Horatio, particularly before the catastrophe. Through his consummate artistry Shakespeare creates within us a sympathy with Hamlet which becomes almost an act of faith—a confidence in the untouched and untouchable core of his spiritual nature. This act of faith, renewed by the great speeches throughout the play, allows us to accept Hamlet's brutality towards Ophelia, his reaction to Polonius' death, his savage refusal to kill Claudius at prayer, and his Machiavellian delight in disposing of Rosencrantz and Guildenstern. Without the memory of the great soliloquies which preceded it, our impression of the closet scene would be vastly different. And, in fact, to attempt to define Hamlet's character by weighing his motives and actions against any system of Renaissance thought is to stage *Hamlet* morally without the Prince of Denmark, i.e., without the felt impression of Hamlet's moral nature which is created by poetic nuance.

Life is mysterious and unpredictable in *Hamlet*. Appearances are deceptive, little is what it seems to be, and no man can foresee the consequence of his acts. Yet we are not left with the sense that Shakespeare's characters move through the mist which envelops Webster's tragic universe. We see with a perfect clarity that the pattern of catastrophe emerges inexorably as the consequence of Claudius's hidden guilt and from his need for deviousness and secrecy. If the ambiguities and the mysteries of *Hamlet* irritate us, it is because we expect an omniscient view of character in drama; we are not used to seeing a play almost entirely from the point of view of a single character. We do not realize that our identification with Hamlet is as complete as with a first-person narrator of a novel. We see little more than he sees; we know little more about the other characters—about Gertrude's crimes or Rosencrantz and Guildenstern's treachery—than he finally knows. If we had to examine objectively the facts of the play to decide whether Hamlet should have had Rosencrantz and Guildenstern executed, then their innocence or guilt would be a crucial matter; but since like Hamlet we identify Rosencrantz and Guildenstern with Claudius' cause, what they knew or did not know of Claudius' plans "does not matter."

It is Hamlet (not the Romantic critics) who creates the problem of his delay in revenge. Were it not for the self-lacerating soliloquies in which he accuses himself of the grossness and insensitivity which he despises in his mother, the thought that he delays would not occur to us. During a performance of the play we do not feel that Hamlet procrastinates or puts off action. From his first appearance, he is engaged in a secret struggle with the shrewd and suspicious Claudius; there is scarcely a moment when he is not fending off one of the King's spies or dupes. In the study a critic can be quite bloodthirsty about Hamlet's failure to dispatch Claudius. In the theater, however, one does not feel that Hamlet should have skewered Claudius at prayer or should have been more interested in Claudius's damnation than his mother's salvation. Nor does one feel that the Hamlet who says, "The interim is mine" is "delaying."

This is not to say that Shakespeare posed an artificial problem in Hamlet's soliloquies in order to make mad the critics and appall the scholars. The problem of action in an evil world is as real in *Hamlet* as in many of the revenge plays of the period. True to his father's command, Hamlet engages in fierce struggle against the world without tainting his mind. False to himself and to his father's advice, Laertes is corrupted and debased by the hunger for vengeance. Although Hamlet commits rash and bloody deeds and comes to take a sardonic delight in flanking policy with policy, he does not, like Vindice, become unfit for life. On the contrary, we feel that he dies just when he is ready to embrace life, when his cloud of melancholy has lifted and he stands before us the very quintessence of dust— beautiful in mind and spirit, noble in thought and feeling, alert, high-spirited, superior to the accidents and passions which corrupt lesser men. We do not feel that Hamlet must die because he has sinned. The inevitability of his death is an aesthetic, not moral, expectation created by the insistent imagery of death, by the mood of the graveyard scene, by Hamlet's premonitions, and by the finality of Claudius's triple-stopped treachery. The calm of the graveyard scene, coming after the feverish action that preceded Hamlet's departure for England, seems a false recovery before death, that brief moment of detachment and lucidity which is often granted dying men. Enhancing this poignant impression are the very simple, quiet responses of Horatio, who attends the final hours of his Prince.

The problem of action in *Hamlet* is posed immediately and ultimately by Death, the philosophical tutor who forces man to consider the value of existence. Because the death of his father has made life meaningless, Hamlet wishes for the release of suicide, which is by traditional standards a cowardly evasion and negation of life. Yet, paradoxically, the willingness and eagerness of Fortinbras' army to die seems to give meaning to a cause that would be otherwise contemptible and valueless. And whether one takes arms against a sea of troubles (an apparently hopeless undertaking) or suffers the arrows and slings of outrageous fortune, there is only one possible conclusion to the action of life, the stillness of the grave. *Hamlet* begins with terrified sentries awaiting the return of the dead. It closes with the solemn march of soldiers bearing Hamlet's body "to the stage." Throughout the play Hamlet faces the most ancient and abiding philosophical problem: He must "learn how to die," i.e., how to live with the fact and thought of death. When he first appears, he seems overwhelmed by his first intimate experience of mortality—the sudden, unexpected loss of his father. Claudius may first address the court on affairs of state and then grant Laertes his "fair hour," but eventually he must deal with the gross insult of Hamlet's ostentatious mourning. In his most suave manner he offers his stepson the consolation of philosophy; he refers to the immemorial fact of mortality and grief, to the commonness and naturalness of death, to the need for the living to dedicate themselves to life. For Hamlet these platitudes have no meaning. He does not mourn because *man* dies; nor is he tormented only by the loss of a father. When he exposes his inner feelings in the first soliloquy we realize that Claudius has completely missed the point. Hamlet's problem is not to accept his father's death but to accept a world in which death has lost its meaning and its message for the living—a world in which only the visitation of a Ghost restores some sense of the mystery and awe of the grave. In his disgust for Gertrude's frailty, Hamlet broods over the debt that the living owe to the dead, the wife to the husband and the son to the father. Gertrude advises her son not to seek his father in the dust, but the Ghost brings the shattering command that the living owe the dead the obligation of vengeance, of taking arms against a world which destroys virtue. Though anguished that the time is out of joint, Hamlet embraces revenge as a dedication which is to give meaning to an otherwise empty existence. And justly or not he accuses himself again and again of failure to carry out his obligation to the dead.

When he returns to Denmark from his sea voyage, however, he is no longer tormented by guilt; his self-laceration and disgust with life have given way to a stoic calm that obliterates the need for immediate action. He has not formulated a new philosophy or come to intellectual terms with life. He has the fatalistic composure possible only to those who have achieved an intimate communion with death—who have killed and have narrowly escaped a mortal stroke. Having passed through a lifetime of experience in a brief span, he seems to share Montaigne's knowledge that men do not require philosophy to know how to die, because life provides all the requisite information and no man has yet failed to pass the test of his mortality. Our life, the action of *Hamlet* reveals, is a process of dying and all roads end where the gravedigger's work begins.

A mind that can trace Alexander's dust to a bunghole can no longer envy the heroic dedication of a Fortinbras. Although still intending to call Claudius to account, Hamlet is no longer obsessed by an obligation to the dead; he speaks mainly now of punitive justice and of his personal conflict with the King. Ironically enough, experience has taught him the sageness of Claudius's platitudes. The young mourner who cried out against the commonness of death now finds solace in its vast equality and anonymity. Counseled before not to seek his father in the dust, he now recoils from the skull of Yorick, who played with him as a father with a child. Compared to the stink of putrefaction, the sins of the flesh seem now more amusing than revolting to Hamlet. Once he hugged death as an escape from the burden of living; now the too too solid flesh melting from the bone no longer seems a consummation devoutly to be wished for. We see in his detached meditations on death a new dedication to life, for he is amused not by the vanity of existence but by the absurd ways in which men waste their precious hours of sentience. What do the living owe to the dead? The coarse familiarity of the gravediggers with the remains of the departed suggests a final answer.

Like all men Hamlet can triumph only over the impersonal fact of death. When he learns that the grave is for Ophelia, his jesting detachment vanishes. As the funeral procession enters the stage, the wheel comes full circle; the play begins again with another mourner in Hamlet's role. Now it is the youthful Laertes who protests with hyperbolic and theatrical gestures of grief the dishonor of his family that is symbolized by the "maimed rites" of death. His emotional extravagance elicits Hamlet's last moment of theatricality: the struggle in the grave that again strips dignity from the ceremony of death.

In the breathing space before the fencing scene there is a haunting moment of repose, of youthful communion, of laughter at Osric's absurdity; there is a poignant sense of recovery and stability. Is there also a more positive religious note? Are we to assume from Hamlet's references to heaven, divinity, and providence that he is now convinced of the great moral design of creation? Or do we see a Hamlet bowing before a universe which defies man's intellectual attempts at comprehension? The sequence of accidents that saved his life appears in retrospect providential, but it provides no guide to future action, no counsel, no direction. Although his restlessness at sea seemed a touch of grace, he shrugs off his misgivings about the fencing match. For to ascribe every premonition to heavenly guidance is to reduce belief to superstition. And Hamlet defies "augury." How much more deeply religious is his surrender to the mystery of his fate than Laertes's concern with the niceties of ceremony. Whether Ophelia deserves Christian burial is a question fit for the mocking and subtle casuistry of the gravediggers. Indeed, if the form of her burial is to determine her ultimate destiny, then she must be eternally grateful to Claudius, who forced the Church to inter her in hallowed ground. Although some modern critics argue like

Laertes over the fine theological issues of the play, the perceptive reader understands that the form of Ophelia's burial matters more to the living than to the dead.

More clearly in *Hamlet* than in *The Spanish Tragedy* or *Tamburlaine* one can see the inner direction which great tragedy takes at the close of the Elizabethan age. For Shakespeare as for Kyd and Marlowe the fact of man's mortality is not the essential pathos of tragedy. That pathos lies in their heroes' anguished discovery of a universe more vast, more terrible, and more inscrutable than is dreamt of in philosophy. In *Hamlet* and Jacobean tragedy man suffers to be wise, and, indeed, his knowledge of reality is a more intense form of suffering than the illustrators of *De casibus* tales could imagine.

CAROLYN HEILBRUN

The Character of Hamlet's Mother

The character of Hamlet's mother has not received the specific critical attention it deserves. Moreover, the traditional account of her personality as rendered by the critics will not stand up under close scrutiny of Shakespeare's play.

None of the critics of course has failed to see Gertrude as vital to the action of the play; not only is she the mother of the hero, the widow of the Ghost, and the wife of the current King of Denmark, but the fact of her hasty and, to the Elizabethans, incestuous marriage, the whole question of her "falling off," occupies a position of barely secondary importance in the mind of her son, and of the Ghost. Indeed, Freud and Jones see her, the object of Hamlet's Oedipus complex, as central to the motivation of the play.[1] But the critics, with no exception that I have been able to find, have accepted Hamlet's word "frailty" as applying to her whole personality, and have seen in her not one weakness, or passion in the Elizabethan sense, but a character of which weakness and lack of depth and vigorous intelligence are the entire explanation. Of her can it truly be said that carrying the "stamp of one defect," she did "in the

Shakespeare Quarterly 8 (1957): 201–06.
[1]Shakespeare, William: *Hamlet,* with a psycho-analytical study by Ernest Jones, M.D. London: Vision Press, 1947, pp. 7–42.

general censure take corruption / From that particular fault,"
(1. 4. 35–36).

The critics are agreed that Gertrude was not a party to
the late King's murder and indeed knew nothing of it, a
point which on the clear evidence of the play, is indis-
putable. They have also discussed whether or not Gertrude,
guilty of more than an "o'er-hasty marriage," had committed adultery with Claudius before her husband's death. I
will return to this point later on. Beyond discussing these
two points, those critics who have dealt specifically with
the Queen have traditionally seen her as well-meaning but
shallow and feminine, in the pejorative sense of the word:
incapable of any sustained rational process, superficial and
flighty. It is this tradition which a closer reading of the play
will show to be erroneous.

Professor Bradley describes the traditional Gertrude thus:

> The Queen was not a bad-hearted woman, not at all the woman to
> think little of murder. But she had a soft animal nature and was
> very dull and very shallow. She loved to be happy, like a sheep in
> the sun, and to do her justice, it pleased her to see others happy,
> like more sheep in the sun.... It was pleasant to sit upon her
> throne and see smiling faces around her, and foolish and unkind in
> Hamlet to persist in grieving for his father instead of marrying
> Ophelia and making everything comfortable.... The belief at the
> bottom of her heart was that the world is a place constructed sim-
> ply that people may be happy in it in a good-humored sensual
> fashion.[2]

Later on, Bradley says of her that when affliction comes to
her "the good in her nature struggles to the surface through
the heavy mass of sloth."

Granville-Barker is not quite so extreme. Shakespeare,
he says,

> gives us in Gertrude the woman who does not mature, who clings
> to her youth and all that belongs to it, whose charm will not
> change but at last fade and wither; a pretty creature, as we see her,

[2]Bradley, A. C., *Shakespearean Tragedy* (New York: Macmillan, 1949),
p. 167.

desperately refusing to grow old. . . . She is drawn for us with un-emphatic strokes, and she has but a passive part in the play's action. She moves throughout in Claudius' shadow; he holds her as he won her, by the witchcraft of his wit.[3]

Elsewhere Granville-Barker says "Gertrude who will certainly never see forty-five again, might better be 'old.' [That is, portrayed by an older, mature actress.] But that would make her relations with Claudius—and *their* likelihood is vital to the play—quite incredible" (p. 226). Granville-Barker is saying here that a woman about forty-five years of age cannot feel any sexual passion or arouse it. This is one of the mistakes which lie at the heart of the misunderstanding about Gertrude.

Professor Dover Wilson sees Gertrude as more forceful than either of these two critics will admit, but even he finds the Ghost's unwillingness to shock her with knowledge of his murder to be one of the basic motivations of the play, and he says of her "Gertrude is always hoping for the best."[4]

Now whether Claudius won Gertrude before or after her husband's death, it was certainly not, as Granville-Barker implies, with "the witchcraft of his wit" alone. Granville-Barker would have us believe that Claudius won her simply by the force of his persuasive tongue. "It is plain," he writes, that the Queen "does little except echo his [Claudius'] wishes; sometimes—as in the welcome to Rosencrantz and Guildenstern—she repeats his very words" (p. 227), though Wilson must admit later that Gertrude does not tell Claudius everything. Without dwelling here on the psychology of the Ghost, or the greater burden borne by the Elizabethan words "witchcraft" and "wit," we can plainly see, for the Ghost tells us, how Claudius won the Queen: the Ghost considers his brother to be garbage, and "lust," the Ghost says, "will sate itself in a celestial bed and prey on garbage" (1.5.56–57). "Lust"—in a woman of forty-five or more—is the key word here. Bradley, Granville-Barker, and to a lesser extent Pro-

[3]Granville-Barker, Harley, *Prefaces to Shakespeare* (Princeton University Press, 1946), I, 227.

[4]Wilson, J. Dover, *What Happens in Hamlet* (Cambridge University Press, 1951), p. 125.

fessor Dover Wilson, misunderstand Gertrude largely because they are unable to see lust, the desire for sexual relations, as the passion, in the Elizabethan sense of the word, the flaw, the weakness which drives Gertrude to an incestuous marriage, appalls her son, and keeps him from the throne. Unable to explain her marriage to Claudius as the act of any but a weak-minded vacillating woman, they fail to see Gertrude for the strong-minded, intelligent, succinct, and, apart from this passion, sensible woman that she is.

To understand Gertrude properly, it is only necessary to examine the lines Shakespeare has chosen for her to say. She is, except for her description of Ophelia's death, concise and pithy in speech, with a talent for seeing the essence of every situation presented before her eyes. If she is not profound, she is certainly never silly. We first hear her asking Hamlet to stop wearing black, to stop walking about with his eyes downcast, and to realize that death is an inevitable part of life. She is, in short, asking him not to give way to the passion of grief, a passion of whose force and dangers the Elizabethans were aware, as Miss Campbell has shown.[5] Claudius echoes her with a well-reasoned argument against grief which was, in its philosophy if not in its language, a piece of commonplace Elizabethan lore. After Claudius' speech, Gertrude asks Hamlet to remain in Denmark, where he is rightly loved. Her speeches have been short, however warm and loving, and conciseness of statement is not the mark of a dull and shallow woman.

We next hear her, as Queen and gracious hostess, welcoming Rosencrantz and Guildenstern to the court, hoping, with the King, that they may cheer Hamlet and discover what is depressing him. Claudius then tells Gertrude, when they are alone, that Polonius believes he knows what is upsetting Hamlet. The Queen answers:

> I doubt it is no other than the main,
> His father's death and our o'er-hasty marriage. (2.2.56–57)

---

[5]Campbell, Lily B. *Shakespeare's Tragic Heroes* (New York: Barnes & Noble, 1952), pp. 112–113.

This statement is concise, remarkably to the point, and not a little courageous. It is not the statement of a dull, slothful woman who can only echo her husband's words. Next, Polonius enters with his most unbrief apotheosis to brevity. The Queen interrupts him with five words: "More matter, with less art" (95). It would be difficult to find a phrase more applicable to Polonius. When this gentleman, in no way deterred from his loquacity, after purveying the startling news that he has a daughter, begins to read a letter, the Queen asks pointedly "Came this from Hamlet to her?" (114).

We see Gertrude next in Act 3, asking Rosencrantz and Guildenstern, with her usual directness, if Hamlet received them well, and if they were able to tempt him to any pastime. But before leaving the room, she stops for a word of kindness to Ophelia. It is a humane gesture, for she is unwilling to leave Ophelia, the unhappy tool of the King and Polonius, without some kindly and intelligent appreciation of her help:

> And for your part, Ophelia, I do wish
> That your good beauties be the happy cause
> Of Hamlet's wildness. So shall I hope your virtues
> Will bring him to his wonted way again,
> To both your honors. (3.1.38–42)

It is difficult to see in this speech, as Bradley apparently does, the gushing shallow wish of a sentimental woman that class distinctions shall not stand in the way of true love.

At the play, the Queen asks Hamlet to sit near her. She is clearly trying to make him feel he has a place in the court of Denmark. She does not speak again until Hamlet asks her how she likes the play. "The lady doth protest too much, methinks" (3.2.236) is her immortal comment on the player queen. The scene gives her four more words: when Claudius leaps to his feet, she asks "How fares my Lord?" (273).

I will for the moment pass over the scene in the Queen's closet, to follow her quickly through the remainder of the play. After the closet scene, the Queen comes to speak to Claudius. She tells him, as Hamlet has asked her to, that he, Hamlet, is mad, and has killed Polonius. She adds, however, that he now weeps for what he has done. She does not wish Claudius to know what she now knows, how wild and fearsome Hamlet has become. Later, she does not wish to see Ophelia, but hearing how distracted she is, consents. When Laertes bursts in ready to attack Claudius, she immediately steps between Claudius and Laertes to protect the King, and tells Laertes it is not Claudius who has killed his father. Laertes will of course soon learn this, but it is Gertrude who manages to tell him before he can do any meaningless damage. She leaves Laertes and the King together, and then returns to tell Laertes that his sister is drowned. She gives her news directly, realizing that suspense will increase the pain of it, but this is the one time in the play when her usual pointed conciseness would be the mark neither of intelligence nor kindness, and so, gently, and at some length, she tells Laertes of his sister's death, giving him time to recover from the shock of grief, and to absorb the meaning of her words. At Ophelia's funeral the Queen scatters flowers over the grave:

> Sweets to the sweet! Farewell!
> I hoped thou shouldst have been my Hamlet's wife.
> I thought thy bride-bed to have decked, sweet maid,
> And not have strewed thy grave. (5.1.245–48)

She is the only one present decently mourning the death of someone young, and not heated in the fire of some personal passion.

At the match between Hamlet and Laertes, the Queen believes that Hamlet is out of training, but glad to see him at some sport, she gives him her handkerchief to wipe his brow, and drinks to his success. The drink is poisoned and she dies. But before she dies she does not waste time on vituperation; she warns Hamlet that the drink is poisoned to prevent his drinking it. They are her last words. Those critics who have thought her stupid admire her death; they call it uncharacteristic.

In Act 3, when Hamlet goes to his mother in her closet his nerves are pitched at the very height of tension; he is on the edge of hysteria. The possibility of murdering his mother has in fact entered his mind, and he has just met and refused an opportunity to kill Claudius. His mother, meanwhile, waiting for him, has told Polonius not to fear for her, but she knows when she sees Hamlet that he may be violently mad. Hamlet quips with her, insulting her, tells her he wishes she were not his mother, and when she, still retaining dignity, attempts to end the interview, Hamlet seizes her and she cries for help. The important thing to note is that the Queen's cry "Thou wilt not murder me?" (3.4.22) is not foolish. She has seen from Hamlet's demeanor that he is capable of murder, as indeed in the next instant he proves himself to be.

We next learn from the Queen's startled "As kill a king?" (31) that she has no knowledge of the murder, though of course this is only confirmation here of what we already know. Then the Queen asks Hamlet why he is so hysterical:

> What have I done, that thou dar'st wag thy tongue
> In noise so rude against me?   (39–40)

Hamlet tells her: it is her lust, the need of sexual passion, which has driven her from the arms and memory of her husband to the incomparably cruder charms of his brother. He cries out that she has not even the excuse of youth for her lust:

> O shame where is thy blush? Rebellious hell,
> If thou canst mutine in a matron's bones,
> To flaming youth let virtue be as wax
> And melt in her own fire. Proclaim no shame
> When the compulsive ardor gives the charge,
> Since frost itself as actively doth burn,
> And reason panders will.   (83–89)

This is not only a lust, but a lust which throws out of joint all the structure of human morality and relationships. And the Queen admits it. If there is one quality that has characterized, and will characterize, every speech of Gertrude's in the play, it is the ability to see reality clearly, and to express it. This talent is not lost when turned upon herself:

> O Hamlet, speak no more!
> Thou turn'st mine eyes into my very soul,
> And there I see such black and grained spots
> As will not leave their tinct.   (89–92)

She knows that lust has driven her, that this is her sin, and she admits it. Not that she wishes to linger in the contemplation of her sin. "No more," she cries, "no more." And then the Ghost appears to Hamlet. The Queen thinks him mad again—as well she might—but she promises Hamlet that she will not betray him—and she does not.

Where, in all that we have seen of Gertrude, is there the picture of "a soft animal nature, very dull and very shallow"? She may indeed be "animal" in the sense of "lustful." But it does not follow that because she wishes to continue a life of sexual experience, her brain is soft or her wit unperceptive.

Some critics, having accepted Gertrude as a weak and vacillating woman, see no reason to suppose that she did not fall victim to Claudius' charms before the death of her husband and commit adultery with him. These critics, Professor Bradley among them (p. 166), claim that the elder Hamlet clearly tells his son that Gertrude has committed adultery with Claudius in the speech beginning "Ay that incestuous, that adulterate beast" (1.5.42ff.). Professor Dover Wilson presents the argument:

Is the Ghost speaking here of the o'er-hasty marriage of Claudius and Gertrude? Assuredly not. His "certain term" is drawing rapidly to an end, and he is already beginning to "scent the morning air." Hamlet knew of the marriage, and his whole soul was filled with nausea at the thought of the speedy hasting to "incestuous sheets." Why then should the Ghost waste precious moments in telling Hamlet what he was fully cognisant of before? . . . Moreover, though the word "incestuous" was applicable to the marriage, the rest of the passage is entirely inapplicable to it. Expressions like "witchcraft," "traitorous gifts," "seduce," "shameful lust," and "seeming virtuous" may be noted in passing. But the rest of the quotation leaves no doubt upon the matter. . . . (P. 293)

Professor Dover Wilson and other critics have accepted the Ghost's word "adulterate" in its modern meaning. The Elizabethan word "adultery," however, was not restricted to its modern meaning, but was used to define any sexual relationship which could be called unchaste, including of course an incestuous one.[6] Certainly the elder Hamlet considered the marriage of Claudius and Gertrude to be unchaste and unseemly, and while his use of the word "adulterate" indicates his very strong feelings about the marriage, it would not to an Elizabethan audience necessarily mean that he believed Gertrude to have been false to him before his death. It is important to notice, too, that the Ghost does not apply the term "adulterate" to Gertrude, and he may well have considered the term a just description of Claudius's entire sexual life.

But even if the Ghost used the word "adulterate" in full awareness of its modern restricted meaning, it is not necessary to assume on the basis of this single speech (and it is the only shadow of evidence we have for such a conclusion) that Gertrude was unfaithful to him while he lived. It is quite probable that the elder Hamlet still considered himself married to Gertrude, and he is moreover revolted that her lust for him ("why she would hang on him as if increase of appetite had grown by what it fed on") should have so easily transferred itself to another. This is why he uses the expressions "seduce," "shameful lust," and others. Professor Dover Wilson has himself said "Hamlet knew of the marriage, and his whole soul was filled with nausea at the thought of the speedy hasting to incestuous sheets"; the soul of the elder Hamlet was undoubtedly filled with nausea too, and this could well explain his using such strong language, as well as his taking the time to mention the

[6]See Joseph, Bertram, *Conscience and the King* (London: Chatto and Windus, 1953), pp. 16–19.

matter at all. It is not necessary to consider Gertrude an adulteress to account for the speech of the Ghost.

Gertrude's lust was, of course, more important to the plot than we may at first perceive. Charlton Lewis, among others, has shown how Shakespeare kept many of the facts of the plots from which he borrowed without maintaining the structures which explained them. In the original Belleforest story, Gertrude (substituting Shakespeare's more familiar names) was daughter of the king; to become king, it was necessary to marry her. The elder Hamlet, in marrying Gertrude, ousted Claudius from the throne.[7] Shakespeare retained the shell of this in his play. When she no longer has a husband, the form of election would be followed to declare the next king, in this case undoubtedly her son Hamlet. By marrying Gertrude, Claudius "Popp'd in between th' election and my hopes" (5.2.65), that is, kept young Hamlet from the throne. Gertrude's flaw of lust made Claudius's ambition possible, for without taking advantage of the Queen's desire still to be married, he could not have been king.

But Gertrude, if she is lustful, is also intelligent, penetrating, and gifted, with a remarkable talent for concise and pithy speech. In all the play, the person whose language hers most closely resembles is Horatio. "Sweets to the sweet," she has said at Ophelia's grave. "Good night sweet prince," Horatio says at the end. They are neither of them dull, or shallow, or slothful, though one of them is passion's slave.

---

[7] Lewis, Charlton M., *The Genesis of Hamlet* (New York: Henry Holt & Co., 1907), p. 36.

CATHERINE BELSEY

From The Subject of Tragedy

In the revenge plays in the half-century before the civil war it is the sovereign's failure to administer justice which inaugurates the subject's quest for vengeance. Hieronimo rips the bowels of the earth with his dagger, calling for "Justice, O justice, justice, gentle king" (*The Spanish Tragedy*, 3.12.63). Titus Andronicus urges his kinsmen to dig a passage to Pluto's region, with a petition "for justice and for aid" (4.3.15). The Duchess Rosaura appeals direct to the monarch:

> Let me have swift and such exemplar justice
> As shall become this great assassinate.
> You will take off our faith else, and if here
> Such innocence must bleed and you look on,
> Poor men that call you gods on earth will doubt
> To obey your laws.
>
> (*The Cardinal,* 3.2.104–9)

In each case, however, the sovereign fails to enforce the law. Indeed, in *Antonio's Revenge* (c.1600), *The Revenger's Tragedy* and *Hamlet* the ruler is the criminal. In the absence of justice the doubt Rosaura defines propels the

From Catherine Belsey, *The Subject of Tragedy* (Methuen, 1985), pp. 111–16. Used by permission of the publisher.

revenger to take in the interests of justice action which is it-self unjust.

Revenge is not justice. Titus is a man "so just that he will not revenge" (4 1.129). Acting outside the legal insti-tution and in defiance of legitimate authority, individuals have no right to arrogate to themselves the role of the state in the administration of justice· "never private cause/ Should take on it the part of public laws" (*The Revenge of Bussy d'Ambois*, 3.2.115–16). Conscience, which permits passive disobedience, forbids murder, and thus makes cow-ards of some revengers (*Hamlet*, 3.1 83–5).[1] Others, more resolute, like Laertes are deaf to its promptings:

> To hell, allegiance, vows to the blackest devil,
> Conscience and grace to the profoundest pit!
> I dare damnation To this point I stand,
> That both the worlds I give to negligence,
> Let come what comes, only I'll be revenged
> Most throughly for my father   (4 5 131–36)

When Hamlet differentiates revenge from hire and salary (3.3 79), he specifies the gap between vengeance and jus-tice Revenge is always in excess of justice Its execution calls for a "stratagem of .. horror" (*Antonio's Revenge*, 2 1 48–50) Titus serves the heads of Chiron and Demetrius to their mother and the Emperor in a pastry coffin. Antonio massacres the innocent Julio and offers him in a dish to his father, after cutting out the tyrant's tongue. Vindice pre-pares for the Duke a liaison with the skull of the murdered Gloriana, and the "bony lady" poisons him with a kiss (*The Revenger's Tragedy*, 3 5 121) Hippolito holds down his tongue and compels him to witness his wife's adultery while he dies.

The discourse of revenge reproduces the violence and the excess of its practice· "Look how I smoke in blood, reeking the steam / Of foaming vengeance" (*Antonio's Revenge*, 3.5.17–18); "Then will I rent and tear them thus and thus, /

---

[1]For an argument to substantiate in detail this reading of the "To be or not to be" speech, see Catherine Belsey, "The case of Hamlet's con-science," *Studies in Philology* 76 (1979): 127–48

Shivering their limbs in pieces with my teeth" (*The Spanish Tragedy*, 3.13.122–23); "Now could I drink hot blood, / And do such bitter business as the day / Would quake to look on" (*Hamlet*, 3.2.398–400); "I should ha' fatted all the region kites / With this slave's offal" (2.2.590–91). As Claudius assures Laertes, it is in the nature of revenge to "have no bounds" (4.7.128). The rugged Pyrrhus—avenging *his* father's death, "roasted in wrath and fire, / And thus o'ersizèd with coagulate gore" (2.2.472–73)—is not, after all, entirely a caricature of the stage revenger.

And yet the act of vengeance, in excess of justice, a repudiation of conscience, hellish in its mode of operation, seems to the revenger (and to the audience?) an overriding imperative. Not to act is to leave crime unpunished, murder triumphant or tyranny in unfettered control. The orthodox Christian remedy is patience: "Vengeance is mine; I will repay, saith the Lord" (Rom. 12:19). *The Spanish Tragedy* offers two contrasting models, dramatizes, in effect, two antithetical worlds, one authoritarian, divinely ordered and controlled, and the other disordered, unjust, incipiently secular and humanist. In Portugal Alexandro is accused of the murder of Balthazar. Alexandro is not permitted to speak (1.3.88), but patience and heaven are invoked in his defence (3.1.31–35). As he is bound to the stake, insisting that his death will be avenged on his accuser, Villuppo, an ambassador arrives with letters for the King which show that Balthazar is alive. Heaven is evidently ordinant in Alexandro's providential last-minute release, and in the consequent execution of Villuppo. In Spain the murder of Horatio initially elicits a parallel response: "The heavens are just, murder cannot be hid" (2.5.57); "Ay, heaven will be reveng'd of every ill" (3.13.2). But when Hieronimo appeals to heaven for justice a letter "falleth" (3.2.23s.d.). Its auspices are uncertain; it is addressed to the subject and not to the sovereign; it reveals the identity of the murderers, and thus inaugurates Hieronimo's quest for justice, which becomes an act of revenge. The place of heaven—or hell—in this process is unclear.

Whatever the requirements of Christian patience, the

imperatives of fiction demand that heaven delays the execution of justice, and in the interim crime continues Belimperia is imprisoned, Pedringano is suborned, Serberine murdered In *Hamlet* Claudius is still in possession of the crown and Gertrude, and is planning the death of the hero in addition Vindice has waited nine years and meanwhile crime at court is met with a travesty of justice. In these circumstances revenge is a political as well as a moral issue Thus Hamlet asks,

> Does it not, think thee, stand me now upon—
> He that hath killed my king and whored my mother,
> Popped in between the election and my hopes,
> Thrown out his angle for my proper life,
> And with such coz'nage—is't not perfect conscience
> To quit him with this arm? And is't not to be damned
> To let this canker of our nature come
> In further evil?   (5 2 63–70)

The question, like most of the questions raised in *Hamlet*, is not answered But even Clermont d'Ambois, model of Stoic virtue, is persuaded by Bussy's Ghost that he has a moral obligation to punish the murder the king leaves unpunished, and so to do in this world "deeds that fit eternity"

> And those deeds are the perfecting that justice
> That makes the world last, which proportion is
> Of punishment and wreak for every wrong,
> As well as for right a reward as strong
> Away, then! Use the means thou hast to right
> The wrong I suffer'd What corrupted law
> Leaves unperform'd in kings do thou supply
> (*The Revenge of Bussy d'Ambois*, 5 1 91–98)

And in consequence, the Ghost concludes, "be above them all in dignity" (99) The bloody masques and Thyestean banquets are hellish, but they have the effect, none the less, of purging a corrupt social body, and in the process installing the subject as autonomous agent of retribution

Revenge exists in the margin between justice and crime. An act of injustice on behalf of justice, it deconstructs the antithesis which fixes the meanings of good and evil, right and wrong. Hamlet invokes the conventional polarities in addressing the Ghost, only to abandon them as inadequate or irrelevant:

> Be thou a spirit of health or goblin damned,
> Bring with thee airs from heaven or blasts from hell,
> Be thy intents wicked or charitable,
> Thou com'st in such a questionable shape
> That I will speak to thee.   (1.4.40–44)

The Ghosts in revenge plays consistently resist unequivocal identifications, are always "questionable" in one of the senses of that word. Dead and yet living, visitants at midnight (the marginal hour) from a prison-house which is neither heaven nor hell, visible to some figures on the stage but not to others, and so neither real nor unreal, they inaugurate a course of action which is both mad and sane, correct and criminal. To uphold the law revengers are compelled to break it. The moral uncertainty persists to the end. Vindice's execution by Antonio either punishes or perpetuates injustice: "You that would murder him would murder me" (*The Revenger's Tragedy*, 5.3.105). Hamlet dies a revenger, a poisoner, but also a soldier and a prince (5.2.396–404). Clermont d'Ambois survives the duel with Montsurry but kills himself thereafter. Antonio, to his (and the audience's?) "amazement" (*Antonio's Revenge*, 5.6.28), is greeted by the Senate as a hero, but the play ends with his retirement to a monastery.

The question whether it is nobler to suffer in Christian patience or to take arms against secular injustice is not resolved in the plays. It is ultimately a question about authority—God's, the sovereign's or the subject's. To the extent that the plays condemn revenge, they stay within an orthodoxy which permits only passive disobedience and prescribes no remedy for the subject when the sovereign breaks the law. But in order to be revenge plays at all, they are compelled to throw into relief the social and political weaknesses of this ethical and political position. To the extent that they consequently endorse revenge, they participate in the installation of the sovereign subject, entitled to take action in accordance with conscience and on behalf of law ·

SYLVAN BARNET

Hamlet on Stage and Screen

Hamlet advises the players, in 3.2.1–4, to "Speak the speech . . . trippingly on the tongue"—but exactly what are the speeches that add up to *Hamlet*? This question will not seem absurd to anyone who has glanced at the textual note on page 145. Briefly, the note explains that *Hamlet* exists in three versions: Q1 (published in 1603), 2,154 lines; Q2 (1604), 3,723 lines; and F (1623), 3,604 lines. (Much depends on how one counts the lines, but that's not important now.) Most scholars agree that F (that is, the version printed in the Folio of 1623) is an *acting* version, i.e., a text somewhat abridged for the stage. They also agree that Q1 is a much more drastic abridgment, apparently prepared from memory by an actor or actors without access to a copy of the manuscript. The text of Q1 is often very poor (sometimes it is gibberish), but occasionally it gives insights into the performance of the play—our topic here—that are not found in either of the fuller and more coherent versions. For instance, only Q1 gives us a stage direction telling us that in 5.1.259 Hamlet leaps into Ophelia's grave.

When people speak of an "uncut *Hamlet*," or of a "full text *Hamlet*," they are speaking of a version that probably never was performed in Shakespeare's time, a version that begins with Q2 (the longest of the three texts) and adds to it the passages in F that are not found in Q2. This composite text, running to about 3,900 lines, takes four or even four and a quarter hours to perform. Most performances of an abridged text run to about three hours, which usually means that about a fourth of the text is cut. For instance, Garrick (1763) used 2,684 lines; Kean (1818) 2,467, Irving (undated promptbook) 2,752, Gielgud (1934) 2,865. There are, roughly speaking, two ways of cutting: one is to leave out some characters (for example, Fortinbras and everything connected with him, including the talk in 1.1 about the quarrel between Hamlet Senior and Fortinbras's father); the other is to keep a little of everything, trimming down longer speeches, especially reflective or descriptive ones. Laertes's advice to Ophelia, Polonius's advice to Laertes, Hamlet's disquisition on drunkenness, his musings on Alexander, and his advice to the players may be reduced to tokens. If one follows the first method, omitting, say, material concerning Fortinbras, one eliminates four speaking characters (Fortinbras, Cornelius, Voltemand, the Captain), and one thus focuses more sharply on Hamlet's problem in a corrupt court. The play becomes more domestic, more personal, and in some ways more manageable, but it necessarily loses its political dimension, for instance in the contrast between the thinking man (Hamlet) and the active man (Fortinbras). It also loses, of course, Shakespeare's ending, which shows order being restored after violence. If one follows the second method of cutting, thinning down the speeches, no single theme may be utterly neglected, but the play loses so much of its complexity or texture or depth that it may seem to be not much more than a melodrama.

The role of Hamlet is long and complex, and *Hamlet* is the most frequently staged of Shakespeare's plays; this short essay can look at only a very few productions, and can comment on only some of their most distinctive features. We must begin by mentioning Richard Burbage (c.1567–1619), a member of Shakespeare's theatrical company, who is known to have played the role—but nothing is really known about how he played it. The next actor of note who performed the role was Thomas Betterton (c.1635–1710), who played his first Hamlet in 1661, when he was about twenty-six, and played his last Hamlet in 1709, when he was in his seventies. Betterton's text was a relatively slight abridgment of the folio text—it deletes about 816 lines, but, as we have seen, the Elizabethans themselves probably abridged the play. It is not known for certain who made this late-seventeenth-century abridgment, but William Davenant is a strong candidate. Among the cuts are the roles of Voltemand and Cornelius, all of the Fortinbras material except the entry of Fortinbras at the end of the play, Polonius's advice to Laertes, Polonius's scene with Reynaldo, Hamlet's advice to the Players, and Hamlet's soliloquy beginning "How all occasions do inform against me." Among the speeches that are thinned out rather than entirely cut are Horatio's explanation of the preparation for war, the king's reproof of Hamlet's excessive grief, Laertes's advice to Ophelia, the Mouse Trap, and the closet scene with Gertrude. Minor changes include some elevation of the diction, in accordance with new ideas of decorum. Thus, instead of "The kettledrum and trumpet thus *bray out* / The triumph of his pledge" (1.4.11–12), we get "The kettledrum and trumpet thus *proclaim* / The triumph of his health."

People who saw Betterton spoke of his "vivacity" and "enterprize," and they described his performance as "manly." Putting together such scraps of evidence as we have, we can say that Betterton's Hamlet (played in the dress of a courtier of Charles II, and later with a cocked hat and powdered wig) was not a neurotic or a weakling but "the glass of fashion," and a vigorous young man—even when Betterton was seventy.

In the middle of the eighteenth century, viewers used pretty much the same words that had described Betterton to describe the performance of David Garrick (1717–79), who first played the role in 1742. In the next thirty years, like his predecessors and his successors, Garrick used a somewhat abridged text, from time to time slightly altering it both by additions and deletions, but in 1772 he made a drastic revision. Although he restored 629 lines that had not been heard for a century (these included such passages as the king at prayer, and the soliloquy beginning "How all occasions do inform against me"), Garrick also in effect rewrote the fifth act, more or less in line with neoclassical ideals of decorum. (As early as 1661 John Evelyn wrote, "I saw *Hamlet, Prince of Denmark* played, but now the old plays begin to disgust this refined age.") Garrick's aim, he said, was to rescue "that whole play from all the rubbish of the fifth act." The rubbish included the gravediggers and (as it must have seemed to eighteenth-century taste) the boorish struggle between Hamlet and Laertes at Ophelia's grave. Clowns did not, in the strict neoclassical view, belong in tragedies, and courtly gentlemen did not engage in fisticuffs at a funeral. Briefly, in Garrick's revision of the fifth act, the king commands Hamlet to go to England, and Hamlet replies by stabbing him. Laertes, seeking vengeance for the deaths of Polonius and Ophelia, mortally wounds Hamlet. Horatio is about to kill Laertes when Hamlet commands him to desist, saying that Laertes has been guided by heaven to give Hamlet the "precious balm" for all his wounds. Hamlet, before he dies, lectures his mother, and commands Laertes and Horatio "to calm the troubled land." But what is most relevant to our purpose here is this: Garrick's Hamlet, though perhaps touched with melancholy, was a man of action. For the rest of the century, Garrick's interpretation remained the touchstone by which other performances of the role were judged.

After Garrick, so many notable actors played Hamlet that this essay can do little more than make what must seem to be arbitrary choices. Our first choice, John Philip Kemble (1757–1823), is summed up in a brief description by the essayist William Hazlitt:

> Mr. Kemble plays [Hamlet] like a man in armor, with a determined inveteracy of purpose, on one undeviating straight line, which is as remote from the natural grace and refined susceptibility of the characters as the sharp angles and abrupt starts which Mr. Kean introduces into the part. Mr. Kean's Hamlet is as much too splenetic and rash as Mr. Kemble's is too strong and pointed.

Kemble was able to play "one undeviating straight line" partly because he cut from the text many of Hamlet's "wild and whirling words"; but what is especially interesting here is that Kemble, who acted the role from 1783 until his retirement in 1817, continued the tradition of a "manly" Hamlet, someone without the signs of weakness, even neurosis, that in the next decades came to characterize the role. True, as early as the late eighteenth century an occasional reader suggested that Hamlet was "irresolute," vainly striving toward manly boldness, but not until Kean did the stage see an active yet angst-ridden Hamlet.

Edmund Kean (1787–1833) first played Hamlet in 1814. We have already heard Hazlitt's opinion that Kean was "too splenetic and rash"; one additional quotation from Hazlitt, describing Kean's first Hamlet, will have to suffice:

> Both the closet scene with his mother, and his remonstrances to Ophelia, were highly impressive. If there had been less vehemence of effort in the latter, it would not have lost any of its effect. But whatever nice faults might be found in this scene, they were amply redeemed by the manner of his coming back after he has gone to the extremity of the stage, from a pang of parting tenderness to press his lips to Ophelia's hand. It had an electrical effect on the house. It was the finest commentary that was ever made on Shakespeare. It explained the character at once (as he meant it), as one of disappointed hope, of bitter regret, of affection suspended, not obliterated by the distractions of the scene around him.

Clearly we do not have the melancholy, indecisive prince of the armchair critics such as Goethe or Coleridge.

The American actor Edwin Booth (1833–93) performed the role from 1853 to 1891. His interpretation was, broadly speaking, in what can be called the romantic tradition, but it is difficult to write coherently about Booth's Hamlet, not because (as with Burbage and Betterton) we possess too little evidence, but because we possess too much; the forest is obscured by the trees. In 1870, the year of Booth's "definitive" Hamlet, a young man named Charles Clarke wrote a sixty-thousand-word description of the performance (Clarke saw Booth perform the role eight times), detailing gestures for almost every line Booth spoke. Charles H. Shattuck has studied this account, as well as other sources, and presented his findings in a book of 321 pages.

Clarke describes Booth's Hamlet as "a man of first-class

intellect and second-class will," but it is difficult to recon-
cile this neat formula with all of the pieces of the evidence,
especially with some of Booth's own statements. Still, a
few generalizations can be offered, even though, as Shattuck points out, Booth modified his Hamlet over the years,
making him somewhat less active, less agonized, and more
stoical. Broadly speaking, Booth's Hamlet was somewhat
"feminine," yet in some scenes "savage." Booth insisted
that Hamlet is always sane, and he played many scenes in a
highly courteous fashion (even when aware of the treachery
of Rosencrantz and Guildenstern he treated them politely if
with irony), yet he played some scenes "wildly," even hysterically. The overall impression on viewers was of a man
haunted by devotion to his father and anguished by the sin
of his mother. When he finally killed the king, he displayed
not a look of triumph but of doubt, even remorse.

Henry Irving (1838–1905), who played Hamlet from
1864 to 1885, somewhat varied his conception over the
years, but essentially his Hamlet was a man overpowered
by his love of Ophelia. (For a thorough discussion of Irving's interpretations of Hamlet, see Alan Hughes, *Henry
Irving*.) In his first version, Irving followed tradition in cutting all references to Fortinbras, but he also cut everything
that seemed to him to diminish Hamlet, for instance Hamlet's bawdy remarks (and of course Ophelia's bawdy songs,
too), Hamlet's callous description of the deaths of
Rosencrantz and Guildenstern, his soliloquy about murdering Claudius under particularly reprehensible conditions
(3.3.73–96), and his claim in his apology to Laertes that he
was mad (Irving at first believed that Hamlet's madness always was feigned). Irving later restored the soliloquy, and
he also (by 1884) allowed that Hamlet was hysterical in
four scenes—after the visitation of the Ghost, with Ophelia
in the nunnery scene, in the queen's closet, and at Ophelia's
grave. And of course he altered some of his stage business
over the years. In the nunnery scene, for instance, in 1885
he added Edmund Kean's business of returning to Ophelia,
after "To a nunnery, go," and kissing her hand. One of Irving's invented pieces of business was severely criticized. In
the closet scene, when Hamlet tells his mother to "Look

here upon this picture, and on this" (3.4.54), the usual business was for Hamlet to call attention to miniature portraits: Hamlet wore a miniature of his father, Gertrude a miniature of Claudius. (An alternate tradition used two framed portraits in the queen's room.) Irving, however, used no real pictures. He gesticulated his hand downstage, as though the portraits hung on the missing fourth wall between the audience and the actors—or existed in Hamlet's mind.

One other point should be made about Irving's *Hamlet*. Staging in the nineteenth century was noted for its spectacle and its illusionism, and Irving's productions were especially known for these qualities. Thus, reviewers comment admiringly on a scene in which the Ghost stands among huge rocks in moonlight, as dawn steals across a great expanse of water. Another especially memorable scene was the procession to Ophelia's grave: All available members of the cast served as priests, monks, and miscellaneous mourners, while a bell tolled and a hymn was played on a harmonium. All of this, of course, took time, which means that the text had to be fairly heavily cut.

Reacting against such productions, in 1881 William Poel, amateur actor and Elizabethan enthusiast, staged *Hamlet* in Elizabethan costumes on a stage with only a few chairs and a platform for the play-within-the-play. This was, he believed, the Elizabethan manner. Moreover, the text he chose for his production was Q1, the so-called "Bad Quarto" of 1603, "bad" because it represents an actor's corrupt abridgment of a performance of *Hamlet*. (See pages 147–48.) But the fact that Q1 is based on a performance made it especially attractive to Poel. He recognized that some passages of Q1 were so corrupt that they were gibberish, but, as he explained in a letter, he also believed that this text "represents more truly [Shakespeare's] dramatic conception than either Quarto 2 or our stage version."

Poel's production, which took only two hours, was reviewed most unfavorably, partly because it offended contemporary taste, and partly because it was indeed a thoroughly amateur affair. (Poel himself played Hamlet; unfortunately, his skill as an actor did not equal his enthusiasm for Elizabethan drama.) In this production, he was more

concerned with the text than with the staging—that is,
more concerned with showing that Q1 is good theater than
with showing how an Elizabethan play ought to be
staged—but critics seized on inconsistencies in his method
of production. Why not, they asked, use boys to play Ophelia and Gertrude? (Poel had in fact used a boy for the Player
Queen.) Why not do the play by daylight? Why not do it in
contemporary—i.e., late nineteenth century—garb, since in
Shakespeare's time the actors wore the clothing of their
own age? The production indeed was inconsistent, and
weak, and it added little to the interpretation of Hamlet—
though Poel did insist that Hamlet is not a sentimental
moper but an Elizabethan gallant; but the production nevertheless marked a milestone in the recovery of Shakespeare's stage, a neutral space that allows one scene to
follow another rapidly.

When reviewers teased Poel by asking why he didn't
stage the play in modern dress, they touched on an important issue. In a sense, up to the late eighteenth century,
Hamlet had regularly been done in modern dress. That
is, the early performers, such as Burbage, Betterton, Garrick, and Kemble wore the clothes of their own period—
Kemble, for example, at first played in modern court dress
and powdered hair. But in the late eighteenth century,
Kemble began to wear what has been called a Vandyck
costume, with a lace collar open at the neck, thus invoking
a somewhat romantic past. Edmund Kean, perhaps from the
late 1820s, wore a sort of stage Elizabethan costume, thus
again evoking a romantic past, and actors later in the century experimented with what were thought to be historically
accurate medieval Danish costumes, though Elizabethan
costume remained popular.

In short, if one goes back to the seventeenth and eighteenth centuries, one finds plenty of productions of *Hamlet*
in the "modern dress," though apparently after the late
eighteenth century there were none until 1925, when Barry
Jackson's Birmingham Repertory opened a production in
London, directed by H. K. Ayliff, with Colin Keith-
Johnston as Hamlet. Reviewers recognized that Jackson
was not offering merely a gimmick; rather, he was trying to

see the play freshly, to think about it not as a period piece
to be declaimed but as something to be spoken naturally.
Hamlet was not only dressed as a modern play, but was
also acted as a modern play. (The negative side is that this
conception encouraged an antipoetic reading of the lines.)
Modern dress did not (for the most part) seem incongruous,
partly because much of the play is set at court, allowing or
even requiring formal dress and military costumes—themselves kinds of theatrical costumes. Thus, in the court
scenes, the ambassadors and Polonius wore tailcoats and
white ties, and Hamlet wore a tuxedo. In other scenes, however, Ophelia wore a short skirt characteristic of the twen-
ties, the young men wore tweeds, and, in the graveyard
scene, Hamlet wore loose sports knickers known as plus
fours.

Modern-dress productions today are so commonplace
that it is hard to realize how novel Jackson's production
was. Since 1925 there has been a fashion for setting *Hamlet*
in some sort of post-Elizabethan period. For instance, in
1948 Michael Benthall directed Paul Scofield in a Victorian
Hamlet at Stratford-upon-Avon. Benthall, having already
done an Elizabethan *Hamlet* in doublet and hose, concluded
that the Elizabethan costume robbed the play of its "essential modern realism." Why Victorian? Because, Benthall
said, the Victorian period was

> near enough to our own to heighten the play's realism, and yet far
> enough distant to give scope for that picturesque romanticism
> modern life has largely betrayed. . . . And I set the play in a mid-
> European court where the juxtaposition of crinolines, uniforms,
> and evening and levee clothes would create the atmosphere of
> color and romance associated with royalty of the period. I hoped in
> this way to retain the grandeur of the tragedy without destroying
> the play's vital contemporary relevance.

Still, a free adaptation of Elizabethan dress seems to remain the favorite costume for productions of *Hamlet*—
partly because of the influence of William Poel and partly
because of the decrease in interest in trying to recreate medieval Denmark. Readers wanting to know more about the

topic should see John Gielgud's essay on costumes for *Hamlet*, printed in Rosamond Gilder's *John Gielgud's Hamlet: A Record of Performance*. (Gielgud is not, of course, an academic specialist on costumes. For more strictly historical discussions of *Hamlet*'s costumes, see an article by D. A. Russell in *Shakespeare Survey* 9, and corrections to this article, by R. Mander and J. Mitchenson, in *Shakespeare Survey* 11.) And it is to Gielgud's Hamlets that we now turn. He played the role in five productions: 1929, 1934, 1936, 1939 (at the royal castle at Elsinore), and 1944, and, as we shall see, he directed Richard Burton in a production in 1964. In the first of these productions, directed by Harcourt Williams in 1929–30, Gielgud was only a little over twenty-five. His evident youth contributed to a sense of Hamlet's isolation in a world of older people, but he was not an especially sympathetic figure, though it is said that in later performances the role gained in dignity and sympathy.

In his next *Hamlet*, in 1934, Gielgud was the director as well as the protagonist. He decided on opulent costumes (rich furs, plumed helmets, decorated armor for the men, and sweeping skirts and tightly laced bodices for the women), basing them on early-sixteenth-century German art. These costumes, in Gielgud's opinion, "suggested admirably the atmosphere of sensuality and crime." Claudius and Gertrude, he said, "looked like a pair of cruel, monstrous cats." The set consisted of various levels, linked by slopes and steps, backed by a bluish-white cyclorama which could be masked with richly decorated curtains for interior scenes. Though not a set Poel would have fully approved of, it allowed for the swift changes of scene that Poel valued. Judging from reviews, this Hamlet was a sympathetic figure: "The glass of fashion and the mold of form." One piece of business that Gielgud invented for this production has become especially famous: the king, praying, puts his sword aside. Hamlet, unseen by the king, picks up the sword and contemplates killing the kneeling king, but does not. Instead, he goes off with the sword. When the king rises from prayer, he finds the sword missing—and the scene fades out with a look of alarm on Claudius's face.

Among the actors who have appropriated this business are Paul Scofield (Stratford, 1948), Michael Redgrave (London, 1949), and Richard Burton (New York, 1964).

Guthrie McClintic saw Gielgud's *Hamlet* in London, and invited him to do yet another *Hamlet*, directed by McClintic, in New York. The production materialized in 1936, with decor by Jo Mielziner, and it is this production that is the basis for Rosamond Gilder's fascinating *John Gielgud's Hamlet*. Of his last *Hamlet*, the 1944 production, Gielgud said that he felt he was giving something of a "hotch-potch" of his earlier performances, but the reviews were good, and it was widely remarked that in this performance Gielgud gave Hamlet more dignity than in his earlier versions. There was very little madness in the interpretation, and a good deal of princely sophistication.

For Richard Burton's *Hamlet*, directed by John Gielgud in 1964, we have a highly detailed record, Richard L. Sterne's *John Gielgud Directs Richard Burton in Hamlet: A Journal of Rehearsals*. This remarkable book summarizes and sometimes quotes at length from tape recordings made during rehearsals. It also includes the prompt-script of the production, an interview with Gielgud, and an interview with Burton. (Also useful is a book by the actor who played Guildenstern, William Redfield's *Letters from an Actor*.) The idea behind the production was unusual: struck by the observation that actors sometimes perform better in a rehearsal run-through, with improvised props and without fancy costumes and sets, than in a public performance, Gielgud conceived of this production as a rehearsal of *Hamlet*. Thus, the play began with some actors (who later played courtiers) bringing a few chairs onto the stage (one of the chairs, an upholstered armchair, served for Claudius's throne); the set was the brick rear wall of the theater (not a real brick wall, but a set looking like a brick wall). The actors wore ordinary clothes—but in fact the clothes were faintly symbolic; Burton wore a black sweater or turtleneck, Hume Cronyn (Polonius) wore a business suit, and Alfred Drake (Claudius) wore a shirt and tie, and a sport jacket. As the play progressed, and pressures on Claudius increased, he loosened his necktie. The lighting, too, pretended to be rehearsal lighting. There were, for instance, no sudden blackouts, but the lights faded or gradually rose where dramatically appropriate. Sterne's transcription of the tapes indicates that much of Gielgud's effort was directed toward restraining Burton's abundant energy—Burton tended to shout—but, even so, the performance was intense rather than sensitive. The production was extremely successful financially, but this success may have been due partly to the publicity attending Burton's recent marriage to Elizabeth Taylor (they had married during the tryouts in Toronto); reviews were mixed.

The last *Hamlet* we will look at, except for the film versions by Laurence Olivier and Kenneth Branagh, is Peter Hall's production for the Royal Shakespeare Company, staged in 1965 with David Warner (only twenty-four years old) as Hamlet. (The fullest account of it is a chapter in Stanley Wells, *Royal Shakespeare,* but there are also useful observations in Peter Davison, *Hamlet: Text and Performance*.) Staged in the turbulent sixties, when university students were vigorously protesting against the Establishment, this Hamlet—with his long, rust-red scarf—was very much a working-class, alienated young man, a sometimes rebellious and sometimes apathetic student, a young man far removed from the princely Hamlets of John Gielgud in the 1930s. Peter Hall could hardly have been more explicit about the relation of the play to the age:

> For our decade I think the play will be about the disillusionment which produces an apathy of the will so deep that commitment to politics, to religion or to life is impossible.

Speaking of politics, it is worth mentioning that in this production Claudius was cool and efficient, and Polonius was no fool (some of his most obviously foolish lines were cut, in order to fit this characterization); that is, the Establishment confronting Hamlet was formidable. To some observers, it seemed inconceivable that this Hamlet, had he lived to rule, would, in Fortinbras's words, have "proved most royal." He seemed chiefly a neurotic young man, not a hero seeking to avenge his father's death, and certainly not a man who at last overcomes great obstacles and succeeds in ridding Denmark of its foul king. The final scene, however, had heroic elements: The duel, accompanied by drums, trumpets, and cannon, was vigorous. Further, Hamlet's attack on Claudius was forceful: First he nicked Claudius in the neck; then stabbed him; then, as Claudius fell, kneed him; and finally poured the poison drink into Claudius's ear. Still, Hamlet's dying words were spoken with no sense of urgency or of accomplishment; here was the "apathy" that Hall said characterized the period. Charles Shattuck, whose monumental work on Booth's *Hamlet* we noted earlier, in *Shakespeare Studies* 3 characterized Warner's prince as "a limp-wristed anti-hero who dies snickering." Clearly, Shattuck saw what Hall and Warner were striving for, but didn't like it at all.

Like several of the productions already discussed, Laurence Olivier's film, made in 1948, has been much written about. (The basic sources are Alan Dent, ed., *Hamlet: The Film and the Play*, and Brenda Cross, ed., *The Film Hamlet*.) Olivier had played Hamlet at Elsinore in 1937, but when he first thought of directing a film of the play he did not intend to take the title role. "I feel that my style of acting," he said, "is more suited to stronger character roles, such as Hotspur and Henry V, rather than to the lyrical, poetical role of Hamlet." (This quotation tells us a good deal about Olivier's conception of the role of Hamlet. It is hard to imagine Burbage, Betterton, or Garrick talking about Hamlet this way.) At the beginning of the film we are told: "This is the tragedy of a man who could not make up his mind," a simplistic view that, fortunately, does not come anywhere near to summarizing the interpretation offered in the film. In fact, the underlying theme really seems to be the Freudian interpretation that Hamlet cannot easily avenge his father's death because he (like everyone) has an Oedipus complex, i.e., he wishes (or wished) to kill his father and to sleep with his mother. Hamlet thus cannot bring himself to act against the man who has done what he himself wanted to do. (Although Freud initiated this explanation of Hamlet's alleged irresolution at least as early as 1900, he did not discuss the play at length. The classic psychoanalytic discussion of the play is by Ernest Jones, in *Hamlet and Oedipus*.) When Tyrone Guthrie directed Olivier in the 1937 *Hamlet* at Elsinore, he drew on Freud's remarks, and Olivier even discussed the idea with Jones. Not surprisingly, then, Olivier returned to this interpretation when he made his film. The most obvious signs of Freud are in the passionate kisses (some of the scenes between Hamlet and Gertrude are virtually love scenes) and in the emphasis on the queen's bedroom, indeed on the bed itself. The text of the play tells us that Hamlet encounters Gertrude in "his mother's closet" (3.3.27), i.e., in a private room. There is no need to think of this as a bedroom—it might well be furnished only with a small writing desk and a couple of chairs—but a bed now seems to have become indispensable. The sexual focus in Olivier's film is sharpened by Olivier's deletion of the entire Fortinbras story; that is, Olivier reduces the political elements in order to concentrate on Hamlet's relationship with his family.

The emphasis on Hamlet's psyche is partly conveyed by the set. Responding to Olivier's desire for a dreamlike cavernous area, the designer provided a castle with vast columns, long (often empty) corridors, and winding staircases, presumably symbolizing the puzzled mind. Exteriors tend to be misty. The camera does lots of panning and tracking, slowing down the action by dwelling on the set. Olivier seems to be trying to make scenes last as long as possible, ending them with dreamlike dissolves—a notable contrast, by the way, to the straight cuts used in the 1964 Russian film version by Grigori Kozintsev. Olivier exploits the camera as fully as possible. For example, the camera moves down from a great height, approaching the seated Hamlet, who then delivers his first soliloquy. Similarly, when the Ghost leaves at 1.5.91, the camera soars into the air (as though with the Ghost), moving above Hamlet, and showing him fainting on the battlement. Olivier also uses the cinematic device of voice-over for parts of some of the soliloquies; that is, we hear Hamlet's thoughts, but his lips do not move. Olivier took advantage also, perhaps needlessly, of the camera's ability to show us scenes that could not be staged, for instance Ophelia's drowning and Hamlet's encounter with the pirates. Olivier's *Hamlet*, in short, is a film, not a filmed version of a stage presentation.

A word about the end of Olivier's film: Laertes unfairly thrusts at Hamlet and wounds him, drawing blood. Having perceived that Laertes's foil is unbated, in the next round Hamlet knocks Laertes's foil out of his hand, retrieves it for his own use, and gives Laertes the bated foil. After wounding Laertes, Hamlet assumes the throne (the courtiers kneel before him), asks Horatio to tell his story, and dies. The film ends with a procession, cannon are fired, the camera goes through the castle, passing the now-empty throne and Gertrude's bedroom, and up to a tower, where Hamlet's bearers are silhouetted against the sky.

Kenneth Branagh's film version (1996, with Branagh as Hamlet, Derek Jacobi as Claudius, Julie Christie as Gertrude, and Kate Winslet as Ophelia) gives us as much text as possible—the longest version (Q2) with the addition of the lines found only in the Folio version. (On the texts of *Hamlet*, see pages 145–61.) It runs three hours and fifty-eight minutes, not including an intermission, whereas Olivier's version runs only 152 minutes. The intermission (after two hours and thirty-five minutes) comes at the end of 4.4, after Hamlet's last soliloquy ("How all occasions do inform against me"), which means that before the intermission we get the whole story up to the time of Hamlet's departure for England. This is a long haul, and after about two hours some spectators find themselves wondering if at *this* screening there will be no intermission.

Branagh's Hamlet—he had already played the role twice on the stage, in 1988, directed by Derek Jacobi, and in 1993, directed by Adrian Noble—is a robust (even a swashbuckling) prince, not a disaffected student. The film is set in a late nineteenth-century kingdom, where the men wear handsome military uniforms (Hamlet in black, Claudius in red, Laertes in white) and the women wear ball gowns. Serving as the exterior of the castle at Elsinore is one of England's baroque masterpieces, the palace at Blenheim Park (1724), and the interior shots show ornate rooms, often with mirrored doors. The visual splendor, doubtless partly an attempt to hold the viewer's interest through a very long film, works

well, though occasionally one feels that the eye is given too
much. There is overkill in, for instance, Hamlet's scene with
the ghost in 1.5, where the earth heaves, and smoke and fire
issue forth. (The music is also a good deal too loud here.)

Doubtless also in an effort to hold the viewer's attention,
during long narrative speeches Branagh sometimes shows
actors silently performing what the character is reporting.
Thus, when the ghost tells Hamlet how he was poisoned, we
see the episode enacted, including the writhings of Hamlet
Senior as the poison takes its effect. Although viewers who
know the play well may wish that Branagh had been content
here to let the words do the work, current dogma insists that
film is a visual medium, and that talking heads are anathe-
ma. There is something to the idea that by showing what a
character is describing at length, a long narrative speech is
not only enlivened but is also clarified. Still, the visual imagery during the ghost's narrative may have the wrong effect; it convinces the viewer that the episode did indeed
happen—we see the episode with our own eyes, and we
therefore conclude that the ghost is indeed an honest
ghost—whereas at this point, although we should be fully
taken by the horror of the ghost's narrative, we should not
yet be entirely certain of its truth. At least we (with Hamlet)
should later be able entertain the possibility that the ghost
was fabricating.

A second and much more offensive added flashback
shows Hamlet and Ophelia nude, copulating. This addition
is merely an attempt to make Shakespeare sexy. Nothing in
the text suggests that they have been to bed, and it is difficult to imagine the dutiful Ophelia would have slept with a
man. It is even difficult for me to imagine that Hamlet
would have seduced her, since he is presented as an ideal
gentleman. (Although audiences today may find the idea risi-
ble, Shakespeare valued virginity; in *Macbeth* [4.3.125–26],
Malcolm—soon to be crowned monarch of Scotland—in assuring Macduff of his fitness to rule says, "I am yet / Unknown to woman.")

Other visual additions in Branagh's *Hamlet*, however, are
of considerable interest, especially the pantomime of the fall
of Troy, narrated by the Player in 2.2.461–529. Branagh has

said that he wished to pay tribute to John Gielgud (Priam) and Judi Dench (Hecuba), and we are glad to see them here, even if they don't speak and the visual addition is not really needed. Several other famous performers, notably Billy Crystal, Gérard Depardieu, Rosemary Harris, Charlton Heston, and Robin Williams play small parts, doubtless in order to attract large audiences.

Branagh's treatment of Fortinbras is both good and bad; good in that Fortinbras has not been omitted (most productions do without him), bad in that he is overemphasized, first near the beginning, when descriptions of him are accompanied by visual images, and near the end, when we see his army invading the palace. The duel between Hamlet and Laertes is intercut with shots of Fortinbras's soldiers advancing on the castle, possessing the courtyard, entering the corridors, and then bursting through the mirrored doors of the great hall. All of this greatly diminishes an immensely important scene, the fatal duel and the deaths of Claudius and Gertrude. And at the very end, when Hamlet's body is carried out, we see Fortinbras's soldiers hacking at a great statue of Hamlet's father, which finally topples, probably reminding viewers of television footage of statues of Lenin and Stalin being pulled down when the Soviet Union dissolved. Strange, that a director who is so eager to give us all of the words of the play should undercut them with irrelevant visuals. After all, who cares about Fortinbras's triumph? (Probably the answer to the question is that Branagh thought that the general public shares the current academic interest in a politicized Shakespeare.) What we care about is Hamlet's trial, and his tragic (woeful and wonderful) success. Still, Branagh's film offers so much that is good, that we must be grateful to Branagh, even as we wish he had left well enough alone.

There are dozens—even hundreds—of other productions that one could talk about, but beyond the few that we have discussed, the rest (for our purposes) is silence.

Bibliographic Note: In addition to the sources already cited within this essay, the following are of special interest. On the 1985 staging of Q1 (the First Quarto) by Orange

Tree, see Bryan Loughrey in *The Hamlet First Published*, ed. Thomas Clayton (1992), and Nicholas Shrimpton in *Shakespeare Survey* 39 (1986): 191–206. On the 1992 production of Q1 by the Medieval Players, see Peter Holland in *Shakespeare Survey* 46 (1994): 159–62. For traditional stage business in productions up to the beginning of the twentieth century, see Arthur Colby Sprague, *Shakespeare and the Actors: The Stage Business in His Plays 1660–1905* (1944).

See also Marvin Rosenberg, *The Masks of Hamlet* (1992, an exhaustive study of the ways in which scenes have been done); Ralph Berry, *Changing Styles in Shakespeare* (1981, on productions from 1948 to the 1970s); Ralph Berry, *Shakespeare in Performance* (1993, a chapter on productions in the 1970s and 80s, and another chapter on the doubling of roles in the play); on modern productions, see Peter Thomson's chapter in Jonathan Bate and Russell Jackson, *Shakespeare: An Illustrated Stage History* (1996); and also Peter Davison, *"Hamlet": Text and Performance* (1983). For general histories, see John A. Mills, *"Hamlet" on Stage: The Great Tradition* (1985), and Raymond Mander and Joe Mitchenson, *"Hamlet" Through the Ages: A Pictorial Record from 1709* (1952).

For film and television versions, see Bernice Kliman, *Hamlet: Film, Television, and Audio Performance* (1988); H. R. Coursen, *Shakespearean Performance as an Interpretation* (1992); and H. R. Coursen, *Watching Shakespeare on Television* (1993). The Olivier and Branagh film versions have been published.

Suggested References

The number of possible references is vast and grows alarmingly. (The *Shakespeare Quarterly* devotes one issue each year to a list of the previous year's work, and *Shakespeare Survey*—an annual publication—includes a substantial review of biographical, critical, and textual studies, as well as a survey of performances.) The vast bibliography is best approached through James Harner, *The World Shakespeare Bibliography on CD-Rom: 1900–Present*. The first release, in 1996, included more than 12,000 annotated items from 1990–93, plus references to several thousand book reviews, productions, films, and audio recordings. The plan is to update the publication annually, moving forward one year and backward three years. Thus, the second issue (1997), with 24,700 entries, and another 35,000 or so references to reviews, newspaper pieces, and so on, covered 1987–94.

Though no works are indispensable, those listed below have been found especially helpful. The arrangement is as follows:

1. Shakespeare's Times
2. Shakespeare's Life
3. Shakespeare's Theater
4. Shakespeare on Stage and Screen
5. Miscellaneous Reference Works
6. Shakespeare's Plays: General Studies
7. The Comedies
8. The Romances
9. The Tragedies
10. The Histories
11. *Hamlet*

The titles in the first five sections are accompanied by brief explanatory annotations.

1. Shakespeare's Times

Andrews, John F., ed. *William Shakespeare: His World, His Work, His Influence,* 3 vols. (1985). Sixty articles, dealing not only with such subjects as "The State," "The Church," "Law," "Science, Magic, and Folklore," but also with the plays and poems themselves and Shakespeare's influence (e.g., translations, films, reputation)

Byrne, Muriel St. Clare. *Elizabethan Life in Town and Country* (8th ed., 1970). Chapters on manners, beliefs, education, etc., with illustrations.

Dollimore, John, and Alan Sinfield, eds. *Political Shakespeare: New Essays in Cultural Materialism* (1985). Essays on such topics as the subordination of women and colonialism, presented in connection with some of Shakespeare's plays.

Greenblatt, Stephen. *Representing the English Renaissance* (1988). New Historicist essays, especially on connections between political and aesthetic matters, statecraft and stagecraft.

Joseph, B. L. *Shakespeare's Eden: the Commonwealth of England 1558–1629* (1971). An account of the social, political, economic, and cultural life of England.

Kernan, Alvin. *Shakespeare, the King's Playwright: Theater in the Stuart Court 1603–1613* (1995). The social setting and the politics of the court of James I, in relation to *Hamlet, Measure for Measure, Macbeth, King Lear, Antony and Cleopatra, Coriolanus,* and *The Tempest.*

Montrose, Louis. *The Purpose of Playing: Shakespeare and the Cultural Politics of the Elizabethan Theatre* (1996). A poststructuralist view, discussing the professional theater "within the ideological and material frameworks of Elizabethan culture and society," with an extended analysis of *A Midsummer Night's Dream.*

Mullaney, Steven. *The Place of the Stage: License, Play, and Power in Renaissance England* (1988). New Historicist analysis, arguing that popular drama became a cultural institution "only by . . . taking up a place on the margins of society."

Schoenbaum, S. *Shakespeare: The Globe and the World*

(1979). A readable, abundantly illustrated introductory book on the world of the Elizabethans.

Shakespeare's England, 2 vols. (1916). A large collection of scholarly essays on a wide variety of topics, e.g., astrology, costume, gardening, horsemanship, with special attention to Shakespeare's references to these topics.

2. Shakespeare's Life

Andrews, John F., ed. *William Shakespeare: His World, His Work, His Influence,* 3 vols. (1985). See the description above.

Bentley, Gerald E. *Shakespeare: A Biographical Handbook* (1961). The facts about Shakespeare, with virtually no conjecture intermingled.

Chambers, E. K. *William Shakespeare: A Study of Facts and Problems,* 2 vols. (1930). The fullest collection of data.

Fraser, Russell. *Young Shakespeare* (1988). A highly readable account that simultaneously considers Shakespeare's life and Shakespeare's art.

———. *Shakespeare: The Later Years* (1992).

Schoenbaum, S. *Shakespeare's Lives* (1970). A review of the evidence and an examination of many biographies, including those of Baconians and other heretics.

———. *William Shakespeare: A Compact Documentary Life* (1977). An abbreviated version, in a smaller format, of the next title. The compact version reproduces some fifty documents in reduced form. A readable presentation of all that the documents tell us about Shakespeare.

———. *William Shakespeare: A Documentary Life* (1975). A large-format book setting forth the biography with facsimiles of more than two hundred documents, and with transcriptions and commentaries.

3. Shakespeare's Theater

Astington, John H., ed. *The Development of Shakespeare's Theater* (1992). Eight specialized essays on theatrical companies, playing spaces, and performance.

Beckerman, Bernard. *Shakespeare at the Globe, 1599–1609* (1962). On the playhouse and on Elizabethan dramaturgy, acting, and staging.

Bentley, Gerald E. *The Profession of Dramatist in Shakespeare's Time* (1971). An account of the dramatist's status in the Elizabethan period.

———. *The Profession of Player in Shakespeare's Time, 1590–1642* (1984). An account of the status of members of London companies (sharers, hired men, apprentices, managers) and a discussion of conditions when they toured.

Berry, Herbert. *Shakespeare's Playhouses* (1987). Usefully emphasizes how little we know about the construction of Elizabethan theaters.

Brown, John Russell. *Shakespeare's Plays in Performance* (1966). A speculative and practical analysis relevant to all of the plays, but with emphasis on *The Merchant of Venice*, *Richard II*, *Hamlet*, *Romeo and Juliet*, and *Twelfth Night*.

———. *William Shakespeare: Writing for Performance* (1996). A discussion aimed at helping readers to develop theatrically conscious habits of reading.

Chambers, E. K. *The Elizabethan Stage*, 4 vols. (1945). A major reference work on theaters, theatrical companies, and staging at court.

Cook, Ann Jennalie. *The Privileged Playgoers of Shakespeare's London, 1576–1642* (1981). Sees Shakespeare's audience as wealthier, more middle-class, and more intellectual than Harbage (below) does.

Dessen, Alan C. *Elizabethan Drama and the Viewer's Eye* (1977). On how certain scenes may have looked to spectators in an Elizabethan theater.

Gurr, Andrew. *Playgoing in Shakespeare's London* (1987). Something of a middle ground between Cook (above) and Harbage (below).

———. *The Shakespearean Stage, 1579–1642* (2nd ed., 1980). On the acting companies, the actors, the playhouses, the stages, and the audiences.

Harbage, Alfred. *Shakespeare's Audience* (1941). A study of the size and nature of the theatrical public, emphasizing the representativeness of its working class and middle-class audience.

Hodges, C. Walter. *The Globe Restored* (1968). A conjectural restoration, with lucid drawings.

Hosley, Richard. "The Playhouses," in *The Revels History of Drama in English*, vol. 3, general editors Clifford Leech and T. W. Craik (1975). An essay of a hundred pages on the physical aspects of the playhouses.

Howard, Jane E. "Crossdressing, the Theatre, and Gender Struggle in Early Modern England," *Shakespeare Quarterly* 39 (1988): 418–40. Judicious comments on the effects of boys playing female roles.

Orrell, John. *The Human Stage: English Theatre Design, 1567–1640* (1988). Argues that the public, private, and court playhouses are less indebted to popular structures (e.g., innyards and bear-baiting pits) than to banqueting halls and to Renaissance conceptions of Roman amphitheaters.

Slater, Ann Pasternak. *Shakespeare the Director* (1982). An analysis of theatrical effects (e.g., kissing, kneeling) in stage directions and dialogue.

Styan, J. L. *Shakespeare's Stagecraft* (1967). An introduction to Shakespeare's visual and aural stagecraft, with chapters on such topics as acting conventions, stage groupings, and speech.

Thompson, Peter. *Shakespeare's Professional Career* (1992). An examination of patronage and related theatrical conditions.

———. *Shakespeare's Theatre* (1983). A discussion of how plays were staged in Shakespeare's time.

4. Shakespeare on Stage and Screen

Bate, Jonathan, and Russell Jackson, eds. *Shakespeare: An Illustrated Stage History* (1996). Highly readable essays on stage productions from the Renaissance to the present.

Berry, Ralph. *Changing Styles in Shakespeare* (1981). Discusses productions of six plays (*Coriolanus*, *Hamlet*, *Henry V*, *Measure for Measure*, *The Tempest*, and *Twelfth Night*) on the English stage, chiefly 1950–1980.

————. *On Directing Shakespeare: Interviews with Contemporary Directors* (1989). An enlarged edition of a book first published in 1977, this version includes the seven interviews from the early 1970s and adds five interviews conducted in 1988.

Brockbank, Philip, ed. *Players of Shakespeare: Essays in Shakespearean Performance* (1985). Comments by twelve actors, reporting their experiences with roles. See also the entry for Russell Jackson (below).

Bulman, J. C., and H. R. Coursen, eds. *Shakespeare on Television* (1988). An anthology of general and theoretical essays, essays on individual productions, and shorter reviews, with a bibliography and a videography listing cassettes that may be rented.

Coursen, H. P. *Watching Shakespeare on Television* (1993). Analyses not only of TV versions but also of films and videotapes of stage presentations that are shown on television.

Davies, Anthony, and Stanley Wells, eds. *Shakespeare and the Moving Image: The Plays on Film and Television* (1994). General essays (e.g., on the comedies) as well as essays devoted entirely to *Hamlet, King Lear,* and *Macbeth.*

Dawson, Anthony B. *Watching Shakespeare: A Playgoer's Guide* (1988). About half of the plays are discussed, chiefly in terms of decisions that actors and directors make in putting the works onto the stage.

Dessen, Alan. *Elizabethan Stage Conventions and Modern Interpretations* (1984). On interpreting conventions such as the representation of light and darkness and stage violence (duels, battles).

Donaldson, Peter. *Shakespearean Films/Shakespearean Directors* (1990). Postmodernist analyses, drawing on Freudianism, Feminism, Deconstruction, and Queer Theory.

Jackson, Russell, and Robert Smallwood, eds. *Players of Shakespeare 2: Further Essays in Shakespearean Performance by Players with the Royal Shakespeare Company* (1988). Fourteen actors discuss their roles in productions between 1982 and 1987.

———. *Players of Shakespeare 3: Further Essays in Shakespearean Performance by Players with the Royal Shakespeare Company* (1993). Comments by thirteen performers.

Jorgens, Jack. *Shakespeare on Film* (1977). Fairly detailed studies of eighteen films, preceded by an introductory chapter addressing such issues as music, and whether to "open" the play by including scenes of landscape.

Kennedy, Dennis. *Looking at Shakespeare: A Visual History of Twentieth-Century Performance* (1993). Lucid descriptions (with 170 photographs) of European, British, and American performances.

Leiter, Samuel L. *Shakespeare Around the Globe: A Guide to Notable Postwar Revivals* (1986). For each play there are about two pages of introductory comments, then discussions (about five hundred words per production) of ten or so productions, and finally bibliographic references.

McMurty, Jo. *Shakespeare Films in the Classroom* (1994). Useful evaluations of the chief films most likely to be shown in undergraduate courses.

Rothwell, Kenneth, and Annabelle Henkin Melzer. *Shakespeare on Screen: An International Filmography and Videography* (1990). A reference guide to several hundred films and videos produced between 1899 and 1989, including spinoffs such as musicals and dance versions.

Sprague, Arthur Colby. *Shakespeare and the Actors* (1944). Detailed discussions of stage business (gestures, etc.) over the years.

Willis, Susan. *The BBC Shakespeare Plays: Making the Televised Canon* (1991). A history of the series, with interviews and production diaries for some plays.

5. Miscellaneous Reference Works

Abbott, E. A. *A Shakespearean Grammar* (new edition, 1877). An examination of differences between Elizabethan and modern grammar.

Allen, Michael J. B., and Kenneth Muir, eds. *Shakespeare's Plays in Quarto* (1981). One volume containing facsimiles of the plays issued in small format before they were collected in the First Folio of 1623.

Bevington, David. *Shakespeare* (1978). A short guide to hundreds of important writings on the subject.

Blake, Norman. *Shakespeare's Language: An Introduction* (1983). On vocabulary, parts of speech, and word order.

Bullough, Geoffrey. *Narrative and Dramatic Sources of Shakespeare*, 8 vols. (1957–75). A collection of many of the books Shakespeare drew on, with judicious comments.

Campbell, Oscar James, and Edward G. Quinn, eds. *The Reader's Encyclopedia of Shakespeare* (1966). Old, but still the most useful single reference work on Shakespeare.

Cercignani, Fausto. *Shakespeare's Works and Elizabethan Pronunciation* (1981). Considered the best work on the topic, but remains controversial.

Dent, R. W. *Shakespeare's Proverbial Language: An Index* (1981). An index of proverbs, with an introduction concerning a form Shakespeare frequently drew on.

Greg, W. W. *The Shakespeare First Folio* (1955). A detailed yet readable history of the first collection (1623) of Shakespeare's plays.

Harner, James. *The World Shakespeare Bibliography.* See headnote to Suggested References.

Hosley, Richard. *Shakespeare's Holinshed* (1968). Valuable presentation of one of Shakespeare's major sources.

Kökeritz, Helge. *Shakespeare's Names* (1959). A guide to pronouncing some 1,800 names appearing in Shakespeare.

———. *Shakespeare's Pronunciation* (1953). Contains much information about puns and rhymes, but see Cercignani (above).

Muir, Kenneth. *The Sources of Shakespeare's Plays* (1978). An account of Shakespeare's use of his reading. It covers all the plays, in chronological order.

Miriam Joseph, Sister. *Shakespeare's Use of the Arts of Language* (1947). A study of Shakespeare's use of rhetorical devices, reprinted in part as *Rhetoric in Shakespeare's Time* (1962).

The Norton Facsimile: The First Folio of Shakespeare's Plays (1968). A handsome and accurate facsimile of the first collection (1623) of Shakespeare's plays, with a valuable introduction by Charlton Hinman.

Onions, C. T. *A Shakespeare Glossary*, rev. and enlarged by R. D. Eagleson (1986). Definitions of words (or senses of words) now obsolete.

Partridge, Eric. *Shakespeare's Bawdy*, rev. ed. (1955). Relatively brief dictionary of bawdy words; useful, but see Williams, below.

Shakespeare Quarterly. See headnote to Suggested References.

Shakespeare Survey. See headnote to Suggested References.

Spevack, Marvin. *The Harvard Concordance to Shakespeare* (1973). An index to Shakespeare's words.

Vickers, Brian. *Appropriating Shakespeare: Contemporary Critical Quarrels* (1993). A survey—chiefly hostile—of recent schools of criticism.

Wells, Stanley, ed. *Shakespeare: A Bibliographical Guide* (new edition, 1990). Nineteen chapters (some devoted to single plays, others devoted to groups of related plays) on recent scholarship on the life and all of the works.

Williams, Gordon. *A Dictionary of Sexual Language and Imagery in Shakespearean and Stuart Literature*, 3 vols. (1994). Extended discussions of words and passages; much fuller than Partridge, cited above.

6. Shakespeare's Plays: General Studies

Bamber, Linda. *Comic Women, Tragic Men: A Study of Gender and Genre in Shakespeare* (1982).

Barnet, Sylvan. *A Short Guide to Shakespeare* (1974).

Callaghan, Dympna, Lorraine Helms, and Jyotsna Singh. *The Weyward Sisters: Shakespeare and Feminist Politics* (1994).

Clemen, Wolfgang H. *The Development of Shakespeare's Imagery* (1951).

Cook, Ann Jennalie. *Making a Match: Courtship in Shakespeare and His Society* (1991).

Dollimore, Jonathan, and Alan Sinfield. *Political Shakespeare: New Essays in Cultural Materialism* (1985).

Dusinberre, Juliet. *Shakespeare and the Nature of Women* (1975).

Granville-Barker, Harley. *Prefaces to Shakespeare*, 2 vols. (1946–47; volume 1 contains essays on *Hamlet, King Lear, Merchant of Venice, Antony and Cleopatra*, and *Cymbeline*; volume 2 contains essays on *Othello, Coriolanus, Julius Caesar, Romeo and Juliet, Love's Labor's Lost*).

———. *More Prefaces to Shakespeare* (1974; essays on *Twelfth Night, A Midsummer Night's Dream, The Winter's Tale, Macbeth*).

Harbage, Alfred. *William Shakespeare: A Reader's Guide* (1963).

Howard, Jean E. *Shakespeare's Art of Orchestration: Stage Technique and Audience Response* (1984).

Jones, Emrys. *Scenic Form in Shakespeare* (1971).

Lenz, Carolyn Ruth Swift, Gayle Greene, and Carol Thomas Neely, eds. *The Woman's Part: Feminist Criticism of Shakespeare* (1980).

Novy, Marianne. *Love's Argument: Gender Relations in Shakespeare* (1984).

Rose, Mark. *Shakespearean Design* (1972).

Scragg, Leah. *Discovering Shakespeare's Meaning* (1994).

———. *Shakespeare's "Mouldy Tales": Recurrent Plot Motifs in Shakespearean Drama* (1992).

Traub, Valerie. *Desire and Anxiety: Circulations of Sexuality in Shakespearean Drama* (1992).

Traversi, D. A. *An Approach to Shakespeare*, 2 vols. (3rd rev. ed, 1968–69).

Vickers, Brian. *The Artistry of Shakespeare's Prose* (1968).

Wells, Stanley. *Shakespeare: A Dramatic Life* (1994).

Wright, George T. *Shakespeare's Metrical Art* (1988).

7. The Comedies

Barber, C. L. *Shakespeare's Festive Comedy* (1959; discusses *Love's Labor's Lost, A Midsummer Night's Dream, The Merchant of Venice, As You Like It, Twelfth Night*).

Barton, Anne. *The Names of Comedy* (1990).

Berry, Ralph. *Shakespeare's Comedy: Explorations in Form* (1972).

Bradbury, Malcolm, and David Palmer, eds. *Shakespearean Comedy* (1972).

Bryant, J. A., Jr. *Shakespeare and the Uses of Comedy* (1986).

Carroll, William. *The Metamorphoses of Shakespearean Comedy* (1985).

Champion, Larry S. *The Evolution of Shakespeare's Comedy* (1970).

Evans, Bertrand. *Shakespeare's Comedies* (1960).

Frye, Northrop. *Shakespearean Comedy and Romance* (1965).

Leggatt, Alexander. *Shakespeare's Comedy of Love* (1974).

Miola, Robert S. *Shakespeare and Classical Comedy: The Influence of Plautus and Terence* (1994).

Nevo, Ruth. *Comic Transformations in Shakespeare* (1980).

Ornstein, Robert. *Shakespeare's Comedies: From Roman Farce to Romantic Mystery* (1986).

Richman, David. *Laughter, Pain, and Wonder: Shakespeare's Comedies and the Audience in the Theater* (1990).

Salingar, Leo. *Shakespeare and the Traditions of Comedy* (1974).

Slights, Camille Wells. *Shakespeare's Comic Commonwealths* (1993).

Waller, Gary, ed. *Shakespeare's Comedies* (1991).

Westlund, Joseph. *Shakespeare's Reparative Comedies: A Psychoanalytic View of the Middle Plays* (1984).

Williamson, Marilyn. *The Patriarchy of Shakespeare's Comedies* (1986).

8. The Romances (*Pericles, Cymbeline, The Winter's Tale, The Tempest, The Two Noble Kinsmen*)

Adams, Robert M. *Shakespeare: The Four Romances* (1989).

Felperin, Howard. *Shakespearean Romance* (1972).

Frye, Northrop. *A Natural Perspective: The Development of Shakespearean Comedy and Romance* (1965).

Mowat, Barbara. *The Dramaturgy of Shakespeare's Romances* (1976).

Warren, Roger. *Staging Shakespeare's Late Plays* (1990).

Young, David. *The Heart's Forest: A Study of Shakespeare's Pastoral Plays* (1972).

9. The Tragedies

Bradley, A. C. *Shakespearean Tragedy* (1904).

Brooke, Nicholas. *Shakespeare's Early Tragedies* (1968).

Champion, Larry. *Shakespeare's Tragic Perspective* (1976).

Drakakis, John, ed. *Shakespearean Tragedy* (1992).

Evans, Bertrand. *Shakespeare's Tragic Practice* (1979).

Everett, Barbara. *Young Hamlet: Essays on Shakespeare's Tragedies* (1989).

Foakes, R. A. *Hamlet versus Lear: Cultural Politics and Shakespeare's Art* (1993).

Frye, Northrop. *Fools of Time: Studies in Shakespearean Tragedy* (1967).

Harbage, Alfred, ed. *Shakespeare: The Tragedies* (1964).

Mack, Maynard. *Everybody's Shakespeare: Reflections Chiefly on the Tragedies* (1993).

McAlindon, T. *Shakespeare's Tragic Cosmos* (1991).

Miola, Robert S. *Shakespeare and Classical Tragedy: The Influence of Seneca* (1992).

———. *Shakespeare's Rome* (1983).

Nevo, Ruth. *Tragic Form in Shakespeare* (1972).

Rackin, Phyllis. *Shakespeare's Tragedies* (1978).

Rose, Mark, ed. *Shakespeare's Early Tragedies: A Collection of Critical Essays* (1995).

Rosen, William. *Shakespeare and the Craft of Tragedy* (1960).

Snyder, Susan. *The Comic Matrix of Shakespeare's Tragedies* (1979).

Wofford, Susanne. *Shakespeare's Late Tragedies: A Collection of Critical Essays* (1996).

Young, David. *The Action to the Word: Structure and Style in Shakespearean Tragedy* (1990).

———. *Shakespeare's Middle Tragedies: A Collection of Critical Essays* (1993).

10. The Histories

Blanpied, John W. *Time and the Artist in Shakespeare's English Histories* (1983).

Campbell, Lily B. *Shakespeare's "Histories": Mirrors of Elizabethan Policy* (1947).

Champion, Larry S. *Perspective in Shakespeare's English Histories* (1980).

Hodgdon, Barbara. *The End Crowns All: Closure and Contradiction in Shakespeare's History* (1991).

Holderness, Graham. *Shakespeare Recycled: The Making of Historical Drama* (1992).

———, ed. *Shakespeare's History Plays: "Richard II" to "Henry V"* (1992).

Leggatt, Alexander. *Shakespeare's Political Drama: The History Plays and the Roman Plays* (1988).

Ornstein, Robert. *A Kingdom for a Stage: The Achievement of Shakespeare's History Plays* (1972).

Rackin, Phyllis. *Stages of History: Shakespeare's English Chronicles* (1990).

Saccio, Peter. *Shakespeare's English Kings: History, Chronicle, and Drama* (1977).

Tillyard, E. M. W. *Shakespeare's History Plays* (1944).

Velz, John W., ed. *Shakespeare's English Histories: A Quest for Form and Genre* (1996).

11. *Hamlet*

In addition to the titles mentioned in *Hamlet* on Stage and Screen (pages 239–56), and those mentioned in Section 9, The Tragedies, the following may be consulted.

For information concerning textual problems in *Hamlet*, consult the editions by Harold Jenkins (1982), Philip Edwards (1985), and G. R. Hibbard (1985), and an essay by Paul Werstine, "The Textual Mystery of *Hamlet*," in *Shake-*

speare Quarterly 39 (1988): 1–26. See also Stanley Wells and Gary Taylor, *William Shakespeare: A Textual Companion* (1987). The three earliest texts of *Hamlet* are assembled in *The Three-Text "Hamlet": Parallel Texts of the First and Second Quartos and First Folio,* ed. Paul Bertram and Bernice W. Kliman (1991).

Alexander, Nigel. *Poison, Play and Duel: A Study of "Hamlet"* (1971).
Bamber, Linda. *Comic Women, Tragic Men* (1982).
Belsey, Catherine. "The Case of Hamlet's Conscience." *Studies in Philology* 76 (1979): 127–48.
Bevington, David, ed. *Twentieth Century Interpretations of "Hamlet"* (1968).
Booth, Stephen. "On the Value of *Hamlet*," in *Reinterpretations of Elizabethan Drama.* Ed. Norman Rabkin (1969), pp. 137–76.
Brown, John Russell, and Bernard Harris, eds. *Stratford-upon-Avon Studies 5: "Hamlet"* (1963).
Charney, Maurice. *Style in "Hamlet"* (1969).
Clayton, Thomas, ed. *The "Hamlet" First Published* (1992).
Conklin, Paul. *A History of "Hamlet" Criticism, 1601–1821* (1947).
Ewbank, Inga-Stina. "*Hamlet* and the Power of Words." *Shakespeare Survey* 30 (1977): 85–102.
Frye, Roland Mushat. *The Renaissance "Hamlet": Issues and Responses in 1600* (1984).
Granville-Barker, Harley. *Preface to "Hamlet"* (1936).
Hattaway, Michael. *Hamlet* (1987).
Honigman, E.A.J. *Shakespeare: Seven Tragedies* (1976).
Jones, Ernest. *Hamlet and Oedipus* (1949).
Kastan, David Scott, ed. *Critical Essays on Shakespeare's "Hamlet"* (1995).
Kernan, Alvin. *Shakespeare, The King's Playwright: Theater in the Stuart Court* (1995).
Levin, Harry. *The Question of "Hamlet"* (1959).
Mercer, Peter. *"Hamlet" and the Acting of Revenge* (1987).
Showalter, Elaine. "Representing Ophelia: Women, Madness and the Responsibilities of Feminist Criticism," in *Shakespeare and the Question of Theory.* Eds. Patricia Parker and Geoffrey Hartman (1985), pp. 77–94.

Slights, Camille Wells. *The Casuistical Tradition* (1981).

Walker, Roy. *The Time Is Out of Joint: A Study of "Hamlet"* (1948).

Wilson, J. Dover. *What Happens in "Hamlet."* 3rd ed. (1951).

Wright, George T. "Hendiadys and *Hamlet*." *PMLA* 96 (1981): 168–93.

WITHDRAWN

Announcing the Annual Signet Classic Essay Contest!

$5,000 in **Scholarships**
for high school
Juniors and Seniors!

Win a
Signet Classic library
for your high school!

Write an essay on a literary classic!

For more information write to:
Signet Classic Scholarship Essay Contest
375 Hudson Street, New York, NY 10014,
or request via e-mail at academic2@penguin.com.

Full details are available on Penguin's
website at www.penguin.com

Penguin Putnam Inc. Mass Market